THE LIGHT AND THE DARK

P.F.M. FONTAINE

THE LIGHT AND THE DARK
A CULTURAL HISTORY OF DUALISM

VOLUME XIII

DUALISM IN ROMAN HISTORY IV

THE STRUGGLE
BETWEEN ORTHODOXY AND HETERODOXY
IN THE EARLY CHRISTIAN CHURCH

J.C. GIEBEN, PUBLISHER
AMSTERDAM 1998

To the memory of my faithful corrector
and good friend John R. Dove,
who died in Amsterdam August 7th 1997

No part of this book may be translated or reproduced in any form, by print, photoprint, microfilm, or any other means, without written permission from the publisher.

© by P.F.M. Fontaine / ISBN 90 5063 558 X / Printed in The Netherlands

"For all things are called
light and darkness"

Parmenides

CONTENTS

In memoriam John Roland Dove   xvii

Preface   xxi

I   A SHORT INTRODUCTORY CHAPTER:
    ON ORTHODOXY & HETERODOXY AS SUCH   1

1. Terminology   1
2. A theory of heresy   1
3. The classical theory challenged   3
4. Distinguishing orthodoxy and heterodoxy   5
Notes to Chapter I   6

II THE APOSTLES AND THE FATHERS ON HERESY   8

1. In the New Testament   8
    a. Two baptist movements   8
    b. Warnings in the Pauline and Catholic Letters   9
    c. Warnings in the Revelation of John   9
    d. The beginnings of a dualistic relationship   10
2. Justin the Martyr on heterodoxy   10
3. Irenaeus of Lyons as an inventorist of heresies   12
4. The work of Hegesippus   12
5. Hippolytus and heterodoxy   13
6. Tertullian in action   13
7. The 'medicine-chest' of Epiphanius   15
8. Augustine and the secular arm   15
9. The ghost let out the bottle   17
Notes to Chapter II   17

III THE APOLOGISTS   20

1. The beginning of the dispute with classical thought   21
2. Pre-Christian Christians   21
3. The Father, the Son, and creation   22
4. The special case of Origen   24
    a. The life of Origen   24
    b. His literary output   26
5. Charges and defenders   26
6. Some disputed theological tenets of Origen   27
    a. The preexistence of souls   27

		b. The fault and the fall	28
		c. Why there is a cosmos	30
		d. Non-existing errors	31
7.	The simple and the perfect		31
		a. Higher Knowledge	31
		b. The 'eternal Gospel'	32
8.	Origen and philosophy		33
9.	Origen in the dock		34
		a. Counsel for the prosecution	34
		b. Counsels for the defense	35
		c. The question of Origen's theological position	35
10.	The Origenist controversy		36
		a. Epiphanius and Origen	36
		b. The beginning of the Origenist controversy	37
		c. The war of the sermons	38
		d. Attempts at mediation	39
		e. Reconciliation	40
		f. Rufinus goes to town	41
		g. The anti-Origenists in action	42
		h. An anti-Origenist campaign	43
Notes to Chapter III			43

IV	ADOPTIONISM: WAS JESUS REALLY DIVINE?		50
1.	The Ebionite position		50
2.	The Docetist position		51
3.	What is Adoptionism?		52
4.	The first appearance of Adoptionism		52
5.	Monarchianism: the unitary position		54
		a. Praxeas	54
		b. Noetus	55
6.	Modalism: no persons but modes		56
		a. What is Modalism?	56
		b. Disturbance in the Church	57
		c. Sabellius	57
7.	The 'Alogoi'		58
8.	The situation in the East		60
9.	Paul of Samosata		60
		a. A secular bishop	60
		b. The teachings of Paul of Samosata	61
		c. The second synod of Antioch and the deposition of Paul	63
10.	Nominalism avant la lettre		64
11.	The dualistic abyss		66
12.	The later vicissitudes of Paulinianism		66
Notes to Chapter IV			67

| V | THE ASCETIC URGE | 71 |

Introductory: Christianity and asceticism 71

PART I ENCRATISM 72

1. What is Encratism? 72
   a. Encratism defined 73
   b. The Encratite way of life 74
2. The Encratite heresiarch Cassianus 74
3. The Encratite heresiarch Tatian 75
   a. What we know of Tatian 75
   b. His works 76
   c. Tatian and philosophy 76
   d. Tatian's theology 77
   e. Tatian's anthropology 78
   f. Orthodox or not? 79
4. 'Horror materiae' 79

PART II 'THE NEW PROPHECY': MONTANISM 80

1. Phrygia the cradle of Montanism 80
2. The beginning of the 'new prophecy' 81
3. The movement spreads 82
4. The new Jerusalem 82
5. The reaction of the bishops 83
6. A new prophetess 83
7. The Roman Catholic viewpoint 84
   a. A Church of ordinary people 84
   b. The Church and her mystics 85
   c. The attitude of the Church towards excesses 86
8. Montanist theology 88
   a. The role of the Holy Ghost 88
   b. The doctrine of successive revelations 90
   c. The eschatological background 91
9. Tertullian the Montanist 91
   a. Where Tertullian agreed with Montanism 91
   b. What Tertullian disliked in Montanism 93
   c. Tertullian and the psychics 94
10. The later vicissitudes of Montanism 95

PART III DONATISM 96

1. The origins of the Donatist controversy 96
   a. The persecution of Diocletian 96
   b. The question of the Martyrs of Abitenae 97
2. Mounting tension 99
3. Donatus 101

4.	Schism in the North African Church	101
	a. The problem of the succession of bishop Mensurius	101
	b. Did the schism have an ethnic background?	104
	c. The ethnic solution under fire	105
5.	Neurosis: a comparison	106
6.	Donatist theology	108
7.	Constantine intervenes	110
8.	The Donatists remain obstinate	111
9.	Bad days ahead for the Donatists	112
10.	Bishop Silvanus accused	114
11.	Donatism tolerated	114
12.	The Donatist Church essentially North African	116
13.	The Circumcellions	117
14.	An extremist view of Christian life	119
15.	Circumcellion terrorism	120
16.	An imperial attempt at rapprochement	122
17.	Imperial action against Donatism	123
	a. Donatism proscribed	123
	b. The Catholic Church as the 'Macarian party'	124
18.	A new chance for the Donatists	125
19.	Donatism repressed again	127
20.	A discussion between Parmenian and Optatus	128
	a. The position of Parmenian	128
	b. Optatus answers Parmenian	128
21.	The rule of Gildo	130
22.	Gildo and bishop Optatus	131
23.	Dissension within the Donatist ranks	132
24.	The unbridgeable chasm	134
25.	The Catholic triumph	135
26.	Donatist resilience	137
27.	The end of Donatism	137
28.	An overview	138

PART IV PRISCILLIANISM 139

1.	Priscillian's sombre view of the world	140
2.	Priscillian dualism	140
3.	Gradations in perfection	141
4.	The final aim of Christian education	141
5.	Christology	142
6.	Priscillian's position in the doctrinal spectrum	143
7.	The Spanish bishops take action	143
8.	The intervention of the Emperor Maximus	144
9.	Priscillianism after Priscillian	146
Notes to Chapter V		147

VI	THE ARIAN CONTROVERSY	164
	PART I THE ALEXANDRIAN ORIGIN OF THE CONTROVERSY	165

1. Arius and his ecclesiastical career — 165
   a. Who was Arius? — 165
   b. A question of martyrdom — 165
   c. Arius's personality — 166
2. How the conflict started — 167
   a. Diverging opinions — 167
   b. The beginning of the conflict — 167
3. Was Arius dependent on Origen? — 168
   a. Origen a disputed theologian — 168
   b. Origen's influence in Alexandria — 169
   c. God's 'aseitas' as a point in common — 169
   d. Arius was not really dependent on Origen — 170
4. A catalogue of Arius's theological tenets — 171
5. Arius's theological position and its consequences — 172
   a. Was there an Arian 'theo-logy'? — 173
   b. Gnostic influences? — 173
   c. Arian philosophy — 174
6. The Arian doctrine of the Trinity — 177
   a. Arius's 'Triad' — 177
   b. The consequences of Arius's abolishing of the Trinity — 177
7. The humanity of Jesus in Arian doctrine — 178
   a. The accent put on Jesus' human characteristics — 178
   b. Texts that seem to support Arius's doctrine — 179
   c. A structural problem — 180
8. The Arian doctrine of salvation — 181
   a. Two divergent views — 181
   b. How can man be saved? — 181
9. Irreconcilable viewpoints — 184
10. The Synod of Alexandria in 320 — 184
11. Canvassing for the Arian cause — 185
    a. The support of Eusebius of Caesarea — 185
    b. The support of Eusebius of Nicomedia — 185
    c. Alexander counter-attacking — 186
    d. Arian propaganda — 187
12. A case of public interest — 187

PART II AN ATTEMPT AT A FINAL DECISION — 189

1. A painful situation — 189
2. A travelling propagandist — 189
3. The Council of Antioch, 325 — 191
4. The Council of Nicaea — 192
   a. The plan for a general council — 192
   b. Why Nicaea was chosen — 192

		c. How ecumenical was the Council?	193
		d. No Acta	194
		e. The opening of the Council	194
		f. Not much support for the Arians	195
		g. A doctrinal formula presented by Eusebius of Caesarea	195
		h. The statement of Eusebius of Nicomedia	195
		j. The attitude of Eusebius of Caesarea	196
		k. The Creed of Nicaea	197
		l. The statement generally signed	197
	5.	The aftermath of Nicaea	198
		a. Banishments	198
		b. The Emperor relents	198

PART III THEOLOGICAL POSITIONS AND TERMS   199

1.	Athanasius bishop of Alexandria	199
2.	Wrangling over the position of Arius	201
3.	The theological stance of Eusebius of Caesarea	201
4.	Problems with terms	203
5.	Eustathius of Antioch as a defender of orthodoxy	204
	a. Eustathius and the Council of Nicaea	204
	b. Eustathius in a middle position	204
	c. The fall of Eustathius	205
	d. The charge of Sabellianism	206
6.	Marcellus of Ancyra as a defender of orthodoxy	208
	a. Who was Marcellus?	208
	b. Attacks and counter-attacks	208
	c. Marcellus seeks to be rehabilitated	209

PART IV A CHURCH DIVIDED   210

1.	The Council of Serdica	210
2.	The case of the bare prostitute	212
3.	The later years of Marcellus	212
4.	Changes in the leadership on both sides	213
5.	Athanasius, leader of the orthodox, the favourite target of the heterodox	214
	a. A curious coalition	214
	b. The mystery of the chopped off hand	215
	c. Athanasius banished for the first time	216
	d. The return of Athanasius	218
6.	A war of Councils	218
7.	Alexandria made safe for Gregory	220
8.	Athanasius in exile for the second time	221
9.	New credal statements	222
10.	Trouble in Constantinople	224
11.	The vicissitudes of Athanasius	225

PART V   THE INTERVENTIONS OF CONSTANTIUS II 227

1. Clouds on the horizon 227
2. Constantius II under ecclesiastical fire 228
3. Constantius II and the reunification of the Church 230
4. Athanasius banished for the third time 232
5. Constantius II hits at his opponents 233
6. The case of Liberius 236

PART VI   A NEW AND RADICAL ARIANISM 237

1. Neo-Arianism 237
2. Was an intermediate position possible? 240
   a. The position of Constantius II 241
   b. The Semi-Arians 241
   c. The Semi-Arian doctrine 241
3. Fruitless attempts at reunification 243
4. The double-faced Council 244
   a. The Council of Rimini 244
   b. 'Rimini' under pressure from the Emperor 245
   c. The Council of Seleucia 245
   d. The Council of Constantinople, 360 247
5. The situation at the death of Constantius II in 361 247

PART VII   THE DEMISE OF THE ANTI-NICENE OPPOSITION 249

1. Julian's religious policy 249
2. The fate of bishop George 249
3. Athanasius' theological position 250
4. The Council of Alexandria in 362 250
5. Athanasius banished again 252
6. Exiled for the last time 252
7. An anti-Arian coalition 253
8. The last stage 254
   a. Imperial measures in favour of orthodoxy 254
   b. A strong pull into the direction of 'Nicaea' 255
   c. The second Ecumenical Council 255
   d. The end of Arianism 256

PART VIII   THE AFTERMATH: GERMANIC ARIANISM 257
Notes to Chapter VI 258

VII   THE STRUGGLE OVER THE NATURES OF CHRIST 280

PART I   APOLLINARISM 280

1. Apollinarism père et fils 280
2. The fate of the literary production of Apollinaris jr. 281

3.	Apollinaris' deviation from orthodoxy	281
4.	Apollinaris' anthropology	282
5.	Two natures, two persons?	283
6.	Apollinaris' answer: one nature, one person	283
7.	The dualism of Apollinaris	285
8.	Apollinarian doctrine disapproved of	286
9.	Questions of terminology	286
10.	The role of Vitalis	287
11.	The Christian community beginning to split	288

PART II   THE THEOLOGY OF THEODORE OF MOPSUESTIA   289

1.	Who was Theodore of Mopsuestia?	290
2.	His literary output	290
3.	Godhead and humanity in Jesus according to Theodore of Mopsuestia	291
4.	Natures and persons	292
5.	Consequences of Theodore's Christology	293
6.	The dualism of Theodore	293

PART III   NESTORIANISM   294

1.	Who was Nestorius?	294
2.	Making enemies	295
3.	Nestorius' literary output	296
4.	The beginning of the theological battle	296
5.	A battle of theses	297
6.	Cyril's epistolary offensive	298
7.	Celestinus investigates	299
8.	The affair entrusted to Cyril	300
9.	The reaction of Nestorius	301
10.	The Council of Ephesus, 431	301
	a. A Council convoked	301
	b. An unruly beginning	302
	c. Cyril's coup d'état	302
	d. The breach complete	304
	e. Imperial intervention	304
11.	A schism prevented	305
12.	Taking stock of the situation	306
13.	Nestorianism in the East	308

PART IV   MONOPHYSITISM   310

1.	Continuing unrest in the oriental Church	310
2.	Cyril and Monophysitism	311
3.	Dioscurus, the guardian of Cyril's spiritual heritage	311
4.	Eutyches steps forward	313
5.	Eutyches condemned	314
6.	Eutyches' counter-attack	314

7.	The 'Robbers' Council'	316
8.	Leo tries to redress the situation	318
9.	A schism averted	319
10.	The Ecumenical Council of Chalcedon	320
	a. The management of the Council	320
	b. Measures against persons	320
	c. The doctrinal result	321
11.	The end of Eutychianism	321
Notes to Chapter VII		

VIII THE BATTLE OVER THE STATUS OF MAN 330

1.	Point and counter-point	330
2.	Who was Pelagius?	331
3.	Pelagius' literary output	332
4.	How Pelagianism began	333
5.	Pelagian doctrine	334
6.	Pelagius confronting Manichaeans and Arians	335
7.	Human nature and grace	335
8.	The necessity of baptism	336
9.	Pelagius under crossfire	337
	a. Jerome contra Pelagius	338
	b. Orosius charges too	339
	c. Allies of Jerome and Orosius	340
10.	What had happened in Carthage	340
11.	An appeal to Rome	341
12.	Zosimus occupies himself with the question	342
13.	Conflict between Zosimus and the North Africans	343
14.	The fate of Caelestius	344
15.	Augustine's doctrine of grace	344
16.	Were Pelagius and Augustine dualists?	346
17.	Semi-Pelagianism	347
	a. Vitalis' protest against Augustianism	347
	b. Monks protesting	348
	c. Allies of Augustine	349
	d. Condemnation of the Semi-Pelagian position	349
Notes to Chapter VIII		350

EPILOGUE

1.	A red-hot issue	355
2.	Why all the fuss?	356
3.	Some general remarks	356
4.	'Horror materiae'	357
5.	Political interventions	358
6.	The lines of dualism	359
7.	The positions of East and West	361
8.	The Roman Catholic Church finally triumphant	362

9.	The non-dualism of the Roman Catholic Church	363
10.	The battle over the doctrinal status of Jesus Christ	363
	a. No Trinity, no Logos	364
	b. No God-man	364
	c. 'Christological dualism'	365
	d. The orthodox solution	367
11.	The dualistic temptation	368
12.	Overcoming dualism	368
	a. The optimism of Pelagius	368
	b. Roman Catholic anti-dualistic statements	369
Note to the Epilogue		369

Chronology 370

Schemes of theological systems 373

Bibliography 381

General index 397

XVII

IN MEMORIAM JOHN ROLAND DOVE

My excellent corrector and good friend John Dove was a Londoner, born on May 10$^{th.}$ 1924. After grammar school he studied theology for a year in a seminary of the Unitarian Church, but he abandoned this study and turned his attention to that of English and American literature in which he remained deeply interested all his life. He went to Oxford University where he graduated in 1949. To continue his studies he travelled to the US, first to Hobart College at Geneva (NY), and later to the University of Texas. Here he gained his doctor's degree with a thesis on nineteenth-century American literature and the work of William Dean Howells, an American novelist.

Remaining true to his literary interests, he taught literature in several American colleges and universities. Later he returned to Europe where he had teaching assignments at the universities of Marburg in Germany and Trondheim in Norway. In 1967 he got a lectureship at the University of Oulu in Finland, where he was to stay for twenty-two years. This university had just started an English Department in which he became an Associate Professor two years later. As the likeable man he was, he was much beloved by his students who had a very good teacher in him. He retired in 1989, when he was sixty-five.

The reader will have remarked that he never had a British appointment. The older he became, the more alienated he was from his native country. In the more than eleven years that I knew him, he only once visited England again, a visit from which he returned disappointed and irritated. Of all the countries where he lived and worked he loved the Netherlands best, so much so that he acquired the Dutch nationality in 1994. As a good Dutchman he learned to speak and read the language. He was really enamoured of

XVIII

Amsterdam where he came to live in the late Sixties. The appartment he had in town was his home-base in all the years that he was teaching at Oulu, returning to it for the holidays.

At some moment in the Sixties he did a brief spell of teaching in a secondary school in Amsterdam, but not being made for teaching youngsters, he soon quit. However, this became the link between him and me, for when I was looking for a corrector in December 1985, a former colleague of his who knew me too, directed my attention to John. I met him for the first time at the end of December 1985, when he was at home for the Christmas holidays. Within no more than twenty minutes we came to an agreement. He showed himself interested in my work, while he found my English satisfactory enough. He told me that he would do no translating and rewriting, but was soon convinced that he could restrict himself to what he called 'cosmetic retouches' - retouches which he always referred to as 'suggestions'. This shows that he was a courteous man who left my text intact. I was sensible enough, of course, to follow his 'suggestions' so that my original text, written directly in English, became more anglicized. He did chapter by chapter; I never had to wait long before he was ready with it. His correcting was accurate and to the point; he always had a good understanding of what I meant. In all he corrected twelve and a half volumes for me with fifty-eight chapters, not to mention the often long prefaces. In eleven years of close collaboration we never had one cross word.

Soon enough we became great friends. During the vacations I visited him in his Amsterdam home and after his retirement more frequently. We had many a 'chat over coffee', as he said. He came to know my wife and was interested in my family. He visited our place; sometimes I took him for a trip through the countryside which he found a great treat, 'enjoying every minute of it', as were his own words.

In the beginning of the Nineties he began to have health problems. First of all, it appeared that he had diabetes which had a bad effect on his legs; his walk became ever more impeded. On December 14th 1996 I met him accidentally in the subway station Wibaut, near his home. He looked so abysmally bad that I anxiously asked what was wrong. Not much, he said, not enough iron is his blood; he had been given some pills to remedy this. But a child could see that there was far more wrong. Then in the first days of 1997 he phoned me to tell me that he could no longer work for me. He was terminally ill, he said, since inoperable stomach cancer had been diagnosticized with him. His condition slowly deteriorated. My wife and I visited him for the last time on May 4th. He clearly meant this as a farewell visit, for what we saw was a man marked by death; his old vigour had gone. He died very peacefully in his own home on August 7th 1997.

John never married and had no children. He lived with a friend, Jan Willem Ruijter, to whom all my sympathy goes. I shall miss John dearly and always commemorate this amiable man not only as a great expert of the English language, but still more as great friend whom I will keep in grateful memory. May he rest in peace.

Piet F.M. Fontaine
Amsterdam NL

PREFACE

Throughout this volume I have used the definition of dualism that I presented in the Preface to Volume I; I have never found occasion to alter it. This definition runs as follows. There is dualism if we are confronted with two utterly opposed conceptions, systems, principles, groups of people, or even worlds, without any intermediate terms between them. They cannot be reduced to each other; in some cases they are not even dependent on each other. The opposites are of a different quality, so much so that one of them is always seen as being distinctly inferior and hence must be neglected, repudiated, or even destroyed. Reduced to the shortest possible notion, dualism is about unsolvable oppositions.

Time and again, in volume after volume, I have cautioned my readers about two frequently occurring misunderstandings about dualism. The first is that it has an Iranian origin, the second that it is only to be found in the field of religion and perhaps also in that of philosophy. This time I leave the task of combating these two misconceptions to an expert on the subject of Mithraism, Samuel Laeuchli. This scholar says that "the dualistic problem has been confused by two rigid assertions. The first limits dualism to an extreme of an Iranian type of two gods, one good and one evil. The second limits dualism to only the metaphysical, religious, or philosophical aspects of such duality. This narrow conception of dualism prevents the observer from grasping the dualistic problem in the ancient world." (Samuel Laeuchli, Mithraic Dualism. Mithraism in Ostia, pp. 61/62. Ed. Samuel Laeuchli (1967)).

XXII

There is yet another misunderstanding, namely that the absolute opposite of dualism would be monism, to the point that the decisive choice would be between either monism or dualism. This would have the curious consequence that the opposition monism-dualism would be dualistic itself. But in previous volumes I have argued more than once that monism and dualism both are unsatisfactory explanations of what is. I do not think that I need explain this for dualism once again. By attempting to subsume all existents under one principle, monism does violence to reality. Reality does not suffer to be categorized in this way. There will always be left a residue that remains outside the monistic system. These elements protest, by way of speaking, against being harnassed into a rigid system. Dualism quite easily originates then.

I found a curious presentation of the pair monism-dualism in a bulky work by the German scholar Gustav Portig who 'flourished' about a century ago. He produced several works. The book I have in mind appeared in 1904 in Stuttgart and is titled 'Das Weltgesetz des kleinsten Kraftaufwandes in dem Reiche der Natur'. What we need is Volume II, 'In der Astronomie und Biologie', and more in particular its Part I, 'Die Grundzüge der monistischen und dualistischen Weltanschauung', § 2 Die philosophischen Grundzüge des Monismus and des Dualismus'. We are led to our subject with German 'Gründlichkeit'.

According to Portig then, the very last or most fundamental principle of all thought is that there are 'dualities', no matter whether these are composed of simple elements or form immense groups of complicated factors. Even God can only think of himself as being part of a duality, namely that of God and the world. There are only two basic forms of dualities; all phenomena in the universe can be reduced to one of these two. Turning to metaphysics, we must speak of these dualities as the monistic and the dualistic world-view.

Monism says : All is One, and One is All. Between the One and the All Portig inserts a duality as an intermediate. He admits that there is a contradiction in this, viz. that something conditional is at once the unconditional; obviously the 'unconditional' here is 'the All' und the 'conditional' 'the One'. It is evident that Portig has no need of a 'block monism';

there must be a measure of flexibility in it so that it does not consist of wholly identical elements. Oppositions are possible, but they are always only of a quantitative nature. Dualism says : the unconditional and the conditional must be there together, but as primary forms of reality they are essentially different. The elements are qualitatively different, quality being understood as something that is metaphysically independent. In short : the monistic world-view has its roots in the primary metaphysical principle of quantity, the dualistic one in that of quality.

According to a monistic world-view, the world process consists only in changes in the quantities and the intensities : hotter or colder, longer or shorter, softer or harder, more or less. Monism means unending becoming, perpetual activity. Were this different, it would not be possible to explain why there is multiplicity in the world. Between the initial absolute One and multiplicity comes activity. However, this unending becoming is a form in which Being, which is rigid, presents itself. The normal situation of the world is rest, so that the world process, which is movement, will always return to rest. Action will always be followed by reaction, and the final result is immobility. I would not be surprised if Portig was thinking here of the law of entropy.

The dominating concept of monism is that of infinite possibilities. But if this is correct, then reality is not truly real, but only apparently so. Everything that is real ends in being a possibility, open to becoming something else. There is no difference between possibility and reality. It will be evident that Portig has no sympathy for monism, since it cannot bring forth a world. It is not creative. But in dualism we find the principle of creativity. There are subjects which cannot be reduced to each other because they are existentially different. Between them there is interaction. Consequently, they possess the power to change a possibility into a new reality (which reality does not finally become a possibility once again). The two primal substances are spirit and matter, and from their fruitful opposition all things result.

I am ready to go along with Portig a long way, but I differ from him with regard to one essential point. He should not have used the term 'dualism' in

XXIV

the manner he does. It leads to confusion. People often subsume all kinds of oppositions under the generic concept of 'dualism'. They would do better to refer to 'dualities'. In a discussion with a Dutch professor of ancient history, she was consequent enough to deny that such a thing as 'dualism' existed. Oppositions, yes, but not dualistic, that is, unsolvable oppositions. Stating that all dualities, all oppositions are dualistic, what Portig does, and holding that there is no dualism means the same thing : that there are no insolvable oppositions. And this is denying an important part of reality.

Although Portig frequently uses the term, he has in fact no room for dualism. His monism does not admit to oppositions; it is one great undifferentiated mass from which things come forth and into which they dissolve again. His dualism is fundamentally creative; it can only produce. But there is no room in it for what does not fit, for what leads to nothing. Let me state categorically that dualism is not creative, that it does not bear fruit. It is negative and destructive. All the twelve volumes of this series have amply born this out, and this thirteenth volume will be no exception to this.

My deceased corrector and friend John R. Dove has corrected the Chapters I-V of this volume. He did this in his usual precise and courteous way, but he had to give up when he had done a few pages of Ch. VI. I have expressed my deeply felt and lasting gratitude to this good man by dedicating this volume to his memory. It would perhaps have been more appropriate to dedicate Volume XII to him, but when he died, that volume was in production already. I praise myself happy for having found, soon after John's stepping back, an excellent new corrector. She is a young woman, Ms Jo Swabe, a native English speaker with a good command of the Dutch language; she is a sociologist who lives in Amsterdam. When this volume was in its last stages of preparation, she received her doctorate on December 5th, 1997. The theme of her doctoral dissertation bears some unintended resemblance to that of the present series : 'The Burden of Beasts. A Historical Sociological Study of Changing Human-Animal Relations and the Rise of the Veterinary Regime'. After we had come to an agreement, she corrected the Chapters VI-VIII, the

Epilogue, and the Preface. Her style of correcting is not essentially different from that of Dr. Dove : accurate, courteous, and leaving my text intact. Somewhere in the margins of her existence my oldest daughter, Dr. Th.A.M. Smidt van Gelder-Fontaine, a philosopher, found the time to read by far the greater part of the text, chapter by chapter in typescript, and to comment on its contents; that she could this time not do all of it was due to very heavy pressure of work. Then my dear wife Anneke came into action; she corrected the one-but-final version of each chapter on typing errors. I must state, however, that everything in this work is my own responsibility, the scholarly contents, the lay-out, and the typing. Finally, Mr. J.C. Gieben, the publisher, stood ready to accept my brain-child and make into a book.

To this volume I add, just as to Vol. XII, a Manual, destined for those readers who are not acquainted with the foregoing volumes; it can help them to find the subjects they are interested in with the help of this thematic catalogue. At the end of this Volume one will find a number of schemes that may assist readers to find their way in the labyrinth of theological opinions.

Vol. XIV will be about 'the enemies of the Roman order'.

Piet F.M. Fontaine
Amsterdam (NL)

MANUAL

This manual is designed for those readers who do not want to read the whole work, but, instead, want to see what is said in it about the subject(s) they are interested in.

I   ON DUALISM AS SUCH

    Prefaces of Vols. I, VI, IX,
    Vol. IV, Ch. IV.4

II   PERIODS AND CIVILIZATIONS

    1. Greece
        Vol. I Archaic and early classical periods
        Vol. II and III Fifth and fourth centuries B.C.
        Vol. VI The Hellenistic world
    2. Egypt
        Vol. IV, Ch. I
    3. Mesopotamia and Anatolia
        Vol. IV, Ch. III
    4. Israel
        Vol. IV, Ch. II
    5. Iran
        Vol. IV, Ch. IV, Vol. V, Ch. I
    6. India
        Vol. V, Ch. II
    7. China
        Vol. V, Ch. III
    8. Roman history
        Vols. X, XI,
        XII, Ch. I.

III   POLITICAL HISTORY

    1. Greece
        Vol. II
        Vol. VI, Chs. I and II
    2. Rome

XXVIII

    Vol. X
    Vol. XI, Chs. I, II, III, IV
3. Egypt
    Vol. IV, Ch. I.1-4
4. Mesopotamia and Anatolia
    Vol. IV, Ch. III.1-9.
5. Israel
    Vol. IV, Ch. II.14
    Vol. VI, Ch. II.11
6. Iran
    Vol. IV, Ch. IV.1-3
    Vol. V, Ch. I.1-3
7. India
    Vol. V, Ch. II.1-11
8. China
    Vol. V, Ch. III.1-5

IV   SOCIAL HISTORY

1. Greece
    Vol. II, Ch. III.3
    Vol. II, Ch. IV.4
2. India
    Vol. V, Ch. II.13-15
Since esoteric religious movements are socially distinct from the rest of the population, we may subsume these too under this heading :
3. The Pythagoreans
    Vol. I, Ch. I
4. Eleusinian mysteries and Orphics
    Vol. I, Ch. IV
5. Yoga
    Vol. V, Ch. II.21
6. Jainism
    Vol. V, Ch. II.22
7. Dao
    Vol. V, Ch. III.25
8. The Essenes
    Vol. VIII, Ch. V
9. Almost all Gnostic movements
    Vol. VII, Ch. III, Vols. VIII and IX
10. The subjected peoples of the Roman Empire
    Vol. XI, Ch. IV
11. The Jews of the Roman Empire
    Vol. XI, Ch. V
12. The Greeks of the Roman Empire
    Vol. XI, Ch. VI
13. The Roman Empire and the Christian Church
    Vol. XII, Ch. I

V   HISTORY OF RELIGIONS

1. Pythagoreanism
   Vol. I, Ch. I
2. The Olympian religion
   Vol. I, Ch. IV.1-8
3. The Eleusinian mysteries
   Vol. I, Ch. IV.8
4. The cult of Dionysus
   Vol. I, Ch. IV.9
5. Orphism
   Vol. I, Ch. IV.10
6. Greek shamanism
   Vol. I, Ch. IV.11
7. Egyptian religion
   Vol. IV, Ch. I.5-7
8. The religion of Israel
   Vol. IV, Ch. II
   Vol. VII, Ch. VI
9. Religions of the Middle East
   Vol. IV, Ch. III.10
10. Iranian religion
    Vol. IV, Ch. IV.4-12
    Vol. V, Ch. I.4-5
11. Mazdakism
    Vol. V, Ch. I, Appendix
12. The New Testament
    Vol. VII, Ch. IV
13. The Essenes
    Vol. VII, Ch. V
14. Hermetism
    Vol. VIII, Ch. II
15. The Veda
    Vol. V, Ch. II.17
16. Brahmanism
    Vol. V, Ch. II.18-19
17. Hinduism
    Vol. V, Ch. II.20
18. Yoga
    Vol. V, Ch. II.21
19. Jainism
    Vol. V, Ch. II.22
20. Buddhism
    Vol. V. Ch. II.23
21. Confucianism
    Vol. V, CH. III.16-21, 23-24
22. Mohism
    Vol. V, Ch. III.22

23. Daoism
   Vol. V, Ch. III.25
24. The Gnosis
   Vol. VI, Ch.IV
   Vol. VII, Chs. I-III
   Vol. VIII, Chs. III-IX
   Vol. IX
25. The Christian Church and the Jews
   Vol. XII, Ch. II
26. The Christian Church and Judaizing
   Vol. XII, Ch. III

VI   PHILOSOPHY

1. Pythagoreanism
   Vol. I, Ch. I
2. Ionic and Eleatic philosophy
   Vol. I, Ch. II
3. Sophists and Socrates
   Vol. III, Ch. II
4. Plato and Aristotle
   Vol. III, Ch. III
5. Hellenistic philosophy
   Vol. VI, Ch. III
6. Indian philosophy
   Vol. V, Ch. II.16
7. Chinese philosophy
   Vol. V, Ch. III.15
8. The philosophy of Philo
   Vol. VIII, Ch. I

VII LITERATURE

1. Greek epics and lyrics
   Vol. I, Ch. III
2. Greek tragedy and comedy
   Vol. III, Ch. I

VIII HISTORIOGRAPHY

1. Greek historiography
   Vol. III, Ch. III.1
2. Old Testament
   Vol. IV, Ch. II.1-6
3. New Testament
   Vol. VII, Ch. IV.1-2.

CHAPTER I

A SHORT INTRODUCTORY CHAPTER :
ON ORTHODOXY & HETERODOXY AS SUCH

1. Terminology

The word 'heresy' is derived from the Greek word 'hairesis' [1] that, in its turn, is the substantive of the verb 'haireoo' = to take, to get, and in its medium form 'to acquire, to choose'. The substantive can mean 'capture, choice, tendency', but also 'party, sect'. Flavius Josephus said there were three 'haireseis' in Jewry, the Sadducees, the Pharisees, the Essenes [2]. By employing the terms 'choice, party, sect' as meanings of 'hairesis', we are hitting upon a fundamental notion. The great Church never saw herself as a party or sect.

2. A theory of heresy

From her earliest days the orthodox Church had to contend with heresy. But what exactly is 'heresy'? Heresy is a doctrine (and often also a practice) that deviates from orthodoxy; heresy and orthodoxy must be defined in relation to each other. But what exactly is 'orthodoxy'? The right, the accepted, the normative doctrine?

There exists something that may be called 'the classical theory of heresy'. It consists, in the description of H.E.W. Turner, of the following elements [3]. 1. "The Church originally kept unsullied and undefiled the teaching of our Lord and the tradition of the Apostles." 2. "The temporal priority of orthodoxy is everywhere assumed." 3. "Heresy was thus, originally, an offshoot from orthodoxy." 4. "The truth as well as the priority of Scripture is confirmed by its prophecy of the rise of heresy." 5. "The root of heresy is personal choice exercised in matters where it does not apply. The personal systems of the heresiarchs are contrasted with the teaching of the Apostles who had 'no faith of their own' and did not choose what they believed." 6. "Confirmation of this estimate of heresy is found in the infinite variety of opinions to which divergence appears to lead" [4]. 7. "Heresy is restricted to relatively few places, whereas the Catholic Church, as the name implies, is world-wide." 8. "The charge is often made that heresy arises from the dilution of orthodoxy with pagan philosophy."

This theory is called 'classical', because all these elements can be found in the Fathers. With regard to our overall theme, it is clear that, on the strength of the classical theory, orthodoxy and heresy are incompatible phenomena, irreconcilably opposed; it is a question of superior and inferior, so that we seem to be in the presence of dualism.

Stating these points does not mean that they are all equally valid. Turner, for instance, shows that it is impossible to find "any substantial justification for the theory that heresy represented a marked philosophical interpretation of Christianity" [5]. But this theory has one great advantage : it concentrated on doctrine, on deviations from supposedly orthodox doctrine, on disagreements over doctrine (and sometimes practice). It held good for ages, although it was never unchallenged.

Deviating groups of Late Antiquity often resented to be dubbed heretical. Some arguments they threw back at the heads of the orthodox. They claimed, for instance, that they themselves relied heavily on the Bible, and contended that even the Fathers were not averse from pagan philosophy, more particularly Platonic philosophy. Heretics not rarely saw themselves as progressives and innovators. The whole idea was sometimes stood on its head when, for instance, during the Reformation the main Church herself was accused by the Reformers as being heretical [6]. It has perhaps escaped the reader that Turner (who was a canon of the Church of England) stressed in his first point that "the Church **originally** (my emphasis) kept unsullied and undefiled the teaching of our Lord". This leaves the possibility open that later, during the Middle Ages, this teaching was sullied and defiled, an abuse that the Reformers set out to redress.

What detracts somewhat from the well-ordered 'classical theory' is 'the fluidity of early Christian thought' [7]. Turner makes it abundantly clear that in the early Church "orthodoxy was a concept the contents and contours of which were only tentatively and gradually fixed". The Roman Catholic Church has for a long period of time considered it authoritative that there are seven sacraments, no more, no less. But the Apostle Peter did not know this. During the Middle Ages it was even thought possible that the foot-washing was also a sacrament [8]. There is 'development of doctrine', to use a favourite concept of John Henry Newman. So, if at first it may not be sufficiently clear what is 'orthodox', it can subsequently not always be clear what is 'heretic'. This applies, of course, especially to the young Church which with her doctrine, her liturgy, her hierarchy, was growing out of the swaddling-clothes.

3. The classical theory challenged

That the Churches of the Reformation did and do not want to be called 'heretical' - which involves also smaller Protestant sects, sometimes called 'the stepchildren of Christianity' - had its consequences for the concepts of 'orthodoxy' and 'heresy'. A climactic event was the publication of Gottfried Arnold's 'Unpartheyische Kirchen- und Ketzergeschichte vom Anfang des Neuen Testaments bis auf das Jahr Christi 1688' (Frankfurt am Main, 1699-1700). In spite of his calling his disquisition 'unpartheyisch' = impartial, the author was not impartial at all. He was far from being a Roman Catholic, but he was no friend of the mainline Protestant Churches either, state-bound as they were. In his eyes there was something incurably wrong with the institutional Churches. His predilection was for the 'ecclesia invisibilis', the invisible community of true believers who needed neither an ecclesiastical organization nor a dogmatics. It will be evident that, in Arnold's view, the distinction 'orthodox-heterodox' loses its meaning.

Arnold was reasoning on the basis of his own spiritualist, mystical, and pietist convictions which were not shared by everyone. But the stone he had set rolling kept rolling. The philosophers of the Enlightenment, the rationalists and the positivists of the nineteenth century, the secularized people of the twentieth, were, and are, not greatly interested in the differences between orthodoxy and heresy, distinctions that they tend to consider theological hair-splitting. What remained, however, was heresy, not as a doctrinal proposition, but as an historical phenomenon.

This modern point of view was only recently expressed by Hans-Dieter Betz in the following terms. "Determining what has to count as heretical or as orthodox respectively depends on the momentary standpoint, on the theological and doctrinal propositions, and on a given situation. The traditional definition of heresy as an arbitrary deviation from a doctrinal norm institutionally represented by a majority does, therefore, not hold good for primitive Christianity ... The phenomena are multiform and cannot be brought together under one formula" [9].

Such a postmodernist point of view makes it very hard, if not impossible, to employ the terms 'orthodoxy' and 'heresy'. What today is orthodox may be heretical to-morrow, and the reverse. Does a criterion suggested by Alfred Schindler who similarly leaves doctrinal contents aside, help us much further? "A heresy is a doctrine that was for some time important and was sustained by persons of consequence or by large groups, or churches, that, in so far as they did not manage to survive as a minority, succumbed to rejection, persecution, or other historical mechanisms of 'disappearing'" [10].

According to this criterion, Arianism would be an heresy, because it had to leave the scene, whereas the Churches of the Reformation are not heretical, because they have come to stay. This criterion is certainly useful and workable, but a less satisfying aspect of it is that it leaves the doctrinal content out of consideration. What it does not explain is why some doctrines or tenets of faith ended on top and others 'ceased into nothingness' or became fringe phenomena. Could this have something to do with content? However, it fits neatly into our present disquisition, since its terms 'rejection, succumbing, disappearance' suggest that we have to do with an unbridgeable opposition, that is, with dualism.

4. Distinguishing orthodoxy and heterodoxy

In his book on the relations between orthodoxy and heresy Turner points out a number of differences between them. The first regards their respective attitudes towards the Bible. Whereas the great Church accepts the whole Bible, both Old and New Testaments, with every letter of it, heterodox groups use a selective method. A drastic instance is how Marcion handled Scripture : he simply dropped the whole of the Old Testament and struck out the greater part of the New [11]. Other heresiarchs were less radical, but they too ignored large parts of the Bible.

A second means of distinguishing both manners of believing is how they understood the meaning of the Bible. The heterodox had a very strong penchant for what Turner somewhere calls a 'wooden literalness', a tendency to accept nothing but the most literal sense of a phrase or passage. They had no eye for context or metaphorical significance. The Arians, who combated the idea that Jesus was the Son of God and held that he was not divine, not the Second Person of Holy Trinity, proved their thesis, for instance, by this saying of Jesus : "Why do you call me good? Nobody is good but God alone" [12]. Didn't Jesus himself state that he was not divine? No attention was paid to the context in which this passage stands; we shall have to come back to this. The Fathers were far more intent upon context, upon structure, upon the use of metaphor. If they sinned, they did so by too much allegorizing, by wanting to find a second and higher meaning almost everywhere. But after all, allegorizing means that we should not stop at the letter.

Another difference is that many heterodox sects, especially the Gnostic ones, were élitist, destined only for those who 'knew'. The main Church "provided a refuge for all souls" [13]; she cared for the sinners and welcomed them. The Gnostics, by contrast, were exactly those who were no sinners, who were redeemed. Sinners were all the others, the great majority.

Orthodoxy also means homogeneity, theological consequence and coherence. Heterodox sects were often as eclectic as they were syncretistic; they, and then again the Gnostics in particular, introduced many pagan and esoteric elements, of the most diverse provenance, into their systems. Some of them contain the grossest contradictions and irregularities. As Turner expresses it : "In no case (can) we discover among the heresies a genuine feeling for the organic wholeness of the Church's Faith" [14].

Not a few heterodox sects were convinced that, apart from what the New Testament reported, there also existed a 'secret doctrine'. Jesus had, according to this opinion, entrusted his disciples with a doctrine that was not to be divulged to everyone but should be handed down, mainly orally, along a line of trusted receivers and be kept hidden from the eyes of the vulgus. The Church, on the contrary, stuck steadfastly to the New Testament such as it was 'published'. Some time elapsed, indeed, before the canon of the New Testament was complete - there was discussion on the question which books belonged to it and which not -, but there never was talk of a secret doctrine. Everything was (and is) open to everyone.

Finally there were differences in practice. Some sects had no Eucharist at all; others celebrated it with water instead of wine. There were sects which permitted women to celebrate it, for instance the Montanists and the Valentinian Gnostics, or, in the Middle Ages, the Cathars and the Waldensians. The main Church considered such customs heretical.

NOTES TO CHAPTER I

1. The German 'Ketzer' and the Dutch 'ketter' have a different origin, namely 'Cathar', the name of the medieval sect, - a word, that in its turn, comes from 'katharos' (Greek) = pure.
2. Flav.Jos., Jew.Ant. 13.171. See Vol. VII, Ch. V8a.
3. Turner, Pattern 3-8.
4. This argument is the leading idea of Bossuet's 'Histoire des variations des Églises protestantes' (1688).
5. Turner, Pattern 230.

6. Even today this idea has not entirely died out. On Thursday November 30, 1995, Queen Elizabeth II of Britain, head of the Church of England, attended a vesper service in the Roman Catholic Westminster Cathedral in London. It was the first time since the reign of King James II that a British monarch attended a Roman Catholic service in Britain. The Queen was warmly applauded by the congregation that included the (Anglican) Archbishop of Canterbury and the Moderator of the Free Church Federal Council. But outside stood Protestants with banners accusing the Queen of betraying her vow to uphold the Protestant Reformed Religion; demonstrators told the press that the Roman Catholic Church was 'corrupt and not a true Church' (The Tablet, December 9, 1995).

7. Turner, Pattern 9.

8. E. Amann s.v. 'Lavement des pieds. Est-il un sacrament?', Dict.théol.cath. 9. Paris, 1926.

9. Hans-Dieter Betz s.v. 'Häresie I'. Theol.Realenz. 14, Lief. 1/2, 313. Berlin, 1985. If this were correct, then there is no telling what was orthodox and what heretical in the early Church. Orthodoxy would be the outcome of much infighting between tendencies and groups in this Church; correct doctrine would be, so to speak, the result of the fortunes of war. Or in other words, orthodoxy would be a more or less accidental end product of theological debate; the term would not refer to a, if not defined, then at least definable, body of unchangeable doctrine, which, I suppose, is precisely the background of Betz's remark.

10. Alfred Schindler s.v. 'Häresie II", Theol.Realenz. 14, Lief. 1/2, 318. Berlin, 1985.

11. See Vol. IX, Ch. II.3.

12. Mt. 19:17; Mc. 10:18; Lc. 18:19.

13. Turner, Pattern 117.

14. Turner, Pattern 231.

CHAPTER II THE APOSTLES AND THE FATHERS ON HERESY

1. In the New Testament

a. Two baptist movements

Seen from the viewpoint of the main Church, there have been heresies right from the start. Already during Jesus' lifetime we can detect deviating tendencies. Christianity is a baptist movement, but John the Baptist was the first to baptize, a well-attested fact in all four Gospels. After having been baptized by John, Jesus himself began to baptize. Some of the followers of the Baptist left him and joined Jesus, Andrew, for instance [1]. John, who had begun baptizing along the lower course of the Jordan, later went more northward, because there was abundance of water there. He baptized many people in that region. So there were two baptist movements in those days. Some of John's followers protested to him that another person (Jesus) was also baptizing and drawing large crowds, but John did not object to this [2]. We also know that Jesus always spoke with the greatest respect of John.

The two baptist movements were not controversial at first. But it is possible, even probable, that John's movement became, after his death, the nucleus of all those baptists sects that later proliferated between the Jordan and the Euphrates and of which the Mandaeans are the last existing offshoot [3]. Since these sects manifest decidedly Gnostic-dualistic traits, we are entitled to speak of an heretical deviation.

b. Warnings in the Pauline and Catholic Letters

In Galatians Paul tells his addressees that they have been 'bewitched', in all probability by Judaeo-Christian teachers [4]. The author of Colossians warns his faithful against 'hollow and delusive speculations ... centred on the elemental spirits of the world', which very probably refers to an astrological cult [5]. The fact that Paul somewhere speaks of 'the attested truth of God' [6] suggests that, in his eyes, there existed something like an accepted body of doctrine. To his wavering Galatians he wrote that there are persons who are 'trying to distort the gospel of Christ' which implies that to him this 'gospel' (doctrine) had a definite character, not to be changed. And he added : "If anyone preaches a gospel at variance with the gospel which you received, let him be outcast!" [7]. This has a dualistic sound : the apostle is clearly of the opinion that in a Christian contrasting and differing doctrines cannot exist side by side.

The author of Philippians too speaks of 'the truth of the gospel' [8]. The author of 1 Timothy wrote of 'subversive doctrines inspired by devils' [9]. Peter states that there is no reason for doubts and deviations : God's "divine power has bestowed on us everything that makes for life and true religion" [10]. Jude, in his short epistle, warns against the danger of false belief.

c. Warnings in the Revelation of John

In his letters to the seven Churches of Asia Minor the author of the Book of Revelation mentions several heretical sects, the Nicolaites [11], 'Satan's synagogue' [12], the 'teaching of Balaam' [13], the 'lures of Jezabel' [14], the 'deep secrets of Satan' [15]. The exact nature of these sects is not always clear, at least not to us, but it is evident that he is speaking of deviants. Although the Apostles and the early missionaries did not have a handbook of dogmatics or a catechism at their disposal, they all seem to be referring to something definite, to an accepted body of insights with regard to the message of the New Testament. If Paul speaks of 'a gospel different from that you have already accepted' [16], he is thinking of a commonly agreed upon set of opinions. My conclusion would be that even in the apostolic Church there was a sort of 'depositum fidei' on which the missionaries drew and which was accepted by the converts. From this deposit deviations - heresies - could originate. It should be stated at the outset that, whereas there were many intermediate links between the Jewish and Christian religions and no small degree of affinity and agreement, there was no middle ground between orthodoxy and heterodoxy. Their relationship was purely dualistic.

d. The beginning of a dualistic relationship

Already in the very first decades of Christianity heresies originated, mainly Gnostic ones. There are allusions to this in several New Testament Letters - 1 Timothy, for instance, warns against persons 'teaching erroneous doctrines' [17] -, but nowhere are they so outspoken as in the Second Letter of Peter. "You will have false teachers among you. They will teach disastrous heresies, disowning the very Master who bought them (= Jesus who also redeemed these selfsame teachers - F.), and bringing swift disaster on their own heads. They will gain many adherents to their dissolute practices, through whom the true will be brought into disrepute. In their greed for money they will trade on your credulity with sheer fabrications. But the judgment long decreed for them has not been idle; perdition waits for them with unsleeping eyes" [18]. This is stated in the form of a prophecy, but in all probability the author was already acquainted with the phenomemon of deviation. It accuses the hersesiarchs of loose living, a point that is laboured upon in great detail in the rest of the epistle. But what is really telling is that the author assumes the dualistic stance that will remain characteristic for the relationship orthodoxy - heterodoxy.

2. Justin the Martyr on heterodoxy

We must now turn to the first Father of the Church who occupied himself with the problem of heresy and was also the first to define an attitude to it, Justin the Martyr, in the middle of the second century A.D. Speaking of attitudes, it should be noted in this context that none of the Gnostic heresies came in for a condemnation by the magisterium of the Church, with one exception. Pope Dionysius (259/260-267/268), in a letter of 262 to his namesake bishop Dionysius of Alexandria, condemned the trinitarian doctrine of Marcion, calling it 'a diabolical teaching' [19].

To return now to Justin, this Church Father is the author of a 'Syntagma adversus omnes haereses' [20] which, alas, is lost. Heretics were to him Simon the Magician, whose influence he ascribed to the working of the devil, Menander, and Marcion, who was equally helped by demons to seduce many people to blasphemy [21]. He also mentions Saturnilus, Basilides, and Valentinus [22]. He was not interested in any way in the personal lifestyle of the heresiarchs [23]. What counts for him is theological content.

Irenaeus very probably quoted Justin directly from the lost Syntagma with the following citation : "I would not have believed the Lord himself, if he had proclaimed another God than the Creator, who is our beginner and our sustainer" [24]. This is directed not so much against those who believed in pagan gods but rather against Gnostic heretics who posited the existence of a second god, the Demiurge, who is the real (often evil-intentioned) creator of the cosmos. Irenaeus adds that "Justin very properly said that before the coming of Christ, Satan never ventured to blaspheme God"; in other words, the idea of a Demiurge did not yet exist. Then follows, apparently from Justin, a dualistic statement. "However, when the Lord had come, he (the Satan) learned from the words of Christ and those of the apostles in all necessary clarity that the eternal fire is prepared for him who turns away from God, and for all those who, without penance, persist in their apostasy ... Those who are full of a demoniacal spirit fling accusations at our Creator who bestowed on us the spirit of life and gave the relevant Law to all ... They invent another Father who is neither interested in our affairs nor gives guidance to them and even falls in with all our sins" [25].

It will be evident that Justin is not speaking here of pagans but of Gnostics. It is all the work of demons, he explains. "Demons incite certain persons to pass themselves off as gods"; in this context he mentions Simon the Magician, Menander, and Marcion, all of them acting under the influence of demons [26].

3. Irenaeus of Lyons as an inventorist of heresies

The first complete work directed against heretical doctrines that we possess is that of Irenaeus of Lyons, the five books of his 'Adversus haereses'; it was composed in the years around A.D. 170. For his opponents he used the word 'heretics' [27]. In his view all heretics are the spiritual heirs of Simon the Magician whether they acknowledge it or not [28]. The doctrine of Valentinus was the arch-enemy: refuting Valentinianism was sufficient to topple all Gnostic systems [29]. From the school of Valentinus 'a many-headed monster came forth' [30].

4. The work of Hegesippus

Around A.D. 180 Hegesippus wrote his 'Hypomnemata' in five books, in which he had a lot to say about heresies. This work would have been an highly useful source for our knowledge of heterodoxy, but only a few fragments of it survive, preserved by Eusebius. This church historian quotes Hegesippus textually where he writes that there were in Israel seven heretical sects; the reader will be surprised to hear that not only the Essenes and the Samaritans, but also the Sadducees and the Pharisees were counted among them. They are classified as heretical because these sects were opposed to the tribe of Judah and to Christ [31]. This means that, in the opinion of Hegesippus, heresy is a combined Jewish-Christian phenomenon. He speaks nowhere of demonic influences. Probably he was a Jewish Christian himself [32].

The ideas of Hegesippus ran as follows. When James, the relative of Jesus, was bishop of Jerusalem, the Church was not yet 'stained by false doctrines'; for this reason she was called a 'virgin'. But after James had suffered a martyr's death, Symeon, another relative of the Lord, became bishop. A certain Thebutis "began to soil her (the Jerusalemite Church)",

13

because he had not become the successor of James; he belonged to one of the seven heretical Jewish sects. According to this version, heterodoxy originated in the personal dépit of a disappointed man, but had at the same time a foothold in Jewish heresies.

Hegesippus then sums up the heretics that followed one another : the followers of Simon, Dositheus, Menander, Saturnilus, and Marcion, and the Valentinians and Basilidians, all different from each other, he says. "From them come the false Christs, the false prophets, and the false apostles who have destroyed the unity of the Church by pernicious doctrines about God and his anointed" [33]. It will strike the reader that in this report Simon the Magician is not the arch-villain.

5. Hippolytus and heterodoxy

Hippolytus too was much concerned with heterodoxy. He composed a 'Syntagma', an 'Adversus omnes haereses'; this work is lost. Much later, around 230, he wrote the 'Refutatio omnium haeresium', also known as the 'Philosophoumena', the greater part of which has been preserved; he had discovered that there were far more heresies (mainly Gnostic ones) than his original thirty-two. In the great Refutatio he was not only firing at the heretics but also at Pope Calixtus I (217-222) whose lax attitude towards Gnostics and towards heresy in general, he found, had encouraged the Gnostics, mainly the Elkasaites, to establish themselves in Rome [34].

6. Tertullian in action

Around 200 the situation of the Church was somewhat confused. This was mainly due to the impact of the Valentinian Gnosis, a system that was far more intelligent and accessible and more coherent than other Gnostic systems [35]. Valentinian propaganda did its utmost to present this doctrine as not really different from orthodox Christianity but as more spiritual, so that not a few Christians were taken in. Irenaeus was already out combating the Gnosis by providing accurate information about it. But it was Tertullian who mounted the main attack, ca. 200, with his book 'De praescriptione hereticorum'. In many other books he wrote against Gnostics and Montanists : five books 'adversus Marcionem', against the Gnostics in general, against the Valentinians and others, and against the Docetists in his 'De carne Christi'. All these books concentrate on theological content, but 'De praescriptione' has a juridical basis (Tertullian was a lawyer), for a 'praescriptio' is an objection, mainly the objection against opening a process. The idea is that Christians should not start a learned (or quasi-learned) discussion with heretics. Tertullian is thinking here mainly of uninformed faithful, not of himself and other theologically schooled persons.

Heresy, says Tertullian, is false doctrine, a deviation from true doctrine in the form of a personal 'choice'. True doctrine comes to us through the Apostles who had it from the Lord himself. "When an angel from heaven would proclaim another Gospel, he would be cursed by us" [36]. The author compares heresy to a fever that lames and corrupts the faith. It is an evil; as long as we are incapable of destroying it, we should shun it. "Heresies work eternal death and the glow of a worse fire ... Heresies have power over those who do not possess a strong faith ... Heresies acquire their power only through the weakness of many people but lose their force when they encounter a really strong faith" [37]. He had to admit that not a few Christians defected to the other side : 'a bishop, a deacon, a teacher, yes, even a martyr' [38].

Tertullian does not seek for the origin of heresy in a person, in Simon or somebody else, but in (pagan) philosophy. "Heresies have their armour from philosophy", a philosophy which is nothing but 'the wisdom of the world'. Here yet another vexing problem looms up : that of the attitude of Christianity towards pagan philosophy. Tertullian would have nothing of it : philosophy is human wisdom, a mimic and falsifier of truth; it is divided into many heresies through the pluriformity of the schools that fight each other. "We do not need speculation since Jesus Christ, no inquiry since the Gospel has been prolaimed. When we believe, we do not wish anything beyond the faith" [39]. There is more than a touch of fideism in this. But let us not forget that Tertullian was thinking all the time of simple Christians who could easily get confused by the manifold propositions of the philosophers.

In the eyes of Tertullian heretics did not deserve the name of 'Christian'. The Church has the 'regula fidei' which it received from the Apostles, the Apostles from Christ, and Christ from God. In their arbitrary way heretics deviate from the regula. "Since they are heretics, they cannot be Christians, because the doctrines they adhere to are their own choice; they have them not from Christ. It is therefore that they are called 'heretics'" [40]. With this categorical statement, says Alfred Schindler, Tertullian presents the 'classical typology of heresy'. Later authors did nothing but fortifying, accentuating, and differentiating this fundamental approach [41]. Many Fathers followed suit, such as Clement of Alexandria and Origen. Since the same arguments are repeated over and over again, we need not go into them.

7. The 'medicine-chest' of Epiphanius

The next great publication in the field of heresiology was the 'Panarion' (374-377) [42] by Epiphanius, bishop of Salamis in Cyprus, with the subtitle 'The medicine-chest against all heresies', a very complete catalogue and encyclopedia of heterodoxy. Although Epiphanius intended to provide unstable faithful with 'medicine', he was not optimistic enough to believe that heresy would ever go away : Church and heterodoxy were doomed to exist side by side. He throws his net very wide : he enumerates non-Christian and pre-Christian heresies, along with pagan philosophies and Jewish factions. Howver, Epiphanius' arch-heretic was not Simon the Magician or any other Gnostic prophet but ... Origen. It was his duty, he thought according to Rufinus, to hound Origen everywhere in every language [43]. This remarkable attitude demands a separate treatment which we will preserve for the next chapter.

8. Augustine and the secular arm

Around 400 Augustine too was active in the fight against heterodoxy. Late in his life he embarked upon an 'adversus haereses', a work that remained a torso. In it he enumerated eighty-eight heresies in a kind of catalogue, all of them with a short description. His intention was to add a treatise of a general nature to it, but nothing came of it [44]. In the course of his enormous output he found endless opportunities for expounding his views on heterodox opinions, but three groups were his favourite targets when it came to browbeating heresy : the Pelagians, the Donatists, the Manichees. More especially it was the Manichees who came under fire; once he had belonged to their Church himself but now he wrote a great many treatises against them.

In contrast to some other Fathers, Augustine did not say that heretics were morally depraved; he was quite ready to admit that there were excellent people among them. This does not mean that he was 'soft on heresy'. Far from it! He once gave a definition of what is a heretic : it is "the one who, because of some worldy advantage and far more in order to win fame and get a dominant position, generates and follows erroneous and new positions" [45]. This was a definition that had come to stay! Augustine did not put too fine a point on it : the opinions in question were false, and heretics were not inspired by religious or spiritual motives.

Augustine was no great admirer of the enormous concentration of power that was the Roman Empire. In consequence, in a very long letter to his fellow-bishop Vincentius - a complete treatise written around 400 - he pleaded against using force (by the secular authorities) against heretics. Although he called such heretics 'atrocious enemies of us, infesting our quiet and peace with various serious kinds of violence and craftiness' [46], he found, nevertheless, that they should be won back by arguments and by the word of God.

However, around 400 there occurred a considerable change in his attitude [47]. He was obviously upset by the persistence of heresy - there were Donatists in his own diocese -, and he felt troubled by the fate that awaited them : eternal perdition. Since he knew how headstrong they were, coercion or punishment by the public authorities might be the ultimate remedy, the last means to save them. But Augustine was not thinking at all of capital punishment.

9. The ghost let out of the bottle

We have now discussed the attitude of the Fathers and the bishops of these centuries with regard to heresies, heretics, and heretical movements. Often doctrinal issues caused enormous commotion in the Church. There can be no doubt that the stance of the Fathers was staunchly dualistic : nulla communio! Between the damnable opinions of the heretics and the orthodox creed no compromise was possible. Of course, not only the heresies but the heretics too, in particular the heresiarchs, posed a problem to the Church; not a few of these movements gained many adherents.

The fight against them had mainly a verbal character. But things began to take a different turn in the fourth century, when Christianity had become a religio licita, and still more when it had become the official religion of the state. The rulers then had a vested interest in defending the cohesion of the faith and the integrity of the Church. It was as of old, in pagan times : the one Empire should have one religion. The Fathers and the ecclesiastical authorities, although not enthusiastic for political power, not even in the hands of Christian rulers, wanted to enlist the help of the state in the repression of heresy. They did not think of and did not ask for capital punishment; they found prohibitions, reprimands, and perhaps banishment, punishment enough.

But by invoking the assistance of the secular arm, they unwittingly let the genie out of the lamp. The state did not need to be told twice to intervene. It did, and it did so in its own way, a way the clerics had not envisioned : by that of physical force. The execution of some Priscillianists, a sad event that has still to occupy us, was the first instance of this, and with it a dismal story began : that of the physical extermination of heretics.

NOTES TO CHAPTER II

1. Jo. 1:40.
2. Jo. 3:22-30.
3. See Vol. IX, Ch. III.

4. Gal. 3:1; see 4:10.
5. Col. 2:8.
6. 1 Cor. 2:1.
7. Gal. 1:19.
8. Phil. 1:7.
9. 1 Tim. 4:1.
10. 2 Pt. 1:3.
11. Ap. 2:6.
12. Ap. 2:9.
13. Ap. 2:14.
14. Ap. 2:20.
15. Ap. 2:24.
16. 2 Col. 11:4.
17. 1 Tim. 1:3.
18. 2 Pt. 2:1-3.
19. Denzinger/Schönmetzer 112.
20. Mentioned by him in 1 Ap. 26.8.
21. Just., 1 Ap. 26.4-6.
22. Just., Dial. 35.6. Obviously he did not see Christians following Jewish customs as heretics, Dial. 47.2. Hilgenfeld, Ketzergesch. 21 : "Eine Häresie des Judenchristentums hat bei Justin keine Stelle".
23. Just., 1 Ap. 26.7.
24. Ir., Adv.haer. 4.6.2.
25. Ir., Adv.haer. 5.26.2.
26. Just., 1 Ap. 26.
27. Ir., Adv. haer. 1.22.2; 4.26.2; 4.34.1.
28. Ir., Adv. haer. 1.27..4 and Book 1, Praef.
29. Ir., Adv. 2.31.1.
30. Ir., Adv. haer. 1.30.5.
31. Eus., HE 4.22.
32. Eus., HE 4.22.
33. Eus., HE 22.6.

34. Extensive treatment in Hilgenfeld, Ketzergeschichte 450-626. A more recent work is that of Klaus Koschorke, Hippolyts Ketzerbekämpfung und Polemik gegen die Gnostiker. Wiesbaden, 1975.
35. See Vol. VIII, Ch. VIII.
36. Tert., Praescr. 6.
37. Tert., Praescr. 2.
38. Tert., Praescr. 3.
39. Tert., Praescr. 7.
40. Tert., Praescr. 37.
41. Alfred Schindler s.v. 'Häresie II", TRE 14, 324. Berlin/New York, 1985.
42. PG 41. Paris, 1863.
43. Hier., Adv.Ruf. 2.21.
44. Aug., De haer. (see Bibliography).
45. Aug., De util.cred. 1.
46. Aug., Ep. 93.1.1.
47. Brown, St.Aug.s Attitude 265/266, believes that we should not think of a sudden 'conversion' here. "It is said that, until 405, Augustine had expressed purely 'liberal' principles by advocating a solution of the (Donatist - F.) schism through free discussion; that he was disillusioned by the unwillingness of the Donatists to listen to reason ... This interpretation is insufficient for many reasons ... We may be dealing less with a volte-face by external circumstances than with a phenomenon common to many aspects of the thought of Augustine - that is, with a sudden precipitation under external pressures of ideas which, previously, had evolved slowly and imperceptibly over a long time." Lamirande, Church 24, is "inclined to side with those who find no evidence that Augustine ever rejected the intervention of secular power because he thought it immoral in itself".

CHAPTER III THE APOLOGISTS

While we studied the reactions of the Apostles, the Fathers, and the ecclesiastical authorities to heresies and heretics, nothing was said of the contents of those doctrines that were considered unorthodox. In the course of the centuries under consideration heretical doctrines were numerous. Mercifully, perhaps, of many of these we know little more than the name. It is not my intention to present a comprehensive catalogue of heresies. They will be passed in review in order to assess their degree of dualism. To avoid the impression that all heresies were dualistic, however, something must be said about the non-dualistic ones.

Quite a number of deviant doctrines have already been treated in depth and in length. The greater part of the earliest heresies were Gnostic in nature. The oldest of these was, in all probability, that of Simon the Magician, with his successors Menander and Saturnilos. Then there were the Barbelo-Gnostics, the Ophites, the Nicolaites, the Carpocratians, and the adherents of Cerinthus. Important sects with a large following were those of Basilides and Valentinus, that of Marcion, preceded by Cerdon and succeeded by Apelles, and above all the Manichaeans. Of all those sects and their doctrines I wrote extensively in the Volumes VII, VIII, and IX. The general tenor of my disquisition on the Gnostic systems is that they were dualistic to the core. I feel I should not repeat myself here. I must, therefore, refer the reader to these volumes I mentioned. I may add that in Volume IX, Chapter V, Part II I explained why, in my opinion, the Gnosis should not be seen as a branch of Christianity, next to and equivalent with the orthodox branch.

1. The beginning of the Christian dispute with classical thought

The threat that the Gnosis presented to the orthodox Church was met by those of the Fathers who were called 'Apologists'; they were called so because they wrote 'apologies', defenses and explanations of the Christian creed, mainly destined for non-Christians. As Wand writes, they were "men of philosophical training who were well fitted to meet the pseudo-science of the Gnostics with genuine rationality" [1]. Their key-concept was 'Logos', a concept authentically biblical, since it was hallowed by its use in the Prologue to the Fourth Gospel; at the same time it was an accepted philosophical concept so that it could be used to make the Christian creed palatable for educated pagans - a creed that, in the second century, was seen by them as fit for slaves and boors only.

The Apologist Fathers - such as Justin, Theophilus, Origen, Tertullian, Athenagoras, and others - were Greeks who are often seen as the founders of Christian theology, that is, of a rational and scholarly account of what Christian doctrine is [2]. Thus began what Pelikan calls 'the Christian Dispute with Classical Thought' [3]. The encounter was not without its dangers; the Apologist Fathers are sometimes seen skating over very thin ice. Not a few ancient and modern theologians found that they occasionally even went through the ice, as we shall see in the case of Origen.

2. Pre-Christian Christians

Since there existed as yet no Christian apparatus of theological and philosophical concepts, these scholars were forced to borrow right and left from pagan philosophy. It pleased them to present the great Hellenic thinkers as, at least partly, pre-Christian. According to Justin the Martyr, all mankind are 'partakers of the Logos'. "Those who lived according to reason are Christians, even though accounted atheists. Such among the Greeks were Socrates and Heraclitus and those who resembled them" [4]. As one sees, this scholar is prepared to go to great lenghts to salvage pagan thinkers for Christianity! The concept Justin employed to this end was that of the 'logos spermatikos', the 'seminal Logos'. This was the idea that, even before the Logos had appeared on earth in the person of Jesus Christ, it had been present as a spiritual force or impulse in Greek thought and poetry; these Greeks were excellent in proportion to the share they had of the 'seminal Logos' [5].

3. The Father, the Son, and creation

The basic tenet of the Apologists was that God is the Creator of all that is, of cosmos and mankind - a tenet that is perfectly orthodox, of course; the creation took place 'ex nihilo'. For the pagan Greeks this solved a problem, since the Olympian religion provided no answer to the question of how and why everything had originated; even their gods had a beginning in time. The fact that the Creator was also the supreme Good suited them well, since for classical thought also the cosmos was good.

The dogma of the Trinity was slow in development; there was a long stretch of time before it was defined in so many words, namely by the Nicene Fathers in 325. Around A.D. 180 Theophilus, bishop of Antioch, was the first to use the term 'trias' for the godhead, although he spoke of Father, Logos, and Wisdom [6]. But this does not mean at all that the idea of a divine Triad was foreign to earlier Fathers or even those who were his contemporaries. It is, for instance, clearly present in Justin. This author, firmly opposed as he was to both Gnosis and Docetism [7], wanted to define as exactly as possible the status of the Son or Logos, especially in relation to creation and redemption. To him, the supreme Father is "too remote and transcendent to be in direct contact with this world" [8]. In fact, Justin's Father is the Demiurge; he uses the very word : 'the Demiurge of the All' [9], 'the Creator of all that is and the intelligent Father' [10]. There is an unsolved anomaly here : the Supreme Being is the Creator, but he does not actually create. To use Aristotelian terms : in God creation is potency (= in his mind) but not act.

This is what Justin thought of the Supreme Being : "The Father who is inexpressible and who is the Lord of the universe, goes nowhere, does not deplace himself, does not sleep and does not rise, but remains in his abode, wherever that may be. His view is piercing, his hearing is sharp, not that he has eyes and ears, but through an indefinable power. He does not move; no place can contain him, not even the whole world, for he was even before the world was made" [11]. The author is combating the anthropomorphism of the Olympians in theologically impeccable terms, but all the same we are much nearer here to Aristotle's Unmoved Mover than to the benevolent Father of Christian devotion.

Justin, therefore, needed an agent who, instead of the Supreme Being, could perform the actual work of creation. Creation was obviously something of a lower order which could not concern the Father. This gives rise to the suspicion that, in consequence, the creating agent was also of a lower order. Justin's idiosyncratic Logos concept saddles him with a problem. The Logos is God, no doubt. "He is called God, is God, and will be God" [12]. But to the Jewish scholar Trypho he explains at great length that the God of the biblical theophanies should not be confused with the Father. We see him skating here on very thin ice. The one Abraham saw near the oak of Mamre was not the Father "who remains ever in the highest heaven (but) another God or Lord different from the Father of the all" [13]. And elsewhere : "That power which the prophetic Logos calls God and angel, is not only nominally different from the Father, as the light is from the sun, but also distinct numerically" [14].

This is not the two-worlds- and the two-gods-dualism of the Gnosis, but we are dangerously near it. The problem of Justin and other Apologists (Theophilus, Athenagoras, Origen, Tertullian) was how to explain "the transition from the absolute state of existence which is the prerogative of God from all eternity to the contingent, the changing and the temporary which characterizes the world we know" [15]. In their theology this transition is not made easily and smoothly.

We see here hovering in the background the figure of a Demiurge who is different from (although in this case not opposed to) the Supreme God. Of course, the Son is in the Father, and the Father in the Son, through the union and the force of the Holy Spirit. "The Son is the Word (Logos) and the mind of the Father" [16]. Nothing could be more orthodox. But although the Son was coeternal with the Father, he was really born only when the cosmos was about to be created, and it was his task to bring it about [17]. Athenagoras even says that the good God is averse to the spirit which is around matter [18]. We are not far from horizontal dualism here. At the same time, the generation of the Son is, in this view, something that happens in time; he is, in consequence, secondary to the Father. It is evident that there is a contradiction between the Son being coeternal with the Father and his generation in time. Theophilus solved this problem by employing two different terms : as coeternal with the Father the Son was 'endiathetos' (= in the Fathers' mind), and as generated he was 'prophorikos' (= spoke, uttered) [19]. Did Theophilus realize that the Son became Logos only by his generation in time, and that he seems to be an emanation from the Father rather than a generated being?

4. The special case of Origen

Origen was the most influential of all the Apologists. As Lohse says : "in the third century the Logos Christology has asserted itself mainly through the influence of Origen" [20]. And Daniélou states categorically that "Origen, with Saint Augustine, is the greatest genius of ancient Christianity" [21]. During the so-called 'Origenist controversy', which I am about to consider, he was postumously accused by his opponents of being heterodox. It is not my intention to go over the whole of the theology of this prolific writer [22], but I will concentrate on a few issues.

a. The life of Origen

Origen was an hellenized Egyptian, born in 184 or 185 into a Christian family of Alexandria [23]. His father Leonidas, a fervent Christian, introduced him to the Bible, in addition to the usual course of studies; the child, says Eusebius, had nothing against it [24]. This gives an idea of how a Christian child was educated in those still pagan days : the three r's, with the rest, were learned in a pagan school, while the instruction in religious matters was taken in hand at home. Origen remained a biblical scholar all his life.

The pious father died as a martyr in 202 during the persecution of Septimius Severus. The boy was seventeen then. Eusebius relates that his mother had to hide his clothes, or else he would have gone after his father [25]. Martyrdom was for Origen the highest expression of the Christian faith; he came very near to suffering it himself. After Leonidas's death the young man had to care for the family which consisted of the widow and six younger children; the family fortune had been confiscated by the authorities [26]. It was his good luck that a wealthy lady took the talented adolescent under her wing and enabled him to pursue his studies so that he became in due time a qualified grammaticus [27].

For a time the young professor taught in a pagan grammar school with mainly heathen pupils. He did not feel wholly at ease there, since he considered the teaching of grammar (and of all that went under this name) incompatible with the 'sacred studies', i.e. with the Bible. Classical tradition and Christian thought were still seen as opposed; a solution for this problem had still to be found. It was, therefore, a relief for him, when bishop Demetrius of Alexandria asked him to become the principal of the catechetical school in town, although he was only eighteen years old. But persecution had depleted the city of Christians who otherwise would have been considered first [28]. Origen retained this office for many, many years, and made himself a great reputation. According to Eusebius, the Empress Julia Mammaea, the mother of the Emperor Severus Alexander, when visiting the Egyptian capital, asked for an interview with him and spoke with him about religious matters [29]. Origen, ascetic, abstinent, puritanical, was a fervent Christian but still a layman then.

His peaceful existence in Alexandria was interrupted by occasional travelling, to Rome, to Arabia, to Palestine, to Greece. Passing through Palestine in 230 he was ordained a priest there by two local bishops, friends of his. He was forty-five or forty-six then. His own bishop, Demetrius, took this very ill. Origen was banned, deposed as head of the catechical school, and again laicized. Was this because of the breach of the ecclesiastical rules? Or was it because an eunuch could not become a priest? For Origen, as a young man, had castrated himself in an excess of puritanism. Or was

Demetrius simply jealous because his protégé had become a celebrity [30]? But one thing stands out, and this is important in our context : heterodoxy, deviant opinions, were not the motive; Jerome states this in as many words. This is the more important since Demetrius succeeded in ranging the greater part of the bishops behind him [31].

Origen retired to Caesarea in Palestine where the bishop was favourable to him and opened another catechetical school there. Engaged in teaching, preaching, and writing, he lived there peacefully until 250 when he became a victim of the great persecution of Decius. He was arrested, horribly tortured, and kept prisoner for some time, but he survived the ordeal [32]. But his health was broken; he died a few years later, in 253, aged sixty-eight or sixty-nine.

b. His literary output

The literary output of Origen was immense. Whereas Epiphanius, his formidable but postumous enemy, speaks of no less than six thousand works [33], Jerome stops at two thousand [34] to which the numerous sermons should be added. During his lifetime Origen complained that some of his writings had been adulterated and that texts circulated that were attributed to him but of which he remained innocent. Rufinus devoted a treatise to these falsifications [35]. Apart from his correspondence and the homilies he delivered (a thousand, it is said), what he produced was biblical criticism, works of biblical exegesis and commentaries, works of apologetics and polemics (for instance the 'Contra Celsum'), theological works, and treatises on asceticism [36].

5. Charges and defenders

Origen's theological insights were just as vehemently attacked as they were hotly defended. Even today he is the subject of scholarly discussion [37]. The burning question, then and now, is : was Origen orthodox or heterodox?

A faithful paladin was Pamphilius of Caesarea (he died a martyr's death in 310), who later headed the catechetical school of his town, and who had the care of Origen's famous library there. He wrote an 'Apology for Origen and his opinions'; although this work is lost, enough fragments and passages have been preserved to give us a fair idea of what was advanced against Origen [38]. Centuries later the omnivorous Byzantine reader Photius drafted a list of fifteen theological tenets in Origen's oeuvre that were allegedly heterodox. I quote some of the most incisive. 1. He did not invoke the Son; 2. The Son is not 'good' without comment; 3. The Son does not know the Father as the Father knows himself; 4. The soul of the Redeemer is that of Adam; 5. The Father is invisible to the Son. It will be evident that the general tenor of these accusations is that Origen held the Son to be of a lesser ontological order than the Father. According to Photius, all these charges are false. Had they been correct, they would have brought Origen in the neighbourhood of Adoptionists and Monarchians.

The objections mentioned by Photius are mainly those formulated by Origen's arch-enemy, the ferocious Epiphanius, in his heresy no. 64 of the Panarion. Origen "says, first of all, that the only Son is unable to see the Father ... He does not want, therefore, the Son to be of the substance of the Father. Far from it! He conceives of the Son as totally alien to the Father, and as a creature." Epiphanius brought forward still other objections which he himself found 'more important' - souls had a preexistence, for instance -, but I for one feel that those concerning the Father and the Son have the greater weight. If these objections were justified, then Origen would not have acknowledged the Trinity and not have propounded a Logos-Christology.

6. Some disputed theological tenets of Origen

a. The preexistence of souls

The great question is whether the heterodox tenets formulated above really occur in Origen's texts. So much one can safely say : in this crude form most of them certainly not [39]. But another question is whether Origen, when he was formulating his theological insights, was not laying himself open to reproaches of this kind. What Epiphanius reproached him with was not so much that he was an heretic but that he was flirting with paganism. The preexistence of souls was, indeed, an idea dear to Pythagoreans [40] and Platonists [41]. This was, found Epiphanius, returning to 'the dreams and trifles of the Greeks', by which he meant pagan mythology and philosophy - in his eyes a graver error than a wrong opinion about the Trinity [42]. The doctrine of the preexistence of the souls does not form part of the 'depositum fidei', indeed. It was condemned as unorthodox by the Church more than once, for the first time (in its Priscillianist form) by the Council of Toledo in 400 [43], that is long after Origen's days.

Origen must have felt that he had good reason to posit the preexistence of souls, namely to combat the Gnosis, especially Valentianism. God had created a great army of souls, all alike, all equal, all good. So there was no (Gnostic) division into races of men, into pneumatics, psychics, and hylics. The souls are spiritual because God is spiritual and incorporeal; they are endowed with reason, because God is reason, and they have a free will, because God is free [44]. All these souls originally contemplated God with an equal fervour.

b. The fault and the Fall

But the problem is that it is no longer so : souls have become very different, ranging from the highest angels to the lowest demons. How is this to be explained? This is where the fault and the Fall come in. What the souls possess they do not own by nature but by grace; free will and reason are gifts from God. They can use these gifts against God (and against themselves); "some of them walk in the way of progress imitating God, others go to the fall through their negligence" [45].

In this way a hierarchy has originated, ranging from the archangels down to the lesser angels who rule the stars and who, physically occupied as they are, are less pure than the highest angels. Other souls have fallen deeper, having committed evil and distanced themselves from God; these others have become the human beings and the demons. To punish the human beings, God has enclosed them in a body [46]. It should be stressed, however, that all creatures, even the highest angels, participate to a lesser or greater degree in the fault. It seems that they became somewhat dissatisfied with their perfection and wanted a change. In fact, no soul has remained wholly untainted, with the exception of the preexistent Spirit of Christ who remained wholly pure [47].

What Origen needed this construction for was his wish to combat the Gnostics. According to them, the fault was something cosmic, a disaster of which man became the helpless victim. It is remarkable that in Origen's model of thought soul and body have a different origin; another remarkable thing is that these origins are also ontologically different, the soul being of a far more exalted nature than the body which is hardly more than an envelope for the soul. We are very close to a soul-body-dualism here.

The freedom of spiritual, and especially human beings, is fundamental in Origen's theology. For him the fault was committed by spiritual beings of their own free will : one can freely choose between being either a child of God or a child of the devil. "Who sins is from the devil; who does not sin is born from God" [48]. It must, however, be stressed that Origen remains rather close here to the Gnostic concepts he is out to combat. Firstly, in the theology of Genesis 3 the fault was committed by humans in a terrestrial setting. In Gnostic ideology it took place in extraterrestrial spheres as a cosmic, non-human drama. In Origen there is no cosmic drama but equally no terrestrial setting. As De Faye writes : "according to him, the Fall takes place in a transcendent world; its actors are not the first couple but transcendent entities; the cause of the Fall has nothing to do with the sin of the first man". It is for this reason that this scholar remarks that Origen "has borrowed from Gnostic theologians the principal elements of his doctrine of the Fall, the pivot of his whole theology" [49]. Where, however, Origen fundamentally disagreed with the Gnostics - and this is the essential front on which he fought them -, is that he does not acknowledge a cosmic drama of which mankind becomes the helpless victim. But let us add that the difference between the children of God and those of the devil at least suggests the existence of two races of men.

c. Why there is a cosmos

The consequence of the Fall is that God needed to create a cosmos. The fallen entities have become more or less material, while the human beings have been clad with a far heavier body than the angels. For these bodies an abode was needed, and this is the world [50]. "With the body the visible world appears. The cosmos owes not only its existence to the Fall of the intelligible entities, but also its present condition", that is, its variety and its changeability [51]. This again is wholly unbiblical. The presupposition is, in all probability, that Origen has strong hesitations in attributing the creation of matter to God [52]. There is no doubt that, on this point, he is close to Gnostic ideology. He does not say, with the Gnostics, that the world, is utterly bad. But he remains prejudiced with regard to nature and the cosmos [53].

It is very curious that in Origen's terminology the coming to be of the cosmos is not really a creation, a 'ktisis'. It seems that the empirical cosmos, as Heimann calls it, is a 'derivation' from the original creation, a cold sediment of it, a 'katabolê'. Origen always speaks of the cosmos as 'katabolê' = foundation [54].

What we have here is the so-called 'double creation', the creation in two stages or tempi. First there was a spiritual creation and after that a physical one. Man existed first as a spiritual entity without a body and only later received his physical shape. Ugo Bianchi stressed that every doctrine of a double creation in which the second creation takes place on the basis of a primordial Fall, or more precisely, of 'antecedent fault', expresses a dualistic mentality, even if it is found in Fathers like Origen and Gregory of Nyssa who admit of a double creation [55]. According to Crouzel, "Origen understood the first two chapters of Genesis not as two different reports of the creation, but as two distinct creations, the first referring to the soul, solely created in the image (of God) (as) the incorporeal soul and invisible image of the incorporeal and invisible Word, and the second referring to the body that is only the container of the soul" [56]. The term 'katabolê' is obviously used in a pejorative sense, in order to denote a downward movement, a displacement from above to below [57]. Heimann states that we find here "a formal affinity with the Gnosis in respect of cosmology that cannot be denied" [58].

d. Non-existing errors

Most of the errors enumerated by Photius have no basis in Origen's writings. In many respects Origen was impeccably orthodox. The Old Testament has not been made superfluous nor is it contradicted by the New Testament. Jesus is the Son of God endowed with a personal existence of his own; the Logos is not a mode of being of the Father. The Logos is preexistent; there is no adoption of the Son by the Father. The Logos became human in every respect.

That errors were imputed to him is partly the result of careless or biased reading, partly the consequence of the fact that Origen was no systematic theologian, partly also because of his use of philosophical vocabulary which was misunderstood or misinterpreted by his opponents. We should also take in account the fact that, with regard to doctrinal orthodoxy, Origen in the second century had somewhat more room for manoeuvring than was the case later. As Elizabeth Clark expresses it : "at the time when Origen composed his theological masterpiece, On First Principles, which was to become one focus of the later origenist controversy, Christianity stood more open to varied expressions of faith than was the case one hundred and fifty years later" [59].

7. The simple and the perfect

a. Higher Knowledge

There is in Origen no flagrant dualism, such as we find in Gnostic ideologies. But there is a certain duality of the simple and the perfect which is not really dualism. He refers often to this distinction in his sermons. The simple believers come no further than the material significance of scriptural texts, their direct sense. No doubt, they too have the faith that will save them.

However, "believing without knowledge (gnosis) is less than knowing" [60]. Those aspiring to perfection want more; they understand such texts in a way that surpasses the traditional dogmas of the creed and the literal sense of the Bible. Origen's opinion was that the true believers should adhere to the dogmas 'with reason and wisdom' - a wisdom that will lead them to true knowledge. There is a suggestion in this that Origen did not accept the dogmas of the Church in an unqualified way.

Origen had the idea - and he did not like this idea - that most of the faithful were quite content with an elementary knowledge of the faith, with a pious reading of the Bible, and above all, with living a Christian life as far as possible in their daily lives. But for the perfect a higher perspective was opened; their faith was not based on miracles but on contemplation of higher things. This reminds one of the Gnostic thesis that there exists a higher Knowledge [61], a Gnosis. The method Origen used to attain this higher knowledge and to lead his hearers to it was allegorizing. His exegetical works and his homilies teem with allegories, with attempts to find a deeper sense in scriptural texts than the literal one; the literal explanation is only the first step in the process of understanding [62].

It seems that he was sometimes flying too high for his hearers. They accused him of presenting riddles to them : "He is everywhere looking for problems, in order to avoid explaining the text to us" [63]. The difference in response comes out clearly here : the audience felt that they got no explanation, while the speaker felt that what he did was to explain. The suggestion of élitism is also present in the same text I am quoting : "Does he want to demonstrate to us that there are 'stars' among us?".

b. The 'eternal Gospel'

Origen sometimes gives the impression that he wants to proceed even beyond this allegorical understanding, that there is an 'eternal Gospel' [64] which surpasses the New Testament just as much as the New Testament surpasses the Old [65]. As Koch wrote, this stressing of the need of a superior, even supreme knowledge is at variance with the saying of Jesus that one who cannot become like a child cannot enter the Kingdom [66].

8. Origen and philosophy

Of course, Origen was laying himself open to misunderstandings in this way, and he was not entirely blameless. Perhaps his fanatical propagating of asceticism and martyrdom, which was not to everybody's taste, also played a role. Add to this his use of philosophy [67]. Using philosophical methods for his catechical and theological work was a constitutive element in Origenism; "from the first Origen defended the use of philosophy in theological reflection, even if this caused tension with the Christian community ... His use of Platonic wineskins for Christian theology has troubled both admirers and critics since his first works in Alexandria" [68].

In a recent essay Theo Kobush called him 'the initiator of Christian philosophy'; he added that Origen had given this philosophy a structure and a character which characterized Christian thought until in the thirteenth century and even beyond [69]. And Hal Koch spoke of him as 'the great mediator between Christianity and pagan thought'. What he was out to do was to bring about a synthesis of both, but this was, as Koch writes, tantamount to uniting in himself 'two opposed worlds' [70].

There were many in the early Church who found these two worlds irreconcilably, dualistically contrasted. Origen himself was initially one of them. When, as an adolescent, he became the principal of the catechetical school in Alexandria, he found the study of philosophy incompatible with applying himself to things divine; as a consequence he sold his library [71]. But when pagan philosophers and Gnostic heretics came to his school, he concluded that the study of philosophy was necessary for a Christian catechete [72]. He came to see secular thought as a propaedeusis for Christian philosophy [73].

What Origen reproached Greek philosophy for was that it was so cerebral; it had no eye for ordinary life where all philosophers should begin. Life is more than concepts, than Ideas. The Platonists, he found, had two different sets of gods : one for daily life (the ordinary Greek divinities), and one in the form of philosophical concepts. For Origen philosophy should be at the same time knowledge of God and adoration of God, a synthesis of theory and practice [74]. The kernel of Origen's philosophy was his Logos-concept, that of the celestial person becoming man in Jesus of Nazareth in whom heaven and earth, divine and human, were united [75]. Without the Logos-concept all contact between the natural and supernatural would have been lost. For Origen stresses the idea of the absolute transcendence of God so strongly that he places him 'in an unfathomable abstraction'; a human being is incapable of reaching God. It is only through Jesus Christ that one can approach him [76].

9. Origen in the dock

a. Counsel for the prosecution

As might be expected, Origen was accused of being more of a (pagan) philosopher than a Christian thinker, of adulterating and alienating the faith by giving in to pagan thought. He was venerated as the great Christian theologian, and at the same time he became a sign of contradiction [77]. The reproaches his ancient colleagues made against him reach into our time [78] - with Harnack as the most erudite and eloquent spokesman [79]. For him Origen was not wrong in some respects, he was fundamentally wrong. In his attempt to dissolve the dualistic tension between pagan thought and Christian faith, he succumbed to paganism.

His theology "has been built up with the help of Philonic scholarship and has doubtless Neo-Platonic and Gnostic features" [80]. This comes very near to saying that Origen's theology was not Christian and, in consequence, no theology. "As an idealistic philosopher Origen has converted the whole content of the faith into ideas" [81]. He even accused him, the theologian who wished to ban Gnostic dualism, of introducing it by the backdoor, albeit in a very subtle way. And indeed, there is at least a shadow of dualism in Origen's idea of there being an esoteric (for the elect) and an exoteric (for the ordinary believers) form of the Christian religion. According to the German scholar, Catholic theology has since Origen a secular, a Greek, i.e. a pagan, overlay from which it was never able to free itself.

b. Counsels for the defense

The Roman Catholic theologian Urs von Balthasar does not agree with Harnack that Christian theology has been led astray by Origen. But he admits that this ancient thinker introduced elements into it which in **this** (his emphasis) form are not to be found in the Bible. It is not that he proposed new dogmas; it is rather a question of an attitude. He quotes Origen's concept of the preexistence of souls as an example [82].

Peter Widdicombe quotes Rowan Williams who spoke of "the uneasy relationship between the two controlling factors in Origen's thought : the given constraint of Scriptural metaphor and the assumptions of Platonic cosmology" [83]. But Widdicombe does not consider this relationship entirely misguided. "Origen seems not to have perceived any tension between his different patterns of the journey to the knowledge of God ... It is the Bible that provides Origen with the basis for linking God as Father to God as good and 'he who is'" [84].

c. The question of Origen's theological position

It is hard to locate Origen with precision on the line running from orthodoxy to heterodoxy, not only in view of what he wrote himself - which is not always unambiguous -, but also in view of what ancient and modern authors thought and think of him. When all is said and done, Origen was, as he himself wrote, a 'homo vere ecclesiasticus'. If one would have accused of heresy, he would have vehemently protested that his whole life was devoted to the service of the Church. Then why all the fuss? one might well ask. Why did he became the object of such vehement attacks? Why did his name split the Church? But some of his opinions were decidedly not orthodox. Does this make him an heretic? "Not every error is an heresy", wrote Saint Augustine [85]. And we should not forget that most of ecclesiastical doctrine had not yet been dogmatically defined [86].

It seems to me that the real problem with Origen is his manner of working with philosophical concepts. "Were there two persons in Origen, a philosopher and a believer? Was there an impregnable partition between these?". As De Faye states : for Origen himself there existed no such opposition : "the philosopher and the believer, the teacher and the priest, were only two sides of the same personality" [87]. But for an ancient theologian like Epiphanius and for a modern one like Harnack, this was not so : in their view the philosopher in Origen suppressed the believer.

The question of Origen's orthodoxy forms part of a wider problem. "Quid Athenis Jerusalem?" Nascent Christianity was confronted by the far older world of pagan wisdom, by its philosophy, its literature, its worldview. After the first innocent decades it became evident that the confrontation could no longer be avoided. There were some like Origen who manfully accepted the challenge; others, like Tatian, rejected the whole classical heritage as evil, as the work of the devil. The problem has never wholly disappeared. Scholastic authors like Thomas of Aquinas are nowadays accused of having adulterated the faith by applying Aristotelian concepts to it. We shall have to come back to the question of how Christian antiquity coped with the problem of the pagan heritage.

10. The Origenist controversy

a. Epiphanius and Origen

I already mentioned Epiphanius as the unrelenting and untiring enemy of Origen. He found his opponent arrogant and blown up by his own opinion and filling the earth with his empty loquacity. It should be remarked that it was an enmity across the grave, for Origen was already dead and buried for more than a century. Epiphanius accused him of having wrong ideas of the relationship between the Father and the Son [88]. He thought that, in Origen's opinion, Christ was only a human creature and no more [89] which was tantamount to saying that he was the father of Arianism [90]. Another reproach brought forward against Origen by the bishop of Salamis was that the mind of his opponent was 'blinded by Greek paideia' [91] by which he meant pagan philosophy. Epiphanius not only fought Origen's theological insights but, more in general, Hellenic scholarship [92].

b. The beginning of the Origenist controversy

Fighting Origen was for the indefatigable Epiphanius obviously a life-task; he never tired of combating him when and where he could. To quote Maurice Villain : "This erudite and polyglot man, a born defender of orthodoxy, had made surveying the horizon of theological studies a speciality of his, with the aim of signalling every opinion that, under whatever guise, looked corrupted, every proposition that seemed to him to soil the immaculate robe of Catholic dogma" [93]. In 393 [94] he was in Jerusalem, probably not accidentally, for the Holy City was a hotbed of Origenism. The bishop of Jerusalem in those days was John, who acted as his host [95]. This bishop was in connection with a group of ascetic monks living on the Mount of Olives; they all studied the works of Origen assiduously. Jerome, who lived close by in Bethlehem, was originally a member of this group, but had become anti-Origenist under the influence of Epiphanius.

In Jerusalem the undaunted Epiphanius ventured into a lion's den. Shortly before his arrival there had been a violent incident. A certain Atarbius had presented himself at the hermitage on the Mount of Olives and pressed Rufinus, the superior or spokesman of the monastery, to renounce the Origenist heresy [96]; Rufinus had chased him away, striking him with his stick, "that same stick with which you (Rufinus) used to chase away the dogs", wrote the indignant Jerome [97]. This was the start of the Origenist controversy in Jerusalem [98].

c. The war of the sermons

Scarcely had he arrived in Jerusalem and after having heard a sermon delivered by bishop John to his neophytes [99], his guest warned him against the Origenists in his entourage, even asking the prelate to anathemize them, especially Rufinus. Then Epiphanius himself took the floor. Preaching in the church of the Resurrection, he indulged in his favourite pastime of inveighing against Origenism. May we believe Jerome, who was present in the audience and who, in this controversy, does not show his most Christian side, the bishop and his clergy sat listening 'with a doglike grimace and contracted nostrils, scratching their heads'. The angered bishop ordered an archdeacon to stop Epiphanius [100].

The next day John himself retorted with a sermon preached in the church of the Holy Cross in which he did not attack Epiphanius directly but, instead, the 'anthropomorphists' : Origen had often accused his opponents of picturing God in a much too human shape. To quote Jerome again, John spoke 'with fury and indignation' : "Your (= John's) eyes, your hands, your breast were turned towards that old man (Epiphanius) in order to suggest that he was guilty of that stupid heresy (namely anthropomorphism)". Epiphanius, who stood in the audience, should take this to heart, found the bishop, although he did not say this openly. At the end of John's sermon, however, his opponent laconically declared that he agreed with everything the bishop had said, including the condemnation of anthropomorphism; only, he should have condemned Origenism too. That the audience burst into laughter shows that Epiphanius had scored [101].

The offensive came from two sides. In a letter Jerome adjured the bishop to remain on the orthodox side. He prayed for him, he wrote : "Lord, grant John that he believes the right things ..., that he preaches the word of truth." And then, addressing him directly : "Turn away from a perverse race, and distance yourself from that heretic, Origen, and from all heresies" [102]. He hoped that "God will liberate you, brother, and all the holy people of God that is entrusted to you, and all the brethern with you, and above all Rufinus, the presbyter, from the heresy of Origen and from all heresies and from the perdition they cause ... For the words of Origen are inimical and worthy to be hated and repugnant to God" [103].

Having implored John, in vain, to desist from his Origenist leanings, Epiphanius fled to Jerome and his monks in Bethlehem, only to flee from it in the night. He went to the monastery of Besan-Duc near Eleutheropolis, on the road southward from Jerusalem to Ascalon (Epiphanius was probably born at Eleutheropolis) [104]. He left two parties behind him : that of bishop John with the monks of the Mount of Olives under the leadership of Rufinus, and that of Jerome and the monks of Bethlehem. Now these monks had no priest among them (Jerome himself was no priest). To help them out, Epiphanius ordained a younger brother of Jerome, called Paulinidas [105]. By doing this he was clearly trespassing on the rights of bishop John in whose diocese Bethlehem lay. John took this very ill and forbade the new priest to enter the Nativity Church in Bethlehem. He refused to cooperate in whatever way with Jerome and his monks, so that these had call in the bishop of another diocese to baptize the catechumens [106]. Between John and Jerome all ties were cut now.

Epiphanius realized that he had gone too far. He wrote a letter to bishop John in which he excused himself; he had acted as he had done only to oblige his friends [107]. It was a humble and deferential letter. But what happened? Jerome made a Latin translation of the original Greek in which he struck out all the soothing and excusing passages. Later the translater excused himself by stating that he had worked in haste with the result that some shades of expression might have got lost in the process. It was a lame excuse, and when Rufinus had the occasion to compare the Greek and Latin versions, he was convinced that Jerome had been partial and dishonest [108].

d. Attempts at mediation

The din caused by the war of the sermons resounded far and wide. The governor of Palestine, Archelaus, offered to mediate, but John refused to collaborate; according to Jerome, who lost no opportunity to blacken his opponent, he excused himself by saying that his services were needed by a sick woman [109]. What the bishop really wanted was to be rid of that cumbersome company of Jerome and his monks, but he could not obtain a decree of expulsion from the governor [110]. This request, wrote the indignant Jerome, really meant splitting the Church [111].

The harassed John then invoked the assistance of Theophilus, the bishop of Alexandria. Now it was the turn of Jerome's monks to say that a foreign bishop was meddling in their affairs [112]. So this mediation began under bad auspices, and to make things worse, Theophilus made quite the wrong choice for the arbiter. He sent a presbyter, called Isidore, who was believed to be an Origenist. This man started his mission in the most tactless way by sending Rufinus a letter in which he declared that he was firmly on his side. The Bethlehemites, he wrote, "would dissolve into the air like smoke, and melt like wax when it is brought near a fire" [113]. Nothing remained secret in this less than edifying quarrel : the letter fell into the hands of Vincentius, a priest, who presented it to Jerome. "Now what is this man", he cried, "an adversary or a legate?" [114].

Jerome mentions an apology by bishop John addressed to Theophilus of Alexandria in which he seems to have tried to influence his colleague against Jerome. There exist only fragments of it in a text by Jerome; it is difficult, as Villain writes, to evaluate it. Anyhow, although John called Isidore 'a most religious man ..., a man of God sent by a man of God' [115], the arbiter could book no success.

e. Reconciliation

The noise of the battlefield now having reached Rome, the ecclesiastical authorities began to feel uneasy about this unpleasant conflict. A friend of Jerome, Pammachius, advised him therefore to write his own apology which he did, in the form of a letter to Pammachius, with his 'Liber contra Joannem Hierosolymitamum'. In the seventh section of this text Jerome enumerates seven heterodox theses of Origen (as formulated by Epiphanius) and required John to repudiate them unambiguously [116]. But as far as is known, there was no response. Only three years later Rufinus, who was not mentioned at all by Jerome, came forward with an apology [117].

In 396 Theophilus succeeded in putting the ghosts back into the bottle. He sent a circular letter to the clergy of Palestine in which, so it seems (for the actual text is lost), he made a far more tactful attempt at mediation. This time Jerome showed himself satisfied [118]. Two pious ladies, Antonia Melania and Paula, prepared the way for a reconciliation. After a mass in the church of the Resurrection Jerome and Rufinus held out hands to one another [119]. It had cost a lot of sweat, sighed Rufinus [120]. There is no talk of John here, but probably he was involved through Rufinus.

I have related this affair extensively to show how high the waves could go in questions of orthodoxy and heterodoxy.

f. Rufinus goes to town

Quiet and peace now having descended on Jerusalem and Bethlehem, with both parties having spiked their guns, Rufinus left his monastery on the Mount of Olives and travelled to Rome. He took up his abode in the monastery of the Pinetum near the city. He was not yet an author, but now he became one, in the Origenist line! Did he not realize that this would fan the flames of a hardly extinguished fire? Perhaps he had some misgivings, for he apologized extensively for having begun to write. He related that a certain Macarius, a philosopher, had come to him wanting to hear what Origen had written about certain difficult questions. Not willing to burn his fingers, Rufinus referred his visitor to an apology by Pamphilius, written in defense of Origen, in which he could find an exposition of the Origenist theology [121].

The problem, however, was that this book was in Greek, a language Macarius did not have command of. He therefore asked for a Latin translation to be made by Rufinus. When this scholar excused himself by saying that his Greek had become somewhat rusty, his interlocutor insisted so long that he finally gave in. When Rufinus had completed this translation, Macarius asked for a translation of the Origenist work on which Pamphilius had based his arguments, the 'Peri archoon' = On principles. Again Macarius insisted so long that Rufinus concluded that this was clearly the will of God, and so he set himself to work [122].

He secured himself against the criticisms he expected. What he believed, he wrote in the Praefatio to the Pamphilian book, was in conformity with the creed of the Catholic Church; with regard to all the things that were preached by John in Jerusalem, he declared : "All this we proclaim and hold together with him" [123]. He knew of course that Origen was frequently accused of heresy, and realized that this blame would probably fall on himself also. To avoid this, he had, as he wrote, 'purged' the original Origenist text so that the Latin reader would find nothing in it that would detract from the creed [124]. He defended Origen against his detractors by positing, as I wrote earlier, that his work had been adulterated by ill-intentioned persons; he even wrote an essay on this subject [125] in which he quoted a letter by Origen himself who complained that his texts had been tampered with.

g. The anti-Origenists in action

Hardly was the ink of the translation dry when part of it was smuggled into the hands of Pammachius, a senator [126]. It was a page in which Origen refuted the thesis of the Anthropomorphists that God is somehow corporeal. The man who brought it to the senator had changed it in order to make it sound more heretical; he was a monk, Eusebius, who already earlier, in Palestine, had stoked the fires between Rufinus and Pammachius. Rufinus was furious [127]. Not without reason : Pammachius was the leader of an anti-Origenist circle with its headquarters in his villa on the Mons Caelius in Rome; this group immediately took action by asking Jerome for a literal translation of the 'Peri archoon' in order to compare it with Rufinus's translation.

They received this new translation already in the spring of 399. Jerome put himself at the greatest possible distance from Rufinus (or really from Origen). "The tenets of Origen are poison; they are not in conformity with the sacred books; they did violence to Scripture." But exactly because they were poison, he deemed it necessary to excuse himself. "Yes, I have read Origen. If it is a crime to have read Origen, I confess I am guilty of this crime. I have exhausted my purse in order to have all these works sent to me from Alexandria. If you believe me, I state I never was an Origenist; if you don't believe me I state that I am no longer one" [128]. Feeling attacked and falsely accused of Origenism, Rufinus began to write an Apology, a work that occupied him for two years [129].

h. An anti-Origenist campaign

A great anti-Origenist campaign was staged. The Mons Caelius-group [130] tried to elicit a formal condemnation by Pope Siricius (384-398) who, however, steadfastly refused. They came further with the next Pope, Anastasius I (398-401), who seems to have issued some sort of condemnation [131]. The real leader of this campaign was Theophilus, the bishop of Alexandria. This is strange since we have seen that he, in the first instance, showed himself favourable to Origenism; but he had obviously made a turnabout and began to harass and persecute all those whom he suspected of Origenism. While he combed out Egypt, particularly envisioning monk settlements in the desert, he asked Jerome to do the same in Palestine where, as he wrote, many Origenists were hiding. He sent a letter to the synod of the Palestinian bishops inviting them to take measures against the heretics, and another letter to Epiphanius, the bishop of Salamis in Cyprus, bidding him to do the same in his diocese. Epiphanius obligingly complied, but his Palestinian confrères answered Theophilus that there were no Origenists in their dioceses [132].

All this did not spell the end of anti-Origenism; there was yet another campaign of this sort in the sixth century. But what I have related shows how the controversy of orthodoxy and heterodoxy could make the seas go high in the Church - so high that we are justified to speak of a dualistic opposition.

NOTES TO CHAPTER III

1.   Wand, Great Heresies 27.
2.   Fisher, History 61.

3. Pelikan, Doctrine 27.
4. Justin., 1Apol. 46.
5. Justin, 2Apol. 13.3.
6. Theoph., Ad Autolyc. 2.15.
7. Docetism is the doctrine according to which Jesus Christ had only a body in appearance, not a physical one.
8. Chadwick s.v. 'Justin Martyr', New Cath. Enc. 8,95. New York (1967).
9. Just., 1Apol. 13.1.
10. Just., Dial. 56.1.10.22
11. Just., Dial. 72.2.
12. Just., Dial. 8.9.
13. Just., Dial. 56.
14. Just., 78. Lohse. Epochen 49, wrote that Justin spoke of a 'second God', but I nowhere found the word 'δεύτερος', only 'ἄλλος' or 'ἕτερος'. On p. 82 he states that "the Apologists did not understand the Logos as the Word of God that appeared in history, but as the intelligence of the world and cosmic principle. They equated, therefore, the preexistent Christ with the Logos concept of Greek philosophy. This might facilitate the entry into Christianity of the educated."
15. Lohse, Epochen.15.
16. Athenag. Legatio 10.
17. This idea is unambiguously formulated by Athenag., Legatio 10, but we find it also in Just., 1Apol. 5.13, 2Apol. 6 and Dial. 61, and in Tatianus, Oratio 5.
18. Athenag., Legatio 24.
19. Theoph., Ad Autolyc. 2.10.22.
20. Lohse, Epochen 82.
21. Daniélou, Origène 7.
22. Strictly spoken, he was no 'writer'. He dictated, and scribes noted down what he said.
23. The most extensive treatment of Origen's life is to be found in De Faye, Origène I Sa biographie et ses écrits (see Bibliography). Further to be consulted is Cadiou, Jeunesse (see Bibliographie), Daniélou, Origène, Chap. I Vie d'Origène, et G. Bardy s.v. 'Origène', Dict.Théol.Cath. 11.2, 1489-1494. Paris, 1932.
24. Eus., HE 6.2.7-11.
25. Eus., HE 6.2.4-6.

26. Eus., HE 6.2.12.
27. Eus., HE 6.2.15.
28. Eus., HE 6.3.1-8.
29. Eus., HE 6.21.3-4.
30. Eus., HE 6.8.4; the jealousy motive in a letter by Jerome, quoted by Rufinus, Apol. 2.20.
31. See Cadiou, Jeunesse, Chap. XI Le conflit.
32. Eus., HE 6.39.
33. Epiph. Haer.fab.comp. 64.63.
34. Hier., Adv.Ruf. 2.22.
35. Rufinus, De adulteratione (see Bibliography).
36. See Crouzel, Origène, Chap. II Les oeuvres d'Origène.
37. A useful overview in Berner (Herausg.), Origenes (see Bibliography).
38. It was in two books in Greek. The Preface and a Latin adaptation of Book I is to be found in Rufinus. Apologia 2. An analysis or short summary is contained in the 'Myrobiblia' or 'Bibliotheca' of Photius of Constantinople (9th century), Codex 117 (see also Codex 118).
39. The provenance of the incriminated texts has been researched more than once, for instance by Naudin, Origène 114-145.
40. See Vol. I, Ch. I.14.
41. See Vol. III, Ch. III.8-10. The prehistory of the concept of the preexistence of souls is sketched by Heimann, Schicksal 13-21.
42. Epiph., Pan. 64.4.
43. Ench. 203.
44. Origen, De princ. 2.9.6.
45. Origen, De princ. 2.9.6.
46. Origen, De princ. 1.8.1.
47. Orig., De princ. 1.8.1.
48. Origen, Comm. in Joa. 20.13. My compatriot Benjamins devoted his doctoral thesis to the theme of freedom in Origen, 'Eingeordnete Freiheit' (see Bibliography).
49. De Faye, Origène III, 90.
50. Origen, De princ. 1.8.
51. De Faye, Origène III, 102.

52. De Faye, Origène III, 106.
53. De Faye, Origène III, 91.
54. Heimann, Schicksal 150.
55. Bianchi, Thème du colloque. Tradizione 24. Sfameni Gasparro, Motivazioni, Tradizione 251/252 : "La struttura di doppia creazione che soggiace a tale formulazioni conferisce un' indubbia connotazione dualistica alle relative antropologie quando distingue, in forme e gradazioni diverse, duo livelli nella natura e nelle modalità di esistenza umana e identifica nel secondo la conseguenza, sia pura mediata, dall' intervento divino, del peccato".
56. Crouzel, Origène 132.
57. Orig., De princ. 3.5.4.
58. Heimann, Schicksal 152.
59. Clark, Controversy 245.
60. Origen, Hom. in Matt. 12.15.
61. There is an unmistakable resemblance here with the typically Gnostic opposition of Pistis and Gnosis. And this too : "Solche Unterscheidung (between Pistis and Gnosis) ruft uns die beiden Erkenntnisgrade in der pythagoreischen Gemeinde in Erinnerung", writes Heimann, Schicksal 22. In Origen there is no dualistic opposition. Those who have Pistis (faith) are not doomed but should develop it so that it becomes an higher understanding, see Koch, Pronoia 86-89.
62. Daniélou, Origène, Chap. II L'interprétation typologique.
63. Origen, Hom. in Lev. 6.8.
64. Origen, De princ. 4.3.13.
65. Koch, Pronoia 88.
66. Mt. 18:2; Koch, Pronoia 86.
67. De Faye devoted the whole second volume of his 'Origène' to 'the philosophical ambiance'.
68. Lyman, Christology 41-42.
69. Kobusch, Origenes 27.
70. Koch, Pronoia 13.
71. Eus., HE 6.3.
72. Eus., HE 6.15 and 19.
73. Kobusch, Origenes 28.
74. Kobusch, Origenes 33/34.

75. The German theologian Hans Urs von Balthasar in his 'Origenes' (see Bibliography) offers a highly useful work by presenting an extensive selection of literal Origenist texts on this and other subjects. I refer the reader to pp. 84-87 Bild des Wortes, and Section II Wort.
76. De Faye, Origène III, 32/33.
77. Crouzel, Origène 7 : "Pendant ces dix-huit siècles, Origène a été le plus étonnant signe de contradiction de l'histoire de la pensée chrétienne".
78. See Crouzel, Origène 223-226 'Les causes des malentendus entre Origène et la postérité'.
79. According to Harnack, Dogmengeschichte 342/343, they even went through the ice. "In der christlichen Apologetik, wie sie bereits um die Mitte des 2. Jahrhunderts aufgekommen ist, stellt sich der Anfang einer Entwicklunng dar, welche hundert Jahre später in der Theologie des Origenes, d.h. in der Umsetzung des Evangeliums zu einem wissenschaftlichen Lehrsystem , ihren vorläufigen Abschluß erreicht hat. Materiell bedeutete dieses Lehrsystem die Legitimirung des Ertrages der griechischen Philosophie auf dem Boden der Glaubensregel ... Eine bunte Menge altchristliche Vorstellungen und Hoffnungen, gewonnen aus den beiden Testamenten, und zu spröde um völlig umgeschmolzen zu werden, umlagerte noch den Kern. Aber das meiste ist hier doch von der theologischen Kunst bewältigt und die überlieferten Glaubensregel zu einem Glaubenssystem umgewandelt worden." This is Harnack's well-known thesis of 'die Hellenisirung des Christentums'. He describes this process a great length in Dogmengesch. I, 496-796, 'Fixirung und allmähliche Hellenisirung des Christentums als Glaubenslehre'.
80. Harnack, Dogmengesch. I, 653.
81. Harnack, Dogmengesch. I, 654.
82. Urs von Balthasar, Origenes 28.
83. Rowan Williams, Arius : Heresy and Tradition, 140. Oxford, 1987.
84. Widdicombe, Fatherhood 120.
85. Aug., De haer., Praef.
86. Crouzel, Origène 344 : "La seule (accusation of not being orthodox) qui reste vraiment fondue concerne la préexistence des âmes, y compris celle du Christ, et la chute qui s'y situe ... A son époque on ne pouvait la taxer d'hérésie, l'Église n'ayant pas alors aucun enseignement sur l'origine de l'âme, sauf que sa création ... vient de Dieu".
87. De Faye, Origène III, 285/286.
88. Epiph., Pan. 63.4. All the charges brought by Epiph. against Origen are analyzed in Clark, Controversy, Ch. 3, 87-104.
89. Epiph., Pan. 64.8.

90. Epiph., Pan. 64.4.
91. Epiph., Pan. 64.73.
92. R. Bonwetsch s..v. 'Epiphanius von Constantia', Realenc. f. Theol. u. Kirche 5, 419. Leipzig, 1898.
93. Villain, Querelle 7.
94. There are differences of opinion as to the exact date of Epiphanius' visit to the Holy City; it migyt also be 395. I am following here the dating of Villain, Querelle 1, arguments in note 2.
95. Hier., Contra Joa. 38.
96. Hier., Adv.Ruf. 3.33.
97. Hier., Adv.Ruf. 3.33.
98. Villain, Querelle 6.
99. We find what John said in his sermon in Hier., Contra Joa. 10.11.44.
100. Hier., Contra Joa. 11 and 14.
101. Hier., Contra Joa. 11.
102. Hier., Ep. 51 (ad Joa.), 3.
103. Hier., Ep. 51 (ad Joa.), 6.
104. Sozomenos, HE 6.32.
105. Hier., Ep. 51.1.
106. Hier., Contra Joa. 41.42.
107. Epiph., Epistola ad Joannem Episcopum (translated into Latin by Jerome, PG 33.
108. Hier., Ep. 57.
109. Hier., Contra Joa. 39.
110. Hier., Ep. 82.10.
111. Hier., Contra Joa. 43.
112. Hier., Contra Joa. 37.
113. Hier., Contra Joa. 37.
114. Hier., Contra Joa. 37.
115. Hier., Contra Joa. 37.
116. Hier., Contra Joa. 7.
117. 'Rufinus' Defense against Charges of Origenism' is analyzed by Clark, Controv., Ch. 4.

118. Hier., Ep. 82.1-3.
119. Hier., Adv.Ruf. 33.
120. Ruf., Apol. 2.37.
121. Apologia Pamphilii Martyris pro Origene (see Bibliography).
122. Pamphilii Apologia, Praefatio ad Macarium. See the translation of Peri archoon in PG 11 with the Prologus in which Rufinus explains how he came to do this.
123. Ruf., Praefatio ad Macarium.
124. Ruf., Prologus in libros Peri archoon.
125. Rufinus, De adulteratione (see Bibliography).
126. Ruf., Apol. 2..44.
127. Ruf., Apologia 1.19.
128. Hier., Ep. 84.2-5, quoted by Villain, Querelle 31.
129. Rufinus, Apologia in S. Hieronymum (see Bibliography).
130. Clark, Controversy, pays in her Ch. I ample attention to what she calls the 'social networks' in the Origenist controversy. Pro- and contra-Origenists had their own, socially different groups of adherents in which a remarkable number of women played their part.
131. But obviously not formal enough to find a place in Denzinger-Schönmetzer.
132. Villain, Querelle 35-37, based on letters by Theophilus, Jerome, and Epiphanius. See also G. Fritz s.v. 'Origénisme, 3. Offensive the Théophile d'Alexandrie'. Dict.Théol.Cath. 11.1571-1574.

CHAPTER IV

ADOPTIONISM : WAS JESUS REALLY DIVINE?

1. The Ebionite position

A deviant sect, but more closely related to Christianity than the Gnostic ones, is that of the Ebionites of which I wrote extensively in Chapter III, no. 3, of volume XII. The Ebionites developed a view of the theological and ontological status of Jesus that would surface every now and then in the history of dogma. It was maintained that Jesus was born as a human being, like everyone of us. However, on the occasion of his baptism in the river Jordan he was 'adopted', either by God or by an angel; this did not mean that he became divine, in the orthodox sense, but rather that he, from then on, was elected as a divinely 'inspired' person.

This ushered in a never ending debate on the person of Jesus Christ : was he only human, was he only divine, or was he both human and divine at the same time? The last position was and is the orthodox one : Jesus is the God-man, not half God and half man, but wholly God and wholly man, two natures in one person, as the Council of Chalcedon later defined it. This means that in the person of Jesus Christ heaven and earth, divinity and humanity, the supernatural and the natural hang together; he is the connecting link between both spheres because he belongs to both. This is the fundamental reason why orthodox Christianity is not dualistic.

Alternative opinions, however, run a fair chance that they are not without dualistic aspects. The earliest form of Adoptianism, in its Ebionite shape, implies that the link between 'above' and 'below' is, if not severed, then at least weakened. Here Jesus belongs basically and first and foremost to the human sphere; he is never made divine but only raised to a position that is more exalted than that of his fellow-men; he remains human.

2. The Docetist position

The opposite opinion, that of Docetism, was also present at a very early stage of Church history. I feel that it would be appropriate to insert a few words about Docetism here. It will set off the Adoptionist and related positions more clearly, because they reacted, at least partly, to this doctrine. The word is derived from the Greek verb 'dokeoo', meaning 'to seem'. If Jesus is presented in the Gospels as human, this only reflects an appearance. The Gnostic systems, as far as they were interested in Jesus of Nazareth, were almost all of them 'docetist' : they denied the humanity of Jesus; to them he was only divine. The gap between heaven and earth, between the supernatural and the natural, is wider in Docetism than it is in Adoptianism - so wide that, when not downright dualistic, it comes very close to dualism. In any case, dualistic doctrine may easily result from it.

It would be wrong to think that only Gnostics were Docetist; many non-Gnostics also denied Jesus' humanity. It seemed to them too earthly, too common, too coarse, to conceive of him as a being of flesh and blood. Already the Letters of John caution the faithful against this idea. "Every spirit which acknowledges that Jesus Christ has come in the flesh is from God, and every spirit which does not thus acknowledge Jesus is not from God" [1]; "many deceivers have gone out into the world, who do not acknowledge Jesus as coming in the flesh" [2]. Ignatius of Antioch in his Letter to the faithful in Smyrna asserts repeatedly that Jesus was human : he was born from a woman, had really suffered, had been really nailed to the cross - "not as certain unbelievers say that he only suffered in appearance" [3]. Theodoretus was the first Father to give them the name of 'Docetists' [4]. Specific Docetist sects are mentioned by some Fathers.

The threat presented to the orthodox Church by Docetism was enormous. If Jesus had not been wholly human, then there would have been no Incarnation : the Word would not have become flesh. And if his suffering and his death on the cross were only apparent, there would also have been no Redemption. The whole fabric of Christian doctrine was in deadly danger; as Bareille writes, the question was one of life and death for the Church [5]. Ignatius adds a personal note to his warnings. "If Christ did only suffer in appearance, ... why then am I charged with chains and do I desire to fight against wild beasts?" [6]. Docetism made the whole Christian creed devoid of sense [7].

3. What is Adoptionism?

The Fathers usually professed what is called a 'pneumatic Christology' according to which Jesus is a celestial, even divine being who appeared on earth, fulfilled his mission, and returned to heaven. In how far and in what manner he united himself with the flesh is not always wholly clear; some thought he appeared in the flesh, others that he took it on (assumptio carnis), still others that the heavenly being and the human form became organically one. In the Adoptionist view it is the other way round : an earthly being was 'adopted' by the Father and raised to a higher status. As Harnack writes, adoptionist and pneumatic Christology exclude each other [8].

4. The first appearance of Adoptionism

According to this same scholar, the first and the only complete and unambiguous expression of Adoptionism is to be found in the Pastor of Hermas. In one of his 'similitudes' Hermas describes a wealthy proprietor who possesses a domain and a great number of slaves. In a part of his fields he plants a vineyard. He then chooses a very faithful servant and entrusts the vineyard to his care; the servant duly makes it grow and flourish. When the master returns, he calls together his son, who is his heir, and his friends, who are his councillors, and in their company praises the work of the slave. In recompense of what he has done, the slave is made co-heir to the son [9].

It is not hard to guess what this means. The master is God, of course, and the domain is the world; the friends are the angels [10]. But who is the son? Is he the Logos, is he Christ? No, he is not! He must probably be indentified with mankind, but it does not become wholly clear what the author means by him. And who is the faithful servant? Is it man who has to guard God's creation? No, he is not! The servant, although not called 'son' in Hermas's parable, is the son of God, who, as a slave, has a very subordinated position [11]. His caring for the vineyard, his weeding out the herbs, is the image of the work of Redemption, but the atoning death on the cross is not mentioned, neither does the author employ the words 'Jesus, Christ', or Logos'. There is in this view an enormous distance between God and the Redeemer, similar to that between a master and his slave.

The son is not the preexistent Son, the second person of the Holy Trinity. Preexistent is the Holy Ghost, who is the real Son. "God has made the preexistent Holy Ghost, who has created all things, dwell in the flesh he has chosen." In consequence, the Incarnation does not mean that the Son took on a human shape, but that the Holy Ghost descended on or into a human being who was not preexistent himself. "This flesh in which the Holy Ghost took up his abode, served the Ghost well; he walked in the way of sanctity and purity, without defiling the Spirit in any way." The term 'flesh' ('sarx'), that is constantly used, makes it clear that we have to do with an earthly being [12]. In recompense of his services the son is made co-heir; this means that he is 'adopted' by God and raised to a higher status.

It is self-evident that Hermas's Christology does not tally at all with the orthodox one. Is it dualistic? In any case, it is not radically dualistic, since the servant is finally raised to the status of co-heir. But it is surely relatively dualistic, because the servant is a slave and is not divine; the Holy Ghost uses him only as his abode. And secondly, it should not be overlooked that the master has many slaves, but that only one is chosen to perform a special task; only part of the earth is planted as a vineyard. We are not far from the Gnostic idea of election, of two races of men, and of the descent of Wisdom into some of them. "Did not the doctrine of a celestial aeon that became incarnated in the Redeemer contain a remnant of the old Gnostic leaven?", asked Harnack [13]. In their fight against an oversimplified Docetism, the Adoptionists fell on the other side.

As Harnack wrote, it is highly significant that the 'Pastor' became so popular in Rome [14]. Eusebius quotes an anonymous author who said that, according to the Adoptionists, their doctrine originated with the Apostles themselves, and that it was the dominating Christology in Rome until the days of Pope Victor I (ca. 189-198/199) [15].

5. Monarchianism : the unitary principle

The Adoptionists objected against theological developments of a binarian or trinitarian kind, that is, the tenet that there are two or three persons in God. They defended the view that God is, so to speak, an unitary principle, numerically too, a 'monê archê', one single beginning. This gave certain heterodox views the name of 'Monarchianism' [16]. It will be clear that Monarchianism excludes the godhead of Jesus.

a. Praxeas

The first Monarchian who emerged in Rome was a certain Praxeas, a very shady figure, who had arrived from Asia Minor. Tertullian, our only source for this, says that he "was the first to bring this kind of perversity to Rome"; he added that he "drove out the Paraclete (the Holy Ghost) and crucified the Father (for it was not the Son but the Father who had suffered - F.)" [17]. He seems to have met no ecclesiastical opposition in Rome, but when he had gone on to Carthage, he was vigorously combated by Tertullian, who reproached him for holding that the Father and the Son are identical, and for stating that 'Son' or 'Word' ('Logos') is nothing but a name given to the Father [18].

Tertullian launched all his powerful eloquence upon the poor man who was forced to retract; he signed a document in which he excused himself, 'after which : silence' [19] Although nothing more is heard of Praxeas, the controversy later flared up again in Carthage; this induced Tertullian to write a treatise 'against Praxeas'.

b. Noetus

The real originator of Monarchianism seems to have been a certain Noetus of whose life we know virtually nothing, except that he lived at Smyrna, or perhaps at Ephesus, between 180 and 200 [20]. He went to Rome where he found the ground somewhat prepared by Praxeas. In the opinion of Noetus God is not only essentially one, but numerically too. In other words, he acknowledged only one divine Person (the Father) which excludes the idea of a Trinity. "What wrong have I done?", he is reported to have asked; "I venerate one God; and apart from him no one else is born, has suffered, has died" [21]. The consequence of this is that, if Christ is God (Noetus did not deny this), he must be the Father, or else he would not be God. If he has suffered, it is the Father who has suffered. This opinion is called 'Patripassianism'.

Of course, Noetus had Bible texts at hand to support his argument, for instance : "I am the first and the last; outside me there is no one else" [22]. A problem was constituted by the Prologue of the Fourth Gospel with its emphatic exposition of the Logos-concept, but Noetus extricated himself by stating that it had to be understood allegorically [23]. Accordingly, those who held that Jesus was the Son, were accused of being ditheists; "there are not two gods, but one", he said [24].

This Noetian doctrine flew straight into the face of orthodoxy. That Noetus, so to speak, brought down the Father from heaven and submitted him to a human fate, not only spelled the end of Trinitarianism but also dealt a heavy blow to the status of the Father. It is as though his place in heaven became empty; the connection between the supernatural and the natural was endangered. There was even a risk - which not all Monarchianists were able to avoid - that this doctrine would slide off towards pantheism [25].

No wonder then that the Church took issue with him. The presbyters of Rome called Noetus before them and had a disputation with him. We don't know whether this was an ordinary assembly or a formal synod of bishops.

In the first instance Noetus managed to exculpate himself. But as he went on spreading his doctrine, the presbyters smelled a rat and summoned him again. This time he did not get off so lightly. The presbyters confronted him with the following statement. "We too honour one God, but we honour him in the right way; we hold that there is only one Christ, but we know that he has suffered and died and is risen and has ascended to heaven and is sitting at the right hand of the Father and will come to judge the living and the dead." This means that the Father and the Son are two different persons; it also implies that it is the Son who connects heaven and earth. Since Noetus refused to retract, he and his adherents were banned from the Church [26].

6. Modalism : no persons but modes

a. What is Modalism?

This did by no means spell the end of Noetism or Monarchianism. We lose track of Noetus after his condemnation, but not of his disciples. Probably shortly before the expulsion of his master, one of them, a certain Epigonus, founded a school, a kind of theological college, in Rome, destined for the spread of Monarchianism there [27]. As head of this school he was succeeded by Cleomenes and later by Sabellius around 220.

The doctrine they taught bears several names : Monarchianism or Sabellianism or Modalism (or Modalist Monarchianism) [28]. If the reader feels confused by the many terms used for this form of heterodoxy, he or she must understand that they do not denote different doctrines; one is more explicit on this point and another on that. 'Modalists' are called so, because they held that the Father and the Son were not two persons in God but two modes of being in God. They could hardly avoid speaking of the Father **and** the Son, since in the Gospels Jesus calls himself the Son, while he addresses the Father as one who is different from him. The Modalists countered the obvious objection rising from this by stating that "on account of this birth that had taken place, he (the Father) confessed himself to be the Son to those who saw him (i.e. to the Jews of Jesus' days - F.), while to those who could receive it he did not hide the fact that he was the Father" [29]. This smacks somewhat of a hidden sense or a secret doctrine.

b. Disturbance in the Church

Modalism spread like wildfire. Hippolytus wrotes that it caused a disturbance in the whole Church [30]. Tertullian states spitefully that the larger part of the faithful adhered to it,"simpletons as they are, not to say imprudent and devoid of learning" [31]. The Modalist party was combated with all his might by Hippolytus who, however, was the leader of only a minority of priests [32]. The Pope of these days was Zephyrinus (198-ca.217) whom Hippolytus calls 'unlearned' and 'avid of money' [33]. In return for a gift, he allowed the faithful to attend the school of Cleomenes whose life style, says Hippolytus, was not exactly that of a churchman [34].

Zephyrinus was wavering in his theological opinions. "I know only one God", he is reported to have said, "Jesus Christ, and apart from him nobody else was born and has suffered". He seems to be approaching the Modalist position here, but he went on to state : "It was not the Father who suffered but the Son" [35]. Probably, as Amann wrote, he did not grasp the danger to orthodoxy that the Modalist position presented [36]. According to Hippolytus, the evil genius of the Pope was Callistus (Calixtus), an archdeacon, whom he describes as being on the side of the Modalists and as 'an arrant villain' [37]. There were heated discussions between Hippolytus and his opponents; to no avail, he sighed, for they always preferred 'wallowing in the same mud' [38].

c. Sabellius

The situation was already confused enough, when Sabellius arrived in Rome, some time before 217. He seems to have been a North African, a Libyan perhaps. Once in the capital, he joined the Modalist faction. He gained the trust of Callistus and had much influence on him. Hippolytus, who hated the archdeacon, says that, disputing with him, he seemed to draw him over to his side, but then Callistus met Sabellius and as a result fell back into his old errors [39]. Hippolytus, who was the principal of a theological college of his own in Rome, desired that Sabellius would be excommunicated, but his wish was not fulfilled. When Zephyrinus died, not Hippolytus, but his enemy the archdeacon became Pope as Callistus I (ca. 217-222/223).

According to Hippolytus, the new Pope accused him of being a 'ditheist' [40]. This made him so angry that he broke with the Church and founded a schismatic community. His report is partial; he accused Callistus of accepting the doctrine of Sabellius, but the reality is that the Pope banned this Modalist spokesman [41]. Hippolytus puts a squarely Modalist profession of faith into the mouth of the Pope [42]; however, the question is whether he is to be trusted in this. Coming from a personal enemy, this accusation should be taken with more than one grain of salt.

What Hippolytus did not see was that Callistus, just like Zephyrinus, honestly sought to avoid a schism in the Church, in which he was not wholly successful, since his opponent Hippolytus broke away. But steering a middle course proved difficult. Callistus saw the preexistent Son as different from the Father, indeed. But when he said that the Father took his abode in the Son who had assumed the flesh, and thus became one with him, he distanced himself from the Logos-theology [43].

The official condemnation constituted a heavy blow for Sabellius. His school subsisted for some fifteen more years in Rome. He seems to have returned to Africa where we are put off his scent [44].

7. The 'Alogoi'

There existed yet another form of Monarchianism, side by side with its Modalist and Sabellian counterparts. Its initiator was a cobbler from Byzantium, named Theodotus, who had a reputation for learning [45]. Hippolytus called him 'a torn off tatter' of the school of the Gnostics and of Cerinthus and 'Ebion' [46]. If this is correct, Theodotus had been in contact with Asiatic heresiarchs. These are dubbed 'Alogoi', a term that was coined by Epiphanius to designate those theologians who rejected the Logos-doctrine and, in consequence, the Fourth Gospel [47]. He gave this name to the Asiatic teachers I mentioned above.

Theodotus arrived in Rome during the pontificate of Pope Victor I, that is, during the last decade of the second century. What he taught there was this. Jesus was just a man (albeit born from a virgin), and lived just like everyone else. Having become extremely pious, he descended into the river Jordan on the occasion of his baptism. There he was transformed from on high into the Christ; a special power flowed into him that had not been there before. This did not mean, however, that he was now God; he was raised to the status of a god only when he rose from the dead [48].

The Greek word for 'power' is 'dunamis', so that this branch of Monarchianism is called Dynamic Monarchianism. It is very close to Adoptionism and is just as unitarian as this doctrine and that of the Modalist Monarchianists with whom they have, of course, much in common. This did not prevent them from being combated, not only by the orthodox, but also by the Modalists. Pope Victor I did not see eye to eye with Theodotus and banned him from the Church [49]. According to Harnack, this is the very first time that disciplinary measures were taken against a theologian [50].

The further fortunes of Theodotus are unknown, but his place was taken by a second Theodotus, a banker or exchange agent. This was during the pontificate of Pope Zephyrinus in the first two decades of the third century. This Theodotus II, knowing that he was not welcome in the main Church, attempted to found a schismatic Church. This shows how great the distance had become between the orthodox and the heterodox [51]. The Theodotians found a certain Natalis prepared to act as their bishop against a monthly salary. But the poor man got plagued by nightmares because of his apostasy; Eusebius piously reports that he repented. Clad in sackcloth and with ash strewn on his head, he threw himself before the feet of the Pope who accepted him again into the Church [52]. So nothing came of a Theodotian Church.

8. The situation in the East

No great future was granted to Adoptionism and Monarchianism in the West, but it was different in the East. There many Unitarians were to be found, of all kinds and shapes; some held that the Father and the Son were one and the same, others that the Son was different from the Father indeed, but only human [53].

Between 218 and 244 an Arabian, Beryllus, was bishop of Bostra, in the Roman province of Arabia. According to Eusebius, he tried to pervert the ecclesiastical rule of faith by introducing new things that were alien to it. Beryllus taught that Christ, before his incarnation, had not been preexistent as a different divine person; the godhead he had received was that of the Father. In other words, he had no divinity of his own. If this report is correct, then this was an Adoptionist doctrine. The commotion among his fellow-bishops in this part of the Empire was great; after having had several disputations with their heterodox colleague, they implored the help of Origen. He came and convinced Beryllus of his error [54]

Since Eusebius is no great doctrinal light, it is difficult to locate Beryllus in the theological spectrum. But that he belonged to the 'Alogoi' is certain. Probably as a sequel to this affair, a synod was convened at Bostra in 244, where the bishops solemnly stated that Christ had not only possessed a human body, but also a human soul [55]. This had Beryllus too denied.

9. Paul of Samosata

a. A secular bishop

In Rome we hear of vehement conflicts, confusion, schisms, and excommunications, whereas in the East events followed a more scholarly course. But this was not to remain so. Around the middle of the third century the leadership of the Alogoi was assumed by a bishop of Antioch, Paul of Samosata [56]. Antioch was in this period a city of the Kingdom of Palmyra that was virtually independent from Rome then and experienced its heyday under its famous Queen Zenobia [57]. During a Persian invasion the acting bishop of Antioch was abducted by the aggressors, and Paul became bishop in his place. He continued to exercize the public functions he already had; he seems to have been a favourite of the Queen [58].

This is what Eusebius has to say of him. "He had formerly been a beggarly pauper, having received no pecuniary resources at all nor an inheritance from his parents nor did he possess any talent that he could put to good use. But he became incredibly wealthy through evil and sacrilegious deeds ... Puffed up by great pride and arrogance, he has secular dignities and prefers to be called 'ducenarius' (= a public office) rather than bishop. He walks proudly about on the public squares, reading his letters and dictating his answers. He stalks along, preceded and followed by guards in great numbers. In this way he is making the faith an object of hatred and envy because of his pomp and the arrogance of his heart" [59]. Perhaps the urge to vilify an opponent, which is quite common in the discussions between the orthodox and heterodox, coloured this portrait somewhat, but it cannot be wholly wrong. It seems a prefiguration of certain worldly bishops of the Middle Ages.

Soon enough his fellow-bishops got uneasy about his doctrinal teachings and his liturgical practices. A synod was convened at Antioch which met in 264 [60]. It was a large gathering, for not only quite a number of bishops came but also many presbyters so that there were six hundred persons present. Paul was accused of heresy and of 'blasphemy against Christ' [61]. But Paul knew how to defend himself and got away scotfree [62].

b. The teachings of Paul of Samosata

What exactly did Paul teach [63]? It must have been Monarchianism or a later version of it. Leontius Byzantinus (Pseudo-Leontius) sketches the Samosatian doctrine in the following terms. "He only spoke of the Father; respecting the Incarnation he stated that Christ was only a man, he found that the Word of God (= the Logos) had not been in him ... He did not see that the Word of God had subsisted in Christ, but that the Word had been some sort of order or mandate, that is, that God had made happen what he wanted through this man."

Leontius also explained what was the difference between Samosatian and Sabellian doctrine. "With regard to the godhead, he (Paul) did not think like Sabellius, for Sabellius said that the Father, the Son, and the Holy Ghost were identical; God was somebody with three names. So he did not recognize the Trinity. Paul, on the contrary, did not say that the Father, the Son, and the Holy Ghost were identical, but he attributed the name of Father to the God who had created everything, the name of Son to somebody who was only human, and that of Holy Ghost to the grace that was present in the Apostles" [64].

This theological concept looks wholly unitarian; there is nothing trinitarian in it [65]. Christ has only a human nature; he acts as the mouthpiece of the Father. However, there are traces of the Logos-theology which make his doctrine somewhat inconsistent. There is in God a 'Logos' which Paul sometimes calls 'Son' and also 'Sophia', but they are and remain impersonal. They are, as Harnack wrote, not persons, but properties of God [66]. This Logos became manifest in Moses, in the prophets, in Mary most of all, and in Christ [67].

In Paul's Christology Christ is human, not divine. "The Word (Logos) is from on high; Jesus Christ, a man, is from here below ... Mary did not bear the Logos, for she did not exist before all ages. She has received the Word but was not older than the Word. She brought forth a man who is the same as we are, but better in all respects, since the grace that is on him, is that of the Holy Ghost, of the promises, and of Scripture" [68].

Paul's problem was that his Christ, although entirely human, had also to be the Redeemer. If he had not kept this theological tenet intact, he would have denied the whole meaning of the New Testament. He, and other Monarchianists, were not prepared to go so far. If they had done so, Jesus would have been no more than a teacher of wisdom, not much different from a Pythagoras or a Socrates. But in order to salvage the redemption he, and others, had to bring in something divine, something supernatural, something 'out there'. This they did, but it brought an illogical element into their theology. In view of this we may ask, was their Jesus then really entirely human? Since there was, according to them, in the last resort something divine in Jesus, it laid them, and Paul not excepted, open to the reproach that they were ditheists.

Was it perhaps a divine element that is present in all men? No, it wasn't, for Paul stated that Christ was different from all others, because Wisdom had taken up its abode in him. This does not signify that Jesus was the Wisdom. Wisdom dwelled in him; Wisdom and Jesus, "they are two"; they do not have the same substance [69]. What made Paul somewhat shifting in his opinions was probably his wish not to fly straight in the face of Scripture. Or else he attempted to make his difference with orthodoxy as narrow as possible. But since the kernel of his theology was that Jesus was divine in no respect, his fate was sealed.

c. The second synod of Antioch and the deposition of Paul

A second synod was convened in 268, equally in Antioch [70]. Seventy or eighty bishops found the affair important enough to travel to Paul's see. His doctrines were thoroughly investigated, but the Fathers were somewhat at a loss, being no theologians. It was good luck for them that a certain Malchion was also present, a sophist, who was the head of a school in Antioch [71]. As a result of his eloquence and learning, Paul was condemned to be deposed [72]. This decree remained a dead letter, since the refractory bishop, protected by Queen Zenobia, did not abandon his see. The faithful became divided into two parties, pro and contra Paul [73]. The importance of the affair for the whole Church was stressed by the synodal Fathers, when they sent the synodal acts, accompanied by a long letter, to 'all the Catholic Churches under the heavens' [74].

Paul could only be deposed, when the Emperor Aurelianus recaptured Antioch in 272. His verdict was that the house (i.e. the see of Antioch) should be adjudged to one to whom the bishops of Italy and the bishop of Rome would give it. A remarkable statement in the mouth of a pagan ruler! "And this man (Paul) was chased from the Church with the utmost shame by the secular power" [75].

10. Nominalism avant la lettre

We should now stop for a moment to determine what we have found so far. Let us first summarize Paul's teachings, since they may stand for all that the Monarchianists, Modalists, Adoptionists, Patripassianists have taught. Although they differ in many details, they are in agreement on the main lines.

The first and most important tenet of Paul's doctrine was the 'monarchy' of God; God is absolutely one so that there are no persons in him [76]. To him God is a being complete and perfect in himself without an inner movement and consequently also without a distinction in persons. The Logos is the impersonal knowledge of the Father. We are entitled to assume that there is a Logos only when he is immanent in the Father, as a spiritual potency and an interior consciousness. The consequence is that the Father must have taken upon himself the role of Creator; the Logos is no more than the instrument he employed. It was not the Logos - in orthodox theology the second person of the Holy Trinity - who became man. It was Jesus, a man, a human being, who from step to step progressed to perfection. Did this progressive development finally make Jesus into God? There were Fathers who thought that Paul had taught this [77]. If this were correct, he would really have been the ditheist some orthodox bishops thought he was.

To the modern secular mind these things may seem nugatory. But in fact they are of prime importance. What was at stake in all these discussions was the essential relationship between heaven and earth, between God and man. When I read in Tertullian that to Praxeas the Logos had no substance - "what is a word but a name, air that is moved, audible to the ear, something empty and inane and insubstantial" [78] -, then the term 'nominalism' thrusts itself upon me. True enough, this term is used for a late-medieval branch of theology, but it equally applies to the teachings of the unorthodox of this period. "When Hippolytus assures us that the real kernel of this (Paul's) false doctrine exists in this that Father and Son represent no reality but are only distinct from one another through nothing but their names, and that both are definitely no more than contentless appellations for one and the same being, appellations to which no reality corresponds, then we are in the presence of a strictly nominalistic logic" [79].

This is certainly correct, but by the same token we are confronted with the sheerest dualism. For what does nominalism denote but the split between reality and the way we speak of it, the terms we use for it? According to late-medieval nominalists, like William of Ockham, there are no 'unversalia', no unities under which a great number of individualities or particularities can be subsumed. Nominalism is the exact opposite of conceptualism according to which there exist concepts with a universal and real validity. But to Ockham cum suis no universal possesses even the slightest degree of reality. It will be evident that rigorous nominalism leads to a fragmentation, to a reduction of the cosmos to 'a system of totally heterogeneous individuals' - a conclusion that Ockham did not shun.

Father, Son, and Holy Ghost, what are they else but names given to the same being, not denoting any substance? Tertullian combats this opinion by arguing that to different names different substances correspond. "Those who are called Father and Son, would they not be different from one another? For all that is given a name must be according to that name; and as they are, they will also be named. It is absolutely not allowable to mix up the diversity of names; if one does, then not only the names, but also the things which they denote, get mixed up" [80]. He adds that it is equally nonsensical that day and night would be the same, as to hold that Father and Son are identical [81].

Hagemann calls Monarchianist theology "a logical individualism to which he is ready to apply the term 'nominalism'. This nominalism transfers reality to the realm of the singular and individual and consequently loses sight of the full reality of the general" [82]. For names connect the individualities with each other. When I say 'Amsterdam is a town', the name 'town' connects it with all similar agglomerations that are so called. But in nominalism the general is severed from the particular and the individual, which makes it hard to understand how they are connected with each other.

Reality fragmented in this way, is made, so to speak, 'molecular'. A dualistic breach in reality, between the general and the individual, cannot be avoided.

11. The dualistic abyss

There is more. If God is absolutely unitary, complete and enclosed in himself, simple, without properties, it will become very hard to see how he communicated himself. In this vision it is extremely difficult to explain the origin of the world. Of course, these theologians say that the Father created the cosmos. But they deny the possibility of a Logos-theology, of the existence of a Logos, a Son who is another person, the godhead, and who is the link between heaven and earth. For Logos too is no more than a name [83].

All these heterodox teachers are balancing on the brink of the dualistic abyss. What connection is there between the immovable God and man? Is there really a connection? They seem to be separated by an unbridgeable chasm. These teachers do not admit as much. They shrink back from this ultimate consequence of their own theology by making use, in spite of themselves, of the Logos-concept. We saw that Paul could hardly avoid being inconsequent, but the alternative was that his God would remain utterly apart from cosmos and mankind. By a narrow margin he established a last link between God and the cosmos, without being wholly convincing.

12. The later vicissitudes of Paulianism

The deposition of Paul and his virtual disappearance from the ecclesiastical scene did not spell the end of Paulinianism. It is, however, extremely hard to follow its later vicissitudes. The Paulinian schism remained confined to Antioch itself and its immediate surroundings, says Bardy [84]. It still existed in the days of the Council of Nicaea in 325, because its Canon 19 occupies itself with Paulinians, or rather with those Paulinians who desired to return to the main Church. They had to be rebaptized and priests should be reordained [85]. We may safely assume that not all Paulinians came over. They are still mentioned during the whole of the fourth century, but in the fifth

Paulinianism must have died out. In the third decade of that century Theodoretus attested that "not the slightest trace of it could be found" [86].

NOTES TO CHAPTER IV

1. 1Jo.4:2.
2. 2Jo.7.
3. Ign., Ad Smyrn. 1-2.
4. Theodoret., Ep. 82.4.22
5. G. Bareille s.v. 'Docétisme', Dict.Théol.Cath. 4.2, 1486 (Paris, 1924).
6. Ign., Ad Trall. 10.
7. The article of G. Bareille, 'Docétisme' in Dict.Théol.Cath. 4.2, is still highly valuable for this subject.
8. Harnack, Dogmengesch. I, 211/212.
9. Hermas, Pastor 5.2.2-11.
10. Hermas, Pastor 5.5.2-3.
11. Hermas, Pastor 5.5.2.
12. Hermas, Pastor 5.6.5.
13. Harnack, Dogmengesch. I, 703.
14. Harnack, Dogmengesch. I, 211. note 2.
15. Eus., HE 5.28.3.
16. This name is somewhat incorrect in so far that the Trinitarians too held that God is a 'monê archê'; they too cannot be accused of ditheism. The distinction between them and the Monarchians is that according to the last mentioned there are no 'persons' in God.
17. Tert., Adv.Prax. 1.
18. Tert., Adv.Prax. 5 and 7.
19. Tert., Adv.Prax. 1.
20. Information about Noetius is to be found in Hippolytus, Contra haer.Noet. which probably formed part of the lost Syntagma, and in Epiphanius, Pan. 57.
21. Epiph., Pan. 57.1.7.
22. Hipp. Contra Noet. 2.
23. Hipp., Contra Noet. 15.

24. Hipp., Contra Noet. 11 and 14.
25. Harnack, Dogmengesch. I, 737.
26. Hipp. Contra Noet. 1; Epiph., Pan. 57.1.
27. Hipp., Phil. 9.7.1.
28. The term 'Modalist' was introduced by Harnack.
29. Hipp., Philos. 9.10.11.
30. Hipp. Philos. 9.6.6.
31. Tert., Adv.Prax. 3.
32. Harnack, Dogmengesch. I, 739.
33. Hipp., Philosoph. 9.7.1-2.
34. Hipp., Philosoph. 9.7.1-2.
35. Hipp., Philosoph. 9.11.3.
36. E. Amann s.v. 'Zéphyrin', Dict.Théol.Cath. 15.2, 3691 (Paris, 1951).
37. Hipp., Philosoph. 9.7.2 and 11.
38. Hipp., Philosoph. 9..7.3.
39. Hipp., Philosoph. 9.12.1-2.
40. Hipp. Philosoph. 9.12.16.
41. Hipp., Philosoph. 9.12.15-16.
42. Hipp., Philosoph. 9.12.16-18.
43. Stuart George Hall s.v. 'Calixtus I', Theol.Realenz. 7, 563. Berlin/New York, 1981.
44. It is hard to gain an exact idea of what he taught. He seems to have progressed somewhat beyond the theology of Praxeas and Noetus. There is, he stated, but one God (and not three) who he called the 'Sonfather', see Didymus Al., De Trin. 3.18. There were, indeed, in the godhead, he said, a Father, a Son, and a Holy Ghost, but he spoke of three 'hypostases' with three different names, just as there is in man a body and a soul and a spirit, Epiph., Pan. 62.1-2. He seems to have been aware of the need to distinguish in some way or other between the Father and the Son, see Pelikan, Emergence 1.179.
45. Epiph., Pan. 54.1.
46. Hipp., Ref. 7.35.1.
47. Epiph., Pan. 51.3.
48. Hipp., Ref. 7.35.2.
49. Eus., HE 5.28.6.

69

50. Harnack, Dogmengesch. I, 711.
51. Harnack, Dogmengesch. I, 711.
52. Eus., HE 5.28; in this same chapter the reader can find the reasons why the orthodox reproached the Theodotians.
53. Orig., Comm. in Joa., 2.2.
54. Eus., HE 6.33.
55. Socrates, HE 3.7.
56. What we know of the life and personality of Paul of Samosata is described by Loofs, Paulus, Kap. I (see Bibliography) and by Bardy, Paul, Chap. III, § III, pp. 168-188 (idem).
57. See Vol. XI, Ch. III.6m.
58. On the relations between Paul and Zenobia see Loofs, Paulus, Kap. I, § 3.
59. Eus., HE. 7.30.7-8.
60. On this first Antiochene synod see Bardy, Paul, Chap. II, § IV.
61. Eus., HE 7.37-38.
62. Eus., HE 7.39.
63. On the traditions about the teachings of Paul, see Loofs, Paulus, Kap. II and III.
64. Leontius, De sectis 3.3.
65. Loofs was convinced that Paul's Christology was a legitimate and necessary return to primitive Christianity. He wrote, Paulus 320, that "der **eine** (his emphasis) Gott, den der Glaube als den Schöpfer der Welt kannte, durch Jesum Christum in einer alle frühere Offenbarung abschließenden Weise zu den Menschen geredet, bzw. (damit die religiöse Wertung des Leidens Jesu nicht ausgeschlossen erscheint) mit der Menschheit gehandelt hat, und daß er durch seinen Geist, den Geist Jesu Christi, die Gemeinde der Christgläubigen mit dessen Gaben ausstattet : das ist unfraglich eine bis in die Urzeit zurückgehende christliche Überzeugung gewesen." What Loofs found so attractive in this formula is that it is not 'metaphysical'. The 'metaphysical' is brought into the doctrine by Tertullian and those who came after him. "Der dreifachen Offenbarung des **einen** (his emphasis) Gottes entspricht hier eine dreifache Entfaltung des göttlichen Wesens selbst (in Father, Son, and Holy Ghost)." But even Paul did not remain wholly free of such 'metaphysical' corruptions (p. 322). "Das gibt ihm in der Dogmengeschichte eine minder rühmliche Stellung." But he "hat der neuplatonischen Flut, der Origenes die Bahn gebrochen hatte, durch sie, die alten Traditionen überschwemmend, in die Kirche eindrang, sich entgegengestemmt. Das ist sein Ehrentitel. Aber er ist von ihr verschlungen worden." It has the appearance that Paul was not

really 'primitively Christian', although Loofs concludes that Paul is so interesting, "weil er in einer Tradition stand, die in einer Zeit vor der hellenistischen Sturmflut wurzelt".

66. Harnack, Dogmengesch. I, 724.
67. Harnack, Dogmengesch. I, 725. This author thinks it possible, even probable, that an **immanent** (his emphasis) Modalist trinitarian doctrine could be ascribed to Paul, I, 724, note 4.
68. Pseudo-Leontius, Contra Nest. 3.
69. Pseudo-Leontius, Contra Nest. 3.
70. On this second synod see Bardy, Paul, Chap. III, § III.
71. On the role of Malchion see Bardy, Paul, Chap. II, § V.
72. Eus., HE 7.29.
73. On the schism in Antioch see Loofs, Paulus, Kap. IV, § 13, and Bardy, Paul, Chap. II, § IV.
74. Eus., HE 7.30.
75. Eus., HE 7.30.19.
76. I am following here Hagemann, Röm. Kirche, 475-478.
77. Athanasius, De synodis 45.
78. Tert., Adv.Prax. 7.
79. Hagemann, Röm.Kirche 347.
80. Tert., Adv.Prax. 9.
81. Tert., Adv.Prax. 10.
82. Hagemann, Röm.Kirche 164.
83. Hagemann, Röm.Kirche 358.
84. Bardy, Paul 412.
85. Gelasius Cyzicenus, Hist.Conc.Nic. 22, no. 19.
86. Theodor., Haer.fab.comp. 2.11.

CHAPTER V

THE ASCETIC URGE

Introductory : Christianity and asceticism

Asceticism has always been a constitutive element of Christianity. The term is derived from the Greek substantive 'askêsis", which means 'training', the exercizes of athletes and soldiers. But in Antiquity it soon also acquired an educational significance, that of training in virtue. The term has no definite content; it can vary from abstaining from certain forms of comfort to masochistic self-torture. Nevertheless, we think of an 'ascetic' as a person who takes this training very seriously, going to great lengths in controlling the body and its normal needs. Although ascetic practices can degenerate into masochism, authentic asceticism signifies, generally speaking, the subordination of the physical, the corporeal to the spiritual [1].

The Roman-Catholic Church has always found certain forms of asceticism necessary for all her members, after the example of Jesus who used to pray and to fast. Even today the period of forty days before Easter is devoted to fasting, prayer, and almsgiving; modern rules of fasting are mild, however, certainly in comparison with the Islamic Ramadan, but also compared with the far more severe customs of the ancient Church. The periods of fasting were longer then; they were also more strict, and they involved sexual abstinence. One should not forget Christians were a minority in these centuries, in many places only a tiny minority. Christian families were surrounded by a sea of paganism, not only by the omnipresent signs and images of the pagan cult but also by pagan customs, by the heathen way of life. This way of life presented many traits that were profoundly unchristian, what with its cruelty, its social and human indifference, its materialism, its love of pleasure. If, as we shall see later, there was a reaction against this even in pagan circles, we should not stand surprised that the Church wanted to preserve her children, many of them 'new-born', from the contagion of the pagan world.

When, in the first centuries of the Church, Egyptian monks withdrew to the desert to live there a life of mortification, of abstinence, of prayer, of meditation and contemplation, when in later times, even in our own days, younger and older people of both sexes join a contemplative order to live in retirement from the world, they do not do so out of horror of 'the world' and its enticements; their entering a monastery is not what the Germans call a 'Weltflucht'. Persons who are running away from their problems are not the most suitable candidates for monastic life. In consequence, there is no dualism in the moderate asceticism as it is found in the Roman Catholic Church.

Asceticism, however, is not without its dangers. As Jan Bergman wrote, "forms of asceticism which are carried through stricter and more consequently are almost without exception based on a dualistic anthropology in which the body is seen as something evil, as a 'prison', as a 'tomb'. Orphism [2], Platonism [3], and Manichaeism [4] are instances of this. The body "must not only be castigated but also fought and finally destroyed". Ascetics of this sort sometimes severely damaged their health and even mutilated themselves [5]. I shall now review the principal ascetic and rigorist sects.

Part I Encratism

1. What is Encratism?

There have always been persons and movements on the fringes of the Roman Catholic Church who were not satisfied with her moderate asceticism, not even with the stricter forms of the early Church. In much of the apocryphal literature total sexual abstinence is propagated, sex being seen as fundamentally incompatible with a life of devotion. There was a movement, called Encratism, the constitutive hallmark of which was the severest asceticism. The term is derived from the Greek substantive 'enkrateia' = self-control [6]. Encratism was one of the worst dangers that threatened the Church in this period, for it struck at the very foundation of its existence.

a. Encratism defined

What it was is defined by the final document of a congress in Milan in 1982 that was entirely devoted to it. "By 'encratism' is understood 'enkrateia' in its radical form excluding the 'gamos' (sexual intercourse - F.) which is immediately identified with 'porneia' (fornication) and 'phthora' (corruption) that it (the gamos) carries with it, and supposes that 'genesis' (procreation) has a negative value. Often this position is accompanied by a specific alimentary abstentionism with regard to meat and wine, together with an 'apotagê' (renouncement) of an a-cosmic character. In addition, this position is characterized by a protological motivation that is its foundation and its justification, namely the doctrine of the virginal Adam or of the uncorrupted soul, which implies that the original essence of man does not contain the sexual element - in the sense that the 'gamos' is held incompatible with the integrity of the soul [7]. This theme determines the whole story of the Fall and the reintegration (of mankind) and gives sense to the manifestation of the Kingdom (of God)" [8]. The creation of Eve, the statement goes on to say, is seen by this doctrine as the breach of a primal pneumatic unity because then the duality of the sexes became manifest; "dualism, the loss of the original unity is the origin of all evils" [9].

"Encratism ... is already present to some degree in the Pastoral epistles, and appears in an explicit and typical fashion in the teachings of Tatian and Julius Cassianus. It is found also in some of the Apocryphal Acts of the Apostles, and in certain sectors of Aramaean Christianity. The tradition of Encratism is present in Manicheism ... It underlies their (of the Encratites) sexual abstinence and their abstinence in matters of food as well as the prohibition to doing harm to the 'particles of light'" [10].

It will be evident that 'enkrateia' is a wide-spread mode of thought and a frequently encountered motivation of behaviour. Some of it may even be found in Origen and his school since this Father of the Church held the opinion that the institution of marriage was 'post-lapsarian', that is, that it came after the Fall (and not before it, as Gen. 2 says), together with the thesis that the creation of the world of sexuality was the consequence of an 'antecedent fault' [11]. It might be supposed that this view of sexuality profoundly influenced the Christian attitude. But this would not be correct. Encratism is not omnipresent in early Christian ideology. A powerful motive in the Christian reservations about sex is the expectation that the end of the world was at hand. Some doubted whether it had sense to bring forth offspring. And finally, there was the wish to serve God with an undivided heart which might imply the idea that it was better not to marry, although marriage (with its sexual side) was not seen as reprehensible [12].

b. The Encratite way of life

Encratites only drank water and never wine, were the strictest of vegetarians (no fish, no eggs), and advocated and practised total sexual abstinence. According to them, this was what the Gospels recommended. Taken literally, the injunction of total abstinence spelled the end not only of the institution of marriage but even of the whole human race. Probably this is what they wanted. For it should be understood that this program was not destined for a few enlightened persons; no, every Christian should live according to these prescripts. The background of this movement is purely Gnostic-dualistic : why save the world and prolong human existence, if they are intrinsically bad, created as they are by an evil intentioned Demiurge?

2. The Encratite heresiarch Cassianus

Very little is known of the one who passes for the first Encratite heresiarch, Julius Cassianus; Jerome calls him 'the fiercest heresiarch of the Encratites' [13]. He lived in the second century A.D., but his dates of birth and death are unknown; he may have been an Egyptian, from Alexandria perhaps. The works he wrote are lost; one of these was called 'Peri enkrateias', about self-control. According to Clement of Alexandria, he had a Gospel of his own, the 'Gospel according to the Egyptians', an apocryphal work [14], a veritable handbook of asceticism. In this Gospel highly woman-unfriendly utterances, attributed to Jesus himself, can be found. "I have come to suppress the works of woman". And also, "the time will come when the great garment of shame, the body, will be trod underfoot".

In view of this abhorrrence of the physical it comes as no surprise that Cassianus is also considered in connection with Docetism. Clement calls him 'the chief of the Docetists' [15]. The idea that Jesus could have had a physical body was repellent to him. He rejected all sexuality, even in marriage; the bringing forth of progeny was the work of the devil [16]. We are confronted here with the fiercest dualism of spirit and matter, almost indistinguishable from its Gnostic counterpart.

3. The Encratite heresiarch Tatian

a. What we know of Tatian

Another 'chief of the Encratites' - so called by Jerome [17] - was Tatian. Irenaeus who knew nothing of Cassianus says he was the one who "introduced this blasphemy" [18]. He was born somewhere along the Euphrates around 120 in a pagan family and received a thoroughly pagan education. For a time he earned his living as a travelling orator; in this capacity he came to Rome where he made the acquaintance of Justin the Martyr whom he greatly admired. He now became a Christian. But, writes Irenaeus, after the death of his master he thought too highly of himself, usurped the title of 'magister', and defected from the Church [19]. Having left the Church, he went to the East where he remained active for a long time. The date of his death is unknown.

b. His works

He is the author of a number of books, some of which are extant and others not. The only text that has been preserved in its entirety is the 'Oratio ad Graecos'. This is an apology for Christianity, for the larger part consisting in a devastating attack on Greek culture which, according to the author, is good for nothing. Another well-known work of his is the 'Diatesseron', a Gospel harmonization in which the four Gospels are artfully woven into one story; this work remained very influential for a long time [20].

For our purpose the 'Oratio ad Graecos' is the important source. It is not an apology in the usual manner, since it does not address the Emperor but 'the Greeks'. Possibly it was a real speech, delivered at some occasion, although we don't know when and where [21]. Although Tatian had no ecclesiastical function, he obviously acts as the spokesman of Christianity, frequently using the word 'we' [22]. Tatian had to admit that he himself had had a (pagan) philosophical education - "I was trained in your (pagan, Greek) doctrines" [23] -; it even seems that he, when still a pagan, took part in Greek mystery cults [24]. He no longer wanted such things : I have "taken my leave of Roman arrogance and the cold cleverness of Athens - incoherent bases of doctrine" [25]; "this was the reason why we abandonded your school of wisdom" [26].

c. Tatian and philosophy

Do these diatribes mean that Tatian would have nothing to do at all with philosophy? Quite the contrary! He considered himself the philosopher par excellence [27], for the Christian doctrine contains the higher, the only valuable wisdom. All the faithful are 'philosophers'. "We reject all that is based on human opinion; not only the rich philosophize, but also the poor enjoy teaching without charge, for there is no comparison in exchange value between the truth of God and this world's recompense" [28]. Elze remarks that, although 'philosophia' was a generic designation for every religious doctrine, the early Christian apologists, with the single exception of Tatian, did not apply it to the Christian faith. This same scholar goes on to say that Tatian behaves towards pagan philosophy in a far more hostile way than the others, but that he nevertheless comes far closer to the pagans in his terminology, since he employs the term 'philosophia' [29]. Tatian ever again "contends that he stands in opposition to Hellenistic philosophy, but especially in the phraseology he is using he shows an inner agreement with this philosophy" [30].

d. Tatian's theology

Tatian was a strict monotheist; his God is absolutely transcendent. "Our God has no beginning in time (in opposition to the Olympians - F.); since he is alone, he is without beginning and is the beginning of all things himself" [31]. For 'beginning' he uses the Greek word 'archê' which is a 'terminus technicus' of Hellenic thinkers; already the Presocratics were looking for an 'archê' [32]. When the transcendence of God is heavily stressed, we may expect to see dualism in the offing, a dualism of spirit and matter, as it was in Origen with his abhorrence of the physical, a repulsion that was shared by God himself, he thought. Elze believes, however, that we do not find this sort of dualism in Tatian, but he argues that this ancient author, in striving to avoid it, manoeuvres himself into an awkward and not wholly logical position.

Initially God was totally alone; there was as yet no creation [33]. Was there already a Logos then? A Logos that was numerically different from the Father? This is doubtful. The Word was 'in him' (the Father); "by his mere will the Word sprang forth ... and became the 'firstborn' work of the Father. Him we know as the beginning of the Universe [34] ... The Word begotten in the beginning begot our creation by fabricating matter for himself" [35]. It seems as though there are two stages in the Logos : first, it is 'in' God; and then it is brought forth as the 'power' to 'establish all things' [36]. It might almost seem as though the Word itself forms part of the creation since it is called a 'work' [37].

For both the Father and the Logos Tatian uses the word 'pneuma' = spirit : the Logos is 'spirit from Spirit' [38]. This means, the Father and the Son are substantially one. But nevertheless, there seems to be pneuma and pneuma, a higher and a lower pneuma. "The spirit that pervades matter is inferior to the more divine Spirit; being on a level with matter it is not given equal honour with the perfect God" [39].

The position of Tatian is certainly not Gnostic, in the sense that in his theology, spirit and matter are not, literally, worlds apart. But in stressing the transcendence of God, he shrinks back from his immanence : the spirit that is present in the cosmos is another spirit than the divine one. Thus a distance is created between the supernatural and the natural. In the same line of thought, his theology nowhere speaks of Jesus of Nazareth. He only once comes near him, when he states that Christians are not "talking nonsense when they declare that God has been born in the form of a man" [40]. Tatian is clearly attempting to combine his idea of God's transcendence with a rejection of spirit-matter dualism, without being wholly succesful. When all is said and done, there is in his theology a kind of screen between the upper and nether worlds.

e. Tatian's anthropology

We detect this also in Tatian's anthropology. "We have knowledge of two different kinds of spirits, one of which is called soul, but the other is greater than the soul; it is the image and likeness of God. The first men were endowed with both, so that they might be part of the material world, and at the same time above it" [41]. But this is no longer so. "The soul cast it (the perfect spirit) away because of sin, fluttered like a nestling, and fell to the ground, and, once removed from heavenly company, yearned for association with inferiors" [42]. The whole purpose of Christian life is "to search for what we once had and have lost, and link the soul to the Holy Spirit and busy ourselves with the union ordained by God" [43]. This return is, so it seems, the fruit of a mental process or of an inner light. "My soul was taught by God", says Tatian of his own conversion [44]. At no point he does mention the sacraments and still less the redemption through the cross. There is surely a Gnostic tinge to this.

There is also something Gnostic in the assertion that "the soul kept a spark, as it were, of the spirit's power" [45]. Furthermore, there are two races of men. "God's spirit is not given to all, but is dwelling among some who behaved justly; being intimately connected with the soul, it (God's spirit) revealed to the other souls what had been hidden. The souls which were obedient to wisdom (sophia) attracted to themselves the kindred spirits; but those which were disobedient ... were clearly shown to be enemies of God rather than his worshippers" [46]. What else is this but the threefold division of mankind, so dear to the Gnostics, into pneumatics, psychics, and hylics?

f. Orthodox or not?

Was Tatian orthodox? Bardy thinks that, when he wrote the 'Oratio', he still was. But this scholar overlooks the fact that some of the material is distinctly suspect. We saw him walking some questionable side-paths, all tending in the direction of the Gnosis. For Irenaeus he was the Encratite par excellence. This Father considers Encratism as one of the eclectic heresies, doctrines composed out of some other heretical doctrines. The doctrinal background of the Encratites, he says, is partly the teaching of Saturnilos and Marcion. Tatian has his own place in the long catalogue of heresies in Irenaeus. According to this heresiarch, marriage is a form of corruption and fornication. "In this he accuses him who created man and woman in order to preserve the human race". It was, however, adds this Father, an idiosyncratic opinion of Tatian that Adam was not saved [47]. And if Adam is not saved, the whole human race is lost. It is for this reason that Irenaeus calls Tatian 'the compendium (connexio) of all the heretics' [48]. For he denies the possibility of the salvation of humanity.

4. 'Horror materiae'

There was in this period of ecclesiastical life an unmistakable 'horror materiae', an aversion to the physical, the same aversion that was so conspicuous in all Gnostic sects. But not only there. We saw that orthodox ecclesiastical authors too were not not wholly free of it. The difference between them and not perfectly orthodox or frankly heretical writers is that the last mentioned go much further in their puritanism and sometimes even condemn sexuality and marriage. Elze, for one, does not think that Tatian's rigorism sprang from a Gnostic source. But there can be no doubt that this scholar is correct in asserting, that he tried to solve ethical problems in a dualistic sense. This is, he goes on to say, "not the principal dualism of the Gnostics, for Tatian sticks invariably to the doctrine of the one principle".

There is, however, a breach between how man was intended to be, his being the image of God, and its realization. "The chorismos, in this form, leaves the principal unity unimpaired, but must be vanquished." The difference with orthodox theology is that it is not through the history of salvation that man will return to his original destination. This is what Tatian means when he says that Adam cannot be saved, not even by Jesus the Redeemer. It is only through his freedom that every individual can vanquish for himself this dualism. This notwithstanding, Elze concludes that Tatian was not a Gnostic. Maybe he is right; after all, we know far too little of his theology to locate him exactly [49]. But I for one do not doubt that he was gnosticizing. The theological influence of Tatian was not great; what remained influential was not the 'Oratio ad Graecos' but the 'Diatesseron'.

Part II The 'new prophecy' : Montanism

1. Phrygia the cradle of Montanism

Phrygia, a region in the west of Asia Minor, had the reputation of being a country with a tradition of prophecy and ecstasis [50]. It was the home of the goddess Cybele, the Earth Mother. She had her own mysteries which displayed orgiastic traits; her priests used to mutilate themselves. Since the missionary work of the apostle Paul Christianity was firmly established in this region, but it had much to suffer from persecutions. Perhaps for this reason chiliastic and apocalyptic expectations were rampant here. In the West expectations of a speedy return of the Lord began already to make place for a resigned acceptance of the fact that the end was not near, but in Phrygia it was different. Around 130, bishop Papias of Hierapolis believed in the coming of the millennium. He testified that a new earth would soon come into being; the days would arrive when not only every vine but even every single grape would yield incredible quantities of wine and every grain of corn ten pounds of white meal. No longer there would be wild and dangerous beasts. Creation would be restored to its original innocent state [51].

Phrygians were reported to incline towards rigorism and puritanism and to be averse to the usual Roman amusements such as circus games and performances in the theaters [52]. They clung tenaciously to their own beliefs and customs and had a predilection for excessive doctrines. De Labriolle states that the history of Montanism presents a new proof of this, one that is highly characteristic [53]. That Clement of Alexandria spoke of the Montanists as 'Phrygians' [54] underlines that there was an ethnic side to Montanism [55].

2. The beginning of the 'new prophecy'

The history of Montanism begins about A.D. 172. In the Phrygian village or township of Ardaban a certain Montanus lived [56]. It is reported that this man, who had earlier been a Cybele priest, was a convert to Christianity [57]. Eusebius quotes an anonymous author of the last decade of the second century who relates that Montanus was seized by an immoderate desire to play a leading role (in the Church). "Moved by a demon, he suddenly became like one possessed and in the grip of a furious ecstasy. He began to say new and unheard of things, to foretell the future and to prophecy, in a manner that was contrary to the customs and institutions of the Church, as they were established by the forefathers and since then ever again propagated" [58].

Together with him two ladies, Prisca (or Priscilla) and Maximilla - 'insane females', says Jerome contemptuously [59] - were seized by the spirit [60]. According to bishop Miltiades, writing around 180 and also quoted by Eusebius, the ladies in question claimed to be the successors of two older prophets, Ammia and Quadratus, who came from Philadelphia [61].

3. The movement spreads

On the fertile and well-prepared Phrygian soil the ecstatic movement spread like wildfire. Montanus' prophecying attracted numerous spectators, many of whom became adherents and followers. He and his two prophetesses, Prisca and Maximilla, addressed themselves directly to their hearers, sometimes exciting them and sometimes condemning them to their faces [62]. It is a curious fact that both adherents and opponents were convinced that their prophecies were genuine. The difference is that the first mentioned ascribed them to the Holy Ghost and the others to demons [63].

They seem to have employed a special technique to bring themselves into a state that Miltiades, quoted by Eusebius, calls 'amathia' = not-knowing [64]. They held that in this state the spirit could freely enter into them; the prophet was no more than an instrument in the hands of the Lord. "See, man is like a lyre", said Montanus, "I fly to it like the plectrum. The man sleeps; I, however, am awake. See, it is the Lord who brings the hearts of men into ecstasy and who gives a heart to men" [65]. What they had to foretell was definitive. Maximilla said : "After me there will come no other prophetess, but the end will follow" [66]. Here we detect the eschatological moment.

Soon a specific Montanist sect came into being [67]. A certain Themison became its treasurer and even its spokesman and propagandist. "In imitation of the Apostle (= Paul) he wrote a Catholic Letter in order to catechize people whose faith was better than his own (= orthodox Christians); he conducted polemics with words devoid of sense, and he blasphemed against the Lord, the apostles, and Holy Church" [68]. Montanus even had salaried missionaries in his service.

4. The new Jerusalem

The end was obviously close at hand; Maximilla prophecied that there would be wars and revolutions [69]. Montanus exhorted men and women to dissolve their marriages; it was said that the prophetesses had already done so [70]. As so often, eschatological expectations assumed an apocalyptic form. Montanus indicated a place where the new Jerusalem would be established, namely in Pepuza and Tymion, two small towns in Phrygia [71] and summoned every adherent of his to go there and join him. History does not tell us whether there really was a great Montanist settlement there, although there seems to have been some sort of centre.

5. The reaction of the bishops

The success of the Montanists in Asia Minor was such that the episcopate of this region began to feel uneasy. In some local churches there seems to have been violent clashes in which people came to blows and Montanist emissaries were molested [72]. Maximilla complained that she "was chased from the sheep like a wolf". But, she added, or rather the spirit speaking through her, "I am not a wolf but the Word, the Spirit, and the Power" [73]. The bishops did not immediately proceed to condemnations but tried to organize disputations. In some cases the Montanists were defeated [74], but in others a regular debate proved impossible. In Pepuza two bishops, Zotikos of Cumana and Julian of Apamea, were prevented from speaking with Maximilla by followers of Themison [75]. When the bishop of Anchialos wanted to exorcize Prisca, he had to beat a retreat [76]. Then synods were held to discuss the problem of Montanism, assemblies in which not only bishops but also laymen took part. The Montanist propositions were investigated and found heterodox; as a consequence the Montanists were banished from the Church [77].

6. A new prophetess

After the death of the Emperor Alexander Severus a terrific earthquake occurred in Asia Minor, afflicting in particular Cappadocia and Pontus; whole towns disappeared into the crevices that suddenly were opened in the earth. The culprits were soon found : the Christians. In 235 the merciless governor of the province began a cruel persecution.

Then, all of a sudden, a prophetess appeared who, in ecstasy, acted as though she was under the inspiration of the Holy Ghost. She attracted many followers among the Christians. She performed amazing things, for instance walking barefoot through snow and ice in a severe winter. This prophetess pretended to have come from Jerusalem and exhorted her adherents to go there themselves. She even acted as a priestess, celebrating the Eucharist and baptizing people; it is said that she did this according to the liturgical rules of the Church. An orthodox cleric tried to exorcize her, but without succes, it seems [78].

Later a much frequented synod was held at Iconium (the modern Konya) which declared such unauthorized baptisms invalid [79]. Enough to show that there were occasional flare-ups of prophetism in the Montanist line. De Labriolle states that the Asiatic episcopate found itself in a difficult position vis-à-vis the Montanist sect. It was a vigorous movement not short of money, with clever propaganda and an abundant literature. Unauthorized persons without an ecclesiastical mandate were setting themselves up as self-appointed reformers. The great danger was that they would find much sympathy in the population with its rigorist and exalted temperament, which indeed proved to be the case [80]. The movement was spreading all over Asia Minor and into Syria; it is said that whole cities defected to the reformers and that soon there were 'prophetic' (i.e. Montanist) churches [81]. Orthodox bishops who attempted to argue with their opponents soon got exhausted by their fruitless efforts which made them feel sick [82]. They then proceeded to exorcize them but were met by loud cries of protest; it sometimes even came to blows [83].

7. The Roman Catholic viewpoint

a. A Church of ordinary people

There is something to this affair that concerns the essential nature of the Roman Catholic Church. This Church is an assembly, a congregation of ordinary people, of persons who, in the vast majority, possess no special religious talents, no aptitude for mysticism, and who have neither visions nor apparitions. They know that they have to live saintly lives; most of them honestly try to do so to the best of their possibilities, sincerely repenting if they fail. The means they have at their disposal are not the promptings of the Spirit but Bible reading, the sacraments, in particular the Eucharist and confession, the communal prayer of the Church and private praying.

In view of this, it is not suprising that the favourite saint of the Catholics of the twentieth century became a very simple girl (but not a simpleton!), Therèse Martin (1873-1897), better known as Saint Teresa of Lisieux, and venerated by the Catholics as 'Little Teresa', the 'Little Flower', and in my country as 'Kleine Treesje', Little Tessie. Little Tessie was a daughter of a French bourgeois family; she became a Carmelite nun with the name of Sister Marie Thérèse de l'Enfant Jésus and never had any function in the Church, not even in her monastery. She died when she was only twenty-four years old. She was not a mystic nor had she ever a vision or a revelation. Her piety was that of the Catholic French family or the nunnery of the late nineteenth century. She was only exceptional in her great holiness, her uncompromising devotion, her total abandonment to God. Although she had led a forgotten life in the Carmel of Lisieux - she called it 'the little way' - , the ordinary faithful immediately after her death recognized that she had been a saint; the Church canonized her in 1925. Since then legions of Catholic girls were baptized on the name of Teresa.

b. The Church and her mystics

There is a place for mysticism in the Roman Catholic Church, of course; visions and apparitions are sometimes recognized as authentic (but not easily). Jeanne d'Arc (1412-1441) had to undergo an unpleasant examination of three weeks before her mission was recognized as authentic. Once taken prisoner by her enemies, she was submitted to an endless series of interrogations by an ecclesiastical court of forty learned jurists and theologians who finally condemned her to death as an heretic, a witch, a sorceress. She was finally rehabilitated by her canonization in 1920.

Teresa of Avila, the 'great Teresa' (1515-1582), was an authentic mystic whose works have remained influential until the present day. All the same she had troubles during her lifetime. Well-meaning confessors tried to convince her that her visions were of diabolic origin. Members of the Spanish Inquisition read her books letter by letter in order to detect only the slightest trace of heresy. But she finally won the day and was canonized in 1622.

The seeress of Lourdes, Bernadette Soubirous (1844-1879), was plagued until her early death in the Carmel of Nevers by investigation commission after commission. But she too was canonized, in 1933.

The real reason for the way the Church treated some of her greatest children is that she is averse to extravagance. Mystical persons, prophets, visionaries, charismatic movements not rarely show a tendency to go to dangerous extremes. With such persons and movements the Church is always on her guard; her touchstone is whether they sincerely adhere to the orthodox 'depositum fidei'. People who don't do this are apt to create confusion by leaning towards heresy and schism. One should never forget that the Church has to cater to the religious needs of innumerable masses of Christian shopkeepers, housewives, artisans, labourers, soldiers, schoolchildren, employees, artists, and scholars like me, all ordinary people with nothing exceptional about them. In the fulfilment of her pastoral duties the Church always follows the 'via tutior', the safer road.

c. The attitude of the Church towards excesses

We are now in the position to understand why the Church turned such a stern face towards the Montanists, whereas there had been sincere attempts to argue with the Paulinians in order to convince them of their errors. Paul of Samosate himself was deposed, but we hear of no unpleasantness against his supporters. The Montanists, however, were harassed right from the start. The reason is to be found not so much in their doctrinal deviations but rather in the ecstatic character of their movement. They wanted to turn the Church into a congregation of exceptional persons, of charismatics, of visionaries, of people in direct touch with the Spirit, which would put off the common run of believers.

Already in the first decades of the Church Paul had given his verdict and set the rules. He had heard that in the young Church of Corinth so-called 'glossolalists' were operating, men and women who uttered strange and incomprehensible sounds, pretending that they were speaking 'in tongues', because the Spirit prompted them to do this. The Apostle was not charmed by this phenonemon. He did not deny that the Spirit might be manifesting himself in this way, but he had great reservations.

"The man who talks in a strange tongue is talking to God, not to men; nobody understands him, he is holding converse with his own spirit." In other words, it is a solipsistic adventure. "By talking in a strange tongue, a man may strengthen his own spirit." This means that he is acting selfishly. There is no sense in it : "Your words will fall on empty air". And he has harsh words for an assembly given to glossolaly. "What will happen if the uninstructed or the unbelievers come in when the whole church has met together, and find everyone speaking with strange tongues at once? Will they not say you are mad?"

Paul felt he was unable to eradicate this custom, but the rules he set were these. In every assembly two persons, or three at the most, were allowed to speak in tongues, and then each one in turn. There should always be somebody to interpret what they said; if there was no interpreter available, there should be no glossolaly at all. In this way the Apostle hoped to neutralize this phenomenon as best as he could. He kept his eye on the whole congregation, mainly consisting of ordinary men and women, not primarily of exceptional individuals. To glossolaly he preferred 'prophecy' by which he meant teaching, instruction in the faith : "by prophecy a man can strengthen the faith of the Church" [84].

Here we hit on the fundamental difference between the main Church and the Montanists. These wanted the Church to be an assembly of visionaries and charismatics, compared to whom the ordinary faithful would be second rank at best. Many of them were high-strung people on the verge of the abnormal and sometimes beyond it. The great danger was that the Church would come to resemble a lunatic asylum rather than a prayerful congregation of quiet believers. Thus we see here opposed to each other two irreconcilable conceptions of what the Church had to be.

8. Montanist theology

What do we know of Montanist theology? The problem is that not one of the Montanist treatises, which must have been numerous, has been preserved, with the exception of those written by Tertullian after he had become a Montanist. We possess, however, a collection of 'oracles', of sayings attributed to Montanus and his prophetesses [85]. And we find a lot of material in orthodox authors, the most informative of whom are Eusebius and Epiphanius [86].

a. The role of the Holy Ghost

The Montanists recognized the absolute sovereignty of God, but they were no Monarchianists, because they acknowledged three distinct persons in the godhead. This was of the utmost importance to them, for they heavily accentuated the role of the Holy Spirit [87]. According to Montanus, the Holy Spirit was especially operative in his generation. The Montanist version of the Passion of Perpetua and Felicitas, two Carthaginian women who died a martyr's death in 202, displays a typical Montanist bias and quotes with agreement the word of the prophet Joel that in the last days the Lord will pour out his spirit upon everyone; visions and dreams will become abundant [88]. And the author proceeds in this way : "Just as we recognize and honor new prophecies, so also we recognize and honor new visions as promised in equal measure, and we esteem the other manifestations of the Holy Spirit for the assistance of the Church" [89]. We are in the presence of a prophetic movement.

This even went so far that Montanus himself could state : "I am the Lord God, the Almighty dwelling in man" [90]. This should not be understood as to mean that the prophet identified himself with God but rather that he felt to be possessed by the godhead [91]. The Holy Ghost, the Paraclete, is the guide par excellence; he leads the faithful to every truth [92]. He is the deputy of the Lord. "What else is the proper office of the Paraclete but regulating the discipline, disclosing the Scriptures, reforming the intelligences, prompting the faithful toward better things" [93]. All this is not really unorthodox, of course, but the Montanists stressed the role of the Holy Ghost so strongly that they were accused of exalting him to the detriment of Christ. Their opponents said that the Montanists imputed every novelty whatsoever to the Paraclete, although, they aded, these fabrications were ultimately inspired by the devil [94].

The Montanists took every precaution to show they remained true to the doctrinal line of the Church. "Montanus, Prisca, and Maximilla do not preach another God nor do they 'dissolve' Jesus Christ or come back on whatever rule of faith and hope" [95]. What the Paraclete teaches does not come from 'another Christ' [96]. Tertullian swears that the rule of faith is absolutely one, unchangeable, and irreformable. This rule of faith is that there is one God, creator of the universe; Jesus Christ is his Son, born from the Virgin Mary, crucified, risen from the dead, seated at the right hand of the Father; he will return to judge the living and the dead.

So far so good. But the attentive reader will have remarked that this author stops before he reaches the article of the creed concerning the Holy Spirit. Instead of proclaiming the Holy Spirit too, he goes on to say that the remaining articles of the creed allow of certain new amendments, through the progressive action of divine grace. "The Lord, knowing that human mediocrity was incapable of receiving all at a time, sent the Paraclete to rectify the rule of faith bit by bit, to regulate it and lead it to perfection by the deputy of the Lord, the Holy Spirit" [97]. They, the Montanists, "are the disciples of the Paraclete, not of men". Tertullian does not omit to tell us who these men were; they were the Roman bishops who leaned on the authority of their predecessors in order to lend force to their decrees, and this did not interest him [98]. Stroehlin rightly remarks that Tertullian is opposing here the rights of tradition to those of truth, rights which, in his view, are irreconcilable [99]. And what to think of this statement that, according to Pseudo-Tertullian, are the very words of Montanus himself : "The Paraclete has revealed greater and better things through Montanus than through Christ" [100]?

b. The doctrine of successive revelations

A few remarks should be made at this point. It is not only the doctrinal authority of the main Church that is denied here. It is equally the case that Christ himself is pushed into the background; his teachings, which obviously are imperfect, have become of secondary importance. Instead, there is a heavy accent on the revelations of the Holy Ghost. We may speak of a 'spiritualizing' of the Christian faith, to the detriment of Christology, of the Logos-doctrine. Prisca declared that the Lord appeared to her in the shape of a female who revealed all wisdom to her [101]. Whoever this apparition may have been, it was not the historical Jesus of Nazareth; the connection with him seems to have been severed.

Some explanation may be found in the doctrine of successive revelations such as it was propounded by Tertullian. The first phase was the Mosaic one; there was as yet no explicit moral code [102]. The patriarchs enjoyed a great latitude; they had concubines and were polygamous [103]. This was, so to speak, the embryonic stage. Infancy began with the Law and the Prophets, especially with the pronouncement of the Decalogue. Youth came with the Gospel [104]. This did not mean that the Law had become less strict; quite the contrary, it was even made more severe [105]. But now the day of the Paraclete has dawned; now it is the time of full maturity [106].

This theory reminds me irresistibly of the doctrine of Joachim da Fiore [107]. This South Italian abbot of the late twelfth century distinguished three stages in the history of salvation : that of the Father (before Christ), that of the Son (after Christ), and that of the Spirit (the future and most perfect era). I don't think that Joachim was acquainted with Tertullian's writings, but we find here the same supremacy of the Spirit. In Joachimite doctrine too there would be no need of Pope and bishops.

c. The eschatological background

The Montanist position should be placed against the background of its eschatology; the expectation that the Lord was to return soon pervaded the whole sect. This explains why they were so severely ascetic : everyone must keep him- or herself pure and untainted for the coming end. There was a heavy accent on fasting and on sexual abstinence. The Montanists must live according to the Holy Ghost, shunning contact with the physical world as much as possible. The believer could even personally somewhat hasten the desired coming of the end by seeking martyrdom. Whosoever attempted to escape from this was an enemy of the Holy Ghost [108].

The idea of an end that was close at hand had not yet wholly died out; the Montanists no doubt made it flare up again. Hippolytus tells us of a certain bishop in Syria who was foolish enough to conduct his faithful, with their families, to the desert to await there the coming of the Lord. They hardly escaped being arrested there for brigandage. Another bishop, this time in Pontus, pretending to be a prophet, persuaded many of his flock to leave their villages and even to sell their fields in view of the coming catastrophe. When nothing happened, they tried to repurchase their property [109]. Events like these cannot have failed to impress the more sensible part of the Asiatic episcopate.

9. Tertullian the Montanist

a. Where Tertullian agreed with Montanism

The Church of North Africa suffered severely from periodically occurring persecutions; she counted many famous martyrs like Cyprian and Perpetua and Felicitas. Consequently, in the eyes of many faithful martyrdom was considered something of exceptional value. No wonder that there was also a wide-spread presumption that the end was near, accompanied by an exalting of the works of the Spirit. It will not surprise us that Montanism was made welcome in this region. Its great mouthpiece and defender became Tertullian.

Quintus Septimius Florus Tertullianus, born in Carthage between 155 and 160, was the son of a pagan Roman officer. He received a very good education in several disciplines and became very fluent in Greek. After completing his studies he established himself as a lawyer. His erudition and intelligence were widely recognized. He spent some years in Rome where he seems to have had a number of erotic adventures. In 195, still a pagan, he returned to Carthage. Not long afterwards he converted to Christianity, deeply impressed as he was by the heroism displayed by the faithful during the persecutions. We have no certain information as to whether or not he was a priest. Anyhow, he wrote quite a number of treatises to defend and propound the creed and to combat the heretics, especially the Gnostics.

And then, in 211 or 212, he joined the Montanists. His writings of the years 211-217 - 'Adversus Praxean, De monogamia, De ieiunio, De pudicitia' [110] - all defend the Montanist position. The conversion did not come all of a sudden; for eight years he had been moving into this direction. As Bardy stated, Tertulllian was a passionate man; moderation meant nothing to him. "As soon as he had an idea, he pushed it to its extreme consequences, without any concern for the claims of everyday life. There was for him no middle way between good and evil, between truth and error" [111]. And De Labriolle found he was 'inexorably uncompromising' [112]. In other words, Tertullian had the mental make-up of a dualist. We detect this in the fierce manner in which he combated all his opponents, the pagans, the Jews, the Gnostics, the heretics, and after he had converted to Montanism, the orthodox Christians too. Add to this that he was a man of great eloquence and a wide erudition; what he wrote did not go unheeded. He was one of the first architects of the Latin theological language.

What attracted Tertullian to Montanism? For instance, the glorification of martyrdom. For a man of his type, dying for the faith must have seemed an act of supreme devotion; it is not hard to guess that ordinary Christians tended to be somewhat less enthusiastic. Then there was the rigoristic moralism of Montanism, its asceticism, compared to which he found the practices of the Church rather soft and laxist. Perhaps he was not comfortably at home in the main Church with her well-defined 'regula fidei'. There was not enough 'prophecy' in the Church for his taste. It seemed to him that a really religious person was allowed a wider scope in the Montanist sect, with its spiritualism, its visions, its prophecies, the Church of the 'new prophecy'. For years already he had exalted the Holy Ghost.

b. What Tertullian disliked in Montanism

There must have been elements in Montanism, however, which Tertullian can only have disliked, the role of women, for instance [113]. He was not exactly woman-friendly. "It is you (woman) who art the gate of the devil; it is you who have broken the seal of the famous tree (in Paradise); it is you who were the first to break the divine Law; it is you who have seduced him whom the devil could not attack (the man) ... It is because of your services - death! so simple is it - that the Son of Man had to die" [114]. He did not mince his words! Women should have no function of any kind in church and should keep mum there. But what did he find in the Montanist Church? Prophetesses! Women went about preaching the 'new prophecy'! Women played a great role in the prophetic movement; they presided over liturgical functions; some even distributed the sacraments.

Then there was the Phrygian origin of the sect. Phrygia enjoyed no great reputation with the erudite part of the population of the Empire; it was considered a region of superstition and of irrationalism. Montanism was and remained for many 'this sect of the Phrygians'. Finally, a well-ordered mind like his must have felt repelled by the anarchism and disorderliness that are common to charismatic movements. All this notwithstanding, Tertullian succeeded in triumphing over his reservations. But perhaps he was not able to pacify his doubts once and for all. Some years later - we don't know when exactly - he took his leave of the Montanists, but this was not followed by a reconciliation with the Church. So this great man was in his life successively a pagan, an orthodox Christian, a Montanist, and, so to speak, a 'free-lance Christian'; whether all this made him happy is the question. The last years of his life are shrouded in mystery. After 220 there appeared no more publications from his hand. It is not known where he died nor where; he is said to have lived to an extreme old age.

c. Tertullian and the psychics

It is a curious thing that Tertullian, the fierce opponent of the Gnosis, nevertheless borrowed some telling terms from it, namely 'psychics' and 'pneumatics'. 'Psychics' - soul-people - were all those Christians who did not adhere to the Montanist tenets; 'pneumatics' - 'spiritales' in Tertullian's Latin, spirit-people - were the Montanists, of course [115]. A 'psychicus' is a Christian who has not the spirit. "On this point there is a problem between us and psychics", writes Tertullian [116], showing that there was a great distance between the two groups. The 'spiritales' are characterized by the charismata of the Spirit; "the psychics are incapable of rejoicing in the things that are of the Spirit" [117].

Tertullian confesses that he would "be ashamed to consort with such people (i.e. the psychics) ... It is they who quarrel with the Paraclete" [118]. He was not chary with his reproaches. "The only thing that remains to you is to abandon God entirely, as far as your power reaches, because he bores you so much" [119]. Psychics are the exact opposite of spiritales : "God himself stated that there are differences between soul and spirit" [120]. What sets us apart from the psychics is our acknowledgement and defense of the Paraclete" [121]. Enough to show that there is, in Montanist opinion, an unbridgeable, a dualistic chasm between them and the ordinary Catholics who are contemptuously called 'psychics'. The conclusion of Stroehlin runs as follows. "The Montanists came to consider themselves as an élitist company in the bosom of each community, as the only Christians worthy of that name, as the pneumatics, in opposition to their adversaries whom they decried as psychics, slaves of the flesh, and whom they accused of rejecting the revelations of the Spirit" [122]. And so we find even in Tertullian that curious division of mankind into two utterly different and opposed races of men.

10. The later vicissitudes of Montanism

In North Africa the Montanists never became very numerous, not even in the days when Tertullian was their spokesman. During the episcopate of Augustine in Hippo, around 400, there still existed a 'Tertullianist' sect at Carthage, with a basilica of its own. Augustine prided himself on having reconciled its adherents with the Church [123]. After 400 nothing more is heard of Montanism in North Africa. It is said, however, that a later sect, the Donatists, inherited much from it.

Montanism gained a foothold in Rome where it showed a certain vitality. Not much is known of its history there, except that at the end of the fourth century Jerome judged it necessary to warn Marcella, a Roman woman, against the 'Kataphrygians' [124]; this proves that there must have been a Montanist party in Rome then. A perhaps not wholly reliable anonymous source relates how, in the middle of the fifth century, a 'Tertullianist' priest arrived from North Africa in Rome; he established a Montanist cult centre at the tomb of the martyrs Processus and Martinianus [125].

In Spain nothing is heard of the sect, but there were Montanists in Gaul, where Irenaeus warned his flock against them; they were false prophets, he said [126]. In Phrygia, the region of its origin, Montanism continued to flourish during the third century, but began to lose ground during the fourth. Ever more it became a fringe phenomenon. All the same it had its adherents and its cult centres, with Pepuza as its holy city. In spite of decreasing numbers they held out for a long time, having retreated into the mountainous interior of Phrygia. Montanists are mentioned for the last time in 722 in a rescript of the Byzantine Emperor Leo III the Isaurian .

The Montanists became the object of official condemnations. Christian rulers issued decrees against it; Constantine the Great, for instance, did this in 331 [127]. After 378 Theodosius I showered one decree after another on them; Arcadius and Theodosius II did the same [128]. Pope Innocentius I (401-417) said that he had discovered a great many of them, banished them from the Church, and shut them up in a monastery [129]. In the same time the Emperor Honorius issued a decree against them, dated February 22, 407; he condemned them severely, ordered the confiscation of their goods, and robbed them of their civil rights [130]. Not much more is heard of them after the middle of the fifth century. There must, however, been Montanists at a later date, for Pope Gregory I the Great in 601 published a ruling on how to reintegrate penitent Montanists into the Church [131].

Part III Donatism

1. The origins of the Donatist controversy

Not chronologically but thematically the Donatist heresy follows that of the Montanists. Geographically there was a connection too; the best-known protagonist of Montanism was the Carthaginian Tertullian, while Donatism had its origin in North Africa. Just like Montanism Donatism was spiritualistic, puritanical, and rigoristic, with a fair dose of fanaticism; in both we find the same exaltation of martyrdom. The Donatists were among the fiercest opponents of the orthodox Church; their offspring, the Circumcellions, even resorted to bloody blows. Whether or not there was a direct link between Montanism and Donatism is difficult to say. It was surely not a direct one; both sects are separated by an interval of more than a century. But both fed on the same rigoristic mentality that was remarkably strong in North Africa (but not only there).

a. The persecution of Diocletian

Scholars agree that the origin of the Donatist defection should be sought in the persecution of Diocletian. This was short but violent; it lasted hardly two years, from 303 to 305 [132]. The conflict that then arose among the Catholics concerned the delivery of the sacred books to the pagan authorities. The first anti-Christian edict of Diocletian ordered the Christians to hand over their sacred books to be publicly burned in the market square [133]. It was unconditionally necessary that the owners handed over the books personally; police were provided with warrants to search even private homes. There can be no doubt that many clergy and laypeople did what was asked of them. Their choice was painful : either ceding to pagan hands books they considered sacred or being arrested and following the path to martyrdom.

Carthage's bishop in those hard times was Mensurius who obviously was on the compliant side; he did what he could to prevent the authorities from resorting to ever harsher measures. He did not deem it necessary that his Christians should rush straight to martyrdom. There were bishops in other dioceses who refused to part with their books, but not many, so it seems. Bishop Felix of Thibiuca [134] kept firm, refused to deliver his books, was arrested, condemned, and beheaded in the summer of 303 [135]. The majority seems to have reasoned that the police would seize their books anyhow; should they refuse and be arrested, their homes would be searched. Not only books were sequestrated but also cult objects and pieces of furniture [136].

b. The question of the Martyrs of Abitenae

The plight of the Christians became still more precarious with the fourth decree of Diocletian ordering everyone to take part in the official pagan sacrificial cult [137]. We know that, when this edict was issued, many faithful lapsed, but in Abitenae, an unidentified town in Africa proconsularis, some fifty of them remained steadfast, in contrast to their bishop, Fundanus, who had handed over the sacred books. In protest against this a number of Christians seceded from the main Church and held conventicles of their own; we see the first germs of schism here. They came together for the celebration of the Eucharist in private houses where the place of the bishop was taken by a certain Saturninus, a priest.

This priest and a number of faithful, fifty in all, some children among them, were arrested during a celebration of the Eucharist. They were conducted in chains to Carthage where they had to appear before Anullinus, the proconsul. Having confessed that they had been present at the sacred office, some of them were most cruelly tortured. Even the children were not spared. Finally, they were locked up in a prison where they got neither food nor drink; one after another they died. Probably, as their 'Passio' suggests, Anullinus simply forgot them [138].

Now this 'Passio' was the work of a Donatist [139]. What strikes us in it is the glorification of martyrdom. The anonymous author speaks deprecatingly of bishop Fundanus who was one of those who had delivered sacred books to the police, the so-called 'traditores', but he had scarcely sufficient words of praise for the martyrs. Of Saturninus he says : "O martyr, who takes precedence over all others" [140]. They all came forward to accuse themselves and went joyfully to the torture chamber. More martyrs followed, like the 'Virgins of Thuburbo', executed on July 30, 304, and Crispina of Thagora, killed on December 5, 304, but their fate was the consequence of their refusal to sacrifice and had nothing to do with the 'traditio', the handing over of sacred books [141].

The black sheep in the eyes of the rigorists was bishop Mensurius of Carthage whom they accused of having delivered his sacred books into the hands of the pagans; their proof was a letter from Mensurius to the primate of Africa proconsularis, bishop Secundus of Tigisis (now Bordj d'Aïn in Algeria) [142]. However, Mensurius had not confessed to this in his letter; he wrote, rather, that he had concealed the books somewhere in a church, leaving in his own church nothing but some heretical works with which the policemen had to content themselves [143].

What probably was a worse offense was that he said he did not understand those who offered themselves so readily for martyrdom. It displeased him that they admitted having books which they would not hand over but for which nobody had asked them; he felt unable to honour them as Christians. In the eyes of his opponents he added insult to injury when he wrote that some of them were criminals or were in arrear with their taxes. He even suggested that the persecution was a fair occasion for such people to quit a life burdened with debts, to wash off their crimes, so to speak, and to enjoy the good offices of Christians, when in custody [144].

The other side retaliated, not without venom. It was rumoured that Mensurius and his archdeacon Caecilianus were guilty of the fate of the martyrs of Abitenae, because they had prevented the Christians from coming to their aid with food. This is not really credible [145]. But perhaps the bishop was overcautious; judging the situation already bad enough, he wanted to prevent more clashes with the authorities. He was against a tumult in front of the prison which could provoke a punitive reaction [146]. The primate of Numidia, Secundus, lectured Mensurius. He had laudatory words for those who had refused to deliver sacred books and replied that he himself had not done so, telling the police : "I am a Christian bishop, not a 'traditor'" [147]. The word 'traditor' is ambiguous : it signifies one who handed over books, but also 'traitor'.

We are confronted with two conceptions of Christian life here, a rigorist one tending towards fanaticism, and a more practical one with perhaps a laxist side to it. These two conceptions were irreconcilable and utterly opposed to each other. The elements for a serious conflict have now been described. The sharpness of this conflict is demonstrated by the following incident. When Lucilla, a rich widow, receiving the cup during the Eucharist, also kissed the relic of a martyr, she was publicly reprimanded by Caecilianus; much nettled, the lady refused to receive the communion [148].

2. Mounting tension

Curious things began to happen in this tense climate, even when the persecution had not yet been called off officially. In Cirta (the modern Constantine in Algeria) the death of the diocesan necessitated the choice of a successor. This must have happened at the end of 304 or in the beginning of 305. The election led to a social conflict between the lower classes and the bourgeoisie. The candidate of the peasants and the quarry workers was a certain Silvanus, who was no more than a subdeacon (that is, not a priest). He was also a 'traditor', for during the perquisition in Cirta, which I mentioned in note 136, he had handed over chalices and cult objects. Obviously he made light of this [149].

The bourgeois had no high idea of this man and opted for a worthier candidate [150]. But the rustics and the labourers proclaimed Silvanus as their bishop; in order to achieve this result, they locked up their opponents in the cemetery of the martyrs [151]. To make things worse, Silvanus was not above being given a sum of money by a fuller called Victor; in recompense this man was ordained as priest [152]. It was, as Frend writes, 'a paradoxical situation' : "A self-confessed traditor had been chosen by fanatical Christian crowds as their bishop" [153]. Perhaps the social conflict offers some sort of explanation, namely, that the populace wanted a candidate utterly different from the one proposed by the bourgeoisie.

The next stage was the so-called 'Synod of Cirta'. Its date, in all probability, was March 5, 305 [154]. Secundus, the Primate of Numidia, convoked it; the occasion was the consecration of Cirta's new bishop. It was not a real synod, rather a meeting of some bishops; it was held in a private house (because the confiscated ecclesiastical buildings had not yet been restored to their rightful owners) [155]. The atmosphere was tense; accusations and even threats were freely bandied about [156]. Bishops who were not in a state of grace, i.e. those who had been 'traditores', would not be allowed to lay their hands on the new bishop [157].

Wanting to ascertain who had remained free of this sin, Secundus interrogated the diocesans who were present; he did this in an inquisitorial and accusing manner, as though he was a counsel for the prosecution. In order to make them feel uncomfortable he praised the martyrs. "What shall we do with the martyrs? They handed over nothing, and this is why they were crowned." But the bishops felt they were not answerable to the Primate; the one after the other begged the question, although they admitted in veiled terms that they had been guilty. In consequence Secundus saw himself compelled to regard them as consecrators.

But things no longer went so smoothly when he came to Purpurius, bishop of Liniata (an unidentified town). The Primate put this cleric harshly in the dock. "They say that you have killed two sons of your sister at Milevis (the present-day Mila in Algeria)." Purpurius did not answer the accusation but counterattacked. "Do you think you can frighten me like the others? You yourself have been arrested by the curator and ordered to give up your books. How is it that you were liberated from their hands, if it were not because you did what you were told? They did not let you go à propos of nothing. Yes, it is true, I have killed, as I will kill those who act against me. Don't force me to say more!" Our Lord has some queer boarders, as a Dutch saying goes!

There was a nephew of the Primate present, also called Secundus, who warned his uncle that Purpurius was ready to cause a schism and carry all the others along with him. He said they were responsible to God alone, and with this the Primate had to remain content. It is evident that a schism could hardly be avoided. Although this did not come to pass immediately, it remained in the offing.

3. Donatus

The term 'Donatism' comes from Donatus, who was an historical person of whom mention is made for the first time in the years between 307 and 312. When he enters the historical record, he was bishop of Casae Nigrae, a no longer existing town, sixty miles south of Thevesti (Tebessa in Algeria) [158]. Donatus a Casis Nigris was a difficult and harsh man, a rigorist, who refused to rebaptize Christians and to reconsecrate bishops who had lapsed. In 313 Pope Miltiades (310-314) condemned Donatus for this and for detaching himself from the Church, i.e. for starting a schism [159]. Frend thinks that, although this sentence dates from 313, it nevertheless refers to acts that Donatus committed when he was still bishop of Casae Nigrae [160].

4. Schism in the North African Church

a. The problem of the succession of bishop Mensurius

Serious problems arose when bishop Mensurius of Carthage died in 311. Since there were now two parties in the North African Church, it goes without saying that there was more than one candidate for the same office. The background was formed by the rivalry and enmity between the Churches of Carthage and Numidia [161]. It was an embarrassing circumstance that, while the Primate of Numidia claimed the right to consecrate the bishop of Carthage, the Carthaginian clergy tried to circumvent this by appealing to an (alleged) African custom that only the bishops of the province in question had the right of consecration [162].

The orthodox candiate, Caecilianus, did not lack enemies. He was an opponent of the rigorists and averse to exalting the martyrs. Soon enough that wealthy widow, Lucilla, who, as the reader will remember, had been publicly reprimanded by him, appeared on the scene again. She had a candidate of her own, Majorinus, one of her servants, who was a lector in the Carthaginian church [163]. Meanwhile Donatus a Casis Nigris was busily scheming against Caecilianus, the candidate of the other party, supported, it was said, by Lucilla's money. When Caecilianus was really elected, it was probably Donatus who informed Secundus, the Primate of Numidia, of this; the Primate was furious, because he felt his rights had been violated. Secundus judged the ordination of Caecilianus as unlawful, among other things because the three bishops who had consecrated him were suspected of being traditores [164]. For the duration of the interim Secundus nominated an 'interventor', a kind of supervisor; if we may believe Augustine, this man was killed by the adherents of Caecilianus [165].

When messengers arrived from Carthage inviting Secundus to go to there and take action against Caecilianus, he decided to strike [166]. Ready for war and with an imposing cortège of seventy Numidian bishops he set out for Carthage where he convened a council [167]. That there was a traditor like Silvanus of Cirta and a man of very doubtful reputation like Purpurius of Limata among them does not seem to have bothered the Primate in the least [168]. When they arrived, they found Caecilianus already functioning. Obviously not being able to use the basilica, they came together in a private house. They then summoned Caecilianus before them, but he refused to appear [169].

Caecilianus now committed a tactical blunder. Probably in the interest of pacification and in order to avoid a schism, he proposed to the council of bishops that he was ready to be ordained as though he were still a deacon [170]. This was tantamount to admitting that even in his own eyes his ordination had not been valid! The reaction of the council was not exactly conciliatory. With his usual violence Purpurius declared that, when he laid his hands on the head of Caecilianus, he would use the occasion to break it - this in spite of the fact that the bishop was his nephew. In his place the council made Lucilla's favourite Majorinus bishop. Optatus scathingly remarks that he was consecrated by the very traditores who had confessed their crimes during the synod of Cirta. And so, he says, "altar against altar was erected"; in other words, the schism became a fact [171].

Augustine adds that the council was supported in this by 'a seditious mob drunken with its own wickedness' [172] on which Frend comments that "an alliance between the Carthaginian lower class and the Numidian clergy which persisted throughout the history of Donatism was coming into being. It is possible that Donatus himself served as the link between the Numidians and the Carthaginian opposition" [173].

None of this makes pleasant reading, the more so because the affair is leaking as a sieve on all sides. It is doubtful whether Secundus, as the Primate of Numidia, really had canonical rights on Carthage; both parties could claim arguments in their favour. What makes the holy indignation of the Numidians bishops against the Carthaginian traditores somewhat suspect is that not a few of them had handed over the sacred books themselves. On the other hand, while it is by no means an ascertained fact that Bishop Felix, who had been one of those who had consecrated Caecilianus, had been a traditor, it is true that Lucilla's money played an considerable role in the affair. Optatus writes that Majorinus was elected 'with the help of Lucilla', leaving it to his readers to guess what this meant [174].

It is anyhow evident that both parties were ensconcing themselves in impregnable positions, in other words, that the situation was assuming dualistic proportions. This was clearly expressed by one of the bishops of the council of Secundus : "Unfruitful branches are to be cut off and cast aside ... Those who being in schism are ordained by traditores cannot remain within the Church of God, unless they are reconciled through penance with contrite acknowledgement (of their fault). Hence, no one ought to communicate with Caecilianus who has been ordained by traditores in schism" [175]. Yet another thing that becomes evident here is that the Donatists considered the main

Church as being schismatic. The outlook did not become better when Majorinus died in 413 and Donatus was elected in his place [176].

b. Did the schism have an ethnic background?

Alfred Schindler [177] shows himself amazed that controversial issues of relatively small importance could cause such ferocious battles (and worse is to come!), lasting for over a century. There was not much theology involved (to which we shall have to come back further on), so that we cannot speak of an outburst of the 'furor theologicus'. How then can such bitterness be explained? Scholars disagree considerably as to the real causes of the conflict. It will have struck the attentive reader that it was Numidia versus Carthage. Could it be that there was a strong ethnic or nationalistic element involved? Several scholars have thought so [178]. In his doctoral thesis of 1893 Wilhelm Thümmel [179] argued that Donatism was 'African nationalism representing inherent separatistic trends prevalent during the Late Roman Empire'. He assumed that Donatism was at home in regions where Punic was spoken, mainly in southern Numidia [180]. If this is correct, the conflict would mirror a fundamental disagreement between a Punic Numidia, always discontented with Roman rule, and a romanized Carthage where Latin was spoken.

Half a century later this thesis was taken up again by William Frend who gave his book 'The Donatist Church' the subtitle of 'A Movement of Protest in Roman North Africa'. This scholar disposed of a lot of archaeological material that was lacking to Thümmel. He himself collected much geographical evidence of which detailed maps at the back of his book testify. His overall conclusion is that of a geographical, linguistic, and social differentiation between the allegedly Donatist and orthodox areas. Donatist areas mainly included southern Numidia that was agrarian in character and where the Berber language was spoken; Roman-Catholic areas included the towns along the coast which throve on commerce and where Latin and Punic were spoken. Furthermore, he held that the Numidian (Donatist) regions preserved older Christian traditions.

Frend entitled his final chapter (XX) 'Two cities .. two Churches'. His conclusion is that "Donatists and Catholic remained divided from each other until both were swept away by Islam. The questions that separated them were those of will and outlook, not doctrine and philosophy ... To contemporaries, the two Churches seemed to stand in relation to each other like two rival societies inspired by contrary wills : an illustration of the everlasting clash between 'the Church of Judas' and 'the Church of Peter'" [181] - the Church of Judas (the traitor) being that of Carthage, of course, and that of Peter (the rock) that of Numidia. Could anything be more dualistic?

c. The ethnic solution under fire

Although there is no denying that the controversy was extremely fierce, Frend's explanation came under fire from other scholars. Six years after the appearance of Frend's work, Jean-Paul Brisson wrote that, in his opinion, the causes of the conflict should be sought in the socio-economic sphere rather than in ethnic oppositions. He did not deny that the Berber country was the cradle of Donatism, but "it was not the past of their race that has pushed the Berbers towards Donatism; it was the retributions, too heavy for their tenures, the indebtedness of the small farmers, the difficulty of finding work for the seasonal workers". In other words, there was a social conflict between the rich landowners (often absentees) and the exploited rural population. "Donatism grew in a province that was driven by its economic oppression by Rome and Italy to isolate itself from its oppressors in order not to die of asphyxiation" [182]. Seen from this point of view, it was for the Donatists a question of life and death.

In the eyes of the Donatists it was not their Church that was schismatic, but rather the orthodox Church that was felt as being foreign to the African soil. There have been long debates among them on the question whether those who came over from the Roman Catholic Church should be rebaptized; there were many who thought that those who had been Roman Catholics should be reintegrated into the proper African community. Donatus himself was of this opinion, but the Donatist council of 337 decided, under the pressure of the Mauretanian Donatist bishops, that rebaptizing was not in all cases necessary.

Brisson sketches the difference in unmistakably dualistic terms. The Donatists hedged their Church hermetically off from their opposite number; they voluntarily used the image of the 'closed garden'. "There was an interior and an exterior. In the interior the virtues and all kinds of sanctity shone; in the exterior there was the darkness of sin. Every sinner crossed the line (i.e. as the result of his sinning), this merciless line of separation, and had no longer anything in common with the interior" [183].

Modern scholarship has toned down Frend's thesis considerably; it is found much too sharp-cut. It cannot be denied that both Churches had much in common. Alfred Schindler refers to African autonomist tendencies; he sees Roman Catholicism in Africa as 'centripetal' (= towards Rome) and Donatism as 'centrifugal' (= away from Rome). 'Rome' should be understood here as the central seat of both state and Church. The disturbing factor in North Africa, he writes, was not Donatism but rather the common attempt of the political power and the Catholic Church to counter African autonomy [184]. But from whatever side we look at it, we have to do with a dualistic conflict.

5. Neurosis : a comparison

I do not feel the urge to present a theory of my own; I have an idea that ethnicism, nationalism, social problems, anti-Roman tendencies, all went into the making of Donatism, and that it is hard to say which factor was the most operative one. However, I want to pay attention to a factor that has been overlooked by modern scholarship, namely the neurotic tension caused by persecution. Population groups which are subjected to severe harassment by authorities, especially if it is a question of life and death, are apt to react in a strange way. I feel I am in the position to say something of this, since I lived through a similar situation. The reader must allow me to go somewhat out of my way, if I try to demonstrate what I mean. I am referring to the German occupation of the Netherlands in the period 1940-1945.

In 1943 I was a twenty-two-year-old student of history in the University of Amsterdam. In the morning of February 6, 1943, a considerable number of students, among them two of my friends, were arrested by Nazi security forces in academic institutes and libraries all over the country; they were lodged in the concentration camp of Vught. It was an attempt to terrify the student population in its totality into submission, since the will to active resistance was stronger among the students than elsewhere.

On March 13 it was announced that all students would have to sign a 'declaration of loyalty' with which they promised to refrain from whatsoever action directed against the occupying power. Those who would sign were to be allowed to pursue their studies; those who didn't had to report for work in Germany. Three days later the prisoners in Vught were released. To sign or not to sign became an awkward dilemma that led to heated, often acrimonious discussions. For weeks on end it was the topic of the day in academic circles. It was argued that there was nothing against signing because it was extorted by force; such a promise was ipso facto invalid. The counter-argument was that the students were the 'spes patriae', and that they had the obligation to give a good example; giving in, if only by appearance, would cause confusion and weaken the general will to resistance.

What made it so hard to take the right decision was that it was by no means a theoretical question. I must admit that I for one for a long time did not know what to do. Refusing to sign was undoubtedly the most honourable, the really patriotic option. But it meant that one had to stop studying for an indefinite period. And then, should one report for work in Germany? Who did not turn up was liable to arrest and could be sent to a KZ. This happened in fact to two of my friends. Going to work in Germany was unpatriotic, of course; it was dangerous too, because of the bombardments. But if one did not report, where to go? It was much too risky to stay at home.

The final outcome was that 86 % of the students refused to sign, I myself being one of them. After the appointed date of April 13 the Germans gave again the opportunity to sign, hoping that the students had become sufficiently nervous by the prospect of having to work in Germany; under this threat another thirteen hundred gave in. Of the non-signers 40 % reported on

May 6 for work in the Reich. The rest went underground, I myself being one of them. In the afternoon of May 6 I left my paternal home, hardly knowing where to go. I must admit that I found it adventurous, but my mother who stood weeping at the door did not see it in this light. During the next two years I several times barely escaped being caught.

I feel there is an obvious resemblance between our situation in 1943 and that of the North African Christians in 305. Both they and we were suddenly startled by a painful question : to sign or not to sign, to hand over or not to hand over. Above both them and us the sword of Damocles hung; a refusal to sign or to hand over would bring it down. The threat made nerves taut, nights sleepless, discussions bitter; lives were thrown out of their ordinary grooves. It made people act strangely, neurotically, abnormally, in ways previously unknown to themselves; they were unable to talk of anything else, getting up with the question, going to bed with it. Relationships were disturbed by it, sometimes for good. What the one called sensible, another called cowardice; what the one called fanaticism, another called courage. What for the one was a question of inevitable accomodation was for another a question of uncompromising principle. The problem was unsolvable; finally, the ways parted, not to meet again.

6. Donatist theology

If there was not much Donatist theology, there was at least some of it, and not of the most superficial sort. "The principal question that was the issue in the discussion between Donatism and the Church was that of the sanctity of the Church as conditioned by the morale of its members" [185]. With regard to this point the Donatists referred voluntarily to Cyprian, bishop of Carthage, a holy man himself, and one to their taste, since he had died a martyr, half a century earlier. He did not make himself a name as a great and original theological thinker; he was rather a practical man, a pastor, who loved to speak mainly of what was of direct importance to his flock, the Church, the sacraments, and the Christian life.

The Church was at the centre of his thought, and in particular her unity [186]. Who did not stick to the unity of the Church could not preserve the faith [187]. "One cannot have God as a father who has not the Church for his mother." Who segregates himself from the Church is an alien, an enemy; he forfeits his salvation [188]. There is no difference at all between heresy and schism, both being fundamentally anti-Christian [189]; the devil himself, disguising himself as an angel of light, is their ultimate source [190]. He was very strict in his opinions.

The Donatists sometimes quoted Cyprian. "They say that Cyprian ... stated that heretics and schismatics, who stand outside the communion of the Church, do not have the baptism" [191]; "you (the Donatists) rejoice in the authority of Cyprian" [192]. But, as Brisson writes, the filiation is to be found in the facts rather than in the quotations [193]. In addition he writes that he feels "inclined to believe that the Donatists continued to profess the same ecclesiology as saint Cyprian, that is, an ecclesiology that was essentially based on the principle of unity" [194]. The unavoidable consequence was that, since there were two Churches in North Africa, the Donatist and the Roman-Catholics, only of one of them could really be the Church; the other simply had to disappear. The wrong of the orthodox was that they had placed an illegitimate bishop in the see of Carthage, an act that made them, in the eyes of the Donatists, schismatics [195].

The sanctity of the Church required that she be pure and irreproachable. "The personal sanctity of the ministers was for them (the Donatists) always a necessary condition for a valid exercize of sacerdotal functions" [196]. A sinful bishop was incapable of mediating between God and the faithful [197]. Augustine makes Petilian, a Donatist, say that "if you (i.e. a sinful cleric) address to the Lord supplications or prayers, this is of no use at all" [198]. It was even the case that this incapacity was, so to speak, hereditary : bishops and presbyters consecrated or ordained by a sinful bishop became sinful themselves, even if they were personally blameless. Bishops like Mensurius and Caecilianus and all who were dependent on them were sinful schismatics.

This is not in accordance with the teaching of the Roman Catholic Church which says that a sacrament works 'ex opere operato' and not 'ex opere operandi'; the validity of a sacrament and the grace it communicates are independent of the moral quality of the spender. But to be precise, the Donatists were not so much thinking of moral qualifications; what interested them was what Schindler calls 'ecclesiological sanctity', consisting in solidarity with the Church of the Martyrs [199]. The 'traditores' and all who were dependent on them stood ipso facto outside the pale of the Church.

7. Constantine intervenes

Let us return to the factual history of Donatism. We now see the secular power intervene. At the end of 312 or in the beginning of 313 the Emperor, Constantine I the Great, wrote a letter to bishop Caecilianus of Carthage. In this he stated that "evil-intentioned persons attempted to turn the people of the holy Catholic Church towards a bad and falsified religion". It is an easy guess that the Donatists are envisioned. The Emperor said that he had notified the local authorities to pay attention to this. He exhorted Caecilianus to denounce persons 'persevering in this madness' to the judges [200].

In March 313 the Emperor addressed himself in writing to the proconsul Annulinus (who, it seems, is not identical with the Anullinus of the persecution period). He wrote that religion was held in disrespect to the great damage of public affairs; he put himself squarely behind Caecilianus [201]. On the 15th of April Annulinus answered that he had received a sealed parcel containing a document coming from the Donatist side and opposing Caecilianus, which parcel he sent to His Majesty [202]. The document in question was signed by five Donatist bishops who wrote that there had arisen a conflict between them and the other bishops; they asked for arbiters from Gaul to decide between them [203]. These Donatist bishops were the first ecclesiastics in this affair to appeal to the secular power [204].

Somewhat later the Emperor wrote to Pope Miltiades because of the great agitation there was in North Africa for what he considered the most minimal of reasons. He thought it best that Caecilianus should go to Rome in person, accompanied by ten bishops from the orthodox side and ten from the Donatist camp, so that the Pope could study the question in detail and give his verdict. He added, however, that the Pope should not tolerate schism or division of any kind [205].

Perhaps Constantine had meant a tribunal, but Miltiades changed the convention into an ecclesiastical council; it assembled on Friday, October 2, 313, in a private house, that of Fausta on the Lateran hill. Present were Pope Miltiades, three Gallic bishops designated by the Emperor, fifteen Italian bishops, and both Caecilianus and Donatus [206]. What a pity there was no tv in those days! Now we don't know how these two behaved towards one another. Did they shake hands? Or even greet one another with the Christian kiss of peace? Or did they studiously neglect each other? In the three days the sessions lasted the two adversaries alternately took the floor. It ended in a resounding defeat for Donatus; his accusations against Caecilianus were judged null and void. Caecilianus was and remained the lawful bishop of Carthage [207].

8. The Donatists remain obstinate

Peace did not return to the harassed province as a result of the Roman verdict. The Donatists were discontented with the sentence of the council and appealed against it to the Emperor [208]. In a letter from the beginning of 314 [209] to Aelafius, the governor of the province of Africa, Constantine spoke again of a 'rather great number' of people who were 'evil-intentioned towards the very holy Catholic religion'. The Emperor had thought that the question had been regulated by the council once and for all. But no, the Donatists maintained that their cause had not really been heard. He therefore ordered Aelafius to send Caecilianus and three of his adversaries to Arles where another synod would be held. The intention of the Emperor was to make an end of the affair as soon as possible and with as little noise as possible. In personal letters Constantine convoked a number of bishops to Arles [210].

On August 1, 314, the convention was opened in the city of Arles. Once again the Donatists bit the dust. The synod, reporting to the new Pope,

Sylvester I, called them 'people with a dechained spirit', impermeable to reason and argument; consequently, they had been condemned and repulsed [211]. Heretics who wanted to (re)join the main Church need not be rebaptized, if the initial ceremony had taken place according to the liturgical rules. And what went squarely against the Donatist position, was the ruling that the ordinations of traditores had not ipso facto become invalid.

Again the Donatists appealed to the Emperor who now obviously became irritated. His response to the bishops assembled in Arles was wholly negative for the opposition. "How many times already have I snowed them under with the answers their incessant appeals merit ... The judgment of the bishops should be considered as though the Lord himself had given the verdict from his throne. Servants of the devil they are" [212]. The Emperor forbade the Donatist bishops present in Arles to return to their sees and had them sent to Rome, to be kept there in a sort of gilded confinement. But he obviously did not intend to push the matter to extremes, for after a few months he allowed them to return to their bishoprics [213].

However sternly Constantine expressed himself, at heart he remained somewhat hesitating. He not only found it good that the recalcitrant bishops resumed their functions but even, most unexpectedly, that they intended a process against Caecilianus in which some of his (the Emperor's) friends would assist them. But in the summer of 315 he changed his mind. The Donatists once again were trouble-makers and totally impregnable to sound reasoning. It seemed best to him that Caecilianus himself would come to Rome [214].

9. Bad days ahead for the Donatists

In the autumn of that same year 315 the Emperor received an official report from North Africa notifying him that the religious troubles were by no means over. He now decided to cross to Africa in person to give his definitive verdict there [215]. Although he did not depart for Carthage, his words show how enormously important he found the Donatist question; it threatened the unity of religion he desired for his Empire. Finally, the opposing parties were summoned to Milan where the Emperor resided in the autumn of 316 [216]. The original acts of this convention are lost, but so much is certain that Caecilianus was definitely vindicated [217]. This time Constantine had taken a stand from which he would never deviate.

Bad days were coming for the Donatists. It was probably in the spring of 317 that the Emperor decided to take action against them; they had to cede the church buildings they had occupied, and the Donatist chiefs would be banished [218]. The consequence of this measure was that the Donatists no longer enjoyed the protection of the state; their religion had now become 'non licita' [219]. Caecilianus tried to avoid the worst by bribing his adversaries with money in order to win them back [220]. But deeply hated as he was [221], he did not meet with success. Pamphlets circulated in which he was branded as 'a butcher more cruel (than the persecutor Anullinus)', this because of his attitude to the Abitene martyrs.

Donatus was not disposed to give in; his view was that the ecclesiastical buildings in the possession of the Donatists had to remain in their hands. Unable to get them back, Caecilianus asked the secular arm for help, and two military commanders held armed forces in readiness for him [222]. Horrid scenes occurred when the soldiers attacked and invaded the Donatist churches. In one of them a regular bloodbath took place; many Donatist faithful who found themselves there were mercilessly butchered. A note in Frend's book tells us that "excavations in this church brought to light a well down which bodies had been flung, together with an inscription dedicated to the martyrs Felicitas and Perpetua" [223]. The bishop of Advocata (or Avioccala, now Sidi Amara in Tunisia), also called Donatus, who was on a visit to Carthage, lost his life in another church [224]. Bishop Honoratus of Sicilibba received a severe wound in his throat from an arrow shot by the commander of the proconsular guard [225]. Never before had such scenes, occurring between Christians, been witnessed! But we may safely assume that it had not been Caecilianus' intention that the soldatesca would commit such excesses. Anyhow, the last chance for a reconciliation between the two parties had now vanished into thin air.

10. Bishop Silvanus accused

In other parts of North Africa the Donatists were left in peace more or less for the time being. But in 320 Silvanus, the bishop of Cirta, got into trouble. Nundiniarius, a deacon, accused him of having been a traditor and of having accepted money from Lucilla (both accusations being only too true). The bishop, a harsh man, had his deacon flogged and excommunicated him. The maltreated Nundiniarius possessed, however, an effective means to hit back. He knew that his diocesan's life was not exactly that of a worthy bishop. He had not been above accepting bribes and of embezzling funds destined for the poor; in general, he proved more interested in financial affairs than in his episcopal duties.

His fellow-bishops tried to keep Silvanus within bounds in his disciplinary measures against Nundiniarius, but shaky though the bishop's position was, he would not listen. When, finally, the grieved deacon had appealed to the law, the case went down for hearing on December 13, 320 at Thamugadi (Timgad in Algeria) before the governor of Numidia, Zenophilus. The Acta of the case, known as the 'Gesta apud Zenophilum', make intriguing reading. But the story is not uplifting since we hear clerics accusing one another. Zenophilus could reach no other conclusion but that Silvanus was guilty of the misdeeds of which he stood accused. He was, therefore, banished from Cirta [226]. The Donatists had a new 'martyr' [227].

11. Donatism tolerated

The Emperor Constantine had more problems on his hands than Donatism alone [228]. Therefore, "those to whom no remedy could give back their normal wits, he left alone, committing them to God" [229]. On May 5, 321 he notified the authorities in North Africa that henceforward the Donatists would enjoy freedom of action [230]. Augustine found this concession 'more than shameful' [231]. It did not, however, signify that Donatism had now become a 'religio licita'; it was only tolerated [232].

Feeling that he had to justify himself for this turnabout in his politics, Constantine wrote to the orthodox bishops exhorting them to exercize moderation and patience and to leave the vengeance to God. Perhaps such clemency would succeed in bringing these 'ensign-bearers of a most miserable quarrel (= the Donatists) to reason' [233]. With this the existence of a schismatic Donatist Church in North Africa was more or less officially admitted, though not legalized. However, the Emperor's sympathies remained with the orthodox bishops. Caecilianus was invited by him to join the Fathers at Nicaea in 325.

Since Constantine had proved powerless to do anything against them, the Donatists had the time of their life. Large Donatist churches were built, for instance, the still standing basilica of Tebessa and that of Timgad. Even in Mauretania (Morocco) churches arose; in Algeria a church was discovered in Castellum Tingitanum (Orléansville) dated 324 . Whether a local congregation was Donatist or orthodox seems to have depended on the bishop [234]. There were Donatist bishops galore, enough to hold synods of their own. In 330 they assembled in Carthage being two hundred and seventy in number, and more than four hundred in 394 and 411 [235]. "Donatus wished to gain all Africa", wrote Augustine [236].

Donatus was the great man now. Optatus said that "he claimed for himself sovereign authority at Carthage; he exalted his heart and seemed to himself to be superior to other mortals, and wished that all, even his own allies, should be beneath him". He behaved "as though he was not human but rather like a god ... Of his bishops he asked that they should venerate him with no less fear than they did God" [237]. He claimed that God himself spoke to him from heaven [238]. One of the differences between the orthodox and the Donatists was that the first mentioned relied on the help of Rome, of the Emperor, that is, while Donatus, to quote Frend, "maintained the African Christian tradition of hostility to what was represented by the Roman authorities" [239].

12. The Donatist Church essentially North African

Attempts to spread Donatism outside North Africa met with little success. Only in Rome was there a Donatist community of some extent, probably among the numerous North African colony there [240]. Donatus sent one of his bishops to Rome, Victor of Garba, one of those who had consecrated Silvanus of Cirta [241]. This Victor set himself up as bishop of Rome [242]; we may consider him as the first antipope of history (although there was simultaneously a Catholic bishop of Rome, Sylvester I, 314-335). However, the real head of the Donatist Church was and remained Donatus of Carthage.

The Donatist Church was not a missionary one; it saw itself as fundamentally North African. As a North African Church it was eminently successful. After 325 nothing more is heard of Caecilianus; his successor Gratus did not make a forceful impression. That Donatism met with no success in other parts of the Empire strengthened its adherents in their conviction that the 'field of God' in this world was North Africa, and this alone. In spite of Donatist successes in the Maghreb, the total number of the saved was only small. Donatus referred to the parable of the wheat and the tares, the tares being the Catholics and the wheat the Donatists; there was an unbridgeable chasm between them. The prospects were sombre, for according to Donatus, the tares were always spreading, whereas the wheat grew ever less [243].

Frend has excellently epitomized the Donatist position in the following words. "It might seem paradoxical that at the moment of the conversion of the Emperor, a Christian leader should solemnly have asserted that the number of Christians had in fact diminished, but the alliance of Church and Roman Empire was not one that appealed to the mass of African Christians. Indeed, such an idea must have seemed blasphemous to the numbers who regarded Christianity in terms of a military service by a chosen few in everlasting combat against the hosts of paganism and idolatry. Donatus' hard and narrow logic carried conviction" [244]. This dualistic attitude vis-à-vis Rome and all that it represented in secular and ecclesiastical respect is mirrored by the never ending series of armed rebellions against Rome in North Africa [245].

There existed a North African specificity of which Donatism was the metaphor. It may also explain why the Maghreb so easily defected to Islam.

13. The Circumcellions

I am writing this in the days when Moslim fundamentalists in Algeria are relentlessly killing, not only westerners, but also and mainly compatriots of them whom they suspect of westernizing. They had their forbears in the Circumcellions. In the half century that followed the death of Constantine the Great in 337 the Donatist Church continued to prosper. It acquired much property and recruited adherents from all sections of the North African population. But however fashionable the Donatist community may have become, a fanatical and terrorist movement originated on its fringes, the Circumcellions. There are several explanations of how this name became theirs, one of these being that it is derived from the words 'circum cellas' = around the shrines. It seems that next to the martyrs' tombs provisions of grain were stored which made it possible to feed many poor people there [246]. People flocked there with a double purpose, to venerate the martyrs and to be fed. But it is also possible that the 'cellae' were the grain depots of well-to-do farmers on which those terrorists threw a covetous eye [247]. Both explanations indicate that the Circumcellions found their members among the destitute sections of the Numidian population, among the non-romanized agrarian masses.

They were a mixed lot of crofters, agricultural labourers, runaway slaves, and poor clerics [248]. Their attitude was composed of religious fanaticism and fierce opposition against those who oppressed them, mainly the great landowners. They saw both the Roman state and the Roman Catholic Church as foreign to the North African specificity. As long as the Empire had persecuted the Christian Church, conversion to it had been a form of protest against romanization, but since state and Church had obviously become allies, adhering to Donatism had become the appropriate form of protest [249]. But although these people were fervent Donatists, or perhaps because of this, they were not really satisfied with the attitude of the leading Donatist circles which basked in their success and in the toleration granted to them by the authorities. This tolerance seemed a form of collusion to the strict.

The Circumcellions harked back to the old North African tradition of the exaltation of martyrdom. Martyrdom was the crowning event of an ascetic Christian life. Tyconius, a Donatist author, wrote of them that "they (the Circumcellions) do not live like the other (i.e. Donatist) brothers, but seek death as from love of martyrdom, in order to secede from life in a violent way so that they may be called martyrs" [250]. They wanted to go down fighting with the cry of 'Deo laudes' on their lips [251] and called themselves 'agonistici' (fighters) [252] and 'milites Christi' [253]. This means that violence was a constitutive part of their way of life.

They saw themselves as a kind of monks, as vagrant monks, that is, for they had no permanent quarters. "They roam and rage over all (North) Africa" [254]; "they go through all the provinces, sent nowhere, nowhere at home, nowhere sedentary" [255]. They carried their possessions with them and wore a sort of monastic habit [256]. They differed from real monks in this respect that they were armed with clubs - not with swords because Scripture forbade these [257].

The Circumcellions took women with them, but abstinence was the rule; marriage was out of the question. These women were called 'sanctimoniales' which meant that they had vowed to remain chaste. But it is possible that sometimes life was stronger than the rule. Augustine, for instance, accuses them of having held orgies, even on the tombs of the martyrs [258]. This accusation was probably for a large part slander - a favourite means of denigrating opponents -, but some of it may have been true. What lends force to this is that the Circumcellions were not averse from drink, to put it mildly. Drunkenness seems to have been a ritual act for them, and dancing too, to honour the martyrs [259].

Standing in the tradition of a deep, even fanatical veneration of martyrdom, the Circumcellions too aspired to it. Augustine said of them that "they lived as robbers, died as Circumcellions, and were honoured as martyrs" [260]. On occsasion they burst in into pagan celebrations, hoping that they would be sacrificed [261]. Others lost their lives when assaulting the villas of the rich and the churches of the orthodox. All those killed were considered martyrs. Another means to acquire martyrdom was to kill themselves. Mass suicides occurred. Several ancient authors report that they threw themselves down precipices [262]; others sought death in a river or in the flames of a fire [263]. A curious way to find death was that a Circumcellion would stop a passer-by on a road, preferably a magistrate, and order such a person to kill him, or else be killed himself [264].

14. An extremist view of Christian life

This attitude to martyrdom, leading to collective suicides, was the extreme, even extremist, consequence of opinions about Christian life that had prevailed in North Africa for a long time. They were the result of what Brisson calls 'a separatist view of the world'. "Already for Cyprian, martyrdom had been in some way the sign par excellence which made it possible to discern the just and the sinners ... The martyr was the supreme form of the struggle of the Christian against the evil that was incarnate in the world of idolatry; by the same token he or she appeared as the clearest mark of the division between the Christian and the idolator. In the eyes of a Tertullian and a Cyprian the world was divided into two irreconcilable blocks : the Church and paganism, the Kingdom of Christ and the realm of the demon ... '(Here begins a quotation from Tertullian) A Christian could not serve two masters ... The oath taken to Christ and the oath taken to a man (the Emperor is meant - F.), the standard of Christ and the standard of the devil, the camp of light and the camp of darkness have nothing in common; the same soul cannot be responsible to two masters, to God and to Caesar' [265].

(The quotation from Brisson continued) Affirming that one could not serve God and the Caesar at the same time made it clear that everyone who had chosen to serve God could no longer form part of the human society that was subjected to the Emperor ... As a soldier of Christ (n.b. the 'miles Christi' of the Circumcellions! - F.), the Christian could only fight the opposite army that was represented by the pagans in the society that was the scene of everyday life; he had nothing in common with the people he met in the street or in the market square : he and they belonged to inimical camps. When he died for having nothing in common with them, he triumphed ... At the moment that Donatism burst out in Africa, the martyrs still constituted that army of Christ that, in the course of the third century, had so often triumphed over the powers of evil" [266].

Thus Brisson excellently summarizes what I wrote so far on the craze for martyrdom that was so conspicuous in North Africa; it also goes a long way to explain the strange behaviour of the Circumcellions. The exaltation of martyrdom that was a characteristic of North African Christianity, was fed by the persecution of Septimius Severus in the beginning of the third century, that of Decius in the middle of the same century, and that of Diocletian in the years 303-305. This exaltation reached its apogee in the actions of the Circumcellions who were the ideological descendants of Cyprian and Tertullian - although these Fathers would not have approved of their terrorism and their suicidal urge. However, these suicides were the logical outcome of a way of reasoning that was followed to its last consequence. The Circumcellions refused to have anything to do with a world that was Roman and Catholic, that was Roman Catholic, a diabolical world in their eyes. There was only one remedy against it : to quit it. Need I add that this is a most drastic example of dualism?

15. Circumcellion terrorism

The Circumcellions acted, in the terms of Schindler, as 'terrorist shock troops' [267]. They fell on Catholic landlords and plundered their possessions; Catholic clerics too became their victims. Churches were robbed and put on fire, but pagan sanctuaries were not spared either. They forced Roman Catholics to have themselves rebaptized.

There was a very strong social element in their activities because they came to the help of the underprivileged and the oppressed. Wherever a movement of protest or discontent among agrarian slaves arose, the Circumcellions were at hand to assist them or even to take the lead [268].

Usurers were forced to release their debtors from their debts [269]; those who refused to do this saw their houses put on fire and themselves maltreated or even killed. On occasion travelling landlords were held up by a Circumcellion band; the proprietor was put before the cart and forced to draw it [270]. On other occasions slave owners were forced to turn their own mill, spurred on by whiplashes [271]. It seems, however, that we have to do with isolated, although frequently occurring, actions, not with a wide-spread and well-planned revolutionary movement [272].

The Circumcellions often suffered severe losses but were never short of recruits. Their fanaticism and their way of living on the one hand, their lust for booty and revenge on the other, attracted many followers. They remained active for a long time in the period between 340 and 420. There was, in general, collusion between the leading Donatist circles and the Circumcellion bands; Augustine reports in many places that Donatist bishops and clerics not only supported terrorist actions against Roman Catholics but not rarely took the lead in these [273].

But not all Donatist bishops were on the side of terrorists; it may reasonably be supposed that the higher they were placed socially and the better their education, the greater would be their misgivings [274]. Augustine also reports that "these things displeased them (certain Donatist bishops) and always proclaimed that they displeased them" [275]. It even happened that collections were organized in Donatist churches for indemnifying people robbed by the terrorists. When the Donatist Macrobius entered Hippo in 409 (where Augustine was the Roman Catholic bishop) to be consecrated as bishop there, he was "greeted by crowds of Circumcellions which mightily displeased him"; he even preached against them [276].

Around 340 the Circumcellion terror reached a peak. Under the command of two 'leaders of the saints', Fasir and Axido, the pillaging and burning occurred on such a large scale that even Donatist bishops took fright that their own co-religionists would not be spared. They asked Comes Taurinus in writing to intervene. This he did. Voluntarily and with gusto. In a town called Octavensis (unidentified) quite a number of Circumcellions were killed or maimed [277]. But this (contraterrorist) action did not spell the end of the unrest.

16. An imperial attempt at rapprochement

In 346 Donatus of Carthage deemed the time ripe for being recognized as the legitimate bishop of this city. He asked the Emperor Constans to grant him this recognition [278]. If the ruler had conceded this, it would have meant the legalization of the Donatist Church. Instead, the Emperor sent two high officials, Paulus and Macarius, to North Africa. Their task was to prepare the rapprochement of the two Churches; Optatus (the author) states expressly that the two men did not come to reunite them [279].

The imperial emissaries clearly showed where their sympathies lay. They worshipped in the basilica of the Roman Catholic bishop Gratus. Their actions were not always calculated to ingratiate them with the Donatists; these accused them, for instance, of putting an image of the Caesar on the altars so that it might seem that the sacrifice was also brought to him [280]. Where they could, they tried to influence the populace in favour of the orthodox. It was widely believed that the two men were acting as though they were bishops themselves [281]. This was not exactly the most tactful manner of operating in the overheated psychological climate of North Africa.

When they were at last conducted before Donatus, this bishop lost his temper and cried : "What has the Emperor to do with the Church?". Optatus even wrote that he (Donatus) considered himself next to God and higher than the Emperor. Anyhow, he wrote to all his bishops telling them not to receive the emissaries [282]. Nothing daunted, Paulus and Macarius travelled on to the lions' den, Numidia. The nearer they came to the Aurès mountains, the more hostile the attitude of the population became. The two men represented in the eyes of the people the political and ecclesiastical imperialism of Rome. Becoming afraid, they requested the armed assistanc of comes Silvester. In his turn the bishop of Bagai, Donatus (another Donatus) summoned the help of the Circumcellions. They came, fought the Roman legionaries, and were massively killed, Donatus being among the dead [283].

17. Imperial action against Donatism

a. Donatism proscribed

Things began to take a wrong turn for the Donatists now. It is thinkable that the authorities intended to make an end of Donatism. "As a consequence of the events at Bagai the toleration which it (the Donatist schism) had enjoyed found an abrupt end", writes Grasmück [284]. Constans issued a decree in which he once again proscribed Donatism [285]. A general return to the main Church was ordered; bishops and clerics who refused to obey had to go into exile and suffer the sequestration of their goods. The Donatist churches were seized. Some bishops lost their lives; some took to flight, toegether with their priests. Others, who were more courageous, remained at their posts, but were arrested and then banished [286].

The authorities made it perfectly clear that they were in dead earnest. The proconsul forbade everyone to shelter a schismatic who remained obdurate. When a certain Donatist, called Maximianus, tore off a poster with the imperial decree in Carthage, he was caught and whipped. An onlooker with the name of Isaac, another Donatist, cried : "Come on, traditores, save the insanity of your unity". He too was arrested; both he and Maximianus were condemned to be deported. But Isaac died before this in a Carthaginian prison. When this became known, the Donatists assembled before the dungeon and required the delivery of the body. On the refusal of the authorities, the crowd stood the whole day and the whole night of August 15, 347 in front of the prison singing and chanting, in order to honour their martyr. On the morning of the 16th the governor had enough of this; he let his soldiers, crack units among them, disperse the crowd; many were wounded during the tumult.

The prisoners, one dead, one living, were brought on a ship that immediately took to sea. The dead body of Isaac and that of Maximianus who was still alive were weighted with sand-bags and thrown over board [287]. The Donatist 'Passio' which relates all these things says that six days later both corpses were washed ashore. Their co-religionists found them and buried them with all due ceremony [288].

How high feelings ran in North Africa is graphically shown by the 'Passion of Marculus' in which for the orthodox only negative terms are used (criminal, raging, serving the Antichrist, Constans the tyrant, Paulus and Macarius two beasts, butchers, rabble) and for the Donatist martyrs only positive ones (saintly, glorious, full of love, disciples of Christ, divinely steadfast). This is only a short selection out of many; the whole text abounds with them, making it into a perfect black-white picture which goes to show how dualistic the situation was [289].

Donatus, the schismatic bishop of Carthage belonged to those who went into exile; he never returned. We don't know for certain whether he was sent to Spain or to Gaul; he is said to have died at some time during 350-355. He had a successor on the see of Carthage in the person of Parmenian [290].

On the whole the anti-Donatist action in Carthage went along smoothly, but Numidia, the heartland of Donatism, proved a harder nut to crack. Paulus and Macarius went there to supervise the operations themselves [291]. Everywhere they were assisted by military detachments [292]; the decree of unity was proclaimed in all the towns. Ten Donatist bishops visited Macarius in Vegesala (now Ksar el-Kelb) in the hope of moving them to leniency. But in vain! He had the dignitaries bound to pillars and beaten with sticks. Their leader seems to have been bishop Marculus whom Macarius took with him to the fortress of Nova Petra (probably Henchir Encedda) where he died on November 29, 347. According to the Donatist version in the Passio Marculi, the soldiers threw him into an abyss, but if we are to believe the Catholics, he committed suicide [293]. Grasmück considers both versions improbable; he thinks that the bishop died when under arrest [294].

b. The Catholic Church as the 'Macarian party'

The operations of 347 dealt the Donatist Church a heavy blow. But it was not wiped out; its position in North Africa was far too strong for this. For the time being, however, it had to keep a low profile. To celebrate the victory, Gratus, the Catholic bishop of Carthage, convened a synod there which was held in 348 or 349. About fifty bishops attended, with perhaps some former Donatists among their number. Its aim was to consolidate the unity of the North African Church. In his opening speech Gratus thanked God that an end had been made of the schism and the Emperor Constans for having effected this. The measures the synod took were moderate. Donatists who rejoined the Church need not be rebaptized. Those Donatists who had lost their lives during the troubles were not to be called martyrs, but their tombs would be left in peace [295].

What was urgently necessary did not take place : there was no thorough reformation of the North African Roman Catholic Church which in many respects was corrupt. There also occurred no profound theological and ecclesiological discussion with the Donatists. These bided their time. What we know of their authors in this period, Petillian, Parmenian, Cresconius, is that they hated the Roman Catholic Church. The days of 347 were called the 'tempora Macariana'; the Church herself became the 'Macarian party', her faithful the 'Macarians' [296].

18. A new chance for the Donatists

The prospects for the Donatists got considerably better when Julian the Apostate became the sole ruler of the Empire in 361; it is well-known that he was a fierce opponent of the Roman-Catholic Church. In order to harass her he favoured everywhere the heretic sects. As soon as the banished Donatists bishops got wind of this, they asked Julian for permission to return to their sees. He answered favourably and also restituted the church buildings to them which had been sequestrated in 347 [297]. The return of their bishops caused a forceful upsurge of the long suppressed anger of the Donatists [298]. Optatus tells us how in Milevis (Mila) congregations that had for years behaved themselves as Catholics suddenly revealed themselves as Donatists again.

As Frend expresses it, "Donatism swept Numidia and Mauretania like a forest fire" [299]. Bands, probably partly composed of Circumcellions, roamed the country. Everywhere ecclesiastical buildings were taken over by force; the religious persons who lived there were expelled and stripped of the signs of their position, like mitres and veils. There was shedding of blood : the bands tried to force people to change their allegiance, to 'become Christians', as they put it; some of those who refused were killed [300]. Many were forcefully rebaptized [301], or rather baptized, for Roman Catholic baptism was not valid in Donatist eyes. The bands committed sacrilege upon sacrilege, in order to show that they held Roman-Catholic liturgy in the deepest contempt. Altars were destroyed, the altar wine drunk, the chalices thrown away. All this was, curiously enough, deemed necessary for making a new start and beginning afresh.

One of the worst incidents took place at Lemellfense (now Khirbet Zembia in Algeria, formerly Toqueville). Since this town was a walled castellum, it had to be taken by storm by a Donatist band under the command of two bishops, Felix of Zabi and Ianuarius of Flumen Piscensis. When the attackers found the church closed, men climbed onto the roof, took off the tiles, and threw them into the building. Two of the deacons who stood ready to defend the altar were killed and others wounded; the church itself was thoroughly sacked [302].

In order to avoid bloodshed, killings, and violation of women in religion, many Catholic communities hastened to change their allegiance. When this happened, the church building were subjected to a ritual cleansing with salt and water, while the altars were whitewashed [303]. Especially in southern Numidia the collapse of Roman Catholicism was greeted with great enthusiasm [304]. Add to this that Julian had Roman officials punished who had oppressed the population, and that he relieved the burden of the taxes, and it will be clear that the Numidians must have had the impression that a new era had begun. The result of all this was that the dualistic rift between the two North African Churches became greater than ever. The split reached deep down into the personal sphere. Donatists and Catholics did not intermarry; they did not even greet one another any longer. Catholics were not buried in Donatist cemeteries [305]. Friendships were terminated, marriages were broken, families fell apart [306]. In the view of the Donatists Roman Catholics were not Christians but pagans [307].

19. Donatism repressed again

And then all of a sudden Julian fell in battle, in far-away Parthia on June 27, 363. His successors Jovianus (363-364) and Valentinianus I (364-375) were orthodox Christians who resumed the religious policy of Constantine, Constans, and Constantius II; for the Donatists "the brief spell of power and Imperial favour ended" [308]. A new highest imperial official was sent to North Africa in the person of comes Romanus, who left a reputation behind him of large-scale corruption and high-handedness [309]. The Donatist author Tyconius wrote that this comes was a revelation of the Antichrist (and that this phenomenon would soon appear in the whole world) [310]. Soon enough Circumcellion bands were active again.

Oppression and heavy taxation caused a revolt to break out in Mauretania. Its leader was a local prince, a certain Firmus who was proclaimed king by the insurgents [311]. Some Romans deserted to him. The Donatists acknowledged him as their legitimate leader; he was wholly on their side, indeed. Aided by Moorish tribes, Firmus succeeded in establishing his rule over large parts of Mauretania where he successfully held out for three years. The Catholics trembled again. In 375, however, Rome replaced Romanus by comes Theodosius [312]. The new comes suppressed the revolt with the help of troops brought over from Italy; when Firmus was on the point of being caught, he committed suicide.

Very strict imperial measures against the Donatists could now be carried through. Rebaptizing was forbidden, and even Donatist services were not allowed [313]. But most of imperial anti-Donatist legislation remained a dead letter, because the successor of Theodosius as vicarius Africae, Nicomachus Flavianus, who came to North Africa in 377, simply did not execute them. Was he perhaps a Donatist [314]? More probably he was a member of the old pagan Roman aristocracy and as such a hater of the Church [315].

Anyhow, for years to come the Donatist Church enjoyed peace and quiet, although Flavianus was no friend of Circumcellion excesses. If the times had now become favourable for the Donatists, they were correspondingly bad for Catholicism. But slowly the relations between the two Churches became somewhat more relaxed. Donatists and Catholics no longer saw one another as lepers; after all, the schism had originated in the time of their grandfathers [316].

20. A discussion between Parmenian and Optatus

a. The position of Parmenian

Parmenian was the successor of Donatus as the Donatist bishop of Carthage. The fact that he was probably not a native of North Africa may have worked to his advantage since, unfamiliar as he was with the inveterate disputes of the Maghreb, he could allow himself to be more moderate. "From all accounts, he was a firm and honourable man, a stranger to intrigue and violence, and contemptuous of the value of brutality. He was a great orator, like nearly all the Donatist leaders, and ... more moderate in his views than most" [317]. He was also an intellectual and an outstanding theologian. He was not inclined, however, to cede an inch to the Roman Catholic Church.

It is a pity that his writings are lost; his ideas must be culled together from other sources, mainly from fragments in books of his opponent Optatus. The title of his book was probably 'Against the Church of the Traditors'. What he reproached the Catholics for was that they had invoked the help of the state, even of the military, against the Donatists. He showed, however, a certain bias in defending violent acts committed by his co-religionists; as Optatus has him say, "soldiers under command are different from consecrated bishops" [318]. If Donatus saw state and Church as squarely opposed and inimical powers, it cannot be made out that Parmenian thought the same way [319]. He found, however, that Church and state had to remain strictly apart.

Speaking of the Church, he had of course the Donatist Church in mind, in his eyes the authentically Catholic one. That the Roman Catholics were no true Christians could be inferred from the fact that they had delivered sacred books to the pagans and, worse still, that they relied on the secular arm.

b. Optatus answers Parmenian

The history of Donatism in North Africa is not only one of rows and blows. Parmenian's treatise was answered in due intellectual form by Optatus, Roman Catholic bishop of Milevis. About the years 366-367 this bishop of whose life we are poorly informed, published a work in six books to which he added a seventh about 385 [320]. It is the most important source for the Donatist controversy we possess, above all because its author constantly refers to official documents. Optatus rejected forcefully Parmenian's accusation that the Catholics had invoked the assistance of the military, with all that this came to imply. Nothing but slander! he wrote indignantly [321]. There was no collusion between the Empire and the Church.

Acting of his own accord as a true servant of God, Constantine had striven to restore the unity of the Church. "One peace should unite the African peoples and the Orientals and the others over the sea (i.e. in Europe); the same unity should melt together the body of the Church for all its members. This would pain the devil who is always tortured by peace among brethren" [322]. Donatus had acted very wrongly when he said : "What has the Emperor to do with the Church? " True enough, the Empire is not in the Church, but the Church is in the Empire, in the Roman Empire that is [323].

It is not accidental but providential that Christianity had its origin in this Empire; it might have begun anywhere, but Christ was born within its confines. Its highest authority is the Emperor who has his power from God; it is God who made him Emperor. Donatus, however, thought that he was more than the supreme ruler [324]. With regard to the Donatist accusation that Macarius had transgressed his competence and had acted arbitrarily, Optatus answered that the Catholic bishops could not be held responsible for what Macarius had done, since he was not a bishop but a layman and an imperial official. If he was guilty, he should be judged by the tribunals of the state [325].

Grasmück whose analysis I am following here, concludes that Optatus stood in the line of Paul : Christians owed obedience to the state, even if it was pagan, because the political order was willed by God. If other Fathers, like Cyprian and Tertullian, were averse to the Empire, this was not the case with Optatus. But the Donatists, and still less the Circumcellions, did not permit themselves to be influenced by Optatus' reasonings [326].

21. The rule of Gildo

Perhaps the reader has got the impression that the opposing parties were now sailing on the quieter waters of intellectual discourse. This impression would be deceptive; the worst was still to come. In 384 or 385 the Emperor Theodosius I nominated a certain Gildo as the highest political and military authority in North Africa; his official title was even more than the usual 'comes Africae', for he became then or later 'comes et magister utriusque militiae per Africam' [327]; one of his daughters, by becoming the wife of a relative of the Emperor, married into the imperial family [328]. All this was not for nothing, of course. Gildo, who belonged to a native Moorish family, had staunchly supported Theodosius I and even fought his own rebellious brother Firmus.

Gildo was a man who understood how to handle power in his own interest. His governorship, which lasted twelve years, made him immensely rich; in this process his hands did not remain clean. This Moorish chieftain, whose own brother Firmus had led a revolt against the Empire, was a liability to the authorities in Rome; out of native tribal warriors he created an army of his own, next to the regular Roman garrisons. In this way he made himself virtually independent of the Empire; he made Rome feel who was boss in North Africa by interrupting the regular corn transports to the capital which was to lead to riots there [329]. As Grasmück remarks, finally "the removal of the comes became a political necessity for the government of Western Empire"

[330]. Honorius was Emperor of the West then, but the man who really wielded power was Stilicho, a German who was the chief minister.

When Gildo threatened to shift his allegiance to the East, he was declared 'hostis publicus' by the Senate [331]. An expedition was sent to North Africa, led by yet another brother of Gildo, called Mascazel; this man fostered a bitter hatred against his brother who had killed two of his children [332]. In the interior of Numidia the two armies confronted each other in the spring of 398; Gildo suffered a resounding defeat and saw his men abandoning him or deserting to his opponent [333]. He himself fled to the coast, hoping to escape, but found his end, either being killed or killing himself.

22. Gildo and bishop Optatus

Gildo's connection with the history of heresy is that he loyally adhered to the Donatists who were his principal allies in his quest for power. In 388 Optatus became bishop of Thamagudi (Timgad) in the south of Numidia; the reader should carefully distinguish this Optatus from the already mentioned one, the orthodox bishop who polemized against Parmenian. This second Optatus was a staunch Donatist; his episcopal see was the strongest bulwark of Donatism in the country. For quite a number of years he held undisputed sway over southern Numidia, in collusion with Gildo who was a Donatist too. On a hill near the town of Timgad the bishop built an enormous cathedral as a visible sign of his quasi-regal power. "The Donatists saw the glory of the Divine Kingdom represented by this church; it served as a symbol of their power in Africa" [334].

Frend states that bishop Optatus was a man with a revolutionary nature, 'bent on accomplishing social as well as religious revolution by violent means'; this author compares him to the Bogomil and Albigensian leaders of later days who "combined religious dissent with social reform" [335]. As the powerful orator he was, he exercized great influence on the Donatist masses. His prop and mainstay were the Circumcellions whom he armed and whose bands he put at the disposal of Gildo and of whomsoever wanted to harass the Catholics. This made the governor an independent warlord rather than a

Roman general. He and Optatus were glove in hand. Optatus established a reign of terror in Numidia; the Catholics and the romanized landowners lived through bad days, robbed as they were of their possessions which the almighty bishop redistributed [336].

Donatism had its heyday in the years between 388 and 398 with a corresponding low ebb for Catholicism. Augustine, then bishop of Hippo, saw his flock crumble and his faithful deserting even in his own town [337]. In February 395 a Donatist jurist could publicly state that "nearly the whole world acknowledged the name and worship of the Catholic (= Donatist) Church, cleansed from error by Donatus of venerable memory" [338]. And indeed, Optatus, the orthodox author, ruefully complained that in North Africa there were few Catholics left [339].

23. Dissension within the Donatist ranks

Optatus' great success was, however, somewhat marred by dissension within the Donatist ranks. In 391 or 392 Parmenian, the Donatist bishop of Carthage died, to be succeeded by Primianus. This Primian, a ruthless man, succeeded pretty soon in making many enemies among his own coreligionists. Opponents gathered around Maximinianus, a deacon who was a relative of Optatus; this lent him a certain prestige. A social division played a part in the conflict since Primian had the crowds behind him and Maximinian the wealthier classes. Soon the conflict ran so high that Primian's opponents convoked a council in which forty-three Donatist bishops took part. Primian was summoned to appear, but the haughty man refused to obey. He made the Carthaginian police search the houses of Maximinian's party; the bishops of the council were threatened by the mob in the church where they assembled; they fled to a nearby village and there condemned Primian. So there was a schism within a schism.

On June 23, 393, a second council convened at Cebarussa (Cabarussa, no longer existing, probably a coastal town). Maximinian's party was quickly gaining support, for more than fifty bishops, perhaps even a hundred, turned up in this town. The chairman was bishop Victorinus of Munatiana. The

Maximinianists had their following mainly in the coastal regions, but were far less strong farther south in Numidia and Mauretania. "The dispute began to take on a regional character, the more conservative and tolerant Romano-Punic cities of the coast and the Tunisian coastal plain protesting against the violence and brutality of the Numidian nominee in Carthage" [340]. This may seem in accordance with Frend's favourite thesis that the whole Donatist affair had an ethnic and cultural background, but already Saint Augustine noted the regional differences [341]. After ample deliberation the council decided to depose Primian; clergy and laity were invited to relinquish their allegiance to him. Fifty-three participants signed the final document [342]. As might be expected, Maximinian was nominated bishop of Carthage to replace the deposed Primian.

But Primian was not the man to give in so easily; a great counter-offensive was staged. A council was convened at Bagai (still existing as Ksar-Bagaï or Baraï); this time we are far from the coast, for this town is in southern Numidia. The strength of Primian's party is shown by the fact that no less than three hundred and ten bishops were present, the first and foremost one of them being Primian, of course. The roles were completely reversed : on April 24, 394 sentence was pronounced on the Maximinianists. They were declared schismatics, adulterers of truth, vipers; Maximinian and the bishops who had consecrated him were excommunicated. The others were given eight months time to return to the fold. Of course, Primian was reinstated as the Primate of Carthage [343].

For the Roman Catholics the controversy within the Donatist ranks was a godsend. The attention of the leading Donatist authorities was not spent on them but on their Maximinianist adversaries. Everywhere Primian appointed new bishops; Maximinian's church in Carthage was razed to the ground [344]. In all his actions Primian was covered by Gildo. His special target was the consecrators of Maximinian. However, three of them clung to their sees, protected by their flocks, two of them successfully. The third was the aged bishop Salvius of Membressa (no longer existing). The authorities ordered the inhabitants of Abitenae (now Medjez el-Bab) to execute the sentence of Bagai against him. They came, hung dead dogs around his neck, and led him triumphantly through his town. This made him immediately into a martyr in the eyes of his own flock; they built him a new church where he officiated for some years more [345].

24. The unbridgeable chasm

The collusion between Optatus and Gildo ended with the latter's defeat in 398. His fate meant the end also of Optatus of Timgad; he too was caught and executed [346]. From that moment the star of the Catholics began to rise again. They were lucky enough to have two competent men at the helm. In 392 Aurelius became bishop of Carthage, an able man who kept the Church of Tunisia on a steady course for quite a number of years. In the same period Augustine was bishop of Hippo, the most outstanding mind of Late Antiquity, perfectly capable of taking up the gauntlet with the Donatists. An additional advantage was that, whereas the Donatist Church was torn apart, even along regional lines, the Roman Catholic ecclesiastical provinces of Africa Proconsularis (Tunisia) and Numidia cooperated in good harmony [347].

Just as Saint Augustine became the great adversary of the Manichaeans, he also put himself squarely in the way of the Donatists. Anti-Donatist tract after tract flowed from his pen. His main argument was that schism within the Catholic Church could hardly be according to the will of God. Augustine's success was great but not complete. Many Donatists returned to the main Church, but Donatism outlasted him, although Empire and Church acted in unison against it.

Frend offers an intriguing analysis of the question why Augustine failed to eradicate Donatism, whether 'more ecclesiastico' or even with the help of the secular arm; this throws light on the relation of the North African Church with the Empire too [348]. Augustine was born into the very milieu that was the strongest support of Donatism; he was a Berber and spent his youth in Thagaste (now Souk Ahras). Possibly the name of his mother, Monnica, latinized Monica, was Berber. "But if Augustine shared a common background and some of the underlying beliefs of his opponents, there was much also that stood in the way of his securing a true appreciation of their ideas" [349]. The chasm between the North African mentality and that of the leading circles of the Empire was virtually unbridgeable; Augustine for one never succeeded in bridging it. His Punic was poor and he did not have a word of Berber; this made it impossible for him to reach the Donatist dispossessed of the towns and the agricultural labourers who did not understand his cultivated Latin nor his way of reasoning. His own family was romanized and formed part of the leading circles I mentioned. His own education as a Latin rhetor and his long stay in Italy alienated him still further from his native background.

His own episcopal see was Hippo Regius (now Bône), a town on the coast of Algeria. His pastoral field of action was and remained the coastal region which was romanized and where the position of the Roman Catholic Church was relatively strong. He never travelled far inland, never visited the Donatist strongholds like Timgad, and did not come to southern Numidia until 422 (and then only going there to see a Roman general, the comes Bonifatius). According to Frend, this highly erudite man made curious mistakes when speaking of Numidia. No olives grew there, he declared [350], while "Numidia was the chief olive-exporting centre of the Mediterranean" [351]. All this makes it clear that this bishop of Hippo was not the appropriate person to tackle the problem of Donatism successfully. It may also explain why he, although really no great friend of the Empire and its power, resorted so readily to the help of the state. His finally fruitless efforts also illustrate perfectly the dualistic gap existing between the official 'romanitas' and North African indigenous culture.

25. The Catholic triumph

Nevertheless, on the surface the Catholic victory seemed complete. In June 410 a North African synod was held at Carthage. Its upshot was that the existing edict of tolerance - from which the Donatists profited - should be rescinded. With this message two fiercely anti-Donatist bishops were sent to the Emperor Honorius. The ruler agreed with this request; he ordered the then comes Africae, Heraclianus, to stamp out heresy and to use 'blood and prescriptions' as his weapons [352]. A special official, Marcellinus, came in order to remove 'the seditious superstition' (i.e. Donatism) [353]. This man began by convoking a great conference which should definitely settle the matter. Primian had no other option than to obey and invited his colleagues to come to Carthage.

On May 18, 411, two hundred and eighty-four Donatist bishops entered Carthage in procession, the last great Donatist manifestation [354]. However, the Catholics could muster two bishops more. Among those present were, on the Catholic side, Augustine, and on the Donatist, Petilian, in all probability the one and only time the two outstanding leaders met in person [355]. The conference took place in the first week of June and was not held in a basilica but in the Thermae Gargilianae, in other words, in a bath-house, perhaps because this was neutral ground. But the atmosphere was not neutral by any standard. Often, when the opponents stood facing each other, the tension was palpable. And no wonder! "The future not only of those who were present but of Christianity itself was to hang on the outcome" [356].

What this outcome would be was never doubtful. The question was settled long before the synod began. The anti-Donatist stance of the rulers in Rome was well-known. In Augustine's view, expressed before this conference, there could be no second final decision; the only thing left to be done was to make it clear to the Donatists that they had lost [357]. Marcellinus, who presided, told the Donatists squarely to their faces that they were the losers : their religion was a 'superstitio', a 'vain error' [358].

The final verdict was pronounced on June 8. There was to be only one legal orthodox Church, the Roman Catholic one. The Donatists stood condemned. Their meetings of every kind were strictly forbidden. Their ecclesiastical buildings were to be restored to the Catholics. Donatist bishops were told that they had to join the orthodox Church. Sticking to Donatism was to be punished as rebellion. This sentence was posted throughout North Africa on June 26 [359]. An appeal of the Donatists to the Emperor Honorius misfired; he did not react directly but on January 30, 432, confirmed the sententia of June 8. Disobedient clerics were to be banished from North Africa. Those who still professed to be Donatists were to be fined rather heavily. But there were no capital punishments [360].

26. Donatist resilience

At this moment of Roman Catholic and imperial triumph nobody knew that Roman rule in North Africa had only another seventeen years to go. Under the leadership of Augustine the Catholics left no stone unturned to win back the Donatists. Their successes were far less spectacular than they may have hoped. Many Donatist bishops remained in their sees and even succeeded in keeping up some sort of network. The stream of Donatists publications did not dry up. The hardest nut to crack was, as may be guessed, Numidia. The roles were often reversed there, for it happened that Donatists harassed those who wanted to choose the other side.

In 420 the Roman magistrate Dulcitius felt strong enough to reduce the Donatist stronghold of Timgad. Optatus, who had been bishop there for so long, was now dead; he had been succeeded by Gaudentius. Dulcitius marched on Timgad and ordered him to surrender his cathedral. By way of an answer Gaudentius, with his flock, took his refuge in the citadel of the town, threatening to burn it down over his head. Not knowing how to act, Dulcitius asked the advice of Augustine who counseled against using force. It is not known how this ended; probably Gaudentius got off scot-free [361]. The conclusion of Frend is that "Donatism may have remained the religion of a large proportion of the African villages in the fifth century as well as in the fourth" [362].

27. The end of Donatism

The history of Donatism in North Africa suddenly breaks off with the coming of the Vandals in 429. The literary sources remain silent about it, but there is some archaeological evidence that it continued to exist, particularly in Numidia. The reconquest of North Africa by the Byzantines in the period after 534, with the ensuing end of Vandal rule, inaugurated a new period of Roman Catholic orthodoxy. At the same time it became clear that there was still a Donatist presence. From the correspondence of Pope Gregory I, it appears that around 593 Donatism was still alive and kicking in its old stronghold

Numidia. He complained that Donatism was steadily progressing; Catholics were having themselves rebaptized [363]. In the town of Macomades there was even a Donatist bishop [364]. The indignant bishop of Rome reproached the Byzantine Praefectus Africae, Panteles, that the Donatists "find under your rule the means of creeping up again into importance ... Not only do they expel with pestilential force the bishops of the Catholic faith from their churches, but they even venture to rebaptize whom by a true confession the water of regeneration has already cleansed" [365].

In August 596 Gregory complained to the Emperor Mauricius that the exarch of North Africa remained inactive against the Donatists. He wrote that "the Catholic faith is publicly put up for sale". The Pope asked the Byzantine ruler "to issue strict orders for the punishment of the Donatists and to arrest with saving hand the fall of the perishing" [366]. After 600 there is no further mention of Donatism in North Africa. In 648 the spearheads of the Moslim armies arrived in Tunisia; in the following decades they conquered, under the green banner of the Prophet, the whole of the Maghreb.

28. An overview

The first element in an overview of the long history of Donatism in North Africa is its incredible resilience and toughness. Whatever Church and state did against it, it refused to go away. This had something to do with its origin, namely that it was a Church of the martyrs, so that its adherents knew and accepted that they would have to suffer for their allegiance to it. Furthermore, it proves how deeply entrenched Donatism was in the mentality of North Africa, more in particular in that of Numidia. It seems as though it was more congenial to the soul of North Africa than Roman-Catholicism. This failed to find the arguments, the symbols, the 'ethnic translation', which might have convinced the Donatists; Augustine was typical in this respect.

Perhaps the origins were forgotten in the long run, when Church was pitted against Church. But an important factor in the disagreement was that the Donatist Church considered herself more pure, more puritan, more prepared for sacrifice and martyrdom, and, in consequence, more truly

Christian than the main Church which, in Donatist view, was more worldly, more compromising, more colluding with the the authorities and, therefore, not really Christian. The Donatists did not set great store by the universalism of the main Church; they were quite satisfied to be and to remain typically North African.

The Donatists claimed that their Church was the only one Catholic Church of North Africa; the main Church, in their eyes a department of the Empire, was alien to its soil. They were fundamentally committed to fight evil and the devil, represented by the imperial and ecclesiastical powers. Need I still point out that the long drawn-out conflict had a dualistiuc character? Each side was convinced that the other simply should not be there; each in its turn tried to do away with the other, both unsuccessfully. The Donatist Circumcellions even resorted to violence. Frend argues that "there was a curious duality in the Donatist leaders. Outwardly they were cultivated men, Latinists ..., moral preachers, ... former lawyers ... Yet at heart they were revolutionary leaders, and their powers of ferocious oratory raised them in the esteem of their congregations whose mother tongue in many cases they could not speak ... The same men who could write dull disciplinary tracts could instill boundless hatred of the Catholics in a Passion of Donatist martyrs" [367]. For three centuries the two Churches remained locked in dualistic battle, until triumphant Islam swept them both away.

Part IV Priscillianism

The very first case of a public process followed by an execution was that of Priscillianus and his companions in 385, the first and the last heretics to be executed in all Antiquity by the secular arm because of their opinions. Priscillian was the father of an heresy that is called 'Priscillianism'. It deviated in important respects from the orthodox creed, for instance, in its doctrine of the Trinity; there are strong Manichaeist tendencies in it (matter is evil, but the spirit is good). The Priscillianists distanced themselves from the great Church and opposed its hierarchy.

1. Priscillian's sombre view of the world

The teaching of Priscillian, a Spaniard, who became bishop of Avila, was stern. He took a very low view of the world and of mankind [368]. The real master of the world was Satan; man is a child of perdition [369]. It is repeatedly said that a Christian should keep the world as far from him as possible : "All friendship with the world is inimical to God" [370], and it is added that "every concupiscence of the flesh and wilfulness of the eyes and the ambitions of human life are not of the Father but of the world". [371] Not only should the faithful desist from lust for money and quarrels [372] but also renounce worldly goods and rather prefer celestial treasures. [373]

Such injunctions are not really heretical, of course, but they ly a heavy, even an unbearable burden on ordinary faithful, stretching as they do the counsels of the Gospel considerably beyond their original meaning. Add to this the Priscillian injunction to abstain from meat and alcohol [374] and a definite preference for the celibate state, [375], marriage being permitted only to those who were too weak to remain abstinent, [376] and we have moved into the orbit of a severely ascetic, puritanical, élitist, and esoteric movement.

2. Priscillian dualism

Priscillianism is not Gnostic, because Redemption, which is possible, is not effected by a special kind of Knowledge, but through baptism and 'the redemption by the divine cross'. [377] This is safely orthodox. The same applies to the statement that God is the author of the Old Testament [378] (most Gnostics rejected the Old Testament or at least the greater part of it). Equally one can agree with a phrase which says that "we bear the image of that which is from the clay and of that which is from heaven." [379]

But we detect also a sharp dualism of the upper and nether worlds. God is veracious and his image is the first-born Christ. [380] However, there also exists 'a wicked nation'; "perdition has its own sons." [381] "There are two sorts of spirits, one of God, the other of the world, leading to errors; [382] ... There are two kinds of wisdom, one of God, the other of men or of the flesh." [383]

"The flesh and its caring for are inimical and should always be kept from God and from every good." [384] That this is ethical dualism will be evident, but it is also bordering on a metaphysical two-worlds dualism.

3. Gradations in perfection

The attitude adopted by Priscillian towards those faithful who were incapable of following his exacting precepts was surprisingly mild. These were not those 'sons of perdition'. "In heaven there are many mansions", he admits. [385] All those baptized Christians who remain more attached to 'the world' (to their families, for instance) than Priscillian likes may be saved, on the condition that they do not waver in their faith. [386]

So far so good. But there are surely gradations in perfection. Priscillian is not far from having his own 'pneumatics'. Some are so inspired by God's spirit that they become the 'sons of God, the heirs of God, the co-heirs of Christ'. [387] These are the truly elected. "Before all ages God has predestined the wisdom hidden in a mystery for our glory, the glory that is of those whom he has chosen before the foundation of the world." [388] That there existed a 'hidden wisdom', only to be divulged to the chosen, was an idea dear to the Gnostics. Many of them held that, apart from the Gospels, there was a 'secret teaching', transmitted orally by Jesus to one of the Apostles, for instance to Peter or to John (but never to Paul). Priscillian does not say so himself, but I feel that he goes even further than that, since his hidden wisdom is eternal, older than mankind, older even than the cosmos.

4. The final aim of Christian education

The final aim of Christian education is the 'new man' who as his image in heaven because he is formed according to the image of God; he is reformed by the grace of God and the light of knowledge (scientia). [389] This Priscillian idea that the 'new man' is the image of God is not biblical, since according to Genesis 1 all human beings without exception are created in the image and likeness of God. Almost imperceptibly some Gnostic ideas are finding their way in : next to the grace of God and on a par with it we detect the 'lumen scientiae'. And here appear the two races of men, for not only the knowledge that is light has its sons, but equally the obscurity of ignorance. [390]

In order to reach the highest summit, an ascetical life is necessary. "To destroy the work of the world, one must be fixed to the cross with a castigated body that should be delivered immaculate to God; that what is divine in us must be preserved impassible." [391] There is a Gnostic ring in this; this divine element reminds us of the 'divine spark' of the Gnostics. Further, a continuous and assiduous study of the Bible is needed all along the upward path. [392] Those who 'know' ('nos autem scientes') "that the Lord is spiritual and that all prophecy needs an interpretation have the God Christ as their exegete." [393] The teaching authority of the Church is not referred to.

5. Christology

With regard to Priscillian's Christology, the question is justified whether it is undilutedly orthodox. "The venerable one God with his threefold power is Christ who is all in all; [394] Christ himself taught his apostles that the name of the Father is Son and that of the Son Father." This comes very close to the anti-trinitarian propositions of the Monarchians and the Modalists. Priscillian nowhere denies that God has become man; on the contrary, he repeats this often enough. Christ has been born from the Virgin and has suffered for us. Once he even states that "to us Christ is the man of men." [395]

But when we hear him say that Christ is 'of divine soul and earthly flesh', then this is not the perfectly orthodox doctrine of 'wholly God and wholly man'. Christ is in Priscillian teaching not so much the historical Jesus of Nazareth, walking about in Palestine preaching and healing, but rather a cosmic principle. What Priscillian has to say of him reminds me of Teilhard's 'cosmic Christ'. "The God Christ is the first principle," [396] ... 'the origin of all' but himself 'without beginning, without end'. [397] He is the vital force working in all nature. [398]

6. Priscillian's position in the doctrinal spectrum

Enough has been said now to assess Priscillian's position in the doctrinal spectrum which runs from orthodoxy to heterodoxy. His tractates and canons are so replete with Gnostic and dualistic elements that there can be no doubt that he was erring on the heterodox side. Was he a Manichee? He was accused of being one, indeed, especially by his enemy, bishop Ithacius. He was no doubt sincere in his convicion that he had nothing to do with Manichaeism. But, as Chadwick remarks, "at the same time he betrays interest in several topics that bring him strangely and disturbingly close to his heretical opponents." [399]

This scholar points to the following items : a great interest in the war of the sons of the light against the sons of darkness - a predilection for apocryphal, non-biblical Acts, especially those which preach sexual abstinence - the idea that married people are an inferior sort - great stress on liberty over against doctrinal authority. Chadwick concludes that all this does not make Priscillian into a crypto-Manichee, but it laid him vulnerably open to attacks from the orthodox side. [400]

7. The Spanish bishops take action

Priscillianism became an affair, of course. Since Priscillian was a Spaniard, the Iberian bishops had to occupy themselves with the affair. In October 380 the Synod of Saragossa condemned his doctrine. But one or another bishop was on his side so that, with the help of bishop Hyginus of Cordoba, he became bishop of Avila. He now considered himself the equal of other bishops. But these invoked the assistance of the Emperor, Gratianus, who issued a decree against the 'Manichaeans'. As a result, Priscillian and some of his adherents left Spain and established themselves at Bordeaux; here they won new converts.

Priscillian was innocent enough to believe that he would be able to enlist the support of the highest ecclesiasticasl authorities. With this aim in mind he and a number of his followers travelled to Rome where Pope

Damasus I (366-384) refused to receive them, and to Milan where bishop Ambrose did not want to see them. [401] What they achieved was the annulment of the banishment decree so that they could return to Spain.

8. The intervention of the Emperor Maximus

In 384 a synod assembled at Bordeaux where one of the bishops who supported Priscillian was deposed; he himself refused to appear. Instead, he appealed to the new Emperor, Maximus. This became his undoing. Priscillian was brought over to Treves where Maximus resided. It soon became evident that this ruler's attitude with regard to heresy was stern and inexorable.

Maximus was proclaimed Emperor by his troops in Britain in 383; havong crossed the Channel, he was soon master of all Western Europe. For the time being he made Treves his capital. But great as his success was, in the eyes of the general public he was a usurper so that he sorely needed props for his position. That the case of Priscillian appeared before his court was a godsend for him. It gave him the opportunity to pose as an orthodox Catholic, ready to save the Church from what he saw as the Manichaean threat. [402] This is what Maximus himself wrote. "We must proclaim that it is our mind and our will that the Catholicn faith must subsist free from all dissensions, unhurt and inviolable, sustained by the bishops serving God in unison." [403]

Whereas the bishops only wanted the Emperor to help them suppress heresy, Maximus set himselfup as the 'defensor fidei' par excellence. He was not the only monarch, Roman or other, to do so. When Ithacius, the bishop of Ossobona, who was ready to act as the counsel for the prosecution, saw what turn things were going to take, he desisted from taking part in the proceeedings. [404] Martin, the renowned archbishop of Tours, pleaded in person with the Emperor so that he would condemn heresy but no the heretic. [405] But Maximus did not feel inclined to clemency. [406] During the proceedings Ambrose arrived at Treves as the envoy of Emperor Valentianus II; it angered him that there was talk of capital punishment, and still more that there were bishops favouring this. He refused to speak with them, upon which the irritated usurper ordered him to depart. [407] When in Treves, Ambrose personally witnessed what happened to another bishop, Hyginus of Cordoba. This old man pleaded to treat Priscillian leniently. As a response, he was spirited away without his mantle and without a cushion in the carriage that carried him away.

Maximus left really no stone unturned to show how resolute a defender of the faith he was! Priscillian and six of his adherents were condemned to death and executed, while two others were banished to a place of exile at the edge of the world, namely the Scilly Islands. These events occurred in 385 but did not spell the end of Priscillianism. [408]

Maximus himself found it necessary to defend his way of acting in a personal letter to Pope Siricius. [409] Perhaps a second intervention by Martin of Tours had made him feel uneasy. When he heard what had happened, the impulsive bishop travelled poste-haste back to Treves, quite ready to weather the imperial storm. When the anti-Priscillianist bishops who were still in town heard that Martin was near, they began to mumble and to tremble, as Sulpicius Severus (a great admirer of the holy bishop) writes. They asked the ruler to send officers to prevent Martin from entering the town, if he did not declare himself in agreement with them. This was asking the impossible, for the day before the Emperor, at their request, had decided to send tribunes to Spain where they had to track down the heretics and deprive them of life and goods.

The intrepid bishop, however, forced his way into the town during the night and in the morning entered the palace. For two whole day Maximus cold-shouldered him, with Martin's enemies imploring him not to give in. But on the third day he had a secret meeting with the bishop, explaining to him that the procedure against Priscillian had been quite normal and legal. But when Martin refused to be convinced, the Emperor got angry, rose to his feet, and departed. On hearing that the tribunes for Spain were leaving, Martin went again to the palace during the night and had a second interview with the Emperor who this time gave in and countermanded the order for the Spanish action. [410]

Some scholars have guessed that Martin had a personal reason for objecting to the punishment meted out to the Priscillianists, namely that he was somewhat of a Priscillianist himself. But, as D'Alès writes, there is not the slightest support in the sources for this supposition. The real reason for his interventions was that "Saint Martin felt horrified by the shedding of blood and would in no case see the Church involved in this." [411]

The Spanish episcopate was not pleased with the fatal course events had taken, but nothing could be done until Maximus, wo ostentatiously paraded himself as an orthodox Catholic, was no longer Emperor. Bishop Ithacius, the accuser of Priscillian, was deposed in 388; the remains of the executed persons were brought over from Treves and buried in Spain.

9. Priscillianism after Priscillian

The execution of Priscillian did not spell the end of Priscillianism. His adherents remained firmly entrenched in Spain's north-western province of Galicia where his shrine attracted many pilgrims. A request by the non-Galician bishops, made about 396, to make an end of this veneration - even miracles were reported - met with a refusal. [412] Under the leadership of Dictinus, the bishop-coadjutor of Astorga, the position of the Galician Church soon enough became schismatic. In Gaul too fierce quarrels raged between Priscillianists and their opponents, In the first years of the fifth century a synod was held at Turin with the aim to restore unity and peace to the Churches of Acquitaine and Gaul. It was not a complete success.

In Spain a synod was held at Toledo in 400 with the object "to put pressure upon the bishops of Galicia to abandon their sympathy for Priscillianism." [413] Once again no wholesale success could be booked. Four bishops refused to give in, or else "they would lose the support of their clergy and people." Some cleric stated loudly in the face of the assembled diocesans that Priscillian was a Catholic, a holy martyr, down and out orthodox, and a victim of persecution. [414] After 407 the imperial chancellery began to take an interest. Priscillianists were outlawed, their goods could be confiscated, their slaves freed; they were debarred form holding office in the imperial service. [415]

But soon enough it became impossible to do anything at all against the Galician Priscillianists. After 409 Galicia, and indeed all of Spain, was overrun by wave after wave of Germanic invaders. Priscillianism managed to subsist for a long time in the new situation. But with the Visigoths now masters of Spain, Arians and fiercely anti-Manichaean as they were, harassment of the Priscillianists began anew. [416] Ever less was heard of them; after 600 there was complete silence.

NOTES TO CHAPTER V

1. Jan Bergman s.v. 'Askese I", TRE 4.196.
2. Vol. I, pp. 235 and 242.
3. Vol. III, Ch. III.6.
4. Vol. IX, Ch. IV, 18b.
5. Jan Bergman s.v. 'Askese I', TRE 4, 196. Berlin/New York, 1979.
6. We find the term for the first time in Ir., Adv.haer. 1.18.1 in the form 'ἐγκρατειης'.
7. The words behind the hyphen are given by Ugo Bianchi, the editor, in a note.
8. Documento finale, Atti del colloquio XXIII.
9. Quispel, Study 74.
10. Documento finale XXIV. Atti del colloquio.
11. Documento finale XXIV. Atti del colloquio 24. Here we listen to Ugo Bianchi; speaking of 'le thème du colloque en tant que problème historico-religieux', he argues that every doctrine of a double creation in which the second creation takes place on the basis of a primordial fall, or, more precise, of an 'antecedent fault', expresses a dualistic mentality even in those Fathers (Origen, Gregory of Nyssa) who admit a double creation. In the same Documento Giulia Sfameni Gasparro, Le motivazione (see Bibliography), 251/252, writes : "La struttura della doppia creazione che soggiace a tali formulazioni (encratitische) conferisce un' indubbia connotazione dualistica alle relative antropologie quando distingue, in forme e gradazione diverse, due livelli nella natura et nelle modalità di esistenza umana e identifica nel secondo la consequenza, sia pure mediata all' intervento divino, del peccato."

12. Documento finale XXIV/XXV. Atti del colloquio.
13. Hier., Comm. in Ep. ad Gal. 3.6 (526).
14. Clem.Al., Strom. 3.13.
15. Clem.Al., Strom. 3.13.1.
16. Hier., Comm. in Gal. 3.6 (526).
17. Hier., Ep. 58 (213).
18. Ir., Adv.haer. 1.28 (107).
19. Ir., Adv.haer. 1.28 (107).
20. Its Greek text has been lost, but there exist Arab, Latin, and even medieval Dutch versions of it. For everything concerning the Diatesseron I refer the reader to a recent work by William L. Petersen, Tatian's Diatesseron. Its creation, dissemination, significance, and history in scholarship. Supplements to Vigiliae Christianae, Vol. XXV. Leiden/New York/Köln, 1994.
21. Elze, Tatian 42 : "Manche Anzeichen sprechen in der Tat dafür, daß es sich um eine wirklich vorgeträgene Rede handelt".
22. Elze, Tatian 54-57.
23. Tat., Or. 42.1.
24. Tat., Or. 29.1.
25. Tat., Or. 35.1.
26. Tat., Or. 1.3.
27. Tat., Or. 42.1.
28. Tat., Or. 32.1.
29. Elze, Tatian 22.
30. Elze, Tatian 27.
31. Tat., Or. 4.1.
32. Vol. I, Ch. II.3-5.
33. Tat., Or. 5.1.
34. Tat., Or. 5.1.
35. Tat., Or. 5.1.
36. Tat., Or. 5.1.
37. G. Bardy s.v. 'Tatian', Dict.Théol.Cath. 15.1, 73 (Paris, 1946).
38. Tat., Or. 7.1.

39. Tat., Or. 4.2.
40. Tat., Or. 21.1.
41. Tat., Or. 12.1.
42. Tat., Or. 20.1.
43. Tat., Or. 15.1.
44. Tat., Or. 29.2.
45. Tat., Or. 13.2.
46. Tat., Or. 13.3.
47. Ir., Adv.haer. 1.128.1.
48. Ir., Adv.haer. 3.23.8.
49. Elze, Tatian 127/128.
50. Schepelern, Mont., Kap. II Die phrygische Herkunft des Montanismus.
51. Ir., Adv.haer. 5.33.3-4.
52. Socrates, HE 4.27.
53. De Labriolle, Crise 11. It is strange and confusing when the opening phrases of this book tell us that the connexion between Phrygia and Montanism has been much exaggerated. This religious movement had, says this scholar, in its primitive phase nothing exceptional. There were analogous phenomena in very different times and civilizations. However, what he writes on p. 11 is clearly in contradiction with this. Recently William H.C. Frend s.v. 'Montanismus'. TRE XXIII, Lief. 1/2, 272 (1994), wrote this : "Nimmt man diese anhaltend prophetische Tradition zusammen mit dem Bestehen einer starken jüdischen Gemeinde und einer angestammten Religion, in der Bußübungen, Bußfasten und orgiastische Gebräuche traditionell waren, erscheint die Ausbruch einer Bewegung wie die des Montanismus kaum überraschend".
54. Clem.Al., Strom. 4.13.93.1 and 7.17.108. Pseudo-Tert., Adv.omnes haer. 7, spoke of a heresy 'according to the Phrygians'.
55. Nathanael Bonwetsch s.v. 'Montanismus', Realenc.prot.Theol. u. Kirche 13, 420 (1905).
56. On the historical existence of Montanus, which is doubted by some (like that of numerous others in Antiquity), see De Labriolle, Crise, Chap. I, § III Montan. Sa réalité historique.
57. Hier., Ep. 41.4.
58. Eus., HE 5.16.7.
59. Hier., Ep. 41.4.

60. On these ladies see De Labriolle, Crise, Chap. I, § IV Maximilla et Priscilla.
61. Eus., HE 5.17.5.
62. According to an ancient author, Apollonius, quoted by quoted by Eus., HE 5.16.9.
63. Schepelern, Mont. 18.
64. Eus., HE 5.17.2.
65. Epiph., Pan. 48.4.
66. Epiph., Pan. 48.2.
67. On the early adherents see De Labriolle, Crise, Chap. I, § V.
68. Eus., HE 5.18.5.
69. Eus., HE 5.16.18.
70. Eus., HE 5.16.9 and 5.18.3.
71. Eus., HE 5.18.2. W.-M. Ramsay, The cities and bishoprics of Phrygia. Oxford, 1897, II 573 and 575, thinks that Pepuza is the modern Turkish village of Boudarli, and Tymion perhaps Dumanli - quoted by De Labriolle, Crise 16, note 1 and 17, note 1.
72. Eus. HE 5.16.12.
73. Eus., HE 5.16.17. The Greek for 'word' is not 'logos' here but '$ῥῆμα$'.
74. Eus., HE 5.16.4.
75. Eus., HE 5.16.17.
76. Eus., HE 5.19.8.
77. Eus., HE 5.16.10.
78. From a letter by bishop Firmilianus, quoted by Cyprianus, Ep. 75.10.
79. Firmilianus in Cyprianus, Ep. 75.19.
80. De Labriolle, Crise 145.
81. De Labriolle, Crise 146.
82. Tert., De praescr. 16.3.
83. De Labriolle, Crise 151.
84. Paul devotes a whole chapter, 1 Cor. 14, to this problem.
85. Heine, Oracles IX/X. See also De Labriolle, Crise, Chap. II, § Les 'oracles' montanistes.
86. Heine, Oracles X.
87. Tert., Adv.Prax. 1. See Stroehlin, Essai 12.

88. Joel 2:28,29.
89. Passio 35.4.
90. Epiph., Pan. 48.11.
91. There are more oracles in the same vein, Heine, Oracles 15, 16, 17 : "I am the Father and the Son and the Spirit". Heine calls their authenticity 'questionable'. Consult for these utterances De Labriolle, Crise 38-53.
92. Tert., De fuga 1.
93. Tert., De virg.vel. 1.
94. Tert., De monogamia 2.
95. Tert., De ieiunio 1.
96. Tert., De monogamia 1.
97. Tert., De virg.vel. 1.
98. Tert., Adv.Prax. 13.
99. Stroehlin, Essai 14.
100. Pseudo-Tert., De praescript. 52.
101. Epiph., Pan. 49.4.
102. Tert., De virg.vel. 1.
103. Tert., Ad ux. 1.2.
104. Tert., De virg.vel. 1.
105. Tert., De exh.cast. 6.
106. Tert., De virg.vel. 1.
107. See for him and his doctrine, Marjorie Reeves, Joachim of Fiore and the Prophetic Future. London (1976).
108. Tert., De corona 1.
109. Hipp., Comm. in Dan. 3.18.
110. Plus a lost work 'De ecstasi'.
111. G. Bardy s.v. 'Tertullien', Dict.Théol.Cath. 15.1, 132 (1946).
112. De Labriolle, Crise 312.
113. De Labriolle, Crise 299-304 Ce qui dût déplaire à Tertullien dans la prophétie nouvelle.
114. Tert., De cultu fem. 1.1.
115. De Labriolle, Crise 359. On pp. 360/361 he presents charts of all the places where Tert. speaks of 'psychics' and 'spiritales'.

116. Tert., Adv.Marc. 4.22.
117. Tert., De monogamia 1.
118. Tert., De ieiunio 1.
119. Tert., De ieiunio 11.
120. Tert., De an. 11.
121. Tert., Adv.Prax. 1.
122. Stroehlin, Essai 32.
123. Aug., De haer. 86.
124. Hier., Ep. 41.
125. An., Praedestinatus 86.
126. Ir., Adv.haer. 2.32.4.
127. Eus., Vita Const. 3.53-56; De Labriolle, Sources no. 72.
128. De Labriolle, Crise 528-531.
129. Liber pontificalis, see De Labriolle, Sources no. 138.
130. Cod.Theod. 16.4.34; see De Labriolle, Sources no. 153.
131. Gregorius, Ep. 11.57, see De Labriolle, Sources no. 198.
132. Eus., De mart.pal. 13.12 (345).
133. Eus., HE 8.2.4.
134. Not be confused with bishop Felix of Aptungi (or Aptugni); Thibiuca is the present-day Henchir Zougitina in Tunisia.
135. Passio S. Felicis, in Maier, Dossier.
136. Alfred Schindler s.v. 'Afrika I' TRE 1, 163 (1977). An interesting record of a requisition is that in the Christian community of Cirta (the modern Constantine in Algeria) where bishop Paulus readily complied with the authorities; even a list of the sequestrated cult objects is given, Gesta Zen. 18.
137. Eus., HE 3.1 and 4.8.
138. Passio Saturnini (see Bibliography); also printed in Maier, Dossier I, 57-92 (annotated).
139. See for its origin Franchi de'Cavallieri, La 'Passio', 3-5.
140. Passio Saturn. 6.210.
141. Passio Maiximae, Maier, Dossier I, 95-105; Passio Crispinae, Maier, Dossier I, 107-112.
142. Aug., Brev. 13.25.

143. Aug., Brev. 13.25; Opt., Hist.Don. 2.
144. Aug., Brev. 3.13.25.
145. Franchi de'Cavalieri, Passio 43, calls this accusation 'inverosimile'. See also pp. 44/45.
146. Opt., Hist.Don. 2.
147. Aug., Brev. 3.13.25.
148. Opt., De schism. 1.16 and 18.
149. Gesta Zen. 22a.
150. It was said that Silvanus had stolen goods from the temple of Serapis, Gesta Zen. 22a; see also Gesta Zen. 21b and Opt., Hist.Don. 3 and 10.
151. Gesta Zen. 23a and 24a.
152. Gesta Zen. 23b.
153. Frend, Don.Church 12.
154. Frend, Don.Church 12, note 3, on the basis of Aug., Brev. 3.17.32.
155. Opt., De schism. 1.14.
156. The story of this synod is related by Opt., Hist.Don. 3 and in the Gesta Zen.
157. Frend, Don.Church 12/13 and note 6.
158. It is an old problem whether there were one or two bishops called 'Donatus', both of whom were 'Donatists'. For Optatus in his History of the Donatists there was only one bishop with this name. Augustine (Retractationes 21.3) initially thought there was one but later came to the conclusion that there had been two of them, a bishop of Casae Nigrae and a contemporary bishop of Carthage. Of these two it was Donatus a Casis Nigris who started the schism, he said. The confusion has persisted until our own days. G. Bareille, for instance, in the Dict.Théol.Cath. 4.2 (1924), has two entries 'Donat' for two different persons. Frend, Don.Church 18, on the contrary, acknowledges only one Donatus, just as, more recently, Alfred Schindler s.v. 'Afrika I', TER 1 (1977), 655. Maier in his Dossier I (1987), 151, note 6, has no clear judgment on this problem. I think it is safest to follow Frend.
159. Opt., Hist.Don. 1.24.
160. Frend, Don.Church 15.
161. Frend, Don.Church 16.
162. Aug., Brev. 3.16.29.
163. Opt., Don. 1.19.

164. Aug., Post coll. 22.38.
165. Aug., Ep. 44.4.8.
166. Opt., Hist.Don. 1.19.
167. Aug., Ep. ad Cath. 18.46.
168. Aug., Contra Cresc. 3.31; Opt., Hist.Don. 4.
169. Opt., Hist.Don. 4.
170. Opt., De schism. 1.19.
171. Opt., De schism. 1.19.
172. Aug., Ep. 43.5.14.
173. Frend, Don.Church 20. There are several problems connected with the origination of the schism. Firstly, the reports we have are from the hands of anti-Donatists, namely Optatus and Augustine; secondly, the contemporary documents are lost, and, thirdly, both Optatus and Augustine wrote long after the events they reported. There is also the problem when exactly these events occurred, in 308?, in 311?, in 312? See the learned discussion in Maier, Dossier I 129-135; this scholar is ready to think of 311/312.
174. Opt., De schism. 1.19.
175. Anon., Contra Fulg. 26.
176. Gesta Zen. 17a.
177. Alfred Schindler s.v. 'Afrika I', TRE 1, 665.
178. The discussion began in 1883 with the publication of a book by Daniel Voelter, Der Ursprung des Donatismus (Freiburg), but the main impulse was given by Thümmel.
179. Wilhelm Thümmel, Zur Beurtheilung des Donatismus. Halle, 1893.
180. Frend, Don.Church XIV.
181. Frend, Don.Church 315.
182. Brisson, Autonomisme 28.
183. Brisson, Autonomisme 141; see for the controversy his Chap. IV Les controverses ecclésiologiques du IVe siècle.
184. Alfred Schindler s.v. 'Afrika I', TRE 1 (1977), 668.
185. N. Bonwetsch s..v. 'Donatismus', Realenc.f.prot.Theol.u.Kirche 4, 796.
186. He devoted a treatise to ecclesiastical unity, De ecclesiae catholicae unitate.
187. Cypr., De unit. 4.
188. Cypr., De unit.6.

189. Cypr., Ep. 7 ad Cornelium Papam.
190. Cypr., De unit. 3.
191. Aug., De bapt. 2.1.2.
192. Aug., Ep. 93.10.36.
193. Brisson, Autonomisme 138.
194. Brisson, Autonomisme 1239.
195. Brisson, Autonomisme 140.
196. Brisson, Autonomisme 143.
197. Aug., Contra ep. Parm. 2.8.15.
198. Aug., Contra lit. Pet. 2.53.121.
199. Alfred Schindler s.v. 'Afrika I', TRE 1, 666.
200. Printed Maier, Dossier I, pp.140-142. It is intriguing to state with Grasmück, Coercitio 28, note 87, that Constantine used to employ the word 'μανία' for heresy and schism, whereas he dubbed the pagan religion 'superstitio'.
201. Printed in Maier, Dossier I, no 14, pp. 143/144.
202. Printed in Maier, Dossier I, no. 14, pp. 145/146.
203. Printed in Maier, Dossier I, no. 15, pp. 146-148.
204. Grasmück, Coercitio 34.
205. Printed in Maier, Dossier I, no. 16, pp. 149-150.
206. Opt., Contra Parm. 1.23.
207. Printed in Maier, Dossier I, no. 17, pp. 151/152.
208. This appeal is not extant.
209. Printed in Maier, Dossier I, no. 18, pp. 153-158.
210. See for instance that Chrestos, bishop of Syracuse, in Maier, Dossier I, no. 19, pp. 158-160. According to Grasmück, Coerc. 57/58, it was not really a council or a synod, but, instead, a tribunal or a court of arbitration.
211. Printed in Maier, Dossier I, no. 20, pp. 160-167; the Acta of the synod have been preserved only partially.
212. Printed in Maier, Dossier I, no. 21, pp. 167-171.
213. Printed in Maier, Dossier I, no. 23, pp. 187-189.
214. Imperial letter to the Donatist bishops, printed in Maier, Dossier I, no. 25. pp. 192/193.

215. Printed in Maier, Dossier I, no. 27, pp. 194-196.
216. Opt., Contra Parm. 1.26.
217. Imperial letter of 10.XI,316, printed in Maier, Dossier I, no. 27, pp. 196-198.
218. The text of the imperial decree is not extant; it is mentioned as 'most severe' by Aug., Ep. 105.9 and Contra lit.Pet. 2.92.105.
219. Grasmück, Coerc. 85.
220. Passio Donati 3.
221. Passio Donati 2.
222. Sermo de passione S. Donati Abiocalensis 2, printed Maier, Dossier I, no. 28.
223. Frend, Don.Church 160, note 2.
224. Passio Donati 11,12.
225. Passio Don. 7. Sicilibba has disappeared from the map.
226. See the Gesta apud Zenophilum passim. Also Aug., Contra Cresc. 3.30.34.
227. Frend, Don.Church 161.
228. A war with his co-emperor was about to break out. Constantine urgently wanted Rome and Italy to remain quiet. Troubles in North Africa would disturb or interrupt the regular delivery of grain to the capital, which would cause unrest there, Grasmück, Coerc. 89.
229. Eus., Vita Const. 1.45.
230. Aug., Post coll. 33.56; Gesta coll. Carth., cap. 549 : "Libertatem agendi tribuit Donatistis".
231. Aug., Post coll. 31.54.
232. Grasmück, Coerc. 90.
233. Constantinus universis episcopis per Africam, CSEL 26, Appendix VIII, also printed in Maier, Dossier I, no. 30.
234. Frend, Don.Church 163.
235. G. Bareille s.v. 'Donatism', Dict.Théol.Cath. 4.2, 1706 (1924).
236. Aug., Ps. contra part.Don. PL 43 on p. 27.
237. Opt. 3.3.
238. Aug., In Jo.ev. 13.17.
239. Frend, Don.Church 165.
240. Frend, Don.Church 164.

241. Frend, Don.Church 164.
242. Opt., 2.4.
243. Aug., Contra ep.Parm. 2.5.
244. Frend, Don. Church 167.
245. See Vol. XI, Ch. IV.6.
246. Frend, Don. Church 173.
247. See Büttner/Werner, Circumcell. 41/42.
248. Alfred Schindler s.v. 'Africa I, TRE 1, 663 (1977).
249. Büttner/Werner, Circumcell. 22/23.
250. Quoted Frend, Don. Church 174.
251. Aug., Ep. 108.5.14.
252. Opt., 3.4.
253. Frend, Don. Church 174.
254. Aug., Contra ep. Parm., 1.11.17.
255. Isidorus, De eccl.off. 2.16.7.
256. Isidorus, De eccl.off. 2.16.7.
257. Frend, Don.Church 174, note 9.
258. Aug., Ep. ad cath. 19.50.
259. Aug., Sermo 311.5.
260. Aug., Ep. 88.8, quoted from Frend, Don.Church 175.
261. Aug., Contra Gaud. 1.28.32.
262. For instance, Filastrius, De haer. 85 and Theodoret., Haer.fab.comp. 4.6.
263. Aug., Ep. 185.4.15.
264. Theodoret., Haer.fab.comp. 5.6.
265. Tert., De idolatria 19.
266. Brisson, Autonomisme 306-308.
267. Alfred Schindler s.v. 'Afrika I', TRE I (19677), 663.
268. Aug., Ep. 108.6.18.
269. Opt. 3.4.
270. Opt. 3.4.
271. Aug., Ep. 185.4.15. See also Büttner/Werner, Circumcell. 58.
272. Büttner/Werner, Circumcell. 51.

273. Büttner/Werner, Circumcell. 57 and notes 281 and 282.
274. Büttner/Werner, Circumcell. 58.
275. Aug., Contra lit.Pet. 1.23.26.
276. Aug., Ep. 108.5.18.
277. Opt. 3.4.
278. Opt. 3.3.
279. Opt. 3.3.
280. Opt. 3.13.
281. Opt. 7.6.
282. Opt. 3.3.
283. Opt. 3.4.
284. Grasmück, Coerc. 117.
285. The text of this decree is lost but it is referred to by not a few ancient authors, for instance Opt. 2.15 and 3.1-4, see Maier, Dossier I, 257, note 7.
286. Opt. 3.1.
287. Grasmück, Coerc. 121 does not believe that Max. was drowned alive; he thinks that he died in prison as a result of the flogging.
288. The whole story in the Passio Maximiani et Isaac.
289. Passio benedicti martyris Marculi.
290. Opt. 2.7. It is supposed that Parmenian was not an African, Frend, Don. Church 181, note 2.
291. Passio Marc.
292. Opt. 3.1.
293. Aug., Contr.lit.Pet. 2.20.46 and Contra Cresc. 3.49.54.
294. Grasmück, Coerc. 125 and note 146.
295. The acts of the synod are printed in Maier, Dossier I, no. 38, pp. 291-296.
296. Aug., Contra lit.Pet. 2.39.92; see Frend, Don. Church 185.
297. Opt. 2.16; Aug., Contra lit.Pet. 2.97.24.
298. Opt. 2.17.
299. Frend, Don.Church 189.
300. Opt. 2.17.18.

301. Aug., Ep. 93.45.
302. Opt. 2.17.18.
303. Opt. 6.6.
304. Opt. 2.18.
305. Opt. 6.7.
306. Opt. 3.10.
307. Opt. 3.11.
308. Frend, Don.Church 193.
309. Amm.Marc.29.5.
310. Quoted by Frend, Don.Church 197, note 3.
311. Orosius, Hist. 7.33.
312. The father of the future Emperor Theodosius I.
313. Law of April 22, 376, Cod.Theod. 16.5.4.
314. Frend, Don.Church 200, quotes Aug., Ep. 87.8, to this effect. But Aug. did not say as much; he wrote that Flavianus was 'a man of your party' - 'partis vestrae homini' -, meaning thereby that he favoured the Donatists, not that he was one.
315. Grasmück, Coerc. 152.
316. Frend, Don. Church 201.
317. Frend, Don.Church 193.
318. Opt. 2.18.
319. Grasmück, Coerc. 141.
320. His work is nameless; the titles 'On the Donatist Schism' and 'History of the Donatists' were given only later to it.
321. Opt. 1.5.
322. Opt. 2.15.
323. Opt. 3.3
324. Opt. 3.3.
325. Opt. 7.6-7.
326. Grasmück, Coerc. 148.
327. Decree of 30.XII.393, Cod.Theod. 9.7.9.
328. For this Gildo see Otto Seeck s.v. 'Gildo', PW 7 (1912), 1360-1363.
329. Grasmück, Coerc. 160/161.

330. Grasmück, Coerc. 161.
331. Claudianus, De bello Gildonico 16.
332. Orosius 7.36.4.
333. Orosius 7.36.
334. Frend, Don.Church 209.
335. Frend, Don. Church 209.
336. Aug., Contra lit.Pet. 2.53.53.
337. Aug., Contra lit.Pet, 2.83.184 for Hippo, 3.57.69 for Rusiccade.
338. Aug., Contra Cresc. 3.56.62, translation Frend.
339. Opt. 7.1.
340. Frend, Don.Church 215.
341. Aug., Ep. 93.8.24 : Maximinianists strong along the coast. See also Grasmück, Coerc. 164/165.
342. What we know of this council we find mainly in Aug., Sermo 2 in Ps. 36 and Contra Cresc. 4.
343. The whole text of the sentence, pieced together out of works by Aug., is to be found in PL 11, 1183-1189.
344. Aug., Contra Cresc. 3.59.65.
345. Aug., Contra Cresc. 4.48.58-59, and Contra Ep.Parm. 6.29.
346. Aug., Contra lit.Pet. 2.92.109.
347. Frend, Don.Church 228.
348. Frend, Don.Church 228-237.
349. Frend, Don.Church 233.
350. Aug., Sermo 46.39.
351. Frend, Don.Church.
352. Cod.Theod. 16.5.51, Aug. 25, 410.
353. Cod.Theod. 16.11.3.
354. Frend, Don.Church 276.
355. Frend, Don.Church 278.
356. Frend, Don.Church 278.
357. Aug., Ep. 88.8, quoted by Frend, Don.Church 278.

358. Gesta coll. Carth. 1.4. The Acts of this synod are collected in PL 11 (Paris, 1845).
359. Grasmück, Coerc. 225.
360. Cod.Theod. 16.5.52.
361. We have this story from Augustine who wrote two books against Gaudentius, PL 43 (Paris, 1861).
362. Frend, Don.Church 299.
363. Greg.Magnus, Ep. 33 (335), PL 11 (Paris, 1845).
364. Greg.Magnus, Ep. 33 (334). PL 11 (Paris, 1845).
365. Greg.Magnus, Ep 32. PL 11 (Paris, 1845).
366. Greg.Magnus, Ep. 34, quoted by Frend, Don. Church 312.
367. Frend, Don.Church 331.
368. Quite a number of writings are ascribed to Priscillian, but the only ones, states Chadwick, Priscillian 57, which "provide a wholly secure criterion by which the doctrine of the movement can be assessed", are the so-called 'Würzburg tractates'; these are contained in a codex of the fifth of sixth century, preserved in the University Library of Würzburg; the collection consists of eleven tractates which are edited by Schepes (see Bibliography). Two other texts are the so-called 'Pauline canons', containing short notes on fourteen Pauline Letters, and a fragment of a letter from Priscillian in Orosius, Commonitorium, ed. Schepes (see Bibliography). Chadwick, Priscillian 37, comments that "the degree of uncertainty will not appear to be uncomfortably high in relation to the canons or the Orosius fragment." For the discussion on the authenticity of Priscillianist scripture I refer to Chadwick, Priscillian 57-70.
369. Tractatus 8.121.
370. Tractatus 4, 75; 9. 122; 10.127.
371. Tractatus 10.127.
372. Tractatus 4.77.
373. Tractatis 1.18-19.
374. Canon 35.
375. Canon 33-34.
376. Canon 57.
377. Tractatus 4.79; 10.137.
378. Tractatus 6.95.

379. Tractatus 10.134.
380. Canon 1.
381. Canon 2.
382. Canon 3.
383. Canon 4.
384. Canon 29.
385. Tractatus 2.43.
386. Tractatus 2.43.
387. Canon 72.
388. Canon 24.
389. Canon 31.
390. Canon 23.
391. Tractatus 6.101.
392. Tractatus 1.7.
393. Tractatus 1.9.
394. Tractatus 2.45.
395. Tractatus 1.28.
396. Tractatus 1.17.
397. Tractatus 6.94.
398. Tractatus 11.144-145.
399. Chadwick, Priscillian 98.
400. Chadwick, Priscillian 98/99.
401. Sulp.Sev., Chron. 2.48.3-4. Priscillian travelled to Rome in the company of two wealthy ladies, Euchrotia and her daughter Procula. This gave rise to rumours about the relations of Priscillian and the girl who was said to have been made pregnant by him and to have undergone an abortion, Sulp.Sev., Chron. 2.48.2-3. Chadwick, Priscillian 37, leaves it undecided whether the incriminated relationship with Procula really existed, but says : "This feminine company with the three bishops was highly imprudent."
402. Babut, Priscillien 170/171.
403. Letter of Maximus to Pope Siricius, CSEL 35.1.Ep.40.
404. Sulp.Sev., Chron. 2.51.1.

405. Sulp.Sev., Chron. 2.50.3-4.
406. The Priscillians were not only accused of heresy but also of indecent behaviour. Sulp.Sev., Chron. 2.50.8, says that Priscillian confessed to have studied 'obscure doctrines', to have held nocturnal sessions with women of low repute, and to have had the habit of praying stark naked. According to Jerome, Ep. 133.3, the conventicles of the Priscillians ended in sexual intercourse.
407. Ambrose, Ep. 26.
408. Sulp.Sev., Chron. 2.51. G. Bardy s.v. 'Priscillien', Dict. Théol.Cath. 13.393-400.
409. Maximus to Siricius, CSEL 35.1. Ep. 40.
410. We find this whole story in Sulp.Sev., Dialogus 2.11-13.
411. D'Alès. Priscillien 69.
412. Chadwick, Priscillian 152/153.
413. Chadwick, Priscillian 170.
414. Chadwick, Priscillian 184/185.
415. Chadwick, Priscillian 188.
416. Chadwick, Priscillian 222.

CHAPTER VI

THE ARIAN CONTROVERSY

It is a very curious thing, from an historical viewpoint, that so soon after her liberation the Church became the prey of an enormous confusion. There had been heresies before, but it was as if only then the woes began from which orthodox Christian doctrine would be born. I am, of course, speaking of the turmoil caused by Arianism. There are two stringent reasons for going into this matter in great depth.

The first is that Arianism created a division in the Church such as had never occurred before. In the words of Rowan Williams, "the crisis of the fourth century was the most dramatic struggle the Christian Church had so far experienced; it generated the first credal statement (i.e. the Nicaean creed - F.) to claim universal, unconditional assent, and it became inextricably entangled with issues concerning the authority of political rulers in the affairs of the Church" [1]. The second is that Arianism became the creed of almost all the Germanic tribes (with the notable exception of the Franks) that invaded the Western Roman Empire which resulted in its decline. The result was that Arianism became "irrevocably cast as the Other in relation to Catholic (and civilized) religion" [2].

Before we embark upon this undertaking it is sensible to take heed of a few caveats uttered by Adolf Martin Ritter [3]. This scholar begins by telling us that the part of the namegiver, Arius, in the whole affair was not so great as may be thought. Secondly, it would be wrong to see in all 'Arians' direct followers or spiritual descendants of Arius; in contemporary polemics the term 'Arian' is somewhat loosely or inappropriately used [4]. Thirdly, it is impossible to describe 'Arianism' as a purely intellectual phenomenon, for it is 'historical' also and has a 'Sitz im Leben' throughout the history of the fourth century.

PART I THE ALEXANDRIAN ORIGIN OF THE CONTROVERSY

1. Arius and his ecclesiastical career

a. Who was Arius?

It is true that Arius himself was not directly responsible for every aspect of what is called after him 'Arianism', but he was the one, after all, who started it all. What do we know of him? Not much really. He probably was a Libyan, born in 265 or some years later. Much later we find him in charge of the parish church of the Baucalis quarter of Alexandria [5]. We know that the Egyptian capital was an unruly city; the local Christian Church was not spared its troubles either. It seems that Arius played an active part in them; Le Bachelet says that his behaviour attests an agitating and somewhat rebellious spirit [6].

b. A question of martyrdom

As so often in the controversies of the early Church, here too a question of martyrdom seems to have been at the root of the conflict. We do not know when exactly Arius arrived in Alexandria, but he was there during the persecution of Diocletian in the years 303-305. He claims a connection with the martyr Lucian who was executed at Antioch on January 7, 312, during the persecution of the co-emperor Licinius [7]. Peter, the bishop of Alexandria, had fled the town; the affairs of the diocese had then been taken care of by Meletius of Lycopolis. He was one of these diehards who found that Christians should unflinchingly face martyrdom. On account of his flight bishop Peter had, in his eyes, become unworthy to retain his see. Meletius paid the price for his doubtless courageous stand when he was sentenced to hard labour in the Phaeno mines, but undaunted, he continued to consecrate bishops and ordain presbyters. Arius took the part of Meletius [8], but when Peter returned, he joined this bishop who made him a deacon in 308. When, however, Peter began taking measures against Meletius and his adherents (as being schismatics), Arius deserted to the other side and was perhaps excommunicated.

c. Arius's personality

The lull in the persecution which had started in 305 came to an end in 312, when the co-emperor Maximinus was after the Christians again. Among the many victims in Alexandria was also Peter who died a martyr's death in the same year. Maybe this convinced Arius that Peter was after all of the right sort. Anyhow, he was reintegrated into the Church by Peter's successor Achillas and was made a presbyter. It was probably the next bishop, Alexander, who entrusted Arius with the Bacaulis parish [9]. One, pro-Arian, report says that Arius supported the election of Alexander, another, less sympathetic, that he had desired to have the see himself and when he did not get it, remained rancunous ever after [10].

The parish priest of Bacaulis seems to have been an imposing man, renowned for his ability to expound the Scriptures [11]. At the age of fifty the years had already begun to tell on him; he looked like an old man [12], pale and worn out [13]. Epiphanius (who said he was 'counterfeited like a guileful serpent') describes him as "always garbed in a short cloak and sleeveless tunic; he spoke gently, and people found him persuasive and flattering" [14]. This brings to my mind a famous dictum of Theodore Roosevelt : "Speak softly, but carry a big stick" , for Arius was certainly a man to be reckoned with. His moral life was impeccable. Being a good speaker, his influence was considerable. On the other hand, he was proud and not without personal vanity [15].

2. How the conflict started

a. Diverging opinions

Soon there was rumor in casa again. The clerics of Alexandria did not see eye to eye; there were divergences of opinion, in theological respects, but also probably of a personal nature. May we believe an ancient source, a certain presbyter Alexander, a deformed man and the second after Arius in the Bacaulis parish, caused the trouble between his parish priest and bishop Alexander [16]. Since these presbyters all spoke publicly from their pulpits, the faithful became fully acquainted with the diverging opinions. To the modern mind such a war of the pulpits may seem a dangerous source of friction. But theologizing was something of a sport then (and long afterwards) in which the public enthusiastically took sides [17].

b. The beginning of the conflict

All dates before 325, the Council of Nicaea, are somewhat conjectural, but we may be fairly certain that the great conflict over Arian doctrine began in the year 318 [18]. We have two different versions of how the conflict started. We may discard Epiphanius' idea that Satan entered into Arius inciting him to throw up a dust-cloud against the Church from which no small fire would result. But he was right when he wrote that the conflict would involve the whole Roman Empire, in particular its oriental regions [19].

Socrates the historian tells us of a clerical assembly in which bishop Alexander spoke of the mystery of the Holy Trinity, insisting on its unity. It is impossible to say what could be wrong with this from an orthodox point of view, but since Socrates adds that the bishop spoke 'with ambition', it might be that he pressed his point somewhat too vigorously. Anyhow, Arius felt challenged to react; he accused his bishop of Sabellianism. Mention was made of this doctrine earlier in this volume : Sabellius held that the persons of the Trinity were not numerically distinct, in other words, that there were no persons at all, but only modes of being of the godhead.

Socrates gives in direct speech what Arius is alleged to have said. "If the Father has generated the Son, he (the Son), having been born, has a beginning of his existence. From this it must be manifestly inferred that there has been a time that there was not yet a Son. From this it necessarily follows that he has been made from nothing" [20]. This amounts to stating that Jesus was not divine and was part of the general creation since he had been made from nothing, like all the rest. "How is he able to be Logos or God who slept as a man, wept, and had to learn by inquiry?" [21]. The Emperor Constantine later wrote that he found Alexander's speech superfluous (he probably meant provocative) and Arius's reaction rash [22].

3. Was Arius dependent on Origen?

a. Origen a disputed theologian

There was in itself nothing new in Arius' attitude on the question of the godhead of Jesus of Nazareth; this had been under discussion from time immemorial. The reader will have found ample evidence of this in the foregoing chapters. The Docetists had held that Jesus could not be fully human, since he had no proper physical body. Modalists of all kinds had ruled that there was no Son at all, since 'Son' was only a mode of being of the godhead or perhaps only one of his names. Much has been made of a possible filiation from Origen to Arius. This may sound strange since Origen was the great propounder of the Logos-docrine according to which the Logos, the second person of the Holy Trinity, had become man in Jesus of Nazareth. But we also saw that the Logos-doctrine was by no means immediately accepted by all theologians; it was combated from many sides and on many grounds. It is the opinion of many scholars that precisely in Alexandria the pro's and contra's had collided very fiercely.

Origen's orthodoxy was, as we saw, doubted by later theologians; it is, therefore, not surprising that Arius was linked with him [23]. Epiphanius, that inveterate enemy of Origen, detected a direct link between this theologian and Arius. "Arius took his handle from this fountain of error", he wrote in a somewhat garbled metaphor [24]. Many a modern scholar agrees with Epiphanius on this point; they regard 'Arius's ideas in a vague and wholesale way as an inheritance from Origen's doctrine', writes Hanson [25]. But this does not apply to Harnack, the most famous of them. With regard to metaphysics, he says, Arius falls in completely with the philosophical ideas of his time and with one part of the expositions of Origen. But then he also stresses that Arianism was a <u>new doctrine</u> (his emphasis) in the Church [26]. Maybe we would know more of a supposed debt of Arius to Origen, if more of the heresiarch's writings had been preserved, but almost all of them are lost.

b. Origen's influence in Alexandria

Although he was considered a controversial figure, Origen continued to exercize great influence during the third century, perhaps most of all in Alexandria. There can be no doubt that Arius was acquainted with the principal tenets of Origenism. It is not too rash to suppose that the catechetical school in the Egyptian capital, of which Origen had been a principal, was a centre of Origenism. This does not mean that there was an Origenist school among theologians, in this sense that his followers faithfully propounded his system. We saw that Origen himself was not much of a systematic theologian and that he was often ambiguous and vague, leaving ample room for speculation about what he really meant. If there were no thoroughgoing Origenists, there were a good many ecclesiastical authors in Alexandria, in Egypt, and in Asia Minor, who interpreted Origen in their own fashion. Perhaps it is in this way that we may view Arius as being linked to the Origenist tradition [27].

c. God's 'aseitas' as a point in common

I believe that the issue on which Arius had most in common with Origen is what later scholastic authors would call God's 'aseitas', his 'aseity'. This means that God needs nothing else or nobody else in order to be; he is wholly and unconditionally 'of himself'. The Father is absolutely transcendent; he is 'a-gennêtos', ungenerated. This is sound orthodox doctrine, of course, but the heavier the accent that is put on it, the greater the risk for the idea of the Trinity and for that of God as creator. The backdrop of both Origen and Arius is probably the anti-materialism that pervades so much of the scholarship of theological writers of the first centuries. They seem instinctively averse to any suggestion that God could bring forth something that might be dubbed physical or material, and sometimes they even exclude the possibility that God would bring forth a Son who would assume the flesh. Arius' fundamental idea was that there could not possibly be two 'a-gennêtoi', two ungenerated beings, at the same time. He found some support for this in Origen who described the Son as 'genêtos', as having come into existence [28]. Consequently, both Origen and Arius saw the Son as a 'ktisma', as a creature.

We must not allow ourselves to be led astray by the fact that Origen used the word 'poiein' - to make, for the way God worked. He applied this word 'to the production of everything invisible and spiritual', whereas the term 'plassein' is used for the making of visible and material things [29]. This sufficiently explains that, when Origen describes the Son as 'made', this does not necessarily mean that he has an origin in time. To him the Son, though distinct from the Father, is coeternal with him; "he only calls him a creature because in him God has formed the ideas of future creation and of all creatures" [30]. Therefore, in spite of appearances, Arius considerably distances himself from Origen with his opinion that the Son, however sublime, is part of creation.

Other resemblances between the doctrines of Origen and Arius are mostly of a superficial sort. For instance, both theologians see the Son as subordinated to the Father. To Origen this was a subordination within the godhead, within the Trinity, whereas to Arius the Son was subordinated to God just as all creation was subordinated to him.

d. Arius was not really dependent on Origen

I feel that it is a fruitless effort to determine just how far Arius was dependent on Origen. Certainly not directly. Arius was no epigon of Origen. Indirectly then [31]? Perhaps, but the differences are far greater and far more decisive than the similarities. Arius may be thought of as being tributary to the theological climate of these centuries of which Origen was such a conspicuous exponent and in which he himself was an outspoken radical. It was a climate of opinion in which the Son was dissociated from the Father, God from creation, divinity from humanity, spirit from matter, heaven from earth, all this in a greater or lesser degree. There is a constant tendency towards dualism in this; not every theologian was able to steer wholly clear of it and not to tumble into some pitfall.

4. A catalogue of Arius's theological tenets

It is now time to present a catalogue of Arius's theological tenets [32].
- 1. Glory be to God alone! He is the only one, without beginning and without end. He is absolutely 'a-gennêtos', unbegotten. Since his eternal being is uncreated, he cannot communicate his being to what is created. This would be an ontological impossibility.
- 2. God has not always been Father. If he had been Father from all eternity, that what is created would be equally eternal, which is impossible.
- 3. God made the Son out of non-existence, ex nihilo, just like everything else. The difference between the Son and all other creatures is that he was made before time existed, while all the rest was made within time.
- 4. The Son is out of God, from God, but only because he is made by God. In no way the Son participates in God's being, since he is a creature with a beginning [33].
- 5. We are only justified in calling the Son Logos and Wisdom, if we are prepared to understand these terms correctly. We should not speak of the Logos as the Prologue of the Fourth Gospel does. Compared with the Father as Logos and Wisdom, these terms, when applied to the Son, can only be used improperly and metaphorically. The consequence is that there are two Logoi and two Wisdoms, of an entirely different order.
- 6. If the Son would have essentially shared the nature of the Father, there would have been two Gods. This would have run counter to Arius's strict

monotheism. The consequence is that the Son is essentially and existentially different from the Father. As Logos he is alien to the divine being.

- 7. The knowledge the Son has of the Father is only imperfect; it is as relative as that of ordinary human beings. The Son does not even perfectly know himself. In principle he is also not perfect in the moral sense. As a creature he is changeable which means that he could have sinned. But God destined him for the good and made him sinless and incapable of sinning.

- 8. All this does not say that the Son is just such an ordinary human being as the present author and his readers. Although the Son is not God, he stands in a very special relationship to him, not by his own merits, but by grace and adoption. All that is has been created through him; he is God's instrument for creating us.

- 9. All that the Gospels say about the Son and his Incarnation must be considered valid. But Arius denies that the Logos, incarnated as Jesus Christ, had a human soul. The fact that he showed human affections - that he was sad, hungry, angry - proves that he was not perfect, although he strove to become so.

- 10. Finally, Arius's position regarding the Trinity. He does not flatly deny it. There is some sort of Trinity, consisting of the unbegotten Father, the created Son, and the Spirit, probably created by the Son and subordinated to him.

5. Arius's theological position and its consequences

To the modern reader such disputes may seem an infantile pastime. But whichever side those orientals took, they all realized that what was at stake was a thing of the utmost importance for the Christian Church of their days. But what they did not realize was that it was also important for the development of Christian doctrine in times to come, and perhaps most of all for the direction that western culture and thought would take.

a. Was there an Arian 'theo-logy'?

Arius stated categorically that God is 'arrhêtos' = ineffable, unutterable, unsayable [34]. This is not false doctrine, if it means that human terms, words, and metaphors all fall short when it comes to 'defining' God. He is altogether too great to be 'defined'. In Christian mysticism there is a trend that is called 'apophatic'; it contends that, leaving all sorts of theological determinations behind us, we should approach God 'in silence'. Nevertheless, a mystic like Dionysius the Areopagite (Pseudo-Dionysius) said that two terms may be applied to God in an absolutely valid way, namely Being and good : God is, and he is good. So in this line of thought he is not wholly ineffable. And Saint Bonaventura added that, while the terms Being and good are properly predicated of God, they are improperly predicated of creatures.

But bishop Athanasius who quoted this line with the 'arrhêtos' literally from Arius, categorized it under his 'blasphemies'. He did this because, in the opinion of his opponent, absolutely nothing can be ascertained of God, and certainly not that he is the creator of all that exists. This leads Hanson to speak of 'a reduced God'. This is not really the appropriate term : God in Arian doctrine is not reduced by any means, but, instead, incomparably great, having 'no equal, none like him, none of equal glory' [35]. Let us rather say that the Arian godhead situates himself at an immeasurable distance from creation. In view of this we are justified in asking whether Arian's doctrine should be called a 'theo-logy', a discourse about God. If God is beyond all human expression, how then can we speak about him?

b. Gnostic influences?

Karin Armstrong asserts that "by the fourth century Christians shared the Gnostic view of the world as inherently fragile, separated from God by a vast chasm" [36]. This statement is, in the form in which she puts it, not wholly correct. If it were true, there would have been no Christianity but only Gnosis - which is far from being the case. What distinguished Christians from Gnostics is precisely the idea that God cares for the world and mankind, of which the whole Bible testifies. Armstrong admits this to a certain extent by writing that "somehow Christ had enabled them to cross the gulf that separated God from humanity" [37], although I take exception to that 'somehow'. Her conclusion is that (for Christians of the fourth century) "either Christ, the Word, belonged to the divine realm (which was now the domain of God alone) or he belonged to the fragile created order" [38].

But it is exactly the gist of the Logos-doctrine, as begun in the Prologue of the Fourth Gospel and fully developed by Origen, that Christ belonged to both worlds : "And the Word (Logos) was made flesh (sarx)" [39]. By stating that the Son is not 'consubstantial' (homoousios, of one being) with the Father, Arius is clearly militating against orthodox doctrine.

If Armstrong means that the Gnosis was exercizing a strong pull at early Christianity, she is surely right. Judaism, or perhaps judaizing [40], was pulling at it from the right, while the Gnosis, or rather gnosticizing, did the same from the left; Origen is a case in point, as we saw. One of the hallmarks of the Gnosis is exactly that it pushes the Father, or whatever the supreme being is called in Gnostic parlance, away from creation, so far even that he has nothing to do with it. To account for the existence of the material world most Gnostic systems need a subordinate being, more often than not evil-intentioned, the Demiurge, who becomes the maker of the cosmos.

In Arian doctrine we do not find such a Demiurge, but here too the Father leaves the work of creation to an intermediate person, in this case the Son. At the bottom of this there is that same 'horror materiae' that bedevils so much of early Christian theology, the consequence of which being that God has to remain innocent of everything that may be called 'matter'.

c. Arian philosophy

It may be considered that the so-called 'Arian controversy' was not of a theological but, instead, of a philosophical nature. The Hellenic and Hellenistic worldviews admit of no creation and no Creator. How everything had come into being remained shrouded in mystery. Even the gods, even the Olympian gods and goddesses, had a beginning and were consequently part of the temporal order. In the Greek worldview there was no generally accepted principle of unity. We see the earliest Hellenic thinkers wrestling with the problem of the 'archê', each of them presenting a different solution [41]. To the Greek mind the cosmos was fundamentally multiple and multifarious. But since all mankind needs coherence and stability, the Greeks stuck to the notion of the polis as being the unifying and organizing element in their collective and personal lives.

This was totally different in Judaism. There all that is started with the Creator God who is essentially one. He is the uniquely unifying element of a world in which everything and everyone depends on him. Just as this notion was alien to the Greek mind, it was an equally foreign idea that the cosmos would have been created 'out of nothing', ex nihilo; for the Greeks from 'nothing' could only come nothing. With the advent of Christianity the idea of a creation out of nothing was sprung on the Hellenistic world [42]. A unifying principle was superimposed on a multifarious world, a God who was not part of creation himself and who was essentially one. As such he stood in contrast to the vast and multiple Greek pantheon.

This Christian notion went a long way to solve the problem of the One and the Many [43], for this is the question that forms the backdrop of the Arian controversy. The Christian notion explained to the pagans "the ultimate unity that lay behind the visible universe and the incalculable variety that exists in the world as we know it" [44]. Arius seems to have feared that the idea of a Trinity in the godhead would make God once again multiple. Perhaps he dreaded that pagans, who still abounded in the Egyptian capital, would have concluded that they were not far wrong with their polytheism.

The dogma of the Trinity presents a great mystery, that of three divine persons who are numerically different but, nevertheless, essentially and ontologically (and not metaphorically) one. It is not suprising that it was sometimes concluded that, after all, there were three gods. Arius may have thought that for this reason pagans would not deem it necessary to become Christians, or that converted pagans might slide back into idolatry. "The Monad existed", wrote Arius, "the Dyad did not exist before it attained existence" [45]. This rather cryptic communication can only signify that God is both essentially and numerically one (a Monad); a Dyad (of the Father and the Son), let alone a Triad (of Father, Son, and Holy Ghost) is not natural to the godhead. In this way Arius attempted to avoid the introduction of the notion of multiplicity into the godhead. In the apex of all existence there is only the One; the Many is of a lower and subordinate order.

Arius had to accept the consequence that in his doctrine the Son was not divine, at least not as divine as the Father [46]. True enough, his Logos was not commonly human either, since Christ had no human soul, but he was not eternal and he was subject to change. In his eagerness to make the Son into more than an ordinary human being, he seems to have tried to have his cake and eat it. For his Son is a curiously hybrid being, neither God nor really man, not as in Christian doctrine perfectly God and perfectly man, the God-man. Arius solved "the difficulty of the One and the Many by proposing a theory of one Supreme Being (the Father) and two inferior deities (the Son and the Holy Ghost - F.)" [47]. Although he referred to Origen for support (and in Origen the Son was subordinate to the Father indeed), he actually chose the opposite way by neglecting Origen's opinion that the Son was eternally generated.

Orthodox thinkers had already exerted themselves to close the gap between God and the world, the chasm that was unbridgeably wide in the Gnosis. Their solution was the Logos-doctrine. Arius did quite the reverse; he was widening the gap again. It is true that he did not say that God remained entirely foreign to creation, but he is not far from this radical conclusion, and later followers were quite ready to draw it for themselves. Arius "protested against any Christological formula that would bring the divine essence into contact with the human suffering incumbent upon bearing a body" [48]. The idea that a divine Logos could have suffered and died was blasphemy to Arius; in his view it was impossible that the incorporeal God could have suffered in a human body [49]. This spells the return of the dualism of God and the world, of God and matter, and, finally, also of God and man. His theory puts the very idea of salvation into jeopardy.

6. The Arian doctrine of the Trinity

a. Arius's 'Triad'

Only a quick glance is necessary to see that Arianism deviates in almost every respect from orthodoxy. In Arian doctrine the godhead is not a Trinity, certainly not in the orthodox sense of the term. We saw already that the Son is a creature, not equal with but subordinate to the Father, while the Spirit in his turn is subordinate to the Son. "Their substances are unmixed with each other, one (namely that of the Father) infinitely more estimable in glory than the other. The essences of the Father and the Son and the Holy Spirit are separate in nature, and are estranged, unconnected, alien, and without participation in each other ... They are utterly dissimilar from each other with respect to both essences (of the Father and the Son) ..." [50].

This leaves no room for misunderstandings! Arius crowns his statement by not speaking of a Trinity but of a 'Triad'. Since he uses dualistic terms to denote the relations within it - 'estranged, unconnected, alien, without participation, utterly dissimilar' -, we may well ask how much of a Triad this actually is.

b. The consequences of Arius's abolishing of the Trinity

The great question that remains is, why did Arius take this destructive and dualistic position with regard to the Trinity? Above I have already presented some elements of an answer, but there is more to it than I said there. The scholars Gregg and Groh formulate it in this way. "It was in order to protect the singularity, the monarchy of God ... This portrait of Christ (i.e. of him as not divine - F.) insured an uncompromised monotheism in which the Son did not vie with the Father for prominence and ruled out the possibility of two 'First Principles', two eternal and unbegotten beings" [51]. Earlier I stated that the age-old question of the One and the Many is involved here. Arius must have felt that these two elements do not go together, that they are separate and even opposed. He was, in fact not speaking of the One and the Many, but of the Monad and the Dyad. The Monad is eternal and unbegotten; the Dyad exists in the temporal order and is made [52].

In Christian orthodoxy, however, the One and the Many, the Monad and the Triad (not the Dyad), belong together in the Trinity, organically, essentially, eternally. God is one, but he is also three in persons. This means that the problem of the endless multiplicity of all that exists, that has been plaguing mankind for so long, is laid to rest. Unicity and multiplicity, the single and the multiple, fuse together in one being; all creation hangs on this. The infinite diversity of created beings and things need not confuse us, for they are bound up with the one unchanging principle of unity.

A graphic expression of this is the institution of marriage in Genesis 2, the crowning event of the creation. It is said there that man and woman, husband and wife, shall become 'one flesh' [53], which means, according to Hebrew parlance, that they will fuse into one existence and that they will share one common life. Later Jesus completed this by saying : "So they are no longer two but one. What therefore God has joined together, let no man put asunder" [54]. What we have here is a triad of God, man, and wife, which is based on and has its raison d'être in the Trinity.

What Arius did by denying the Trinity was tearing apart the existential and essential connection of the One and the Many, of unicity and multiplicity, in the bosom of the godhead. It also meant that mankind lost its bearings to which Christian teaching had learned it to trust. This is already an extremely drastic and far-reaching consequence of Arius's doctrine. There is yet another.

7. The humanity of Jesus in Arian doctrine

a. The accent put on Jesus' human characteristics

It may seem that Arius, by making Jesus less divine and more human than he is in orthodox doctrine, he is bringing him nearer to us. But in spite of the appearance of the contrary, the bond between Jesus Christ and human beings is loosened. Arius portrayed him as 'one of many brothers' [55], but this is the crux exactly. In orthodox Christianity Christ is not only man but also God;

only so can he be effective for mankind. He can do what no mere man could do. In Arian doctrine he is not really different from us. Is he, as an ethical example, more important, more necessary than other teachers of morality, a Pythagoras, a Socrates, a Zoroaster?

Arius is sometimes accused of being disinterested in the Bible, but he in fact assiduously scrutinized the Gospels. However, he did this mainly in a negative way, that is, in the hope of finding texts which proved that Jesus was not divine. The Arians selected and singled out all those texts - and there are a good many of them - that stressed on his humanity. How can, for instance, a person who, like everybody else, is sometimes tired, be divine [56]? Athanasius said that the Arians were looking for the 'anthropina', the human characteristics of Jesus [57].

b. Texts that seem to support Arius's doctrine

Even a few texts may be picked which seem to flatly deny that Jesus was God. A pivotal one in this respect is : "What do you call me good? Nobody is good but God alone" [58]. Does Jesus himself not deny here that he was God? It is, however, an example of what Turner called the 'wooden literalness' of much heterodox exegesis. Arians had no eye for the context. There is one here, as always. A wealthy young man comes to Jesus and asks him : "Good master, what must I do to achieve eternal life?". And then Jesus rebukes him for calling him 'good'.

There can be no doubt that this young man saw in Jesus no more than a human being, albeit an exceptional one, a gifted teacher of wisdom, just as the Arians did. Jesus gauged this but did not retort with the claim that he was God. For a long time he was extremely reticent with this. Instead, he refers him directly to God as though he would say : It is not all about me, about the wise rabbi you prefer to see in me. I only came to reveal the Father to you and to reconcile you with him. This is my mission. If you are unable to see anything else in me but a man, because faith is failing you - and the young man did not have sufficient faith in Jesus to follow him, for he loved his riches better -, than raise your eyes to God.

There are more texts of this tenor. "That day and that hour you speak of (= when heaven and earth shall pass away - F.), they are known to none, not even to the angels in heaven, not even to the Son" [59]. If Jesus were the Son of God, equal to the Father, why then does he not know what the Father knows? When the mother of the sons of Zebedee, John and James, requested of Jesus to make them sit to the right and left of him in his kingdom, he answered : "A place on my right hand or my left is not mine to give; it is for those for whom my Father has destined it" [60]. If Jesus is God, why then is he unable to determine what is to happen in heaven?

Jo. 14:28 : "My Father is greater than I", takes pride of place. If all three divine persons are God in the same measure and equal to one another, how then can the Father be 'greater' than the Son? This text is especially important because it occurs in John, and only there. If one were to take it at face value, as a flat denial of divine Sonship in Jesus' own mouth, it would be wholly at variance with the tenor of the Fourth Gospel; the evident aim of its author is to prove that Jesus is God in the fullest sense of the word. Here the context to which no attention is paid is the whole book. It is not really probable that John would insert a text that says the exact opposite of what he was trying to state. Jesus is here speaking at the Last Supper; he reproaches his disciples for their desire to keep their master with them and not wanting him to go 'to the Father'. They still have to learn that his mission is of a limited duration and that he has to go through suffering and death. On earth, in his human shape, Jesus is self-evidently not as 'great' as the Father; he will only become so through the cross when he has entered his glory and has seated himself 'at the right hand'.

c. A structural problem

The Arians handled scriptural texts in an arbitrary way in order to arrive at a preconceived goal. They "pieced together a picture of the earthly Christ which emphasized the existential and psychological aspects of creaturely existence in the ministry of Jesus" [61]. The upshot of this is that we are here confronted with a 'structural' problem. Handling Scripture in this reductionist, even negativistic way, the Arians did not realize that a number of selected texts do not add up to a structure, that is, to a theological doctrine, for they set out, in opposition to orthodoxy, to find out what is not, instead of what is. This saddled their doctrine with a basic weakness which ultimately made it lose out to orthodoxy.

8. The Arian doctrine of salvation

a. Two divergent views

I feel that it is necessary to go deeper into the question of the place of salvation in Arian doctrine. There are for two reasons for this. First, because orthodox Christianity and Arianism appear to have totally divergent ideas of salvation; secondly, because my contention that Arius put the idea of salvation at risk is flatly contradicted by two scholars, both experts in this field, Robert Gregg and Dennis Groh, in their book 'Early Arianism'. This book carries in its title the words 'A view of salvation' which makes it perfectly clear that, in the opinion of these scholars, salvation was at the core of early Arianism. They "contend that early Arianism is most intelligible when viewed as a scheme of salvation ... At the centre of the Arian soteriology was a redeemer, obedient to his Creator's will, whose life of virtue modelled perfect creaturehood and hence the path of of salvation for all Christians" [62].

b. How can man be saved?

With his thesis that Jesus, whatever else he might be, was not divine, Arius landed himself in very great difficulty. Regarding redemption there were two fundamental options in the days of Arius, that of the Gnosis in which redemption is worked by Knowledge, and that of Christianity in which it is the fruit of Jesus' redemptive and salvific death on the cross.

Were I to describe the Christian creed in the shortest shorthand possible, I would do so in the following terms. Man, made powerless by his innate sinfulness, is reconciled with the Father through the cross of his Son

Jesus Christ in the power of the Holy Spirit. This formula contains the principal tenets of this creed in an nutshell. God is a Trinity, a unity of three persons, Father, Son, and Holy Ghost, numerically different but ontologically one. Man is sinful and oppressed by sin; incapable as he is to free himself, he has to be redeemed. In order to save him, the Father sent his divine Son who became man in the person of Jesus of Nazareth; Jesus Christ effectuated the work of redemption by his death on the cross. Now all men can follow the path of salvation, helped in this by the Holy Ghost.

As Anselm of Canterbury would explain in his 'Cur Deus homo?' eight centuries later, it was necessary and inevitable that the Redeemer of mankind had to be divine. Guilt-ridden humanity, condemned by God, was incapable of freeing itself of its guilt. How could it, since man, a creature, is guilty towards its Creator, towards the One upon whom he is totally dependent? To expiate this guilt somebody was needed who was at once totally innocent and greater than a mere man. This person was the God-man, the divine Son of the Father. If emphasis is laid "upon a more metaphysical view and thought of salvation (i.e. than was the case in Arian doctrine - F.) as the radical change from sin to holiness, from mortality to immortality, from the human to the divine, then Jesus must be perfectly man in order to be completely associated with the whole of our human nature, and then perfectly God to change it into the divine likeness" [63].

In Arian theology this argument lost all its force since there was no longer a divine Son to take the guilt of mankind upon himself. The crucifixion acquired a significance totally different from that in orthodoxy, having now become the ultimate proof of Jesus' submission to the will of his Father and the great result of his continous growth in virtue. How then is mankind to be saved? For Arius did not deny that it had to. That "the Jesus of Scripture had to be a creature ... , a creature totally dependent on the will of his Creator", implied "the closest possible link between Christ and his fellow-creatures" [64]. What is true of the redeemed is true of the Redeemer : they are all changeable beings which signifies that they are improvable, that they can change for the better, Christ no less than others, this in spite of the fact that he could not sin. Gregg and Groh point out that Arius was influenced by the Stoa and its ideal of ethical perfection. Jesus too, changeable as he was, chose resolutely the way of improvement 'along the lines of Stoic advance' (i.e. towards perfection in virtue) [65].

Jesus's growth in virtue had as its final result that he was 'adopted' by God, and this is what all true believers may hope too, that they will also be adopted, for "adoption is common to us and the Son, and this is the salvation for which Christians hope" [66]. In Arian perspective the salvation of Christians is effectuated by following the moral example of Jesus, i.e. along ethical lines. Who succeeds in this will steadily grow in perfection and will finally be 'adopted' in the same way as Jesus. There is, however, a problem involved here. Jesus, who was changeable, could have sinned, if he had chosen to do so. But he did not sin, he never did. "God would have not created him in the first place had he been the kind to rebel. He was created precisely because he was of a kind to be obedient and so become a son" [67].

Now where in this reasoning can the existential link between a Jesus who was sinless, and all other human beings who are sinners be found? If they are to follow Jesus' example and aspire to perfection in order to be 'adopted', Jesus has, so to speak, an unfair advantage. Would it not have suited Arian doctrine far better if he had been a sinner who, by heroic exertions and a life of mortification, had arrived at perfection? It is true that in orthodox doctrine and practice the faithful are invited to follow Jesus' example, but this is made possible for them only by his sacrificial and expiating death on the cross, and through the grace that flows from it.

In Arian doctrine there is a vague resemblance to the Gnosis. In both the Gnosis and Arianism redemption is not worked by the death on the cross, but whereas it is in the Gnosis effectuated by Knowledge, in Arianism it is the fruit of ethical behaviour. Arius's teaching is more 'democratic' than the elitist Gnostic system, because it says that every Christian can choose the path of Jesus. But since there is no ultimate sacrifice of the Son of God, redemption is brought about in Arianism by one's own ethical exertions. What we are concerned with is self-redemption. From an orthodox viewpoint this is a contradiction.

9. Irreconcilable viewpoints

Bellini [68] describes the controversy between bishop Alexander and his parish-priest Arius in the following terms. "For Alexander Christian reality is a mystery which makes man approach life in respectful adoration, without any pretension to comprehend it : man only knows that the life communicated to him is divine and that Christ who is God is the source of it, Christ who is God like his Father and 'the perfect image of the Father'. For Arian, by contrast, Christian reality is a wisdom and a perfect human morality of which Christ is the master and the model : man is capable of knowing this and live it and express it in a satisfying manner". For this reason, this Italian scholar describes the conflict between bishop and presbyter as one between faith and ideology. He concludes his short disquisition on this conflict by stating that here "are opposed 'the man of his time' who sacrifices the faith to current opinions (or who has been made incapable by them to understand the peculiarity of his faith), and the man who, so to speak, is prepared to sacrifice everything in order not to compromise the transcendence of his Christian hope."

It will be evident that the Arian and orthodox standpoints are squarely opposed. Arius was hammering away at the very foundations of the Christian faith and radically severing the bonds that united God with his Son, with creation, and with mankind, just as the bonds that connected Jesus with humanity [69]. As Wand wrote, "it was not only the doctrine of God that was destroyed by such teachings, but the whole Christian scheme of salvation" [70]. No wonder then that the orthodox reacted!

10. The Synod of Alexandria in 320

And react they did! In 320 Arius's bishop Alexander convened a synod of some hundred Egyptian and Libyan bishops [71]. The Acts of this synod are lost [72]. Sozomenos says that Alexander, who was in the chair, vacillated, praising now this side, now the other, probably because he wanted to avoid a schism. Arius was asked to retract, but this he refused. He then was excommunicated, together with a party of his adherents, consisting of the bishops Secundus of Ptolemais and Theonas of Marmarice, five presbyters and six deacons [73].

It is not wholly clear what happened next. Epiphanius tells us that Arius fled to Palestine and from there travelled on to Nicomedia, the capital of Bithynia and in that period an imperial residence [74], where the bishop, Eusebius, was on his hand. Later, however, we find him in Alexandria, still under the ecclesiastical ban [75].

11. Canvassing for the Arian cause

a. The support of Eusebius of Caesarea

Arius quickly gained support in Egypt and Libya; "whole provinces and towns were grazed quite bare" [76]. Alexander had every reason to feel uncomfortable with the course that events were taking, the more so because Arius was seconded by two influential churchmen, both called Eusebius, the one the historian, the bishop of Caesarea in Palestine, and the other the bishop of Nicomedia. Two letters from the hand of the former have been preserved. Taking up the pen on behalf of Arius, he wrote to Alexander that he (the bishop) was calumniating his presbyter in his letters [77].

In a second letter he addressed Euphration, the bishop of Balanae (on the Syrian coast). In this he repeated his main doctrinal thesis, namely that the Son is not coeternal with the Father and that he is inferior to him; rather cryptically he added that "the Son is God but not the true God" [78]. Did he add this phrase to save appearances? Anyhow, the support of such an influential man as the historian was very valuable for the presbyter - although the issue remains as to how much of an Arian Eusebius really was; perhaps he did not know this himself.

b. The support of Eusebius of Nicomedia

Probably when travelling to Asia Minor, Arius wrote to the second Eusebius, the bishop of Nicomedia. This ecclesiastic has the reputation of being a schemer, which would not have been suprising since he lived almost next door to the imperial residence. Perhaps he was a member of the imperial family himself; he had much influence with Constantia, the sister of Constantine the Great and the wife of his co-emperor Licinius. He had known Arius when they both had sat at the feet of Lucian in Antioch [79].

Writing to his old fellow-student, now risen so high, Arius made short work of the doctrinal tenets of Alexander. He accused him of having condemned in the same breath quite a number of bishops, among them Eusebius of Caesarea and Paulinus of Tyrus, in an attempt to drive him (Arius) into an isolated position. "We are condemned", he concluded, "because we said that the Son has a beginning, but that God is without beginning" [80]. The Nicomedian did not tarry to take his friend's side : "You are thinking well. Pray for all who may feel thus" [81]. In him Arius had won a very influential supporter, one who was at home at the imperial court.

Full of energy, Eusebius of Nicomedia began canvassing for the Arian cause. He strew letters left, right and centre to his colleagues across the Orient and Asia Minor, asking them to come out in favour of Arius and to put pressure on Alexander to rescind his sentence. Exemplary of this is the letter he sent to Paulinus of Tyrus in which he proved himself a convinced Arian, bent on proselytizing [82]. We see here already an Arian party in the making, headed by an ambitious churchman with political instincts and connections.

c. Alexander counter-attacking

But Alexander too held up his end. He is said to have written some seventy letters to fellow-bishops in which he clarified his doctrinal position and warned against Arius and his adherents [83]. However, his attempts proved somewhat counterproductive, because some bishops felt inclined to contest their colleague of Alexandria, most of all Eusebius of Nicomedia. Alexander received some protesting reactions, but also others concurring with his view [84]. A second party, the orthodox, was not slow in organizing itself. The Arian question was quickly becoming a hot item in the Church.

d. Arian propaganda

It is far from improbable that Arius wrote his main doctrinal work, the 'Thalia', during his stay in Nicomedia [85]; as I said already, very little of it remains; so we have no clear idea of its contents. Anyhow, it was written partly in prose partly in poetry, because he hoped in this way to reach the masses.

As the acting head of the Arian party Eusebius of Nicomedia convened a synod in the Bithynian capital the participants of which put themselves firmly behind Arius; they wrote to all the bishops (i.e. in the East) asking them to accept the supporters of Arius as people of the right opinion; they were ready to intercede with Arius's own bishop so that he could establish ecclesiastical communion with the Arians [86]. We know that Eusebius of Caesarea did so indeed [87]. Paulinus of Tyrus did not act but received a letter from his Nicomedian colleague prompting him to do so [88]. This time Paulinus did what he was asked [89].

Probably at the instigation of the Nicomedian bishop, Arius and those who were with him in Bithynia wrote a conciliatory letter to Alexander in which he toned down his opinions as much as possible without becoming unfaithful to himself [90]. Perhaps he did this to facilitate his return to the Egyptian capital, but Alexander did not react.

The party now moved to Palestine where Arius consorted with several bishops, among them Eusebius of Caesarea and Paulinus of Tyrus; they petitioned Alexander to reinstate him as presbyter in the Alexandrian diocese. A number of Palestinian bishops authorized Arius to assemble the faithful as they had done in former days, with all due respect for their bishop [91]. What this really meant is that the Alexandrians, together with their bishop, were invited to join the Arian party.

12. A case of public interest

In our days theological disputes do not lead to a media hype. What people find interesting are the clashes between what they use to call 'the Vatican' and theologians whom they dub 'progressive'. The contents of the dispute leave them cold; usually they have no inkling of what it is about. For this reason, it is extremely hard for the modern mind to grasp what an enormous stir Arius's tenets caused in the Church of the fourth century, among the theologians and the bishops to be sure, but no less among the common run of the faithful. Gregory of Nyssa, referring to the Council of Constantinople in 381, gives us some fascinating vignettes of the heated debates that took place in the streets of the oriental towns, where people, unburdened by theological knowledge, stood discussing the issues with the ardour that people today expend on football results.

I quote this passage in full. "Sailors and travellers were singing versions of popular ditties that proclaimed that the Father alone was true God, inaccessible and unique, but that the Son was neither coeternal nor uncreated since he received life and being from the Father. If you ask for the exchange rate, the man begins to philosophize on the nature of the begotten and the unbegotten. If you want to be informed on the price and the quality of bread, the baker says that the Father is the greater one and the Son subordinated to him; if you say that the bath is excellent, the bath-attendant states that the Son is generated from nothing." And he adds that he does not know how to dub this evil : madness or fury [92].

Everybody was interested and everybody took sides. Both parties viewed each other with so much hostility that Theodoretus could speak of a 'war' ('polemos'). Harsh words flew around. There were nasty quarrels everywhere; it sometimes came to blows. Hearing the sermons from both sides, the faithful made themselves the judges of the question, favouring this opinion or the oppposite one. "It was really a tragedy, worthy of sorrow", wrote Theodoretus mournfully; "now no longer external enemies fought the Church, but people of the same race, sharing one roof and table, direct bitter words against one another instead of spears. Although they were members of the same body, they mutually armed themselves against one another" [93]. It is evident that we are confronted with a dualistic situation. This was an occasion of great mirth for the pagans; in their theatres the quarrels of the Christians became an occasion for ridicule and laughter [94].

PART II AN ATTEMPT AT A FINAL DECISION

1. A painful situation

Now that the Arian controversy was in full swing, disturbing the civil peace of the Orient, Licinius, Constantine's co-emperor for the East, saw reason to intervene, He curtly forbade the bishops of both sides to convene synods [95]; this must have been in 322.

The situation was painful and confusing indeed. Bishop Alexander paints a vivid portrait of the state of affairs in his diocese in a lettter to his namesake Alexander who was the bishop either of Constantinople or Thessalonike [96]. 'The Arians", he complains, "are daily stirring up divisions and harassments against us, both troubling the law-courts by the pleas of disorderly females whom they have duped, and also discrediting Christianity by the way in which the younger women among them immodestly frequent every public street ... (They are) both demolishing Christianity publicly and striving to exhibit themselves at the law-courts and to the best of their ability rousing persecutions against us where no persecution was" [97]. The bishop adds that the Arians did much proselytizing and that they met continuously 'in their robbers' dens'. They intrigued with other bishops in order to have themselves readmitted into the communion of the Church. He asked his colleagues not to support them in this, and invited his fellow-bishops in Egypt, Libya, Syria, and other countries to express their adherence to his position in writing.

2. A travelling propagandist

I have identified several bishops as supporters of Arius, but these men were tied to their sees and could not travel around spreading the new notions. One who was free to move about, however, was a certain Asterius; as a sophist he had the habit of wandering. He had so severely damaged his reputation as a Christian by apostatizing during the persecution of Diocletian that he could never become a presbyter. Thus he had no official function in the Church. He belonged to those who had studied with Lucian in Antioch. It is, therefore, possible that he was personally acquainted with both Arius and Eusebius of Nicomedia. In the years between 320 and 325 he published a defence of Arianism called the 'Syntagmation' of which only fragments remain [98].

Hanson says he was a good homilist, one of the best of the fourth century. "He presents us with a pleasing picture of a preacher who is seriously concerned with presenting the Christian faith as he understands it to his people" [99]. Asterius was something of a theologian in his own right. He does not wholly dissociate the Father from creation since he says that he had a pre-existent capacity to produce, just as a physician who has, before he cures, a capacity to heal [100]; this does not imply that the Father actually performed the work of creation. The first one to come into existence, created by God's abundance, was Christ [101]. The Son is not brought forth by the Father as an earthly man brings forth his child, that is, from his own substance [102], but by his will [103]; in other words, the Son has no divine substance.

Asterius advances a curious reason why God did not create himself : "He saw that nature could not endure to experience his unmediated hand" [104]. As Hanson expresses it : "The Father must not be compromised by the Incarnation, as the Son could be" [105]. Therefore, the Father "first makes and creates, himself sole, a sole being, and he calls this Son and Logos so that through this as a mediator the rest could be created" [106]. It is as though God is not allowed to soil his hands with the work of creation.

The Son is not called so because he is the second person of Holy Trinity but "for the sake of those who are made sons", i.e. the human beings [107]. If he is one with his Father, this is not because he has the same substance, but because he is obedient to his Father's will and shares his teaching [108]. His power and wisdom are of a different order than the power and the wisdom of the Father [109], so that the Father and the Son are two different 'hypostases'. But the Son is not fully human either since he is a spiritual being [110]. Christ has the same indefinite status in Asterius' opinion as he has in that of Arius. If Asterius said that Jesus 'became man', "this does not of course imply that Jesus Christ was a complete man" [111]. The great problem, for Asterius as well as for Arius, was that a mere man could never have effectuated the redemption; in consequence, Jesus had to be something more than a mere man. This was the message Asterius spread travelling through the Orient.

His words fell on fertile ground. The end of the persecutions and the acceptance of the Christian creed by the Emperor had led many new converts to the Church. We should not suppose that they had themselves baptized after a thorough study of Christian doctrine. Many of them must have remained somewhat unsure about certain difficult tenets, for instance, the Trinity and the divine-human status of Jesus Christ. There were so many opinions about such points, defended by erudite and eloquent scholars, so it must have been hard to know which way to decide. A Christ who was, as a spiritual being, somewhat greater than human, rather than a God-man, a redeemer who redeemed along the ethical way rather than through the cross, will have appealed to hellenized people more strongly than the orthodox point of view.

3. The Council of Antioch, 325

In the meantime Licinius had disappeared from the scene. He had fallen out with Constantine; a war between Emperor and co-emperor followed, and Licinius was defeated in 324. In the course of the ensuing events he lost his life a year later. Constantine was now the sole boss, and the Arian controversy fell to his lot. He had a residence in the East and had obviously heard enough of the quarrel to conclude that it was a matter 'of futile relevance'. At the end of 324 he sent a letter, probably from Nicomedia, to the main contestants, ordering them to come to a reconciliation [112] which was easier said than done. But for the Emperor ecclesiastical unity was a precondition for political harmony.

By now Constantine had appointed a personal counsellor for ecclesiastical affairs, bishop Ossius of Cordoba. He sent this man on a fact-finding tour to Egypt, with the letter I mentioned [113]. Of course Ossius failed dismally in his attempt to establish peace and harmony in Alexandria [114]. It will have become clear to him, and through him to the Emperor, that it was more than a question of quarrelling clerics. Travelling back to Nicomedia, he arrived in Antioch where the episcopal see happened to be vacant. More than fifty bishops, even from as far away as Arabia and Cappadocia, convened there early in 325. This Council of Antioch nominated a radical anti-Arian, Eustathius of Beroea, to the see of the Syrian capital.

The deliberations resulted in an anti-Arian statement which was accepted by fifty-six of the bishops who attended and rejected by three of them; one of these three was Eusebius of Caesarea. They were promptly excommunicated, but only provisionally, until an all-Church synod could convene [115]. One of the greatest anti-Arian champions, Arius's own bishop Alexander, was not present in Antioch. But as Hanson states, "the doctrine promulgated in the Statement (of Belief) is very like his doctrine" [116].

4. The Council of Nicaea

a. The plan for a general council

What Constantine above all needed was peace and quiet in his Empire. He already had enough ecclesiastical problems on his hands, what with the Donatist troubles in North Africa; he was not in need of yet another crisis, this time in the East. He felt that a general council might end the controversy, if only it was really general, and an 'imperial synod', truly 'ecumenical'. But who suggested this idea to the ruler? Was it Ossius, his ecclesiastical adviser [117]? Or was it bishop Alexander [118]? Or could it have come from Silvester I, the bishop of Rome [119]? Or perhaps the Emperor himself woke up one morning with this idea.

b. Why Nicaea was chosen

And why was Nicaea chosen? The fact is that the original choice was not this town but Ancyra (the modern Ankara), but the Emperor had ruled Ancyra out. Why? We do not know. In the Edict of May 23, 325, in which he called the Fathers to Nicaea [120], he said that Ancyra, on the highlands of Anatolia, was too far away for bishops from Italy and Europe. Nicaea was easier to reach.

But valid as this argument was, there may have been unspoken others. Did the Emperor fear that a gathering so far away would escape his control? Or did he fear that the anti-Arian party would dominate the great council as it had done at Antioch? Not that Constantine was an Arian - I suppose that his theological ideas were somewhat hazy -, but with the situation in North Africa before his eyes, he did not want to see the eastern situation whipped up still further. Nicaea was nearer to Nicomedia, the imperial residence. As a special enticement he noted in his decree that Nicaea had 'a fine mixture of air'.

c. How ecumenical was the Council?

Bishops streamed to Nicaea from everywhere. How many there were present shall never be known exactly; ancient authors mention varying numbers. Tradition has fixed it at three hundred and eighteen [121]. Hanson thinks that the number of those present "probably fell between 250 and 300" [122]. Whatever the case, it was the greatest (and most important) synod so far.

How 'ecumenical' was it? Pope Silvester I did not take part in person, but sent two presbyters as his representatives. Few bishops from the western Empire attended. Did they not realize what was at stake? Had the din of the theological battle not yet reached western ears? Going to Nicaea would have meant a journey, easy nowadays - an episcopal charter flight perhaps -, but in those days it would have been long and arduous. North Africa was probably too preoccupied with Donatism to send more than one representative, Caecilianus of Carthage.

Pro-Arian Fathers came marching in, like the two Eusebius's, and also anti-Arians, like Alexander and Eustathius. Arius himself was present too. And not to mention an unknown deacon from Alexandria, not yet a presbyter, under the name of Athanasius. Who also came because his presence was absolutely necessary was the Emperor in person. Strange enough, he, nominally not a Christian, not yet baptized, was the driving force behind it all.

d. No Acta

The Council of Nicaea is one of the two best known synods of ecclesiastical history, the second being that of Trent (1545-1563), with Vaticanum I (1869-1870) as a good third. All the more surprising is it that so little is known of its proceedings. There are no Acta; no official report of discussions was made. We have only the final products, namely twenty canons, and further, of course, the ultimate doctrinal statement, the famous Creed of Nicaea. For more information, although not of an official character, we have to rely on ancient historiographers, Socrates, Sozomenos. Theodoretus, Rufinus, and others still.

It is, however, known where the sessions were held : in the great hall of the imperial palace where seats were ranged on both sides so that every participant could have his own place [123]. This made it possible for the Emperor to keep an eye on the proceedings without having to displace himself.

e. The opening of the Council

Nothing much could be done before the arrival of the Emperor who came in the middle of June. It is the communis opinio that the Council was entirely dominated by Constantine, and that it was he who spurred the Fathers on. But Eusebius of Caesarea who was present in the assembly room, has hardly anything to say of the Emperor's role in his 'Life of Constantine'. However, he does give the speech with which the ruler opened the sessions. It was in Latin, rendered into Greek by an interpreter [124]. In his short speech Constantine did not speak one word of a doctrinal nature. Instead, he said that this unrest in the bosom of the Church seemed to him something much graver than whatever war. He therefore admonished the bishops to restore general peace and concord [125].

f. Not much support for the Arians

We possess no clear picture of the proceedings. If Sozomenos reports that some would stick to the traditional beliefs, while others were not ready to accept the opinion of the ancients without investigating them [126], this is only what might be expected. It soon became evident that the great majority of the Fathers did not support Arius; the minority that defended him was restricted to seventeen or twenty bishops [127]. It is, however, possible that a middle ground was taken by Eusebius of Caesarea and Paulinus of Tyre, for neither of them was a fervent Arian. The Arian party had every freedom to express its opinions [128].

g. A doctrinal formula presented by Eusebius of Caesarea

Eusebius of Caesarea tried to rescue for the Arian party what could be saved. He proposed a doctrinal formula the preamble of which spoke of the faith received 'from our predecessors at our baptism, the faith we, as bishops, still have and confess'. Obviously there was nothing new under the sun. The statement then said that "we believe in one God and that everything comes from God". This looks innocuously orthodox but it provided a loophole for the Arians. For if everything is created by God, then the Logos too is a creature. If this was a trap, the majority did not step into it. They held that the Son is not a creature but is from the substance of the Father and is truly God [129].

h. The statement of Eusebius of Nicomedia

The other Eusebius, the bishop of Nicomedia, also presented a doctrinal letter which was read to the Council [130]. In this letter he gave as his opinion that, if the Son would be really uncreated, he would be 'homoousios' = of one substance with the Father [131] which, in his view, was perfectly impossible. Ambrose says that the use of this famous Greek term 'homoousios' brought about the Fathers to insert it into their final document.

When this, what Theodoretus calls, 'blasphemous document' (namely Eusebius' letter) was read to the assembly, it caused an enormous tumult. In the shortest possible time the Fathers demolished it, covering it with scorn. The incriminated letter was torn into pieces in front of all. This seems to have been a turning-point in the deliberations, for Theodoretus writes that many Arians were so intimidated by the uproar that they swung over to the opposite side, in fear of being excommunicated [132]. Sozomenos remarks that during these discussions the Alexandrian deacon Athanasius increasingly began to profile himself as the spokesman of the anti-Arian party [133].

Meanwhile, the Emperor sat there and patiently listened how the bishops hurled invectives at each other's heads [134]; the question is how much he understood of the rapidly and angrily spoken Greek, abounding with theological terms. Anyhow, at a certain moment he ordered that the mutual invectives should cease and that the libels which were circulating should be burned [135].

j. The attitude of Eusebius of Caesarea

One of those who repeatedly changed sides was bishop Eusebius of Caesarea. If we may believe what he wrote himself, he presented a credal statement of impeccable orthodoxy to the Council. In this he called the Lord Jesus Christ 'the Logos of God, God from God, Light from Light, Life from Life, first-born of all creation, begotten from the Father before all ages", etc. etc. Exception might be made at that 'first-born of all creation' which has a slightly Arian ring to it. He hastened to assure his readers - he was writing to those at home - that the Emperor himself was the first to acknowledge the theological correctness of his statement [136]. Perhaps he may be pardoned for stretching the limits of bare truth somewhat, for he felt he had compromised himself. His stark leanings towards Arianism were commonly known; at the Synod of Antioch, a few months earlier, he had been provisionally excommunicated. He did not want to share the fate of Tertullian, an author as famous as he himself, to wander about without a spiritual home for the rest of his life. So he did what he could to escape the definitive excommunication [137].

k. The Creed of Nicaea

How little we may know of the actual goings-on at Nicaea, all the more famous became its concluding document, the Symbolum Nicaeanum, the Creed of Nicaea [138]. It is still recited or sung in all Roman Catholic churches every Sunday as an integral part of the Mass. The texts on the Father and the Holy Ghost are short and crisp, but that on the Son is elaborated and extensive. It repeats sevenfold that the Son is God like the Father : 'begotten as the only-begotten of the Father, of the substance of the Father, God of God, Light of Light, true God of true God, begotten not made, consubstantial with the Father". The statement is almost obsessively repetitive because it was the Fathers' intention to hammer in that one great truth that the Son was God just as much as the Father. It was concluded with a formal condemnation of the Arians. "With regard to those who say, there was a time that the Son was not, because he had not yet been brought forth, or that he was made from nothing, or with regard to those who say of the Son of God that he is from another hypostasis or substance, or a creature, or changeable or mutable, they are anathemized by the Church" [139].

l. The statement generally signed

"Thus for the first time the official teaching of the whole Church was set forth in an authorized formula, and that formula was regarded as primarily a test creed for bishops" [140]. With only two exceptions all the Fathers rallied to this formula, even die-hards such as Eusebius of Nicomedia; whether they did so whole-heartedly may be doubted. The two recusants were the bishops Secundus of Ptolemais and Theonas of Marmarike, both Libyans, and among the earliest supporters of Arius. These two incurred the threatened excommunication. Philostorgius reports that Secundus left the assembly room vehemently accusing Eusebius of Nicomedia who obviously was a traitor to the cause to him; he reproached him for his cowardice and prophesied that he would follow him into exile within a year [141].

5. The aftermath of Nicaea

a. Banishments

Secundus was banished from his see by the Emperor, to be followed by, as predicted indeed, Eusebius of Nicomedia [142]. It did not help Eusebius that he had adhered to the final document, since the ruler suspected him of remaining in contact with the Arian party; he therefore had to depart into exile, to Gaul, so it seems [143]. Several Arian presbyters were banished along with them. And what about Arius himself? He had been present at the Council, at the express command of the Emperor, it is said [144], but not as a participant, being neither a bishop nor playing a conspicuous role. He too had to exchange his comfortable existence in the Egyptian capital for a place of exile in Illyria and was forbidden to reenter Alexandria [145]. Alexandrians who possessed his writings were impelled to hand these over so that they might be burned [146]. The next year Constantine decreed that the privileges the Christian religion enjoyed should be accorded only to the orthodox, with the exclusion of the Arians, that is [147].

b. The Emperor relents

The victory of orthodoxy seemed complete. Arianism had been trodden underfoot; Arius himself and his most influential supporters vegetated in inhospitable corners of the Empire. But after some years had passed the stern Emperor began to relent. Eusebius and his likewise banished colleague Theognis composed a letter which they sent to a number of fellow-bishops; this was probably intended as a kind of public statement of their position. They were not heretics at all, they wrote, they did not protest against the verdict of Nicaea. They asked only for a chance to explain themselves, for, as they stated, this opportunity had already been conceded to Arius [148]. It worked : they were allowed to leave their places of exile and could return to their sees; the two bishops who had replaced them had to go [149].

199

Arius himself at the end of 327 wrote a short letter to the Emperor, mainly consisting of a credal statement that was wholly innocuous; he stated that he believed what the Church believed and Scripture taught; no exception could be made at what he said of the Son [150]. On receipt of this letter Constantine invited him to come to his court by public transport in order to be reconciled with the ruler and return to his country [151]. Arius travelled to Constantinople, got his pardon, and returned to Egypt. It is a moot point what happened next. Was there a second, much more restricted Council of Nicaea in 328 or perhaps in Nicomedia, to officially reinstate Eusebius and Theognis and rehabilitate Arius? It is not certain [152].

We have more certainty about what may have been the backdrop to Constantine's unexpected volte-face. The sister of the Emperor, princess Constantia, had in her retinue a cleric who was a convinced Arian. He influenced the princess in favour of Arius, telling her that he had become the victim of bishop Alexander's jealousy, because he was invidious of his presbyter's popularity with his flock. When, in the autumn of 327, Constantia lay on her death-bed, her brother visited her. She asked a favour of him, namely that he would receive the presbyter Arius in audience; she feared that her brother would suffer from it if he went on harassing innocent people. According to Rufinus, it was because of this intervention that the Emperor sought contact with Arius [153]. This story is not improbable, since we indeed need some explanation why the Emperor so suddenly and so easily changed his mind. One who was not so easily taken in was bishop Alexander. He refused to readmit his troublesome presbyter [154].

PART III THEOLOGICAL POSITIONS AND TERMS

1. Athanasius bishop of Alexandria

The precise date of the death of Alexander, that most dogged opponent of Arius so far, is not known, probably 18th April, 328. His successor on the see of Egypt's capital was Athanasius, who was to become the great spokesman of the anti-Arian campaign. This cleric was an Egyptian, perhaps an

Alexandrian, born in all probability in 297 [155]. He received a thorough education with that same combination of classical and biblical studies we also found in Origen. It is far from impossible that Athanasius spent some years in the desert with the godfather of all hermits, Saint Anthony. In the Church of his home town he first became a lector and later the secretary of bishop Alexander. It was during that period that his first books appeared. In the Arian controversy he stuck to the orthodox side from the very outset; in this respect he never hesitated in the slightest. And from the very beginning too he became the target of Arian hatred. As we saw, he was present in Nicaea; Cyrillus of Alexandria mentions 'his subtle mind, of an imcomparable perspicacity' [156].

He was elected bishop on 8th June, 328. As might be expected, loud protests followed immediately. At thirty-one years, he was too young, some said [157]. Moreover, he was only a deacon or only a presbyter - a defect that was soon remedied, of course. Of greater weight was the accusation, made by the Arian party, that his election had been irregular; two authors, Sozomenos and Philostorgius, claim that heavy moral pressure had been exercised in order to get Athanasius chosen [158]. Athanasius himself brings forward a statement by all the bishops of Egypt that he was unanimously chosen, and that his own flock had asked him to be their bishop with one voice [159]. There was thus unpleasantness right from the start, a sure sign that the Arian controversy was far from over.

Assessments of Athanasius' character differ widely. To the historians of the eighteenth and nineteenth centuries he was a great man; even Gibbon, no great friend of the Roman Catholic Church, had praise for him. But scholars of the twentieth century highlighted the darker sides of his nature. He is accused of organizing pogroms, of being the initiator of an ecclesiastical mafia, of stirring up trouble everywhere, and of being a politically ambitious man rather than a theologian. This obviously signifies a fundamental change in the intellectual climate. Could it be that past historians were more ready to give orthodoxy the benefit of the doubt, whereas those of our own century feel more inclined to favour heterodoxy? Which in both cases colours their judgment of Athanasius' character.

We find the same watershed already in Late Antiquity. Philostorgius did not have much good to say of the bishop whom he describes as arrogant, lawless, unscrupulous, and not averse of using violence, even murder. Ammianus Marcellinus, a pagan author, joins in by saying that the bishop did not respect the law, stepped out of his own peculiar (i.e. episcopal and pastoral) sphere, and even resorted to magic [160].

2. Wrangling over the position of Arius

Athanasius was certainly courageous and steadfast. Soon after his inthronisation he received a letter from Eusebius of Nicomedia, asking him, nay, ordering him to readmit Arius and his party to the Alexandrian ecclesiastical community; in case he refused those who brought this letter to him were to threaten him. But the young bishop refused indeed [161], saying that he would have no communion with those who had been condemned by the Council of Nicaea. Eusebius then appealed to Constantine who, in a letter to Athanasius, told him to accept into his flock whoever asked for it; if he did not obey, he would be deposed and exiled. But the bishop sent a letter to the Emperor with which he convinced him that the Church should not hold communion with heretics [162]. It will be evident what was the real issue : readmitting Arius and his party as ordinary faithful would signify not only their personal rehabilitation but also that of their doctrine.

3. The theological stance of Eusebius of Caesarea

It will be evident that there was now a war on the fronts of which were becoming clearly delineated. If Athanasius was the leader of the anti-Arian army, Eusebius of Caesarea became the commander-in-chief of the opposite side, at least as long as that other Eusebius, the bishop of Nicomedia, did not take over. I have already quoted the letter Eusebius wrote from Nicaea to his flock at home in which he interpreted the outcome of the Nicaean discussions rather freely; Athanasius later said that he explained it as he saw fit [163].

Eusebius began his letter [164] with the credal statement he himself had presented to the Council. From this statement the term 'homoousios' = consubstantial (the Son with the Father) is conspicuously absent. He next presented to his faithful the Creed of Nicaea in which that 'homoousios' has pride of place. Since there is a glaring difference between the 'Creed of Caesarea' and the authoritative credal statment, Eusebius felt he had to explain something. The Nicaean term 'of one substance or being with the Father' meant solely that the Son came from the Father, not that he shared the essence with him. He had only accepted the term 'consubstantial' for the sake of peace; in other words, he had withheld his assent in foro interno. "Homoousios' signified that the Son was similar to the Father in every respect. The term 'born, not made' said that the Son is not entirely similar to all other human creatures, but that he is of a better substance (than humans) [165].

No wonder that Eustathius of Antioch accused Eusebius of adulterating the Creed of Nicaea! It is impossible to say whether the Caesarean bishop was simply dishonest in presenting the case in this way, or that he naively believed that there was no real difference between his opinion and the Creed of Nicaea. But even to a non-theological mind it must be clear what he was doing, namely, widening the distance between the Father and the Son by suggesting that the Son was more of a creature than Nicaea had intended to say. Eusebius riposted the reproach of Eusthathius by accusing his fellow-bishop of Sabellianism, that is, of holding that God is numerically one, with no essential difference between the Father and the Son [166].

Socrates, the historian, summarizes very precisely what was at stake. "Those who rejected that word (homoousios) felt that the others in this way introduced the opinion of Sabellius and Montanus, and treated them as impious people, because they denied the existence of the Son of God; by contrast, those who stuck to that 'homoousios' thought that the others would introduce the plurality of gods of which they had as great an aversion as though the others would reestablish paganism". And so the positions were taken, and warfare went on in what Socrates calls a 'night-battle', since "neither side sufficiently understood why they were calumniating one another"
[167]

A famous Dutch football coach, Rinus Michels (of the Ajax team), once coined the lapidary phrase : 'Football is war'. It seems that theology too can be war. For it was not so that 'Nicaea locuta, causa finita'; the verdict of the Council did not make an end of Arianism. Quite the contrary! It flared up again with new vehemence, fuelled, perhaps, by Constantine's leniency.

4. Problems with terms

In favour of the quarrelling Fathers it must be conceded that the Nicene Creed offered some ground for further debate, because it was not a theological treatise by any standard but rather a formal (and short) doctrinal statement. What was exactly meant by 'ousia' = substance? What exactly by 'homoousios' = consubstantial? And what exactly by 'hypostasis'? There was what Hanson calls considerable 'semantic confusion', caused by the fact that people "holding different views were using the same words as those who opposed them, but, unawares, giving them different meanings from those applied to them by their opponents" [168]. Add to this that the theological discussion was bedeviled by questions of a personal or juridical nature and by ecclesiastical politics. It is evident that the battle over theology was creating casualties, all the more so because the imperial family remained interested.

For instance, were the terms 'hypostasis' (essence) and 'ousia' identical and interchangeable? To the occidentals, including the Egyptians with Athanasius, they were synonyms; yet to most orientals they were not. They were of the opinion that the word 'homoousios', the 'consubstantial' of the Nicene Creed, weakened the idea of a Trinity, because it did not make a clear enough distinction between the Father and the Son. Once again the accusation of Sabellianism, of that notion, mentioned before, that the godhead is both numerically and ontologically one, was present [169]. We shall now see that three theologians, Eustathius, Marcellus, and Athanasius, stood up in defence of orthodoxy. Whether their own orthodoxy was really impeccable remains to be seen.

5. Eustathius of Antioch as a defender of orthodoxy

a. Eustathius and the Council of Nicaea

Eustathius was a Pamphylian, a native of the town of Side, born between 280 and 285 [170]. After having first been bishop of the Syrian town of Beroea, he went on to take up the see of Antioch in 325 [171]. He was present in Nicaea and participated in the discussions. His role there was conspicuous; he presided over plenary sessions [172]. He is quoted as a staunch upholder of the orthodox faith [173], as the first and foremost in the Council [174]. In this important role he acted as a convinced anti-Arian, speaking of his opponents as 'Ariomaniacs' [175]. We shall now see if it is true what Sellers wrote, namely that the bishops of the party to which Eustathius belonged, "while they were not Arians, ... were certainly not Sabellians" [176].

b. Eustathius in a middle position

It is probable that many orientals returned home after the Council somewhat flabbergasted, uneasily pondering the question of whether they had signed something which they originally had no intention of signing. It was the word 'homoousios' that caused the main problem. We see Eustathius battling on two fronts, against the Arian party, to be sure, but also against those whom he suspected of Sabellianism. He took a middle position which required the utmost tact, but tact was not his strongest point. It must be admitted that his position was difficult, because he was one of the few committed anti-Arians in the East. He refused to admit quite a number of aspirants to the clergy whom he suspected of deviating opinions, among them a number who later became bishops themselves [177].

We have already seen that he accused Eusebius of Caesarea of adulterating the Nicene Creed. But Eusebius was not his only enemy, he had many more, Arian or Arianizing bishops, of course. "Having retained possessing of their episcopal seats by the most shameful deception (i.e. by signing the Nicene Creed without fully adhering to it - F.), although they ought rather to have been degraded, they continue, sometimes secretly, sometimes openly, to patronise the condemned doctrines, plotting against the truth with various arguments ... But we do not believe that these atheists can ever thus overcome the Deity" [178]. He was not one to mince his words!

c. The fall of Eustathius

According to Eusebius (no friend of Eustathius) and Sozomenos, the Church of Antioch had split into two from top to bottom as a result of Eustathius' actions. Eusebius even thought that it would have come to blows if the Emperor had not intervened. He sent count Musonianus to Antioch to calm down the troubles. Eustathius was considered to be the main instigator of all that unrest. An episcopal synod was held at Antioch, presumably with Eusebius in the chair, which deposed him [179]. But when did this happen, in 326, 327, 330, or 331? It seems that the first or the second date is the best candidate [180].

On the orders of Musonianus the deposed bishop was arrested and sent to Nicomedia there to appear before the Emperor. But before he could plead his cause, Eusebius arrived with a party of his sympathizers. He informed the ruler that his enemy had been deposed, because he was a tyrant; there was some truth in this accusation [181]. He added, to make completely sure, that Eustathius had been vilifying the Empress-Mother Helena [182]. This spoilt any chance the bishop might have had with the Emperor.

He was not only deposed but also had to go into exile, accompanied by part of his clergy. Several authors state that he was sent to Traianopolis in Thrace (now in ruins) [183], but Theodoretus has it that he was deported to somewhere in Illyricum [184]. Undaunted, he kept up his artillery-fire on his opponents, the Arians and the partisans of Eusebius from his place of exile. He died in exile, probably before 337 [185] and was buried at Philippi in Macedonia [186]. Eustathius had left behind him a deeply divided community, torn apart between pro- and anti-Eustathians; many clergy and faithful did not acknowledge his successor.

But what exactly was the cause of his deposition? If I may venture a guess of my own, Eustathius irritated friend and foe by lashing out left, right and centre with his sharp tongue. A powerful coalition was brought about by his attacks on the Eusebian party which became his undoing [187]. There was no lack of charges against him, though some of them were trumped up [188]. His high-handedness in his dealings with his adversaries was played against him, and then there was a charge of Sabellianism brought forward [189]. On both sides no quarter was given.

d. The charge of Sabellianism

This charge of Sabellianism brings us to the climactic question of Eustathius' theological stance - climactic because it was fundamentally this that ruined him. Authors ancient and modern have joined hands in defence of his impeccable orthodoxy. And indeed, if we peruse the fragments, there seems to be nothing wrong with them. The Son, the Logos, is just as much God to him as the Father. "The divine unity is clearly insisted upon, and at the same time the duality between the Father and the Son is strictly maintained." He rarely speaks of the Holy Ghost, but it should be inferred that he "must have thought correctly of the Trinity" [190]. Socrates rightly concluded that Eustathius confessed God in three persons ('hupostaseis') and the Son as having 'a person and an existence of his own' [191]. So there seems to be absolutely no ground for an accusation of Sabellianism.

Nevertheless, there is some reason for doubt. Hanson points to Eustathius' 'anxiety to protect God from human experiences' [192]. Did the bishop really believe, with the Prologue of the Fourth Gospel, that the Logos became flesh, that is, that he fully assumed a human shape and existence? In other words, did he confess the God-man? Or as Sellers puts it, "does Eustathius posit a true incarnation" [193]? If Paul says that Christ was 'born of a woman' [194], this meant, thought Eustathius, that what was born of Mary was a man; this man was already in Mary's womb united with the Logos [195]. In other words, the divine element was not congenial to Christ but was added to his manhood.

Since Eustathius was averse to think of one who was perfectly God and perfectly man, he had to coin another expression than 'God-man', which he found in 'God-bearing man' [196]. Who was it that was crucified? The God-man? Impossible! We should not 'attribute human experiences to the Divine' [197]. The one who hung on the cross was the man Jesus, not the divine Logos [198]. For Eustathius "the divine in Christ was not the personal Son of God, but merely God in his activity ... All he can teach is a mere conjunction of the divine and the human in the person of Christ, where the two natures are joined together because the human soul (of Christ) always wills what is in harmony with the divine" [199].

So there is in Christ no organic unity or fusion of the divine and the human, but "nothing more than a moral union of the Man with the impersonal Logos which proceeds from the one Divinity" [200]. It will not surprise us that Eustathius did not exactly give the Redemption pride of place in his theology. "All thought of Redemption vanishes. The Man of Christ is but an example of godly life, who has prepared for us the way of heaven" [201].

Can it be that all those ancient and modern authors who praise the orthodoxy of Eustathius so loudly are perhaps being somewhat too rash? Anti-Arian as he doubtless was, he sometimes comes dangerously close to his opponent on such fundamental issues. If Arius uses the term 'Dyad' for the relation of the Father and the Son, Eustathius does the same [202]. Lorenz says that his Christology constantly shows a dualistic trait. The divine and the human do not fit together in Christ. Inwardly his person is Christ and really the Son from the nature of God, but outwardly he is clad with the immaculate Temple of the body [203]. Perhaps Eusebius of Caesarea was not far wrong in his accusation of Sabellianism. Whatever the case, this whole affair shows how hard it was in those days to assume a perfectly orthodox position.

6. Marcellus of Ancyra as a defender of orthodoxy

a. Who was Marcellus?

Another theologian whom Eusebius, rightly or wrongly, accused of Sabellianism, of not carefully distinguishing between the Father and the Son, was Marcellus of Ancyra. He was born around 280; by 314 he had already become the bishop of Ancyra. He must have been a man of prestige since, as we saw, the original idea was to convene the great ecumencial council in his city. He was of course present at Nicaea in 325 where his role as an anti-Arian was conspicuous. When, in the aftermath of the Council, Constantine began to waver, Marcellus stuck to his guns. He steadfastly stood on the side of Athanasius in his refusal to reincorporate Arius into the Alexandrian Church. In every respect Marcellus was a champion of anti-Arianism.

b. Attacks and counter-attacks

Some time after the Council of Nicaea Marcellus composed a book which is lost and of which not even the title is known. All we know of it is that in this book he polemized against the theology of Asterius; it seems that he also charged against the two Eusebius's, against Paulinus of Tyre, all of whom he suspected of Arianism or Semi-Arianism, and, over their heads, against Origen [204]. He obviously mastered the gentle art of making enemies. In this age of theological strife it was never hard to find a devastating accusation. At the Council of Jerusalem it was imputed to him by his opponents that he had fallen into the error of Paul of Samosata. What this error was is graphically expressed by Socrates the historian, namely that Paul had held that Jesus was 'a nude man', a mere man, that is; the assembled bishops ordered him to change his opinion. Shamefacedly, says Socrates, he promised to burn his book [205]. What should we make of this accusation? Since we have only a few fragments of Marcellus' book, we are unable to verify it. But if he really was such a staunch anti-Arian, he can never have said that Jesus was 'a mere man'.

Not mincing his words, Marcellus counter-attacked. Within the great war between Arians and contra-Arians there were many mini-wars. In his 'Opus ad Constantinum Imperatorem' of 336, dedicated and presented by himself to the Emperor, he lashed out against his opponents whom he accused of being followers of the Gnostics Valentinus and Marcion. Of this work one hundred and twenty-eight fragments remain. Probably not knowing what to do with it, Constantine (who was near his death) entrusted it to a synod held in Constantinople in 336. This synod was dominated by adherents of Eusebius of Caesarea. The result may be guessed : when Marcellus refused to retract, he was deposed. If we believe Sozomenos, the reason for his disgrace was that he was alleged to hold that Jesus took his beginning from the Virgin Mary (not from eternity, that is), and that his reign would not be eternal but would have an end [206].

c. Marcellus seeks to be rehabilitated

Probably hoping or supposing that Constantine had a personal pique with him, Marcellus returned to his see after this Emperor's death in 337 [207], but his coming to Ancyra led to tumultuous scenes [208]. He was banished again by Constantine's son and successor Constantius II (337-361) who was 'arianizing' or even an Arian. A second synod of Constantinople condemned him anew; this was in 338 or 339.

Marcellus now hoped to be rehabilitated by the bishop of Rome, Julius I (337-352). He personally went to Rome and found himself there in the company of many other ecclesiastical exiles and refugees, one of these being Athanasius. For a long time he had to await his chance. Then, in 340, he wrote to the Pope in defence of his orthodoxy [209]. Careful reading of this statement may raise the question of whether he was really as orthodox as he maintained.

In his eagerness to avoid the impression that he might be considered a ditheist, he fell into another trap. "If anybody divides the Son, that is the Logos, from almighty God, he must either think that there are two gods, which has been judged foreign to the divine doctrine, or confess that the

Logos is not God, which also appears foreign to the correct faith." But he then went on to state that "the Father's Power, the Son, is undivided and unseparated" [210]. Did Marcellus really see the Father and the Son as ontologically and numerically different? Discussing theological questions in those days was like walking a tight-rope! Marcellus' protestation notwithstanding, Julius convened a synod that acknowledged him as perfectly orthodox. The Pope directed an encyclical to the bishops of the East to notify them of this decision. "Regarding Marcellus, what you (the orientals) wrote about him, we affirm to be false" [211].

PART IV A CHURCH DIVIDED

1. The Council of Serdica

The papal rehabilitation of Marcellus did not imply that he could now regain possession of his see. When a synod was held at Serdica (Sardica, the modern Sofia, the capital of Bulgaria) in 343, he went there. This Synod had an official, an imperial character, since it was convened by the Emperors Constans and Constantius II. The story of this Council proves how deep the rift in the Church was, a rift that was also one between East and West. It was Constans who took the initiative [212], "with the intention of resolving the tension between East and West in the Church". The city of Serdica was "carefully chosen as standing between the Eastern and Western halves of the Roman Empire" [213]. But the high hopes of this Emperor, together with those of Pope Julius, were dashed.

In the autumn of 343 bishops of East and West assembled at Serdica in almost equal proportions, ninety occidentals and eighty orientals. The orientals were conducted by two imperial officials, one of them being count Musonianus. Some of the occidentals had come from far-away dioceses, from Lyons, Treves, Carthage, for instance; their leader was Ossius, who had been the ecclesiastical adviser to Constantine the Great. Pope Julius sent three representatives, two presbyters and a deacon. Constans, accompanied by Athanasius and other deposed bishops, came too.

The convention was doomed from the start. Hanson says, it was 'a débacle rather than a council' [214]. Constans, who feared trouble and unpleasantness, kept the two factions carefully apart, as though they formed two enemy camps. The orientals, who had not wanted to come at all [215], were lodged in the imperial palace and virtually forbidden to consort with the westerners who were housed elsewhere in the town. The orientals began by posing a preliminary condition. The non-Arian bishops who had been ejected from their sees - Athanasius and Marcellus, for instance - were not to take part. It was inconceivable that the westerners would be ready to accept this. Attempts by Ossius to reach a compromise misfired, and the orientals left Serdica. The Council had not even begun.

The easterners retired to Philippopolis and from there sent an encyclical around [216]. In this document they accused the others of disturbing the peace in the Church for the sake of Athanasius and Marcellus. The dualistic character of the fray is finely expressed in the following phrase of the letter [217]. "Whatever the oriental bishops have decided emphatically in a council is scratched open by the western bishops; equally, what has been decided by the bishops from the West is dismissed by the orientals." By way of conclusion the bishops gathered at Philippopolis excommunicated Pope Julius, Ossius, Marcellus, Athanasius, and several others [218].

To this encyclical a credal statement was added [219]. By means of this document the assembled bishops intended "to reject Arian doctrine equally with Sabellianism ... Their profession of faith cannot possibly be described as Arian. But neither it is intended to be a supplement to N(icaea). It is the production of men who were searching for a substitute for N(icaea)" [220]. Since this war was fought with words rather than spears, the bishops who had remained at Serdica did not stay behind; they produced no less than eight documents. Two of these were letters to Pope Julius and the Emperor Constantius. The most important is an encyclical letter to all Churches (in East and West), because this contained a credal statement [221]. There was no lack of such professions in those days! It rejected the main tenets of Arianism, but it seems that its authors put this and Origenism in the same boat which confused matters. Needless to say that the Serdicans rehabilitated

Athanasius and Marcellus and exommunicated the leading Eusebians. The net result of the Council of Serdica was a situation that came very close to a schism.

Even the spectre of civil war was not far off. When the returning Eusebians passed through Adrianople, they were molested by opponents; it rained blows on them. They complained to the Emperor who had ten laymen put to death [222] - the first fatal victims in the whole controversy. Another was Lucius, the bishop of Adrianople, who sided with the Athanasians; bound with chains round his neck and his hands, he was sent into exile where he soon died. Also banished were two oriental bishops, a Palestinian and an Arabian, who in Serdica had joined the western side [223]. The fronts had to remain clearly delineated!

2. The case of the bare prostitute

A highly unedifying episode took place in 344 at Antioch; it not only demonstrated how great the hatred was but also how deeply some were prepared to stoop. At Easter of that year two occidental bishops, Vincentius of Capua and Euphrates of Cologne, arrived in the Syrian capital on a peace mission; they came as deputies of the Council of Serdica and were provided with letters of recommendation by the Emperor Constans. In Antioch the worthy bishop Stephanus set a trap for them. During the night he introduced a prostitute, completely naked, into the sleeping-room of Euphrates, 'and this in the most holy Easter days', added the indignant Athanasius. The idea was that, when the bishop made approaches, she would begin to scream as the offended party and alarm the servants. But the design was discovered and the attempt misfired. It cost the bishop of Antioch his episcopal see; the cleric who succeeded him was an Arian [224].

3. The later years of Marcellus

By now the reader will probably have completely forgotten that we were speaking of Marcellus of Ancyra. The Council of Serdica put him in a very dubious position, rehabilitated as he was by the West but rejected, although himself an oriental, by the East. In his person the East-West split becomes apparent. After 343 he still had some thirty years to live (he died around 374), but we hear almost nothing of him henceforward. Athanasius seems to have had his doubts about this somewhat uncertain ally with his 'ambiguous pronouncements' [225]. According to Epiphanius, whenever the name of Marcellus was mentioned to him, Athanasius only responded with a mild smile [226].

4. Changes in the leadership on both sides

In the years after 335 important changes in the leadership on both sides occurred. Arius disappeared from the scene. He had never been reintregated into the ecclesiastical community of Alexandria. In 336 Eusebius of Nicomedia got the Emperor Constantine the Great so far that he accorded another interview to Arius. When interrogated in Constantinople by the Emperor in person, he swore that he stuck to the Catholic faith upon which the ruler said : "If your faith is the true one, you swore well; if not, and you swore nevertheless, God may judge you".

The Eusebians now wanted to bring Arius into a church so that he might receive holy communion there, as a token of his reconciliation with the Church, but Alexander, the bishop of Constantinople, adamantly refused to admit him. With the blessing of Constantine, the Eusebians threatened the bishop either to give in or to be deposed. But he remained steadfast. At the appointed hour, a Saturday evening, Arius proceeded not without ostentation through the town on his way to the ceremony; suddenly seized by a natural necessity, so the report goes, he had to absent himself, and there he suddenly died. Probably he suffered a stroke or a heart attack [227].

Arius's death left Eusebius of Nicomedia the virtual head of the Arian party; that other Eusebius, the bishop of Caesarea and historian, died in 339. The Nicomedian booked another success when he could baptize Constantine on his death-bed, 22nd May, 337. He crowned his career by becoming bishop of Constantinople, late in 338 or early in 339. To achieve this the acting bishop, Paul, the successor of Alexander, had to be sent into exile which Constantius II benevolently did for him [228].

Within a short time four great protagonists in the Arian controversy had left the scene : Arius himself, his bishop Alexander of Alexandria, Eusebius of Caesarea, and Constantine the Great. The Eusebians seemed supreme, with Eusebius of Nicomedia now bishop of the eastern capital and, so to speak, one of the family at the court. He was close to the ruler of the East, Constantius II, who was either an Arian already or arianizing. Two other sons of the deceased ruler shared the West between them, Constantine II and Constans; both were orthodox, which does not necessarily say that they were exemplary Christians.

5. Athanasius, leader of the orthodox, the favourite target of the heterodox

a. A curious coalition

By mentioning the name of Athanasius we are introducing the man who was the main target of Arian fury; the Arians rightly saw in him the great leader of the orthodox party, formidable through his erudition, his eloquence, and his energy. Five times in all he was banished from his see. When he became bishop in 328, he was himself confronted with an alliance of Melitians and Eusebians. Perhaps I should refresh the memory of my readers somewhat. Meletius, bishop of Lycopolis in Egypt, had been very severe on those faithful who had lapsed during the persecution of Diocletian in 303-305. His conflict with the then bishop of Alexandria, Peter, who was more liberal, led to a schism; Meletius and his adherents stood apart from the main Church, but there was no doctrinal issue involved [229]. In his younger years, Arius had been a supporter of Meletius. The Meletians were certainly no Arians and were not involved in the anathemas of Nicaea. The Council permitted him to remain in his city, on the condition that he should not ordain presbyters; he was to have no authority or jurisdiction [230]. But they were and remained an opposition party. Athanasius relates how after the death of bishop Alexander in 328 they began to harass the Alexandrian Church once again. The Meletians opposed the election of Athanasius.

At that moment the Meletians joined hands with the Eusebians. They were strange bedfellows, since the Meletians, although refractory, were theologically orthodox and the Eusebians not. Barnard says that the Meletian schism was "a puritanical, indigenous movement against laxity in the Catholic Church, much as Donatism was in North Africa" [231]. Both parties could use an ally in their quarrel with Athanasius. Eusebius of Nicomedia had a pique with the new bishop, since he had failed to persuade him to readmit Arius into the Alexandrian fold. And, as Newman says, "being bent on the overthrow of the dominant Church, they (the Meletians) made a sacrifice of their own principles" [232]. The new coalition directed a heavy barrage of accusations on Athanasius; they accused him of abuse of power and high-treason, no mean things. Athanasius was called to Nicomedia in order to appear before the Emperor. He duly went there, but succeeded in wholly exonerating himself [233]; he returned home vindicated since the ruler had called him 'a holy man' [234].

b. The mystery of the chopped off hand

The Meletians were not convinced; a new plot was hatched to bring the bishop down. He had, so it was alleged, given an order to kill a Meletian bishop, Arsenius [235]. Athanasius' enemies pretended that they had found a hand of the poor man in the episcopal palace, for use in magical practices; they paraded this chopped off hand everywhere as a proof of the prelate's murderous designs. The affair reached the ears of the Emperor who sent a member of his family to investigate. But agents of Athanasius who, as Martin Tetz writes, had 'an excellently functioning ecclesiastical information service' [236], discovered the man in a monastery in the Thebaid where he was hiding; he did not miss a hand.

Exposed as he was, Arsenius fled to Tyre, but he had Athanasius' men on his heels who found him there and identified him in the presence of Paul, the bishop of the town [237]. At that moment Constantine stood squarely behind Athanasius. John Arcaph, who had become the leader of the Meletians after the death of Meletius, was ordered by the ruler to make his excuses to the bishop which he did, and was summoned to Nicomedia in order to be reprimanded [238].

This was in 332. But soon the wind began to blow from another direction. I have alread mentioned how Arius succeeded in gaining the favour of the Emperor, how the ruler wrote a letter to Athanasius in his usual peremptory tone in which he ordered him to readmit Arius, and how the bishop refused to comply. This was in 333. Dissatisfied with the continual exclusion of Arius, the opposition party convoked a council at Caesarea; Athanasius disregarded a summons to appear there [239]. Perhaps this convention did not even take place. A year later, however, it was reopened at Tyre with sixty bishops and an imperial deputy present; sternly ordered to do so by Constantine, Athanasius appeared.

This was not really a Council but rather a court with 'the Meletians being the accusers, and the Eusebians the judges in the trial' [240]; Athanasius, instead of being an ordinary participant, sat in the dock. The curious thing is that, although the Eusebians disagreed with the bishop in doctrinal matters, the only issue at stake was his conduct. All the old charges were brought against him again, even the murder of Arsenius; the incriminated hand was shown to the convention. But this accusation rebounded like a boomerang, for Arsenius, who meanwhile had made his peace with Athanasius, appeared in the hall in person, with both hands intact.

c. Athanasius banished for the first time

The Eusebians did not give up so easily. A synodal commission was sent to Egypt, under military escort, on the pretext of investigating the charges, but in reality to collect evidence against the accused. Since the commission consisted of his declared enemies, suitable evidence was found. When the commission returned to Tyre in September 335, Athanasius was no longer there; he had gone to Constantinople to seek the help of the Emperor. This was not very prudent, since his departure was taken as a confession of guilt. The Council duly condemned him for misbehaviour, but the charge of murder was dropped; nor was there a word said of doctrinal questions. The assembled bishops wrote to all their colleagues asking them to sever communications with the condemned [241].

On October 30, 335, Athanasius entered Constantinople. The Emperor himself related in a letter to the Council of Tyre how he, riding on his horse through the town, had suddenly met Athanasius, to his immense amazement [242]. What the bishop requested of him during an audience was to convoke another Council at Tyre, more favourably disposed to him, of course. Although the ruler rejected this request, he banished John Arcaph, because this man had been instrumental in the Arsenius affair; the Emperor took this very ill [243].

Perhaps Athanasius might have won the Emperor over, if a new accusation had not been brought forward the source of which was Eusebius who had come to the capital too (at that moment he was still bishop of Nicomedia). It was alleged that Athanasius had impeded the passage of the cornships in the harbour of Alexandria. The Emperor was very sensitive on this point, since shortage of grain might cause riots in the densely populated cities of the West; in his eyes this amounted to high treason. The irascible old man banished the bishop to Treves, on the very outskirts of the Empire. It was the first time Athanasius went into exile, but certainly not the last [244].

Athanasius' disappearance left the field free for his opponents who triumphed in all Egypt; the cleric who was nominated to the see of Alexandria, Pistus, an inconsequential man, was an Arianizer. The banished prelate left the eastern capital on 11th July, 335; travelling via Rome, where he must have stayed some time, he arrived at Treves only on 6th November, 336. Treves was the residence of Constantine II, a son of Constantine the Great; both he and Maximinus, the bishop of the town, showed themselves to be favourable towards the exile, who remained in correspondence with friends and adherents back home.

d. The return of Athanasius

When Constantine the Great had died on 22nd May, 337, all the banished bishops were allowed to regain their sees [245]. Athanasius left Treves armed with a letter of recommendation from Constantine II, now one of the three Emperors [246]. The bishop took his time. He did not choose the shorter sea route but instead travelled home through the Balkans, Asia Minor, Syria, and Palestine. At Viminacium in Bulgaria he met with Constantius II, another co-Emperor, an Arian [247]. Everywhere he replaced Arian bishops by orthodox ones. By the time that he arrived in Constantinople, he found the episcopal see empty, since bishop Alexander had died a short time earlier. The Christian community was divided between an Arian candidate and an orthodox one, Paul, who had the blessing of Alexander, was chosen; Barnes believes that Athanasius was one of the bishops who consecrated him [248]. But when Constantius arrived in the town, he was furious, deposed Paul, and replaced him, as already mentioned, by Eusebius of Nicomedia [249]. Athanasius made his triumphal entry into Alexandria on 23rd November, 337, after an absence of thirty-two months.

6. A war of councils

There was no plain sailing ahead for Athanasius. He had been sent back to his see by Constantine II, who held no jurisdiction over Egypt; this country fell under the sway of Constantius, no great friend of the bishop. The opposition, led by Eusebius, now of Constantinople, was still strong and vociferous. During the winter of 337/338 a synod was held at Antioch - Constantius was then present - that declared the deposition of Athanasius, as ordained by the Council of Tyre, still valid; it repeated that his election in 328 had been irregular and accused him of acts of violence, both old and new (referring to his actions during his journey from Treves to Alexandria).

All such events had their repercussions throughout the whole Empire. The Antiochene Synod sent a letter to the three Emperors reminding them of the fact that Athanasius had been officially deposed. The Fathers also dispatched a presbyter to Pope Julius I in Rome to tell him that he ought not hold communications with Athanasian bishops and least of all with Athanasius himself; they stated that the true bishop of Alexandria was Pistus [250]. Nothing could be more apt to illustrate how deeply the dualistic rift ran through the Church (and the Empire). Julius did not react, but Constantius gave a warning shot across the bows, indicating that he had not forgotten the charge of high-treason [251].

Athanasius reacted to the Council of Antioch by convoking an all-Egyptian council in his town, with more than a hundred bishops present. It cleared Athanasius of all accusations [252]. Deputies were sent to Rome in order to notify Julius of this decision. But the delegation from Antioch was the first to arrive and told the Pope that Pistus was the legitimate bishop of Alexandria. Then the Alexandrian delegation appeared. Obviously in the presence of the other delegation, it told Julius that Pistus was an Arian and that he had been ordained by Secundus, an excommunicated bishop. The Antiochenes were unable to deny these irrefutable facts. Julius could do nothing else than conclude that Pistus's election as a bishop had been invalid [253]. Attempting to remain as impartial as possible, he convened a synod in which both Athanasius and Eusebius should be present [254].

It is possible, even probable, that Athanasius travelled to Caesarea in Cappadocia in order to have an audience with Constantius II. It is certain that the bishop spoke with the Emperor on three occasions [255], the first, already mentioned, being the encounter at Viminacium in 337, and the third in Antioch in 346. Barnes presents circumstantial evidence that the second meeting, that at Caesarea, took place in the spring of 338. The Emperor was far too busy with the problems of the eastern frontier to go into the matter deeply, and Athanasius returned to his town unscathed. His condemnation by the Council of Antioch remained without effect. Back home, he enlisted the support of the famous hermit Anthony who really left his desert to come to the noisy capital; in a public sermon he obligingly condemned the Arians [256]. But as Barnes writes, "such a demonstration was needed showed the fragility of his (Athanasius') hold on power" [257].

7. Alexandria made safe for Gregory

The opposition, sensing that Constantius sympathized with it, charged again. A second synod of bishops met in Antioch during the winter months of 338/339. It untiringly repeated the old charges against Athanasius, adding that his return to Alexandria had been unauthorized. Again the result was as might be expected. Athanasius was for the second time declared deposed. Although there was already a substitute for him, namely Pistus, the synod ignored the poor man entirely and nominated a certain Gregory, a Cappadocian with a reputation for learning, as Athanasius' successor; he was not foreign to the Alexandrian scene since he had studied in the Egyptian capital [258].

Since trouble might be expected - not from Pistus who ceased into nothingness, but from the followers of Athanasius -, strong support for Gregory was needed. Constantius played his part by virtually summoning the faithful of the town to accept the newcomer. But a harder hand proved necessary. The arrival of the new bishop was preceded by that of a new imperial prefect who came with a band of soldiers. On 18th March, 339, he made it publicly known that everyone must acknowledge Gregory as their legitimate bishop. His soldiers then marched on the church of Theonas where Athanasius happened to be baptizing; their aim was to arrest him, but he escaped and went into hiding somewhere near the town.

The soldatesca was then let loose on the town. Several churches and baptisteries went up in flames; the legionaries attacked the faihful with cudgels and swords. Virgins in religion were publicly robbed of their garments and molested; monks were trodden underfoot or pelted with discs. Christians were stripped bare and forced to repeat obscene words; others had to blaspheme and even to deny their faith under heavy pressure. Pagan soldiers made mock sacrifices on the altars. The wounded were numerous and there were fatal victims [259].

On 23rd March Gregory himself arrived, but he soon discovered that he was less than welcome. The man must have been a paragon of tact! One day during Lent he entered a church accompanied by the bloody prefect and a number of pagans; when the faithful in the church murmured against this intrusion, Gregory showed who was boss by having twenty-four ladies and gentlemen from high society arrested and whipped [260]. Acting on behalf of the new bishop, the prefect conquered Alexandria manu militari for the sake of Arianism; all churches in the capital were sequestrated and put in the service of the Arians [261]. The worst days of the persecution period seemed to have returned. In the meantime, Athanasius had succeeded in finding a ship that brought him to Rome. His second period of exile had thus begun [262].

8. Athanasius in exile for the second time

In Rome a group of exiles gradually came together, Athanasius and friends, Marcellus and friends, and others. The troubles caused flotsam to drift about. The exiles hoped for action from the side of Pope Julius, but they had to wait for a long time. Important political events intervened. In an attempt to dislodge his brother Constans from the part of the Empire that had been allotted to him, including Italy, Constantine II invaded the valley of the Po but was defeated and killed [263]. Of Constantine the Great's three sons two now remained, Constans (in the West, an orthodox Roman Catholic) and Constantius II (in the East, an Arian).

Already before the events occurring in Alexandria, Julius had written to the Eusebians in the East inviting them to a Council to be held in Rome. This council I mentioned earlier in connection with Marcellus' problems. This proposal did not appeal to the Eusebians; Rome was in enemy territory. Their answer that came only much later is not extant, but Hanson reconstructs it as follows [264]. The Eusebians denied the Pope the right to act as arbitrator between East and West and threatened with a schism if he continued to communicate with Athanasius and Marcellus [265].

When the political situation had quieted down, Julius was able to hold his synod in the beginning of 341. It investigated the conduct of Athanasius and the orthodoxy of Marcellus and acquitted them both. Since this council was manned mainly by western bishops, Julius had to communicate the outcome to the Eusebians in writing [266]. The Roman bishop was highly critical of the way in which Gregory had been parachuted into Alexandria and of how he had behaved there. In his view it was all totally unwarranted. Finally, he claimed that the bishop of Rome had jurisdiction over the sees of Alexandria and Ancyra.

This last argument was perfectly apt to enrage the orientals who loathed any intrusion by the West, including moves by the bishop of Rome. As Hanson states, "the Greek-speaking Eastern and the Latin-speaking Western areas of the Christian Church were now heading for a major rift" [267]. I should say that the dualistic rift was already there; what failed was its official confirmation in the form of an east-west schism. Hanson goes on to say that "the cause of this was not primarily the doctrine of Arius. Theoretically at this point the Arian Controversy had been settled". We have seen that this was far from being the case. According to this scholar [268], the troubles had three chief causes in this stage : the intrigues of Eusebius of Constantinople, the opportunism of Julius of Rome, and the misconduct of Athanasius of Alexandria, with this as the major cause. Does this cholar believe himself? Is it conceivable that clerical rows on the personal level were sufficient to turn the whole Church upside down?

9. New credal statements

Hanson's bold thesis is belied by yet another Council of Antioch, held in 341, which resulted in several doctrinal statements. During the summer months of that year some ninety bishops had assembled in the Syrian capital to celebrate the the dedication of a splendid new church, the 'Dominicum aureum'. The attendants were all orientals which does not necessarily mean that they were Arians to the last man, but there was certainly a powerful Arian minority with such leading authorities as Eusebius of Constantinople, Gregory of Alexandria, and the theologian Asterius. Constantius II too was in town and present in the assembly hall. This Council of Antioch acted as a counter-council to that of Rome. Its practical result was that both Athanasius and Marcellus were and remained condemned.

In their first credal statement the bishops denied in as many words ever having been Arians. They explained this by an argument that was perhaps not wholly ingenuous : "How could we as bishops have followed a presbyter?" [269]. But the statement contained no formal rejection of Arianism. The second formula is far more important [270]. Newman writes that "it is in itself almost unexceptionable, and, had there been no controversies on the subjects contained in it, would have been a satifactory evidence of the orthodoxy of its promulgators ... An evasive condemnation was added of Arian tenets, sufficient as it might be to delude the Latins, who were unskilled in the subtleties of the question" [271].

But there had been controversies. On careful reading it appears that the word 'homoousios' does not figure in this text. Those present in Antioch seem to have tried to have it both ways : reconciling the West with an apparently harmless formula, and going back to a credal statement prior to that of Nicaea, for instance that of Eusebius of Caesarea [272]. Hilary of Poitiers thought that with this formula the Antiochene Fathers protested against those who held that there were not three persons in the Trinity, but only that the Father had three names [273]. This points to the ineradicable suspicion of the orientals that the use of the 'homoousios' in fact meant a denial of the Trinity.

On the initiative of bishop Theophronos of Tyana yet another formula was drawn up. This was less conciliatory since its main object was to condemn Marcellus (along with Sabellius and Paul of Samosata) [274]. This was an attack on Pope Julius who time and again proclaimed the innocence of the bishop of Ancyra. This statement was followed by a fourth one, drawn up somewhat later in a new meeting of bishops; it is called the 'Macrostich' or 'Long-Liner' because of its length [275]. It contains ten long paragraphs [276]. Since it was meant to reconciliate the West, it was not really tactful to repeat Marcellus' condemnation [277]. The Macrostich is certainly not a declaration of Arianism. But once again the terms 'homoousios' and 'ousia' were avoided with which these Fathers once again seemed to be taking their distance from the Nicene Creed. Their aversion to these terms brought the Antiochenes into a quandary, since they did not prove themselves capable of producing another equally useful term which could have satisfied the orthodox.

A delegation of oriental bishops was dispatched to bring the Macrostich to the West; they had the good luck that they could present it to a council that was in session in Milan in 345 [278]. Although they were politely received, they failed in their mission. The Fathers of Milan did not understand why the orientals had produced such a spate of doctrinal formulas. Wasn't the once-and-for-all Nicene Creed sufficient? Did they, the orientals, whole-heartedly back 'Nicaea'? It seemed not. And if they accepted Nicaea as it should be accepted, that is, with the 'consubstantial', with the 'homoousios', why then did they keep Athanasius, the great protagonist of Nicene orthodoxy, away from his see [279]? The western Fathers were unable to overcome their suspicion that the orientals were not entirely honest in professing their good intentions. In order to make sure, the Council asked the delegation members to condemn Arius. This they refused, departing in anger [280].

10. Trouble in Constantinople

In the meantime the Arian party was bereft of its energetic leader. Bishop Eusebius of Constantinople (formerly of Nicomedia) died around the turn of the year 341/342. His death led to a great turbulence in the eastern capital. Two bishops were chosen; the orthodox elected Paul, who had earlier been banished in order to make place for Eusebius, while the Eusebians opted for Macedonius. From this double choice, sighs Socrates, "a tribal war between Christians arose; there were numerous riots in the city, and many perished because of this violence" [281]. When Constantius heard this, he sent his general Hermogenes with orders to expel Paul, but when the man attempted to do this, he met with heavy resistance among the population. The house where he was lodged was set on fire; the general himself was dragged by his feet into the street and killed. Constantius, who could impossibly let this pass, rushed on horseback from Antioch to Constantinople in the middle of the winter, changing horses all the way. On arrival he immediately chased Paul out of the town. To punish the rebellious city he put it on a meagre diet by halving the grain supply. And he put Macedonius on the episcopal see, of course, then returning to Antioch [282].

11. The vicissitudes of Athanasius

To take up the vicissitudes of Athanasius' career again, the bishop remained in Rome for three years, not without lobbying for support in the West. He had a very good friend in Maximinus, the bishop of Treves, and another in Paul, the banished bishop of Constantinople, who had gone to that western city. These two prelates had the ear of the Emperor Constans, who had his residence there. On the basis of their entreaties this ruler invited Athanasius to meet him in Milan. "The western emperor", writes Barnes, "had become the champion of all the eastern bishops who were in exile in the West, convinced that their deposition imperiled Christian orthodoxy" [283]. His attitude certainly imperiled his relation with his non-orthodox brother Constantius II. At the instigation of, among others, Pope Julius, Constans conceived the idea of convoking a great ecumenical council that would once and for all end the disagreement between East and West. When Athanasius came to Milan in 342, the Emperor was already planning this [284]. The banished bishop now had an Emperor on his side.

Constans wrote to his brother in the East several times to convince him of the necessity of an ecumenical council. Constantius reluctantly agreed; he probably did not believe in a favourable outcome; anyhow, he was fully occupied by a war against the Persians. All the same, Serdica was appointed as the place where the Fathers would assemble. Athanasius met Constans again in Treves in July 343 where the Emperor briefed both him and Ossius for the council. After this second interview the two prelates accompanied Constans to Serdica where the proposed council was to take place. It was opened late in the summer of 343 [285].

I have already related that nothing came of Constans's pious intentions; East and West went different ways, figuratively as well as literally. For the East the stumbling-block was the presence of Athanasius and other exiles, who came with the western Emperor. Ossius proposed that he himself, as the chairman of the Council, after having listened to the objections of the orientals, would decide on the fate of Athanasius. But the opposition found him too much a stooge of Constans to entrust him with so delicate a task [286]. After this the orientals withdrew, as we have seen, to Philippopolis. The rump council at Serdica declared Athanasius innocent; the synod at Philippopolis condemned him and asked all the bishops to sever communications with him.

Athanasius, still an exile, returned to the West. He seems to have taken up his residence in Aquileia (the present-day Venice) [287]. Early in 345 he had a third audience there with Constans [288]. It is evident that he could reckon with the unwavering support of this ruler who was intent on bringing him back to his see. Since Alexandria fell under the jurisdiction of Constantius II, and since this ruler was not exactly crazy about the idea of having Athanasius back there, hard-fisted measures were necessary to get him so far : Constans even threatened war against his brother if he did not comply [289]. This is a highly intriguing detail. It not only proves just how fierce the tension generated by the Arian controversy was, but that it could even spill over into imperial politics and dualistically pit East and West against each other in a civil war.

As a result of the pressure exerted by his brother, Constantius wrote to Athanasius from Edessa, permitting him to regain his see [290]. After the receipt of this letter the bishop had a fourth and last interview with his protector in Treves, late in 345. Constantius' decision was facilitated by the fact that bishop Gregory of Alexandria conveniently died on June 26, 345 [291]. He also wrote twice to the population of the Egyptian capital announcing the return of Athanasius [292]. He really had no choice since, as Barnes states, "the normal procedure of an episcopal election in Alexandria would have produced no result other than the reelection of Athanasius" [293]. So he made 'bonne mine au mauvais jeu'.

Athanasius was slow in returning; it was only a year later that he was in Alexandria once again. Perhaps he did not trust Constantius. In the meantime he was with Pope Julius in Rome, another great friend, and later he met with Constantius in Antioch. This encounter was a resounding success for the bishop. All previous measures against him were rescinded; if we may believe Athanasius himself, the Emperor even swore to never again lend his ear to malignant reports about him [294]. From Antioch he took the land route south through Syria and Palestine to Egypt. He was still a hundred miles away from the capital, when an enthusiastic crowd met him to escort him all the way home; on 21nd October, 346, he triumphantly entered Alexandria to regain possession of his see [295]. He had been away for more than seven years.

PART V THE INTERVENTIONS OF CONSTANTIUS II

1. Clouds on the horizon

Perhaps a somewhat superficial and all too optimistic observer may have believed that at that moment the controversy was over. Athanasius, the great anti-Arian champion, was completely rehabilitated and had both Emperors behind him. Of course, there were still Arians and Arianizers, but what could they do now the tables had been turned against them? Our contemporaneous observer might perhaps be forgiven for his superficiality, since there had been an incredible amount of fuss about the bishop's position, which now seemed safe. But what was at stake was not the personal fate of a bishop, however important; the fundamental issue, although it sometimes seemed to recede into the background, was still the doctrinal disagreement.

  For some years indeed Athanasius could act as he wished. Bishops far and wide rallied to him [296]; even declared enemies hoped to enter into communion with him [297]. But then the first cloud appeared on the horizon. Early in 350 Constans was murdered by an ally of the usurper Magnentius. This left Athanasius bereft of his staunchest and most powerful friend. For the time being there arose no danger from the side of Constantius. He wrote a friendly letter to the bishop telling him that he should not believe any rumours (namely, that the Emperor planned to depose him - F.), "for it is our resolve that, in accordance with our wishes, you shall be bishop in your place for all time" [298].

Another prop of Athanasius fell away when Pope Julius I died on April 12, 352; he was succeeded as bishop of Rome by Liberius (352-366) who seems to have been somewhat less favourably disposed towards the bishop of Alexandria. Anyhow, he did not consider the Athanasius file closed. Acting as he said, from a desire for peace in the Church, he invited Athanasius to come to Rome where his case would be heard. In a letter to the oriental bishops (which he wrote in 357) he stated that he had threatened Athanasius with excommunication if he did not come [299]. Barnes, however, is doubtful whether he really had uttered this threat way back in 352 [300].

Threat or no threat, Athanasius did not go to Rome; he probably found that his case had already been heard sufficiently. He responded to the papal invitation with a Council of Alexandria bringing up to eighty bishops together who, as may be guessed, proclaimed his innocence. A report on the proceedings was sent to Rome, and Liberius read it to a council of Italian bishops [301]. The outcome was probably that the Italian bishops were not wholly convinced because they asked Constantius to convoke a larger council [302]. It is here that Constantius comes into the picture again.

After the violent death of Constans the usurper Magnentius hoped to become Emperor of the West, officially recognized by the Emperor of the East, Constantius II. But Constantius waged war on him. In the campaigns of 352 and 353 he drove his enemy from Italy to Gaul. Considering his situation hopeless, Magnentius killed himself at Lyons on August 10, 353, the result being that Constantius II was now the sole ruler of the Empire. And he was an Arian! This new situation made the outlook for Athanasius (and the orthodox party) less rosy still.

2. Constantius under ecclesiastical fire

How much he was feared by the Athanasians appears from the barrage of abuse that was directed against him. Hilary, bishop of Poitiers, writing to Constantius, expressed the opinion that a ruler who did not heed the divine commands was an Antichrist [303]. His later diatribe 'Contra Constantium Imperatorem', written in 360, begins with a clarion-call : "It is time to speak out" [304]. By now he had convinced himself that Constantius really was the Antichrist [305]. With him the times of the great persecutors, of Nero and Decius, had returned [306]. "You are fighting God, you rage against the Church, you persecute the saints, you hate those who preach Christ, you take religion away", and so on, and so forth [307]. "Your tribunes have penetrated into the holy of holies ... and have dragged away the presbyters from their altars" [308]. In short, "you are the enemy of religion" [309].

On what really was at stake bishop Ossius of Cordoba, far gone in years - "I could be your grandfather", he wrote to Constantius [310] - had interesting things to say. "Remember you are a mortal man; fear the day of judgment ... Do not meddle into ecclesiastical affairs, don't send us precepts regarding these, but rather learn such things from us. God gave you the imperium; he entrusted us with the affairs of the Church ... We are not allowed to reign the world; you do not have the power to offer sacrifices" [311]. Ossius is clearly drawing the line : here the Church, there the state.

The reproach made to Constantius is succinctly expressed by Lucifer of Calaris (the modern city of Cagliari in Sardinia) [312] who says that the Arians considered the Emperor an 'episcopus episcoporum', as a kind of temporal Pope [313]. What the moderate Ossius and even the more fierce Hilarius had to say of Constantius is mild in comparison with the abuse Lucifer heaped on him. The vehemence of such authors as Hilarius, Lucifer, and also Athanasius himself with regard to this ruler, may be partly explained, as Girardet says, by the fact that the orthodox were not prepared for an Arian ruler [314]. How great the shock was, provoked by the sudden reversal of fortune, is proved by the invectives Lucifer hurled at him. To the bishop of Calaris Constantius II is hardly better than the bare devil; he is never short of abuse and compares him to everyone who is wrong or criminal in the Bible : Holophernes, Antiochus IV Epiphanes, Herod, Judas, the Sanhedrin, you name them [315]. The worthy bishop was quite sure that he himself would once be in heaven from which vantage point he would see how the Emperor was roasted by the flames of hell [316].

Athanasius did not stay far behind Lucifer in vilifying the Emperor. He deeply resented the ruler's meddling into the affairs of the Church. "If it is a matter of judging bishops, what business has the Emperor with this? ... When did the Emperor have a right to judge the Church, or was his judgment in these matters ever recognized?" [317]. This is still business-like, but occasionally he adopts another tone. He too compares him to Herod and says he is a persecutor of the Church and an enemy of the Christian faith. Constantius kept this bad reputation until in the present time [318].

Both Hanson [319] and Girardet take up Constantius' defence saying that he did not deserve the slurs directed at him by his ecclesiastical opponents. This may be true or not; I am not going into this. For, as I wrote earlier in this series, dualism is, like beauty, in the eye of the beholder. In the opinion, correct or not, of the ecclesiastical spokesmen of those days there was an immense, a dualistic distance between the orthodox Church and the Emperor, and this is the fact with which we have to reckon.

3. Constantius II and the reunification of the Church

After his victory over Magnentius Constantius spent four years in the West, in all those years only once visiting Rome, in 357. He had much work on his hands, especially with the defence of the north-western frontiers against the Alemans, but he saw it as another important task of his to reunify the Church. On the initiative of Pope Liberius he convoked a synod [320]. Liberius would have preferred Aquileia for its sessions, but in fact it assembled at Arles in the Provence, mainly because the Emperor resided there at that time. It is not perfectly clear what Constantius was bent on when convoking a council. Did he want to bring the western bishops into line by making them condemn Athanasius, or did he want more, for instance a doctrinal statement with an Arian slant [321]?

But, as Le Bachelet writes, the occidental Fathers stood so firmly behind the Nicene Creed that there could be no question of dislodging them from their doctrinal position [322]. Not many bishops came to attend; those who took part were mainly orientals, and some from Gaul. The Fathers at Arles were not conspicuous for their courage. There was neither a doctrinal statement nor a condemnation of Arius, but the Emperor succeeded in obtaining a condemnation of Athanasius from them. It is true that they had to be bullied into it : those who refused to sign would be banished [323]. There was only one bishop who refused to sign, Paulinus of Treves, who consequently was sent into exile; he died far from his see [324]. Pope Liberius was deeply ashamed when he heard that one of his own legates had also signed.

Since far more eastern than western Fathers had been present at Arles, Constantius was not satisfied with the little support he had got from the West. In order to get more occidental Fathers on his side, he convoked a Council at Milan that convened in the summer months of 355, with the Emperor present in the town. It is difficult to tell how great the attendance was this time; it was probably not very numerous [325]. This Council too had one overriding aim : to gain general support for the condemnation of Athanasius. All the Fathers present duly concurred, with the exception of two of them, the combative Lucifer of Calaris and bishop Eusebius of Vercellae.

A very telling incident took place during the sessions. Eusebius of Vercellae declared himself ready to sign the condemnation of Athanasius if only the Council was prepared to discuss the doctrinal issue; what he meant with this is that the Fathers would agree with the Nicene Creed. This was a significant move. For the real issue, namely whether or not this Creed would be generally accepted as it stood, was obfuscated by the long drawn-out quarrel over the position of the Alexandrian bishop. 'Back to the basics!', was what Eusebius intended; it had come to his knowledge, he said, that several of the participating bishops were tainted with heresy.

He found a partisan in bishop Dionysius of Nicaea who sat down in order to sign the Creed. But Valens, the bishop of Mursa (now Osijek in East Slavonia, former Yugoslavia) and an outstanding leader of the Arian party at that time, wrenched the pen and the Creed from Dionysius' hands screaming : "It shall not be that anything of this kind happens here!". In other words, Valens did not want to discuss the far wider and more important matter of the acceptance of the Nicene Creed; instead, he desired the issue to be restricted to the smaller question of Athanasius' position. The incident became known in the town and caused unrest.

"Because the judgment of the people was feared", the Council withdrew from the church building where it convened to the imperial palace, under the stricter control of Constantius, of course [326]. Athanasius reports that when it was publicly said that the Emperor went against the 'canon', the rule of the Church, he retorted : "But what I wish, that must be the rule ... So now either give in or you will be exiled" [327]. It does not matter whether the Emperor really said this, which Hanson finds unlikely, or that he 'in effect intended it' [328]; it clearly shows just how strong a grip Constantius really had on the episcopate. The three recusant bishops, Lucifer, Eusebius, and Dionysius, were indeed banished [329]. Athanasius must have felt very lonely, deserted as he was by almost all his fellow-bishops.

4. Athanasius banished for the third time

The Emperor, fortified by what he must have seen as the support of the whole Church, now opened the attack on the bishop of Alexandria. He sent a notarius who busied himself for four months on end to dislodge the bishop, but this was in vain; if the Emperor had the support of the bishops, Athanasius enjoyed that of his faithful. Since this notarius could show no written orders, Athanasius was able to hold out [330]. He left the town in December. An attempt to arrest the bishop during a service in a church had failed. A harder hand was needed.

Syrianus, a Roman general, entered the town in January 356 with a considerable body of troops. This man too brought no written orders with him. Athanasius protested that he was in the possession of a letter from the Emperor of 350 guaranteeing him that he would remain in his see undisturbed. He would only go at the express orders of Constantius. With no such orders having yet arrived, Syrianus, in the night of 8/9th February, encircled the church of Theonas, where Athanasius was at that moment, with five thousand legionaries, as if he were beleaguering an enemy fortress. At midnight the doors were forced open and the soldiery stormed in. Heavy blows were dealt, many were wounded, others trod underfoot; the bowmen shot with arrows at the faithful. The bishop remained sitting on this throne but was spirited away in time by some of the faithful, more dead than living [331]. He found a hiding-place in the town for some days but then he made good his escape. His third period of exile had thus begun. He had been in possession of his see this time for a total of nine years, six months, and nineteen days [332].

5. Constantius II hits at his opponents

Perhaps Athanasius had hoped to regain Rome, but the arrest of Pope Liberius made him change his plans. This arrest dealt another severe blow to the position of the orthodox in general and that of Athanasius in particular, for although Liberius had seemed to vacillate in the beginning of his pontificate, he was now squarely behind the orthodox. Constantius was evidently aiming to get rid of all his ecclesiastical opponents. During the course of the year 355, after the Council of Milan, a certain Eusebius, an imperial official, arrived in Rome. This man told the Roman bishop that he had to condemn Athanasius and restore communication with the Arians. He showed the Pope the presents he had brought, took the bishops's hands, and said : "Obey the Emperor and take this". When Liberius firmly refused, Eusebius left furiously with his gifts [333]. A few days later he returned to the Lateran palace where Liberius lived and had his escort abduct him in the middle of the night. The Pope was conducted to Milan to appear before the Emperor. However surreptitiously this was done, the Roman population got wind of it and tried to prevent the abduction. Eusebius succeeded in his design only 'with great difficulty', as Ammianus Marcellinus writes [334].

As soon as Liberius was brought before Constantius, the ruler took up his favourite theme : Liberius should condemn Athanasius. "You are the only one to support this impious man. You are jeopardizing the peace of the whole world. If you do what I am asking you, I am ready to send you back to Rome. You have three days for deliberating with yourself whether you will sign (i.e. the condemnation) and return to Rome; or else tell me where you will be deported." Liberius answered : "A respite of three days will not make me change my mind. Send me where you want". When the Emperor again interviewed the bishop two days later and saw that he had indeed not changed his mind, he gave orders to deport him to Beroea in Thrace. Later Constantius sent somebody to bring him fifty golden coins to cover his expenses. But Liberius said only : "Go away and take this back to the Emperor". On the third day he departed to his place of exile. I can only advise the reader to read for her- or himself the fascinating literal transcription of the conversations between the head of the state and the head of the Church, as we find them in Theodoretus, much longer than this short excerpt [335]. It reminds me of the interview the Emperor Napoleon I had in June 1812 at Fontainebleau with another abducted Pope, Pius VII.

Constantius II hit at yet another great champion of orthodoxy, Ossius, bishop of Cordoba, formerly the ecclesiastical adviser of Constantine the Great and now an extremely old man, perhaps almost a hundred years of age. In spite of this, the Emperor forced him come to Sirmium and presented him with his obsessive demand : that he too should condemn Athanasius. Although he was kept for a year at Sirmium, Ossius steadfastly refused to do so. However, he signed some sort of Arian formula; Athanasius says he did this because of the blows that rained on him [336]. It seems that Ossius was allowed to return to his see where he died soon after, not without having condemned Arianism in extremis and having warned all faithful against it [337].

The Emperor wanted to make sure of Egypt too, yet another strategic position in this dualistic struggle. This proved a hard nut to crack, for popular resistance was strong in the country of the Nile. He first of all had to bully the pro-Athanasian episcopate into submission. Ninety Egyptian bishops were supporters of Athanasius. Of these, sixteen were sent into exile; a number of others took to their heels. The rest were sufficiently cowed to keep a low profile [338]. But there was also a laity. Important laypeople sent a letter of protest around; it ended with the assertion that Constantius had promised with letters and with oaths that Athanasius would be their bishop and that, in consequence, they must have him back [339]. For four months still the Athanasians remained in undisturbed possession of their churches. But on 10th June, 356, a new prefect, Cataphronicus, and a new general, Heraclius, arrived with more troops. Four days later the orthodox were chased out of their churches which were given to the opposite party [340].

Since the see of Alexandria was empty, the populous diocese needed a new bishop, the fateful Gregory having died some time ago. It lasted a long time, however, before he arrived; he was Georgius, a Cappadocian, like Gregory, but just as illiterate as Gregory had been erudite. He appeared in the Egyptian capital on 24th February, 357 [341]. The new bishop, who was highly impopular, could never have remained in his see without the military support of Sebastianus, the commander of the Roman garrison; this man posted his troops all over Egypt in order to keep the orthodox under and the Arians up. On 29th August, 358, when Sebastianus was not in the country, adherents of Athanasius attacked George in the Church of Dionysius; he could be rescued by the police only with difficulty [342]. Judging his position to be hopeless, George left Alexandria on October 2nd. Nine days later the Athanasians profited again from an absence of Sebastianus to recover all their churches. On Christmas Eve, however, the commander returned and immediately restored the buildings to the Arians [343]. It is evident that they would not have been able to keep their own without official and, above all, military support. George only dared show his face in Alexandria again on 26th November, 361, three years and three months after his flight [344].

But where was Athanasius all that time? In Egypt! Even in Alexandria for some time during the winter of 357/358. For the rest of his exile he found hiding-places with the monks all over the country. Although many people knew where he stayed, nobody betrayed him. The police were at his heels often enough, but he always succeeded in escaping their clutches. Tall stories were told of his adventurous life. All this irritated Constantius II enormously; we know that no love was lost between the Emperor and the bishop whom he called 'a pest' and 'utterly wretched'. In a letter to the Alexandrians he played on the theme that his opponent was allegedly of low descent, someone 'from the lowest depths of society, ... not different from artisans". He was guilty of the most horrible crimes and deserved to be killed [345].

6. The case of Liberius

In Rome the episcopal see was empty after Liberius' departure into exile. But after some time the archdeacon Felix was made bishop, in an irregular manner, according to Athanasius [346]. Felix was supported by part of the clergy but not by the mass of the faithful. When the Emperor visited Rome in 357, he received a deputation of ladies from high society who asked him to give the Church a pastor, for the one they now had was not the right one. Constantius was ready to acquiesce to this request, if only Felix and Liberius would rule the Church conjointly. When this curious demand was read to the public in the circus, some acclaimed it as just, but to others it led to an outburst of hilarity. Almost unanimously the public cried : 'One God, one Christ, one bishop' [347]. In 358 Constantius, sticking to his rule of a common rule of the Church, allowed Liberius to return; he asked the faithful of Rome to not molest Felix any longer. Liberius was received in Rome amidst great rejoicing, 'as a triumpher', writes Jerome [348]. Soon enough Felix's position proved untenable; he, therefore, retired to some other city [349].

The case of Liberius, however, is not as simple as it seems and has given rise to a great deal of controversy. In his place of banishment in the backwoods of Thrace he felt lonely and desolate. Demophilus, the bishop of the town where he lived, Beroea, was a Eusebian. This bishop and Fortunatanus, bishop of Aquileia, a friend of the exile, put pressure to bear on him. Their argument was that he was sacrificing himself neither for the glory of God nor the welfare of the Church but solely for Athanasius, a private person who had been condemned over and over again. So there was really no need for Liberius to make a martyr of himself [350].

Jerome tells us that the exile, vanquished by the tedium of his banishment, subscribed to an heretical proposition [351]. This is known as the 'fall' or the 'capitulation' of Liberius, but it is uncertain what exactly he signed. What is fairly certain is that he subscribed to the deposition of Athanasius. There exist several letters allegedly from the hand of the Roman bishop, but the great question is whether they are actually authentic [352]. In these he stated that he had signed some sort of credal formula [353]. Probably he subscribed to the so-called 'first formula of Sirmium' of 351. It cannot be said that this formula was overtly Arian, but it sinned by omission, that is, by avoiding the term 'homoousios'. This would signify that at that particular moment Liberius did not put himself squarely behind the Nicene Creed. Newman calls this a 'miserable apostasy' [354]. Later Liberius came to regret this. In a letter of 366 to the bishops of Macedonia he declared in as many words that the Creed of Nicaea was and remained 'integral and unshaken'; it contained the perfect truth. This Creed refuted 'all the crowds of the heretics' [355]. All is well that ends well, but to Athanasius the temporary defection of the bishop of Rome was to be yet another heavy blow.

PART VI A NEW AND RADICAL ARIANISM

1. Neo-Arianism

In those days the Arian party came under the leadership of a new champion of Arianism, Aetius [356]. This Aetius was an Antiochene, born around 313 and of humble origin. An early orphan, he seems to have spent his youth as a slave-boy. As an adolescent he became a goldsmith, or a tinker, as others say of him. Whatever the case, he picked up enough knowledge of medicine and philosophy to act as a travelling sophist. In 350 he was ordained a deacon by bishop Leontius of Antioch and given a teaching assignment. In 357 we see him in Alexandria in the wake of bishop George. There he made the acqaintance of Eunomius who became his disciple and his friend. A year later he returned to Antioch after which he had a chequered career. He was banished several times but was rehabilitated by Julian the Apostate and even made a bishop. He died in one of the years 366-370. Only one book of his survives, although he is known to have written more.

His disciple and secretary was Eunomius, a Cappadocian [357]. The date of his birth is unknown; his father was a simple peasant. But his son was intent upon making a career and worked his way upwards. Kopecek says that he "had in common with George (the bishop) and Aetius low birth, an intense devotion to education, and a strong ambition to make his way in the world" [358]. From 358 he collaborated closely with Aetius. After the death of his friend and master he remained the leader of the radical Arian party for thirty years. His career too was chequered. He had been banished and forced to leave Constantinople, but was later pardoned. On the orders of Theodosius I he was again deported. He died in exile in his native Cappadocia, spending his last years polemizing against the Nicene Creed [359]. Jerome says that his admirers valued his writings more than the Gospels [360]. However, very little remains of his numerous books, for the Emperor Arcadius (395-408) ordered them to be burned. In spite of this, we still have three complete treatises together with a number of fragments.

The party headed by Aetius and Eunomius is known by several names, Aetians, Eunomians, or Anomeans. They may be seen as the extreme left flank of Arianism. They would hear nothing of the Nicene 'homoousios', the consubstantial (of the Father with the Son) nor of the 'homoiousios', the similar (the similarity of the Father and the Son). It is therefore that they also are called 'anomeans' (= an-homoios, no similarity of any kind). Their doctrine was the ultimate consequence of that of Arius. Although their teaching does not fundamentally differ from the original one, they are sometimes called 'Neo-Arians' [361].

Both Aetius and Eunomius profess one God who is not engendered and has no beginning; he exists strictly for himself and by himself. It is absolutely and ontologically impossible that he could communicate his own substance to something or somebody else. So there can never be consubstantiality. The Son is created from nothing through the will of the Father. He is, therefore, inferior to the Father but superior to all other creatures because he is the first of them all and the instrument through which they are made [362]. This is common Arian ground, of course; the tone, however, is different, because Aetius and Eunomius constantly refer to Aristotelian categories. As Gregory of Nyssa said, Eunomius converted everything into these categories [363]. In other words, he was turning the faith into philosophy, perhaps in order to make it more palatable to educated pagans. Stressing the 'aseity' of God would be a thing they understood. Of course, the idea of a Trinity and of a Son consubstantial to the Father would be alien to them, but a Son begotten in time would be less hard to comprehend. His strong penchant towards dialectic gave Eunomius the nick-name the 'logic-chopper' [364].

In this new garb Arianism was moving still further away from the depositum fidei and even from the very idea of faith as ordinary faithful understood it. Must one become a skilled dialectician in order to be a believer? Hanson is quite right in stating that Aetius "is not in the least concerned to appeal to the Bible, nor even to mention the name of Jesus Christ. His sole concern is philosophical ... Rationalism is in fact Aetius' outstanding characteristic ... His main purpose is to preserve the correct metaphysics" [365]. Eunomius he characterizes as a 'philosophically eclectic theologian' [366] who, for instance, was not concerned with the Incarnation [367]. "It is the all-prevailing rationalism of Eunomius ... which makes the strongest and last impression on those who read the remains of his work" [368].

It is not wholly certain whether the term 'anhomoios' = unlike, was the watchword of the Neo-Arians. Theodoretus says it was [369]. But Philostorgius reports that when Aetius, in the presence of the Emperor Constantius II, was accused by Basil, the later famous bishop of Caesarea in Cappadocia, but then still a deacon, of applying the term 'anhomoios' to the relationship of the Son with the Father, he vigorously defended himself [370]. The term Aetius preferred was 'heteroousios' = of a different substance. Does this make much of a difference? Whatever term was used, the Son was still thought not to be of the substance of the Father.

The radicalism of the Neo-Arians becomes apparent in their baptizing practice. They not only baptized converted pagans but also Roman Catholics and even Arians of other denominations who were won over by them. Epiphanius says they used another baptismal formula than the biblical one : "I baptize you in the name of the uncreated God and of his created Son and of the sanctifying Spirit procreated by the created Son" [371]. The most radical aspect, however, of Eunonius' teaching, and this especially with regard to the main theme of this work, is its transcendentalism, or perhaps we might also say its essentialism. God is entirely cut off from the work of creation which he leaves to the Son. He no longer is a Providence nor is he a Father. He possesses, as Ritter writes, 'no personality or activity' [372], but becomes a mere abstraction. The dualistic chasm between God and all that is not God - cosmos, creation, humanity - that was already apparent in Arius's original teaching becomes highly conspicuous in the radicalized doctrine of Eunomius. He could not say with Paul "the humanity of our God has appeared to us" [373] which is what the Incarnation signifies.

Kopecek asks the important question of why Aetius (and we may add, also Eumonius) drew 'such a sharp distinction between the fleshless, immortal God of Christianity and its enfleshed, dying Lord'. He sees this as part of Aetius's reaction against Athanasius' rather literal Father-Son language. "We know the Neo-Arians feared this language ... If God should be construed as in any way the literal father of the one who bore flesh and endured bodily death on the cross, one would be forced to admit that God, too, was bodily and, hence, passionate ... Consequently, he (Aetius, and once again Eunomius also - F.) posited a radical distinction between the Ungenerated's fleshless and immortal mode of being and the Generated's mode of being which included incarnation and bodily death" [374]. In this ontological distinction the dualism becomes apparent.

2. Was an intermediate position possible?

The theological situation was becoming ever more confused. We saw how hard it was for an eminent dignitary such as Liberius to follow a straight course. There were the orthodox under the leadership of Athanasius who, although an exile, managed to keep in contact with his party. On the other side there were the Arians with their, so to speak, two denominations, the traditional Arians, the old followers of Arius, and the Neo-Arians, the adherents of Aetius and Eunomius. It will surprise nobody that, in view of the ever more radicalized and dualistic opposition of the orthodox and Neo-Arian doctrines, people were looking for an intermediate solution, a bridge between the two opposed standpoints. If this would have been feasible, there would no longer have been a dualistic opposition. But, as the English columnist Julian Barnes writes [375], "received wisdom states that those who occupy the middle of the road in politics risk getting run down from both directions". Would this be different in theologics?

a. The position of Constantius II

One of those who attempted to steer a middle course was the Emperor Constantius II himself who obviously hoped that it would be possible to reunify the Church. Was there not a compromise formula conceivable that would satisfy both parties? What he did not realize was that such a formula was not only practically but also politically impossible. His theological stance is not wholly transparent, perhaps not to himself either. Was he an convinced Arian? Or an Arianizer? One thing is certain : he was not orthodox as his obsessive persecution of bishop Athanasius proves; he was leaning strongly to the Arian side. But on the other hand, the peace and harmony of the Empire were dear to him. Just as his father Constantine the Great he saw in a unified religion the political cement of the state, and since this unified religion had to be Christianity, it had to be one.

b. The Semi-Arians

Apart from the Emperor, there was also a group of theologians and bishops who judged it possible to occupy an intermediate position. They are called the 'Semi-Arians', an illogical term that defeated itself, for one was either an Arian or one was not [376]. Their key-word was the term 'homoeusios' = alike in substance, in contrast to the 'homoousios' = of the same substance, of Nicaea. Semi-Arians must not be thought of as an homogeneous group, for there were important shades of opinion among them. What united them was their common opposition to the Nicene 'consubstantial' [377].

c. The Semi-Arian doctrine

The leading mind of this group was bishop Basil of Ancyra, for which reason the Semi-Arians are sometimes called 'those around Basil'. Originally a doctor,

Basil became bishop of Ancyra in 336. Twenty-two years later he convened a synod in his city. Although there were only twelve bishops present, all from Asia Minor, it was a mile-stone in the history of Arianism, for it produced a programmatic statement which became the charter of the Semi-Arian party. Its publication meant that the anti-Nicene opposition was now split up into a radical and a moderate wing [378].

The Fathers of Ancyra carefully took their distance from Sabellianism (there is no Trinity) as well as from radical Neo-Arianism. We should not, like the Aetians and Eunomians, speak of the relationship of the (uncreated) Creator and the created, but of that of Father and Son. The Son is like ('homoios') the Father. Whoever (the Eunomians, that is) is not ready to speak of a Father-Son relationship is left, not with a Son, but with something impersonal. The statement does not use the term 'consubstantial', but declares instead that the Son is the image of the substance of the Father - which means that the Semi-Arians did not accept the proposition of the Nicaea, although they did not openly reject it. In some way or other the Son remains subordinate to the Father. It was expressly stated that likeness in substance did not necessarily mean identity of substance.

In Sozemenos we find a highly revealing remark [379]. These oriental bishops, he wrote, could not conceive of consubstantiality as something of a spiritual nature. "They understand the consubstantial as proper to material things, that is, to humans and other living beings, and to trees and plants which all take part in the similar (homoion) and generate from it. But 'like in substance' has its place in incorporeal things and in God and the angels, both of whom are to be understood as separate with regard to their proper substance". We can detect in the Ancyrene statement more than a shade of that 'horror materiae', of that radical distinction of spirit and matter, that was no rare occurence in those centuries. As Hanson states, the 'homoousios' was 'invoking undesirable corporeal ideas' [380].

3. Fruitless attempts at reunification

With this statement in their baggage Basil and two other Ancyrene Fathers travelled all the way to Sirmium to present it to Constantius II [381]. The Emperor realized at once that he had unexpectedly come into contact with an intermediate group, a half-way station between the Athanasians and the Eunomians. Suddenly enraged against the latter, he banished both Aetius and Eunomius to towns in Phrygia [382]. It was then that Liberius was allowed to return to Rome. A synod was held in Sirmium of which not much is known but that in all probability jettisoned the term 'homoousios' [383].

The brutal Basil, who had been instrumental in the banishment of his opponents, had however overplayed his hand. More moderate bishops persuaded the Emperor that he was endangering the peace of the Empire by such severe measures. Never knowing exactly where he stood, the ruler retraced his steps and called back Aetius, Eunomius, and the other exiles. The idea now was to convene a great ecumenical council. Nicomedia was thought of and also Nicaea, but this whole region was hit by an earthquake. Finally, it was decided to hold two synods, one for the occidentals at Arimimium (Rimini) and one for the orientals at Seleucia in Cilicia [384]; obviously the eastern and western worlds were still so far apart that it was judged preferable to not allow them to confront each other directly.

In preparation of this double-faced 'ecumenical' council, a credal statement was framed under the guidance of the Emperor, called the 'Dated Creed', because we know that it was decided upon after intense discussions in the night of 22nd May, 359. It was a carefully worded document couched in terms that might reconcile the opposing parties [385]. Among those who composed it were Basil of Ancyra and George of Alexandria. They had great difficulty in reaching agreement; it was only under the pressure of the Emperor that they came to a conclusion. This boded ill for the future.

The doctrinal text was in almost all respects unexceptionable from an orthodox viewpoint. But then came a remarkable passage. "Since the term 'ousia' (substance, essence) was adopted by the Fathers (the reference is to the Council of Nicaea - F.) without proper reflection and, not being known by the people, causes confusion, because the Scriptures do not contain it, it has been resolved that it should be removed and in the future there should be no mention whatever of 'ousia' in God, since the divine Scriptures nowhere refer to essence (when speaking) about Father and Son. But we declare that the Son is like the Father in all things (homoion kata panta), as the holy Scriptures indeed declare and teach." It was a curious supposition that the Nicene Fathers would have acted unthinkingly! The crux of this statement was, of course, that with the 'ousia' the 'homoousios' too had to go which would make the Nicene Creed invalid. It was a bold attempt to bury it once and for all.

4. The double-faced Council

a. The Council of Rimini

The degree to which this ecumenical Council was an imperial affair is shown by the fact that Flavius Taurus, the prefect of Italy and Africa, was ordered to prepare the western section of it. He offered free transport to all bishops who were willing to come; it must be said that almost all bishops of Gaul did not accept this, because they wanted to keep their hands free. About four hundred Fathers assembled in Rimini in July 359, with perhaps eighty Arians among them [386]. The non-Arian majority were not intent on pleasing the Emperor. When they had heard the Dated Creed read to them, they did not see a formula of compromise in it. Rather the contrary! Why was a new Creed needed to replace the Nicene one? They stuck to this and declared it unchangeable; it had to remain exactly as it was (with the 'homoousios', that is). The doctrine of Arius was all wrong and was condemned [387]. This outcome was a resounding defeat for Arians of all denominations but also for the Emperor himself who saw his hopes for a compromise dashed.

b. 'Rimini' under pressure from the Emperor

But this was not to remain so. A deputation was sent from Rimini to Constantius whom they found on the 10th of October at Nike in Thrace. The ruler was not at all amused by the news from Rimini; not wanting to see his religious policy thwarted, he brought heavy pressure to bear on the delegates. There also arrived a second delegation, a small group of sympathizers with Arianism who had the Emperor's ear. They outwitted the orthodox deputation, for as Sulpicius Severus mournfully states, they were shrewd and very clever [388]. They told Constantius that they were the true defenders of the Catholic faith and they were ready to do as he wanted, namely to make all talk of 'ousia' stop [389].

The orthodox delegates were brought to their knees and subscribed to a doctrinal statement in which the hotly debated term 'ousia' did not figure. The bishops who were still in Ariminium were prohibited to depart by Taurus, acting on the orders of the Emperor who was determined to force the Council come to a conclusion that suited his policy [390]. The bishops became impatient because they wanted to return to their sees before the winter set in. When the non-orthodox delegation came back, they at first refused to have contact with them. But Taurus was just as ruthless as his master; he made them feel who was boss. One after the other the Fathers yielded; about twenty of them made a last stand but finally these too gave in. By the end the non-Nicene formula was unanimously accepted. Sulpicius Severus, an orthodox author, says contemptuously that they succumbed partly from sheer stupidity, partly because they found their prolonged stay so boring [391]. They had indeed been detained in Rimini for seven long months, exposed to the winter weather now and short of everything [392]. A delegation was sent to Constantinople to announce the conciliar decision to the Emperor.

c. The Council of Seleucia

The Council of Seleucia drew one hundred and fifty or sixty bishops; two high imperial officials were also present to keep an eye on the proceedings [393].

The sessions began on 22nd September, 359. The discussions had barely started in earnest or the split became evident. The majority were prepared to accept the Nicene Creed, if only the consubstantial was left out; they favoured the 'homoiousios'. A minority of forty, under the leadership of bishop Acacius of Caesarea, and with George of Alexandria among their number, would have nothing of it. The debates grew heated, the tone often was acrimonious, accusations were hurled around. On the third day, 29th September, the leading imperial official, comes Leonas, convened all the Fathers and read a credal statement to them that was framed by Acacius [394]; it had been adhered to by forty-three Fathers [395]. It avoided all difficulties by simply not speaking of them; it ignored 'homoousios' or 'homoiousios', and also 'anhomoios'; 'homoios' (like) was enough. "We confess that the Son is like the Father." It was a text as bloodless as possible; of course, it satisfied no one.

The next day Acacius was put through his catechism on what exactly his 'like' meant. Well, it meant that the Father and the Son had the same will, that they willed the same, but not that they were similar in substance ('ousia'). The majority protested and the temperature of the debate rose so high that Leonas thought it wise to adjourn the sessions. The Council foundered in the greatest possible confusion. Regular sessions no longer took place. The majority deposed George, Acacius, and many others. Finally the two factions sent each a delegation to Constantinople to inform the Emperor. This Council had been an impressive flop [396].

Hilary offers an interesting insight into how the theological opinions were divided among the oriental bishops; he was knowledgeable since he was personally present. Of those attending the great majority, about a hundred and fifty Fathers, favoured the 'homoiousios' (similar in essence) and about nineteen the 'heteroousios' (dissimilar in essence); only a minority, the Egyptian bishops minus George, were in favour of the 'homoousios' (identical in essence) [397].

d. The Council of Constantinople, 360

The Emperor was extremely irritated by the non-result of Seleucia [398]. He waited until the deputies from Ariminium had arrived and then forced the Seleucians to sign the credal statement to which the Ariminians had submitted [399]. Since he wanted to have it as legal and official as possible, Constantius convoked yet another Council which came together in Constantinople in January 360; seventy-two bishops attended, one of them being a hellenized Goth, the famous Ulfilas (Wulfila), who acquired fame through his translation of the New Testament into Gothic. The driving force in this Council was Acacius; the Emperor pushed him, because he hoped that this bishop would be able to reunite the Church according to his own formula.

The doctrinal text adopted by the Council was almost identical to that of Nike : the term 'ousia' was considered confusing and causing offense and should, therefore, no longer be employed [400]. The Fathers completed their task by going through the Church with a broom; everywhere opponents of Acacius were deposed, among them Basil of Ancyra and Cyril of Jerusalem [401].

5. The situation at the death of Constantius II in 361

This confused episode was brought to a sudden end by the death of Constantius II on November 3, 361 at Mopsukrene in Cilicia. He was succeeded by Julian the Apostate (361-363). It is well-known that this Emperor, although baptized and raised as a Christian, became a pagan as an adolescent. So, for a short while, the series of Christian rulers, whether Arian or orthodox, was interrupted by a non-Christian one.

This is an appropriate moment to stop and see how the land lay. At first sight it may seem that the non-orthodox, the anti-Nicene party, was scoring very well. It had enjoyed the almost overt sympathy and support of Constantius II; their leading opponents, Athanasius first and foremost, had been deposed, banished, and silenced. Everyhwere Arian and Arianizing bishops had been installed. The old Arianism had acquired a new and powerful lease of life in the form of Neo-Arianism.

In a long chapter Kopecek describes how this Neo-Arianism had transformed itself from a party into a sect [402]. At the end of that chapter I find the following conclusion which I shall quote in full. "Much had happened to Neo-Arianism during the period A.D. 360 to A.D. 377. Its founder (Aetius) had died, his second in command (Eunomius) had been put on trial twice (at Constantinople in 360 and at Antioch in 361 - F.) and exiled twice; it (Neo-Arianism) had been attacked by Arian and non-Arian alike. Yet, the Neo-Arians had managed to weather the storm and to consolidate themselves in a theologically and organizationally integral and self-conscious sect. They were even self-confident enough to go on the theological attack themselves. Despite their non-enjoying either continuing imperial favour or the favour of any of the most powerful bishops of the eastern Roman Empire, the Neo-Arians had established themselves as a force in eastern Christianity to be reckoned with" [403].

But on closer inspection we see that a considerable body of faithful had remained orthodox, not only in the West, also in the East. The attentive reader will have remarked that a quite incredible number of synods and councils had been held over the Arian question, gatherings which produced statement after statement and creed after creed, most of them not in accordance with the basic creed, that of Nicaea. It will not have escaped the reader that constant political pressure had been needed to bring these anti-Nicene successes about. But the further we come in time, the more the heterodox party gets fractionized; it became divided into sects, not always on friendly terms with each other, each with its own slogan : homoiousios, homoeusios, anhomoios, with the Emperor all the time pleading for the 'homoion' as the magical unifying formula.

The orthodox had to keep a very low profile; their greatest theologian, Athanasius, was forced to trudge the bylanes of his country for years. But he spent this time writing a number of important theological works which strengthened and clarified the orthodox position. The Athanasian party had the great advantage of being unified. It stuck to the Nicene Creed that, whatever the opposition might say of it, was legally accepted by a truly ecumenical Council; this Creed became and was to remain the official doctrine of the Roman Catholic Church. The pivotal term in it was the 'homoousios', the consubstantial; it had, whatever the opposition might object, unanimously been agreed upon, even by many who later began to combat it. From a political point of view orthodoxy seemed to be at a low ebb. But looking at it from a theological perspective, the future lay before it.

PART VII THE DEMISE OF THE ANTI-NICENE OPPOSITION

1. Julian's religious policy

One of the new Emperor's first measures was to lift the banishment of the bishops living in exile [404]. Hilary returned to Poitiers, Lucifer to Cagliari, and Athanasius to Alexandria to quote only the best known. Why was Julian, no friend of the Christian Church, so accomodating? It has been supposed, for instance by Newman, that he did so in order to foster the discord in the Church. "The object of Julian in recalling the banished bishops, was the renewal of these dissensions, by means of toleration, which Constantius had endeavoured to terminate by force ... (He was) persuaded that Christianity could not withstand the shock of parties, not less discordant and far more zealous than the sects of philosophy" [405]. But this is probably taking a far too Machiavellian view of Julian's religious policy. I do not think that he was really interested in the theological disputes of the Christians which, with all the rest of Christianity, he had left behind him. Together with abolishing all the privileges the Church enjoyed, he put an end to the discriminatory measures taken by his predecessor.

2. The fate of bishop George

When Athanasius took possession of his see again on February 21, 362, he found it empty : George, the man who had usurped his place, had been murdered. He had been a political prelate rather than a pastor; his flock saw him rarely and, when he came, rioted against him. "He depended for his security on Roman spears" [406]. He was not only impopular with the faithful of the town but still more with its pagans, for in so far as he showed any religious zeal, it was in harassing the pagans and attacking their shrines with the assistance of the garrison [407]. This led to his undoing. When it became known in the town that Constantius was dead, a pagan mob dragged George from his home and threw him into a prison. On the day before Christmas 361 they brought the unhappy man onto the street and killed him. His corpse was paraded through the streets on a camel's back [408].

3. Athanasius' theological position

It is important to take now stock of Athanasius' theological stance since he was the greatest champion in the fight against Arianism [409]. He wrote a lot, especially during his periods of exile, but we should not think of him as a systematic theologian. We find his insights scattered over all his works. The heart of his theology was the doctrine of the Incarnation, of the Son of God, the second person of Holy Trinity, having become man. Allow me to quote Le Bachelet. " It is above all from this side that he attacked Arianism, showing that negating the divinity of the Word was at variance with the most intimate sentiments of true Christians; that it raised an insurmountable barrier between God and us, because according to Scripture we know the Father only through the Son; that it annihilated in fact the work of redemption, because no one else was able to renew in us that what was destroyed in us as a consequence of sin, and to make us children of God again" [410]. There was, as I have argued before, dualism in this : the drawing apart of God and man. The Church Father elaborated this theme specifically in his treatise 'On the Incarnation'.

4. The Council of Alexandria in 362

Since it was highly important to end the theological dispute once and for all - it had already lasted more than half a century and had almost turned the

Church upside down -, Athanasius convoked a council in his town that convened in the summer of 362. It was only a small synod with twenty-one bishops taking part; it is called 'the synod of the confessors'. The letter of convocation mentioned four subjects for it : the condemnation of the Arian heresy, the unconditional acceptance of the Nicene Creed, the rejection of the doctrine that the Holy Spirit is a creature and of one being with the Son, and the reiterated condemnation of the heresies of Sabellius, Paul of Samosata, the Gnostics Valentinus and Basilides, and of the Manichaeans [411].

A special problem was that there were so many arianizing bishops. The Council of Alexandria was preoccupied by it. Should harsh measures be taken against them? Some bishops advocated measures of this kind, but under the leadership of Athanasius a more moderate line was followed. Those arianizing bishops who were ready to sign the Nicene Creed were allowed to remain in their sees; only those who had been public defenders of Arianism were reduced to the lay-state (though not excommunicated) [412].

On the doctrinal level Athanasius had some difficulty in keeping the Fathers in one line. Although there were no Arians or Arianizers among them, there were divergent opinions regarding certain aspects of the Incarnation. Not all of them were thoroughly thrashed out; after all, a council is not a theological seminar. Finally Athanasius unified the Fathers on this formula : "The Word has not come into a holy man, as it had come into the prophets, but the Word itself has become flesh" [413].

This Council of Alexandria, small though it was, became the starting-point for a general resurgence of orthodox doctrine. Many, many councils were held in its wake in East and West, and innumerable bishops signed the Nicene Creed. Some differences of expression remained in existence, however, without dividing the Church again. The Latins preferred the term 'personae' for the members of the Trinity; the Greeks were in favour of a more philosophical term, namely 'hypostases' (realities) [414].

252

5. Athanasius banished again

And out he went again! The Emperor Julian, who was busy reestablishing the waning paganism as the leading religion, could do without a competitor who was instrumental in revigorating orthodox Christianity. In his eyes Athanasius was 'an enemy of the gods', of his pagan gods. "The nicest thing I might hear from you", he wrote to the prefect of Egypt, "is that this miserable Athanasius, who during my reign has dared baptize Greek ladies of distinction, is banished from all regions in Egypt" [415]. "I learn that this audacious man ... has returned to what they call the episcopal throne, to the great displeasure of the religious people of Alexandria. Therefore, we communicate to him the order to leave the town" [416]. When the greatly displeased religious people of Alexandria protested against this measure, Julian laid his soul bare by writing that "the impious school of Athanasius ... exercizes a dangerous influence on a great many men of distinction among you" [417].

The bishop left the town to begin his fourth period of exile on October 24, 362 with the words that it was 'only a small cloud that would soon pass away'. Persecuted on the Nile by the river flotilla of the prefect, he succeeded in escaping in a bold and dangerous manoeuvre [418]. He did not leave Egypt, but again sought refuge with the monks of the desert [419]. On 26th June, 363, Julian fell against the Persians; Athanasius himself relates how he heard this news when he was on the verge of perishing with a Nile boat in a spell of rough weather [420]. Jovianus became Emperor and the bishop was back in his town on September 5, 363. The new ruler, with whom he had a meeting in Antioch [421], was favourably disposed towards him; he addressed an exposition of his doctrine to him [422]. But the reign of his protector was of short duration, for he suffered a sudden death in the night of 16/17th February 364.

6. Exiled for the last time

The succeeding ruler, Valens, was an Arian. He renewed the decree of banishment of orthodox bishops issued by Constantius II but revoked by

Julian. Apprehending what was to come, Athanasius left the capital on 5th October, 365, beginning his fifth and last period of exiled. It was just in time, for in the following night the military broke into the church of Saint Denys where he used to pontificate [423]. These occurrences caused an uproar in Alexandria. Valens was so afraid of this - for he knew how rebellious the Alexandrians were - that he gave orders to bother the bishop no longer. Athanasius returned to his town on 1st February, 366. He had still seven years of undisturbed possession of his see before him; having been a bishop for forty-five years, he died on 2nd May, 373 [424].

7. An anti-Arian coalition

While the East had an Arian Emperor for another fifteen years, the West was ruled in the meantime by an orthodox Christian, Valentinianus I. Refusing to meddle in ecclesiastical politics, he left the controversy to disentangle itself. In the West the Arians had never been particularly strong and now they were definitely on the wane there.

In the East the situation was different. In Egypt there was still an Arian party which succeeded in arresting Peter, the successor of Athanasius, in 374 or 375 [425] and in making their own candidate, Lucius, bishop [426]. This Lucius was authorized to banish all who adhered to the Nicene Creed [427] of which facility he made an ample use [428]. In Asia Minor too the orthodox went through hard times; bishops were deposed, for instance, in 395, the famous theologian Gregory, bishop of Nyssa (a no longer existing town), who was replaced by an Arian [429]. The attentive reader will perhaps have remarked that Cappadocia, the heartland of Asia Minor, had been the nursery of Arian theologians; Asterius was a Cappadocian just as Gregory and George of Alexandria, Eudoxius of Constantinople, and last but not least, Eunomius.

It is equally curious that Athanasius' real successors with respect to the defense of orthodox doctrine were also Cappadocians, forming what Le Bachelet calls 'the most efficacious anti-Arian coalition' [430], consisting of the brothers Basil of Caesarea and Gregory of Nyssa (to say nothing of their sister Macrina) and their friend Gregory of Nazianze (an equally no longer existing town). In their bulky tomes as well as in their correspondence with each other they further clarified and elucidated the fundamental issues of the relations within the Trinity and of the Incarnation, defining the necessary theological terms with great precision. They gained an influential ally in the West when the Arian bishop of Milan was succeeded by Ambrose in 374.

8. The last stage

a. Imperial measures in favour of orthodoxy

The last stage of the Arian controversy started when Valens fell in the Battle of Adrianople against the Visigoths on 9th August, 378. Both his successors were orthodox Christians, Gratianus in the West and Theodosius I in the East. By this time the West had already almost unanimously adhered to Nicene orthodoxy. On 27th February, 380, Theodosius issued a decree from Thessalonica that goes by the name of 'Cunctos populos' [431]. It stated that the Nicene Creed was henceforward to be the official doctrine of the Roman Empire as being the faith taught by bishop Damasus I of Rome and bishop Peter of Alexandria. It was the first time that the Roman Empire was declared to have an officially accepted Christian doctrine. This helped the orthodox doctrine to triumph, of course, but whether this was an altogether happy development is another question.

That Theodosius meant business was clearly demonstrated when he took possession of his eastern capital. He was hardly within its walls when he ordered Demophilus, the Arian bishop of the town, to subscribe to the Nicene Creed; if he did not do so, he would have to go. Demophilus went, applying to himself the Gospel word : "If you are persecuted in one town, fly to another" [432]. Lucius also, the Arian bishop of Alexandria, had to cede his see to Peter, who was orthodox [433]. On 10th January, 381, the zealous Emperor issued yet another decree against the Arians [434]. The Arians, in their different denominations, were not allowed to possess any churches, nor were they permitted to hold meetings within the walls of whichever town. Although Arianism was not officially proscribed, this measure came very near to a prohibition. Henceforth, the only good Christians were the orthodox : "He who professes the Nicene faith is to be thought of as the genuine worshipper in the Christian religion". said the decree.

b. A strong pull into the direction of 'Nicaea'

A strong current was pulling into the direction of 'Nicaea', and this not only because of imperial measures. In 378 or 379 a synod was held at Antioch in Caria attended by a great number of Arian and semi-Arian bishops. They did not present a united front. A minority stuck to the 'homoiousios', the similarity of the Son and the Father, and would not hear of the 'homoousios', the consubstantiality of the Father and the Son. But without any political pressure being exerted, the majority adhered to the Nicene Creed [435]. Later some one hundred and fifty oriental bishops, assembled in the Syrian capital Antioch, wholeheartedly accepted the dogmatical prouncements of Pope Damasus which meant that they adhered or returned to the orthodox creed; they made this public by sending a synodal letter to the bishops of the West in which they acknowledged their univocal acceptance of orthodoxy [436]. Arianism was clearly on the wane, and East and West, once so far apart, were approaching each other once again.

In the West the last Arian bishops were deposed during these years. Pope Damasus judged the time had come for drawing the line between orthodoxy on the one hand and all heresies on the other. A Roman synod, under his chairmanship, framed a 'confessio fidei catholicae'; this statement contained twenty-four anathemas, all directed against oriental heresies. It condemned the Arians and the Eunomians, but also the Sabellians and the doctrine of Marcellus of Ancyra, and a lot of heterodox opinions that do not figure in these pages [437].

c. The second Ecumenical Council

The time was ripe to hold a second Ecumenical Council which met in Constantinople from May to July 381 [438]. Its coming together in the imperial capital signified that the Emperor Theodosius I wanted to keep an eye on it. He received the Fathers in this throne-room in the palace, but did not attend the sessions as his predecessors had done; they were not held in the palace either. That the shadow of the ruler fell over the sessions is shown by the fact the later ones were chaired by an imperial official, a certain Nectarius, a catechumen, who had not yet been baptized. The hundred and fifty bishops who were present acted wholly in the line of Pope Damasus : the Nicene Creed was unanimously agreed to, and the condemnations of the Roman confessio fidei were repeated. The precedence of the bishop of Rome was recognized but the bishop of Constantinople was to be the second in the ecclesiastical hierarchy [439].

d. The end of Arianism

After the Council of Constantinople Arianism was moribund. We are informed by Sozomenos [440] that, to use Kopecek's words, "after Eunomius' banishment, ca. A.D. 383, the Neo-Arian movement began to suffer serious internal traumas and, as a consequence, schisms [441] ... The movement even began to split apart over exegetical problems ... Its demise to nothing but a historical curiosity was obviously well on its way by the time of Theodosius' death in A.D. 395" [442]. Imperial decrees helped to dig Arianism's grave. Theodosius who wanted to restore ecclesiastical unity in his Empire put himself squarely behind the decisions of the Ecumenical Council. On 30th July, 381, he decreed that all Christian churches should be handed over to the orthodox [443]; by 19th July, he had already forbidden the heretics to build new churches [444]. On 25th July, 383, he forbade the Arians and Eunomians to propagate their faith [445], followed in 391 by a prohibition on heretical assemblies [446].

The Arians of the West may have put their last hopes on Justina, the widow of Valentinianus I; she governed the West in the name of her infant-son Valentianus II. She was an Arian, combated by Ambrose, the bishop of Milan. After her death, probably in 388, the cause of Arianism in the West was lost. Valentinianus II was an orthodox Christian.

The decisions of the Council of Constantinople, together with the imperial decrees, may be considered the virtual end of Arianism in the Roman Empire. Fifty-six years after the Council of Nicaea the wheel had come full circle. An orthodox creed had been unanimously agreed to in 325 but it had been so vigorously combated from all sides that more than once it had seemed on the way out. All Emperors of the fourth century pursued a policy of ecclesiastical unity, although some of them thought that Arianism should be its expression. Now, in 381 and after, 'Nicaea' had come back into its own, with the support of the then Emperor. Nobody will believe that Arian, Semi-Arian, and Neo-Arian ideology did vanish completely. A great number of Arian sects remained in existence, all very small and fighting each other to their hearts' content.

PART VIII THE AFTERMATH : GERMANIC ARIANISM

There was, however, an aftermath. We know that the imperial armies of the fifth century were to a large extent composed of Germans; among these the Goths were extremely numerous. Now these Goths were Arians. Being indispensable for the defence of the tottering Empire (against other Germans), they had to be cajoled; no problem was made of their heterodoxy.

Mentioning those Arian Goths brings us to the subject of the Arianism of other Germanic tribes. While in the West Arianism had virtually died out during the reign of Valentinianus II, it returned in force with the Germanic invasions. Quite a number of Germanic tribes had been converted to Christianity by zealous missionaries who were, however, Arians. As a consequence, the Visigoths, the Ostrogoths, the Vandals, the Burgundians, the Longobards all became Arians. When they invaded the western Empire and conquered most of it, a new Arian wave swept across Europe and Africa [447]. Famous Germanic kings like Alaric, Euric, Genseric, Gondobald, Theodoric, were Arians. Carried forward by the Vandals, Arianism even penetrated into the Donatist stronghold, the Maghreb. Of course, the new Germanic rulers favoured the cause of Arianism, while some of them actively persecuted orthodox Christians.

Theologically, Germanic Arianism was of no importance whatsoever. The Germans of this historical period produced no theologians or authors - with the exception of course of Bishop Ulfila who was an hellenized Goth, favoured by the eastern Emperors. German Arians thrived on the classical texts of Arianism, adding nothing of their own. Why did most Germanic tribes accept Arianism rather than the orthodox creed? We do not know; we possess no documents that could answer this question. It could be that they found it easier to understand that the Son was inferior and subordinate to the Father, as more in accordance with their own patriarchical ideas, than the absolute equality of the Father and the Son. Or perhaps they found Roman Catholicism too 'Roman' for their taste and Arianism more 'regional', more adapted to their peculiar circumstances. Le Bachelet supposes that it was 'the first great manifestation of the antagonism between the two great races of the West, the Latin and the Germanic' [448]. Maybe the Germanic tribes prided themselves on having a religion of their own, different from that of the Roman master-race.

But Germanic Arianism was without a future. One of the Germanic tribes, that of the Franks, had remained pagan for a long time. At the end of the fifth century they went straight from paganism to orthodox Christianity, skipping the intermediary stage of Arianism. The decisive event was the baptism of their king Clovis at the end of the fifth century [449]. Fate would have it that the Roman Catholic Franks became the new master-race of the West. They conquered the greater part of western Europe, subjecting the other tribes to their rule; their king Charlemagne. crowned by the Pope in 800, became the 'Roman Emperor', the universal ruler of the West. Under Frankish rule Germanic Arianism disappeared everywhere to make place for orthodoxy. For nine centuries long nothing more was heard of Arianism, until it surfaced again, under other names like Socianism, at the time of the Reformation.

NOTES TO CHAPTER VI

1. Williams, Arius 1.
2. Williams, Arius 1.

3. Adolf Wilhelm Ritter s.v. 'Arianismus', TRE 1 (1978), 693.

4. Several modern scholars show themselves averse to using the terms 'Arian' and 'Arianism' at all. Hanson, Search XVII/XVIII, for one, finds the term 'Arian' "scarcely justified to describe the movement of thought in the fourth century that culminated in the Nicene-Constantinopolitan Creed". R.D. Williams, quoted from the Scottish Journal of Theology 45 (1992), 102, by Wiles, Archetypal Heresy 4, goes even further by stating that the term 'Arianism' should preferably be relegated to oblivion; if it should be used, than best between inverted commas. Wiles himself, on p. 6, sees Athanasius, as is the great fashion nowadays, as the evil-doer. "Arius had been excommunicated at the Council of Nicaea. The name 'Arian' carried guilt by association. It was an invaluable polemical tool". And he concludes that the Bishop of Alexandria was 'responsible for creating the concept of Arianism'. Wiles says this in a chapter entitled 'What is Arianism?'. All the same Wiles uses the term 'Arianism' freely and not between inverted commas. D.H. Williams gave a volume of essay edited by him with Barnes the title 'Arianism after Arius', as late as 1993. And where Hanson had ex cathedra declared that the term 'Arian controversy' is a 'misnomer', Kopecek, Neo-Arianism, gives his first chapter the title 'The Early Arian Controversy'. And what else should we do? Speak every time of 'the movement of thought in the fourth century that culminated in the Nicene-Constantinopolitan Creed'? Or disfigure our texts with endless series of inverted commas? In the paragraph belonging to this note I present some caveats with regard to terminology and I hope that these will be kept in mind throughout the rest of this work.

Yet another word with regard to the stance taken by Athanasius towards Arius and his doctrine. In their blind zeal to denounce him as the obsessive vilifier of Arius and Arianism, solely responsible for the bad name he and his doctrine earned, modern scholars overlook the fact that he was not the first to accuse Arius. This was bishop Alexander of Alexandria, the man under whose jurisdiction the Bacaulis parish of which Arius was the parish priest came. Writing 'to all bishops', that is, to the universal Church, he calls Arius and his partisans 'iniquitous men, enemies of Christ', and their teaching 'an apostasy that may be considered ... a forerunner of the Antichrist'. He calls it 'an enormity, a curse'. This encyclical letter was signed not only by Alexander but also by seventeen presbyters and twenty-four deacons from Alexandria and nineteen presbyters and twenty deacons from other parts of Egypt, in Opitz, Urk, I.4b, from Socr., HE 1.6.4. Writing to his colleague and namesake Alexander who was bishop of Thessalonika or Constantinople, Alexander of Alexandria calls Arius and his friends 'evil-intentioned' and 'made furious by the devil who operates in them'. "They have built robbers' dens in which they continuously hold their meetings ... (as) a workshop for combating Christ." Their doctrines are 'ruinous' and their actions 'bad'. "Their diabolical activities should be condemned to the flames." At the end of this long letter Alexander mentions that he had received many letters of approval from his colleagues and that many of them had signed 'the document', Opitz, Urk. I.14, from Theodoret., HE 1.4. It is not clear whether this document was the encyclical letter quoted before or another statement. What is evident is that Alexander organized a movement of protest against Arius that involved the whole Church. When Athanasius began to polemize against Arius, he found the ground prepared. It should moreover not be ignored in silence that almost all church historians of this period were inimical to Arius and his school : Epiphanius, Socrates, Sozomenos, Theodoretus, the one and only exception being Philostorgius. The influential Eusebius of Caesarea who supported Arius at first, let him fall coolly when the presbyter was condemned by the Council of Nicaea in 325.

5. Epiph., Pan. 69.1.

6. X. Le Bachelet s.v. 'Arianisme', Dict.Théol.Cath. 1.2, 1779 (Paris, 1923).

7. Letter of Arius to Eusebius whom he calls 'truly a fellow-disciple' (of Lucian), Epiph., Pan. 69.6. With this 'fellow-disciple' is probably meant that Arius, together with Eusebius, studied with Lucian in Nicomedia, Epiph., Pan. 69.5. We have for this connection only one word to go by, the 'sulloukianista' in Epiph. It is unclear whether Arius was Lucian's fellow-student or his disciple. However, he had been studying in Antioch or Nicomedia in the time that Lucian was there, see Williams, Arius 31. There has been much speculation on the question whether Arius was influenced by the teachings of Lucian. The problem is that we know virtually nothing of Lucian's doctrine. Gustave Bardy wrote extensively of him in his 'Recherches sur Saint Lucien d'Antioche et son école' (1926); we find a shorter exposition by Bardy's hand in the Dict.Théol.Cath. 9.1 (Paris, 1926), 1024-1031, in which he admits that very little is known of Lucian's doctrine. It is not even wholly certain whether Lucian the teacher and Lucian the martyr are one and the same; some scholars doubt this, one of them being Bardy. See for this point Hanson (who assumes the identity), Search 81/82. Newman, Arians 7, said that there was 'a doctrinal connexion between him and the Arian party', although he did not specify this. He also points to the historical connection : "In his school are found, in matter of fact, the names of most of the original advocates of Arianism, and all those who were most influential in their respective Churches throughout the East: Arius himself, Eusebius of Nicomedia, Leontius, Eudoxius, Asterius, and others".

8. Several scholars, see Williams, Arius 263, note 82, are convinced that the Arius of Meletius and Arius the heretic are one and the same person, but Williams himself, Arius 36-40, argues to the contrary, concluding that "the Meletian Arius, so beloved of several modern scholars, appears to melt away under close investigation". The nevertheless remarkable circumstance that there were two troublesome churchmen with the same name in Alexandria in the same period, is explained away by the communication that Arius was quite a common name. Hanson too, Search 5, finds that the identification "rests on rather frail evidence".

9. Sozom., HE 1.15.
10. Theodoret., HE 1 (726).
11. Theodoret., HE 1.1.9.
12. Epiph., Pan. 69.3.
13. In a letter of Constantine the Great, quoted by Hanson, Search 5.
14. Epiph., Pan. 69.3.
15. X. Le Bachelet s..v. 'Arianisme', Dict.Théol.Cath. 1.2, 1780 (1923).
16. Philostorgius, HE 1.4.
17. Epiph., Pan. 69.2.
18. See for the question of the chronology Hanson, Search 129-134. Williams, Arius 48 : "Recent scholarship has generally accepted the order and dating proposed by Opitz for the documentary remains of the early years of the crisis". The first document printed by Opitz in his collection is a letter from Arius to Eusebius of Caesarea which he dates 'ca. 318', Opitz, Urkunden, Lief. 1. no. 1. Opitz would have become one of the greatest experts on Arianism, if he had not fallen in the early stages of World War II. Williams, who is nothing if not critical, sifts the evidence in his 'Arius', Part I B The Nicene crisis : Documents and Dating, 1. The controversy to 325, and concludes (p. 56) that "at no point we possess any exact dates for our pre-Nicene fragments, and it is therefore impossible to date with any precision the outbreak of the controversy". Enzio Bellini presents a useful collection of sources (in Italian) in his 'Alessandro e Ario' (see Bibliography).
19. Epiph., Pan. 69.2.
20. Socr., HE 1.5.
21. Athan., Or. contra Ar. 3.27.
22. Eus., Vita 2.69.
23. Williams, Arius 131, suggests that Marcellus of Ancyra was the first to say that Origen was 'the ultimate source of Arius' heresy'.In fact, Marcellus nowhere mentions Arius in his attack on Origen, Eus., Contra Marc. 1.4.17-19.
24. Epiph., Pan. 64.4.
25. Hanson, Search 62.
26. Harnack, Dogmengesch. II Die Entwicklung des Dogmas I, 220.
27. See Williams, Arius, Part II B Alexandria and the Legacy of Origen, especially 131-57.
28. Or., On princ. 1.2.2.
29. Hanson, Search 63/64.

30. Hanson, Search 64, referring to Or., On princ. 1.2.2.

31. Lorenz, Arius jud., 4 Kap. 1 Vergleich arianischer Sätze mit der origenistischen Logos- und Trinitätslehre : "Der Vergleich zwischen Origen and Arius zeigt, daß eine Reihe von Aussagen beiden Theologen gemeinsam ist (p. 92) ... Arius behält unverkennbar Stücke des origenistischen Systems bei (p. 93)".

32. The sources are Arius's book 'Thalia' which is lost but fragments of which have been preserved in the works of Athanasius, and the letter of Arius to Eusebius of Caesarea, Opitz III.1, Urk. 1; there is also a confession by Arius, in Opitz III.1, Urk. 6, also one in Socr., HE 1.26 = Sozom. HE 2.27. Furthermore, there are utterances by Arius in direct speech preserved in the writings of opponents, bishops Alexander and Athanasius of Alexandria. See Harnack, Dogmengesch. I, 198, note 20. I concocted my list from Harnack, Dogmengesch. I, 198-2-2, Lorenz, Arius jud. 37-49, and Hanson, Search 20-23.

    Some scholars doubt whether the testimonies by Athanasius of Arius's opinions in the fragments presented by him are really verbatim reports; it is sometimes thought that Athanasius misrepresented Arius's doctrine. An exception, however, is made for the 'blasphemies', because they possess 'a distinctive style and vocabulary, and a probably consistent metrical pattern', while they are 'free of offensive expressions', see Williams, The Quest 1.

    Hall, The Thalia, is much milder in his judgment. He thinks (p. 37) that the bishop's "exposition of the Thalia consists of a general framework of allegedly Arian ideas, upon which has been superimposed elements of what Athanasius believed to be the written Thalia of Arius". This scholar feels (p. 157) that Athanasius acted in good faith. Since he (Athan.) quoted several items "directly from Arius, he was probably quite satisfied that he had given the devil his due, and told his readers what Arianism was about".

    It is rather startling for an innocent student of Arianism to discover that Father Charles Kannengiesser, The Blasphemies, has a quite different opinion. He says (p. 59) that, "while the De Synodis passage is in truth a quotation and is integrated as such by Athanasius, the Blasphemies only pretend to express the genuine doctrine of the Alexandrian heresiarch". His conclusion (p. 74) is that the Blasphemies were not written by Arius but are from a later date, "as a kind of remake of Arius' Thalia. They are a fine Alexandrian produce, probably by a fervent Arian scholar, influenced by the teaching of the local neo-Arian masters". All the same, he thinks that the Blasphemies were circulated as a genuine part of Arius's Thalia and that Athanasius took them as such.

    Isn't this scholarship run wild?

33. Hanson, Arian Doctrine 182 : "Arianism in all its forms assumed that the Incarnation was a dispensation on the part of God which necessitated a reduction or lowering of God so that it had to be undertaken by a being who, though divine, was less than fully divine.

263

       The inferiority of the incarnate Logos to God was necessary to take place at all".

34. Athan., De synodis 15.3.
35. Athan., De synodis 15.3.
36. Armstrong, History 127.
37. Armstrong, History 127/128.
38. Armstrong, History 128.
39. Jo. 1.14.
40. See Vol. XII, Ch. III.
41. See Vol. I, Ch. II.
42. If Armstrong, History 127, says that "Genesis had not made this claim", namely that the world came 'out of nothing', but that it said that the world had been made 'out of primordial chaos', this is not entirely correct. The notion of 'nothing' is an highly abstract one and as such not to be expected in the Genesis account. Instead, Gen. 1.2, uses the Hebrew term 'tohuwabohu', disordered and unstructured chaos, just as formless as a sea swept by a hurricane. This 'tohuwabohu' is the metaphor Genesis uses to indicate 'nothing'. The text does not say that this was God's elementary material.
43. See the General register of Vol. I s.v. 'One (the) and the Many' and and of Vols. III and VI s.v. 'Monism'.
44. Wand, Heresies 38.
45. Athan., De synodis 15. Lorenz, Arius jud. 66 : "Hinsichtlich der Verwendung der Begriffe Monas und Dyas steht Arius der Gottes- und Logoslehre des Origenes näher als dem eigentlichen Platonismus".
46. This is graphically expressed by Wiles, Archetypal heresy 13 when he speaks of 'the relationship of the Word and the Father, between god and true God'.
47. Wand, Heresies 43.
48. Gregg/Groh, Early Arianism 4.
49. Arius to bishop Alexander, Opitz III.1, Urk. 6.5.
50. Athan., De synodis 15.
51. Gregg/Groh, Early Arianism 44/45.
52. Athan., De synodis 15.
53. Gen.2:24.
54. Mt.19:6.
55. Title of Ch. 2 of Gregg/Groh, Early Arianism.

56. Athan., Or. contra Ar. 3.26 presents a list of such quotations.
57. Athan., Or. contra Ar. 3.35.
58. Mt.19:16-22; Mc.10:17-22; Lc.18:18-23.
59. Mt.24:36; Mc.13:32. It deserves attention that the incriminated words 'not even to the Son' fail in Matthew, while Luke and John do not have the passage at all.
60. Mt.20:20-23. Mc.10:40 says: "for those for whom it has been destined". Luke and John omit this passage.
61. Gregg/Groh, Early Arianism 12.
62. Gregg/Groh, Early Arianism IX.
63. Wand, Heresies 70/71.
64. Gregg/Groh, Early Arianism 12/13.
65. Gregg/Groh, Early Arianism 18.
66. Gregg/Groh, Early Arianism 56.
67. Gregg/Groh, Early Arianism 29.
68. Bellini, Alessandro 9.
69. Newman, Arians 219-235, made the following objections against Arian doctrine. 1. (219) "The unscriptural character of the arguments upon which the heresy was founded ... (220) They (the Arians) took only just so much of it (Scripture) as would afford them a basis for erecting the system of heresy by an abstract logical process." Newman calls this (221) 'disputing instead of investigating'. 2. The Arian doctrine is rationalistic. 221 "They assumed as an axiom, that there could be no mystery in the Scripture doctrine of the nature of God." In other words, they were incapable of accepting the concept of the Trinity, of the essential unity of the three in the one. 3. The Arians were versatile in their manner of reasoning (226-230). Sometimes they use allegories to explain what they mean ; in other instances they stick to the literal sense, just as it suits them. 4. Their arguments are shallow and evasive, never far short of sophistry. Newman's conclusion is (230) that Arian doctrine leads "to the establishment either of a sort of ditheism (namely of viewing the Father and the Son as two separate gods - F.), or, as the more practical alternative, of a mere humanitarianism as regards our Lord".
70. Wand, Heresies 12/13.
71. It is possible that the bishop first wrote to Arius and his party, which would be the so-called 'Depositio Arii', PG 18 (Paris, 1857), but some scholars regard this as a falsification.
72. With the exception of the letter with which Alexander invited his colleagues to join him in Alexandria, Socr., HE 1.6 (10-14).

73. Sozom., HE 1.15 (32); Theodoret., HE 1.3 (748); Depositio Arii; Epiph., Pan, 68.4.
74. Epiph., Pan. 68.4 (720).
75. Eus., Vita 2.6 (642); Sozom., HE 1.15.
76. Socr., HE 1.16 (10).
77. Interpretatio Synodi VII generalis - Actio VI. PL 129, col. 429 (Paris, 1853).
78. Opitz III.1, Urk. 3.3 (dated by Opitz ca. 318).
79. X. Le Bachelet s.v. 'Arianisme', Doct.Théol.Cath. 1.2, 1781 (1923); G. Bareille s.v. 'Eusébe de Nicomédie', Dict.Théol.Cath. 5.2, 1539 (1924).
80. Opitz III.1, Urk, 1..5.
81. Opitz III.1, Urk. 2.
82. Theodoret., HE 1.5 (751-754).
83. Epiph., Pan. 69.4. We still have the letter he wrote to bishop Alexander of Thessalonike, a very long one, Theodoret., HE 1.3 (728-748). Theodoret. himself has : Bishop of Constantinople. The ascription to a bishop of Saloniki is on the authority of Hanson, Search, 136, note 24, who says that there was no Alexander bishop of Constantinople.
84. Socr., HE 1.6 (14); Sozom., HE 1.15 (632).
85. Lorenz, Arius jud., 2.Kap.§ 2 Die Abfassungszeit der Thalia, thinks that the Thalia were written when Arius was still in Alexandria, 'zwischen der ersten Ausschließung des Arius und der großen Synode' (p. 51).
86. Sozom., HE 1.15 (330.
87. Opitz III.1, Urk. 7.
88. Opitz III.1., Urk. 8.
89. Fragments in Opitz III.1., Urk. 9.
90. Opitz III.1, Urk. 6.
91. Sozom., HE 1.15 (33).
92. Greg.Nyss., De deitate, col. 557.
93. Theodoret., H.E. 1.5 (754).
94. Eus., Vita 2.6 (472).
95. Eus., Vita 51.1.
96. Opitz III.1, Urk. 14, uit Theodoret., HE 13.
97. Translation Hanson, Search 136.
98. Hier., De vir.ill. XCIV.

99. Hanson, Search 38.
100. Athan., De synodis 19.
101. Athan., De synodis 19.
102. Athan., Or. contra Ar. 2.28.
103. Athan., De synodis 19.
104. Athan., Or. contra Ar. 2.24, translation Hanson, Search 34; this scholar presents a list of Asterius fragments, 33-37.
105. Hanson, Search 37.
106. Athan., Or. contra Ar. 2.24.
107. Athan., Or.c.Ar. 2.38.
108. Athan. Or.c.Ar. 3.10.
109. Athan., De synodis 18 and Or.c.Ar. 1.32.
110. Athan., De synodis 19.
111. Hanson, Search 38/39.
112. Opitz III.1, Urk. 17.
113. Eus., Vita 2.63, where the name of Ossius is not mentioned; Socr., HE 1.7 (15); Sozom., HE 1.16 (34).
114. Eus., Vita 1.73.
115. Hanson, Search 146.
116. Hanson, Search 149. For the document see Opitz III.1, Urk. 18; this document is in Syriac, but it is accompanied by a Greek translation made by E. Schwarz.
117. Sulp.Sev. 2.40.5 (95).
118. Epiph., Pan. 68.4.5.
119. An idea that is generally 'honourably' dismissed by Roman-Catholic scholars, as Hanson, Search 154, puts it.
120. Opitz III.1.2, Urk. 20, in Syriac with a Greek translation by E. Schwarz.
121. Mansi II presents a list of 318 names. Hanson, Search 156, states that this is 'the same number as the men of Abraham's household whom he led out to rescue Lot' (Gen.14:14).
122. Hanson, Search 156.
123. Eus., Vita 3.10.
124. Eus., Vita 3.13. Perhaps the Emperor did not trust his Greek enough, although he could speak it, to use it in such a solemn occasion.

125. Eus., Vita 3.13. Eustathius of Antioch responded to the speech, Mansi II, 663/664.
126. Sozom., HE 1.17 (36).
127. On the authority of Philostorgius, HE, Suppl. PG 65, col. 623.
128. Athan., De decr.Nic.syn. 3 (165).
129. Athan., Ep. ad Afr.Ep. 5 (217).
130. This Eusebius, and not the other one, is mentioned as the author of this statement both by Ambrose, De fide 3.125, and Nicephoras Callistus, HE 8.18.
131. Ambr., De fide 3.125.
132. Theodoret., HE 1.6 and 8.
133. Sozom., HE 1.17 (36).
134. Eus., Vita 3.13.
135. Sozom., HE 1.17 (35).
136. Letter to the faithful at home, June 325, Opitz III.2, Urk. 22.
137. See for the question of the 'who is who?' of the two Eusebius's Hanson, Search 161.
138. Furthermore, twenty canons were drawn up, among others one regarding the date of Easter, Mansi II 667-692.
139. Opitz III.2, Urk. 24.
140. Wand, Heresies 50.
141. Philost., HE 1.10.
142. Philostorg., HE 1.10; Sozom., HE 1.21; Socr., HE 1.9.
143. Philostorg., HE 2.1; Socr., HE 1.9 (37). Constantine justified his action in his usual brutal terms in a personal letter to the faithful of Nicomedia, Opitz III.2, Urk. 27, 9-14 (Nov./Dec. 325.
144. Rufinus, HE 1.1.
145. Sozom., HE 2.16 (64).
146. Sozom., HE 1.21 (40).
147. Cod.Theod. 1.16.
148. Socr., HE 1.14; Sozom., HE 2.16.
149. Sozom., HE 2.16 (64).
150. Opitz III.2, Urk, 30, from Socr., HE 1.26 (61).
151. Opitz III.2, Urk. 29, from Socr., HE 1.25 (60-61).

152. Hanson, Search 176-178.
153. Rufinus, HE 1.11 (236-237); Socr., HE 2.35; Sozom., HE 2.27.
154. Opitz III.2, Letter of Constantine to Arius, 333, nos, 9-11; Arius had obviously complained of this to the Emperor.
155. Hanson, Search 247.
156. Cyr.Al., Ep. 1 (4).
157. Chron.Athan. 3; Socr., HE 1.23.
158. Sozom., HE 2.17; Philostorg., HE 2.11.
159. Athan., Ap.c.Ar. 6 (101/102).
160. Amm.Marc. 15.6-10; see for this passage Hanson, Search 239-241.
161. Socr., HE 1.23.
162. Athan., Ap.c.Ar. 59-60.
163. Athan., De syn. 13 (581).
164. Epistolae Eusebii 1.
165. Ep.Eus. 1.5-7.
166. Socr., HE 1.23.
167. Socr., HE 1.23 (57).
168. Hanson, Search 181.
169. X. Le Bachelet s.v. 'Arianisme', Dict.Théol.Cath. 1.2, 1801 (1923).
170. The most recent article on Eust. is that of Rudolf Lorenz s.v. 'Eustathius von Antiochien', TRE 110 (1982).
171. Hier., De vir.ill. 85.
172. Theodoret., Ep. 151 (1312).
173. Facundus, Pro def. 8.1.
174. Facundus, PG 18 (1857), col. 692.
175. In a fragment of his Homily on the Proverbs, quoted by Theodoret., HE 8.
176. Sellers, Eustathius 31.
177. Athan., Hist.Ar. 4.
178. Quoted from Eust., Hom. on the Prov. 8.22 by Theodoret., HE 1.8.
179. Eus., Vita 3.59; Sozom., HE 2.19 (69).

180. Chadwick, Fall 35, who discusses the chronological issue extensively, comes to the conclusion that Eustathius was deposed in the autumn of 326.
181. Theodoret., HE 1.21.
182. Athan., Hist.Ar. 4. Sellers, Eust. 48, note 2, suggests that Eust. may have been unwise enough to repeat the rumours about Helena's doubtful past. Chadwick, Fall 34 : "The Emperor's mother had a past which could provide an easy opportunity for some sarcastic references on the part of the Bishop of Antioch".
183. Hier., De vir.ill. 85; Jo.Chrysost., Laud.Eust. 2; Philost. HE 2.7.
184. Theodoret., HE 1.21.
185. Rudolf Lorenz s.v. 'Eustathius von Antiochien', TRE 10, 544.
186. His body was transferred to Antioch in 482 and buried there with great honour.
187. Sellers, Eust. 45.
188. The story found in Theodoret., HE 1.21, that Eusebius produced a woman who named Eust. as the father of her child, is in all probability apocryphal.
189. Socr., HE 1.24.
190. Sellers, Eust. 86.
191. Socr., HE 1.23 (58).
192. Hanson, Search 12.
193. Sellers, Eust. 102.
194. Gal. 4:4.
195. Spanneut, fr. 18.
196. Spanneut, frs. 42 and 59.
197. Spanneut, fr. 27.
198. Spanneut, fr. 25.
199. Sellers, Eust. 111.
200. Sellers, Eust. 111.
201. Sellers, Eust. 111.
202. In his polemic against Origen, 'De engastrimytho', 24, quoted by Hanson, Search 214.
203. De engast. 3.1.10. Rudolf Lorenz s.v. 'Eustathius von Antiochien', TRE 10 (1982), 545.

204. Eus., Contra Marc. 1.4 passim.
205. Socr., HE 1.36 (72).
206. Sozom., HE 2.33 (91).
207. Athan., Hist.Ar.8.
208. Athan., Ap.c.Ar. 33.
209. Epiph., Pan. 72.2 (834-836).
210. Epiph., Pan. 72.3, translation Hanson, Search 231.
211. Athan., Ap.c.Ar 32.
212. Athan., Ap. ad Const. 4.
213. Hanson, Search 293.
214. Hanson, Search 295.
215. Socr., HE 2.20.
216. Hilarius, fr. 3.
217. Hil., fr. 3.26.
218. Hil., fr. 3.27.
219. Hil., fr. 3.29.
220. Hanson, Search 298/299.
221. Theodoret., HE 2.8; Athan., Ap.c.Ar. 44-50.
222. Athan., Hist.Ar. 18.
223. Athanas., Hist.Ar. 15.
224. Athan., Hist.Ar. 20.
225. Hil., fr. 2.21.
226. Epiph., Pan. 72.4.
227. Athan., De morte Arii; the spokesman of Athan. was Macarius, a presbyter, who was present in Constantinople when these events took place.
228. Athan., Hist.Ar. 7.
229. Barnard, Meletian schism 181.
230. Opitz, Urk. III.2, 23.
231. Barnard, Meletian Schism 188.
232. Newman, Arians 281.
233. Chronicon, PG 26 (1857), col. 1352.

234. Athan., Ap.c.Ar. 62.
235. Hanson, Search 257, says that it is not certain whether this Arsenius was a Meletian or a Eusebian.
236. Martin Tetz s.v. 'Athanasius von Alexandrien', TRE 4 (1979), 336.
237. Sozom., HE 2.23; Socr., HE 1.29; Athan., Ap.c.Ar. 63, 65.
238. Athan., Ap.c.Ar. 70.
239. Sozom., HE 2.25 (78).
240. Newman, Arians 282.
241. Athan.' own story in Ap.c.Ar. 73-81; further Eus., Vita 4.42 (letter of Constantine about the sending of his deputy); Sozom., HE 2.25; Socr., HE 1.31-32.
242. Socr., HE 1.34.
243. Sozom., HE 2.31.
244. Athan., Ap.c.Ar. 87; Socr., HE 1.35; Sozom., HE 2.28.
245. According to Athan. Hist.Ar. 8.1, this was decreed by the three Emperors together.
246. Athan., Hist.Ar. 8.2; Ap.c.Ar. 87.
247. Athan. Ap. ad Const. 5.2.
248. Barnes, Athan. 36.
249. Athan. Hist.Ar. 7.
250. Athan., Ap.c.Ar. 19,20.
251. Athan., Ad Ep. ad Episc.Eg. 18.
252. The documents are to be found in Athan., Ap.c.Ar. 3-19. Barnes, Athan. 37-40, presents us with a handy summary.
253. Athan., Ap.c.Ar. 24.
254. Athan., Ap.c.Ar. 22.
255. Athan., Ap. ad Const. 5.
256. Athan., Vita Ant. 69.
257. Barnes, Athan. 45.
258. Athan., Ap.c.Ar. 29,30.
259. Athan., Ep.enc. ad episc. 3.
260. Athan., Ep.enc. ad episc. 4.
261. Athan., Ep.enc. ad episc. 5.

262. Socr., HE 2.11. In accordance with the anti-Athanasius slant of modern historiography, Barnes, Athan. 49, says that the bishop's report in the Encyclical Letter is biased. "Athanasius suppresses the fact that there was violence on both sides ... It is highly improbable that his partisans failed to resist the imposition of a new bishop with all the force they could muster." This is simply guess-work. If Athan. did not mention the violence of his partisans, how do we know it occurred? And if Barnes says that the faithful resisted with all the force they could muster, we may well ask how much force these civilians could muster against Roman legionaries.

263. See Vol. XI, Chr. III.5.

264. His cources are Socr., HE 2.17, Sozom., HE 3.8, and Epistula Julii in Athan., Ap.c.Ar. 21-35.

265. Hanson, Search 269.

266. The Epistula Julii mentioned in note 261.

267. Hanson, Search 272.

268. Hanson, Search 273.

269. Athan., De synodis 22; Socr., HE 2.10.

270. Athan., De synodis 23; Socr., HE 2.10.

271. Newman, Arians 286/287.

272. X. Le Bachelet s.v. 'Arianisme', Dict.Théol.Cath. 1.2, 1811 (1923).

273. Hil., De synodis 24.

274. Athan., De synodis 24.

275. Ekthesis Makrostichos = Long-Lines Manifesto, so already by Socr., HE 2.19.

276. Athan., De synodis 26.

277. In § 6.

278. Athan., De synodis 26.

279. Newman, Arians 288.

280. Letter of bishop Liberius to Constantius II, ca. 354, Hil., fr. 5.4.

281. Socr., HE 2.12.

282. Socr., HE 2.13.

283. Barnes, Athan. 69.

284. Athan., Ap. ad Const. 4.

285. Athan., Ap. ad Const. 4.

286. Athan., Hist.Ar. 44.
287. Athan., Ap. ad Const. 4.
288. Athan., Ap. ad Const. 3.
289. Constantius II admitted that he had given in because of this threat, Lucifer Cal., De Athan. 1.29.28.
290. Athan., Ap.c.Ar. 51.
291. Athan., Hist.Ar. 21.
292. Socr., HE 23 (114-115).
293. Barnes, Athan. 90.
294. Athan., Hist.Ar. 22.
295. Index ao. 346.
296. Athan., Hist.Ar. 26.
297. Athan., Hist.Ar. 26.
298. Athan., Ap. ad Const. 23.
299. Epistula Liberii ad orientales episcopos 1.
300. Barnes, Athan. 110.
301. Epistula Liberii ad Constantium 2.
302. Epistula Liberii ad Ossium (353/354).
303. Hil.Pict., Ad Const. 8.1.
304. Hil.Pict., Contra Const. 1.
305. Hil.Pict., Contra Const. 5.
306. Hil.Pict., Contra Const. 4.
307. Hil.Pict., Contra Const. 7.
308. Hil.Pict., Contra Const. 11.
309. Hil.Pict., Contra Const. 27.
310. Athan., Hist.Ar. 44 (292).
311. In Athan., Hist.Ar. 44 (293).
312. For the little we know of his life see Tietze, Lucifer 59-66; for his literary output see Tietze, Lucifer, Ch VII.
313. Lucifer Cal., Moriendum 13 : "adclamantes Arrianae dogmatis tuae episcopi episcopus te esse episcoporum".
314. Girardet, Konst. II, 96.

315. Lucifer was so liberal with his invectives that it is an endless task to quote them. I refer the reader to Tietze, Lucifer, Ch. VIII, who had enough patience to catalogue them.
316. Luc.Cal., De non parcendo 33.
317. Athan., Hist.Ar. 52.
318. Girardet, Konst. II, 95/96.
319. Hanson, Search 321/322.
320. Epistula Liberii ad Constantium, Hil., fr. 5.
321. Hanson, Search 329-331.
322. X. Le Bachelet s.v. 'Arianisme', Dict.Théol.Cath. 1.2, 1819 (1923).
323. Sulp.Sev., Chronicon 2.39.1-3.
324. Athan., Ap. ad Const. 27.
325. Hanson, Search 332; Barnes, Athan. 117.
326. Hil.Pict., Textus narrativus 2.3 (8).
327. Athan., Hist.Ar. 33.7.
328. Hanson, Search 333.
329. Athan., Hist.Ar. 31-34; Socr., HE 1.20; Sozom. HE 4.9.
330. Athan., Ap. ad Const. 22.
331. Athan., Ap. ad Const. 25; Index ao.356. The whole story is told by Athan., Ap. ad Const. 22-28; Hist.Ar. 48, and in the Hist.Ak. 1.
332. Hist.Ak., 1.11.
333. Athan., Hist.Ar. 36-37.
334. Amm.Marc. 5.7.9.
335. Theodoretus, HE 2.13; Athan., Hist.Ar. 40.
336. Athan., Apologia de fuga sua 5.
337. Athan., Hist.Ar. 45. Hanson, Search 336, note 82, doubts whether Ossius really recanted, but Barnes, Athan. 126, has no such doubts.
338. Athan., Ap. ad Const. 27.
339. Athan., Hist.Ar. 81.
340. Hist.Ak. 2.1-2.
341. Hist.Ak. 2.2. Hanson, Search 342, writes : 358, but this cannot be correct, see Hist.Ak. 2.2.
342. Hist.Ak. 2.3.

343. Hist.Ak. 2.3-4.
344. Hist.Ak. 2.5-6.
345. Letter of Constantius II to the Alexandrians in Athan., Ap. ad Const. 31.
346. Athan., Hist.Ar. 75.
347. Theodoret., HE 2.14.
348. Hier., Chron. ao. 352.
349. Sozom., HE 4.15.
350. Hier., De vir.ill. 97. See Newman, Arians 320/321.
351. Hier., Chron. ao. 352; De vir.ill. 97.
352. É. Amann s.v. 'Libère : authenticité de quatre lettres attribuées à Libère. Dict.Théol.Cath. 9.1, 646-651 (1926).
353. Letter of Liberius to the oriental bishops, CSEL 65, p. 169.
354. Newman, Arians 322.
355. Socr., HE 4.12.
356. For his life see Philostorgius, HE 3.15 sqq; more information in Gregorius Nyssenus, Contra Eunomium 1.
357. See X. Le Bachelet s.v. 'Eunomius'. Dict.Théol.Cath. 5.2 (1924); Loofs s.v. 'Eunomius', Realenc.prot.Theol.u.Kirche 5 (1898); Adolf Maria Ritter s.v. 'Eunomius' TRE 10 (1982).
358. Kopecek, Neo-Arianism I, 146.
359. Photius, Bibl. 137, 138; Philost., HE 3.22, 4.5, 5.3, 6.1-4, 8.2, 8.12, 9.3-8, 10.6.
360. Hier., Contra Vigilantium 8.
361. It is obviously hard to give them the correct name. Newman spoke of 'Anomaeans' and X. le Bachelet of 'Anoméens', art. 'Anoméens', Dict.Théol.Cath. 1.2 (1923). Barnes, Athan., Ch. XV, does not mention this term, but says that Aetius and Eunomius should not be called 'Neo-Arians' and less still 'Neo-Platonists'. Hanson, Search, Ch. 19, seems to prefer 'Neo-Arians' ; in his opinion 'anhomoians' is not satisfactory; this term dates only from the beginning of the twentieth century. On several occasions he says (p. 598) that the Arians denied that the Son was 'unlike' (anhomoios) the Father.
362. X. le Bachelet s.v. 'Anoméens'. Dict.Théol.Cath. 1.2, 1324 (1923). The sources are Eunomius, Liber Apologeticus, Appendix, and 37 'Capita Aetii', preserved by Epiph., Pan. 76.
363. Greg.Nyss., Contra Eunomium 12 (col. 906/907).

364. The term was coined by Greg. of Nyssa, quoted Barnes, Athan. 137. Whether or not Eunomius deserves this epitheton is discussed by Wiles, Eunomius : hair-splitting dialectician or defender of the accessibility of salvation? (see Bibliography).
365. Hanson, Search 610/611.
366. Hanson, Search 636.
367. Hanson, Search 627.
368. Hanson, Search 632.
369. Quoted Hanson, Search 600.
370. Philostorg., HE 4.12.
371. Epiph., Pan. 76.
372. Ritter s.v. 'Eunomius', TRE 10, 526 (1982).
373. Titus 3.4. Greg.Nyss., Contra Eunomium 1 (col. 426-429), argued against Eun. that we should accept the revealed doctrine that God is Father indeed and is rightly called so for which reason we can pray 'our Father' ...". And this Father is none other than the eternal one who is before all and everything, the same as the eternal and incorruptible God that Eunomius proclaimed.
374. Kopecek, Neo-Arianism I, 159/160.
375. Quoted by Ian Buruma, NY Review, 21.III.1996, p. 25.
376. The term was coined by Epiph., Pan. 73.1 (845).
377. They did not use the term 'homoiousios', although this has the same meaning as 'homoeusios'.
378. This long statement is to be found in Epiph., Pan. 73.2-11.
379. Sozom., HE 3.18.
380. Hanson, Search 356.
381. Sozom., HE 4.13.
382. Sozom., HE 4.14.
383. Sozom., HE 4.15.
384. Sozom., HE 4.16.
385. Text in Greek (but the lost original was in Latin) in Athan., De synodis 8.
386. Sulp.Sev., Chronicon 2.41.
387. Athan., De synodis 11; Collectanea antiariana parisiana A IX 3, CSEL 65.

388. Sulp.Sev., Chronicon 2.41.7.
389. Sulp.Sev., Chronicon 2.41.5 says that in Ariminium they had seceded from the main body and had come together in another building. Their letter to Constantius in Coll.Antiar.Par., Series A VI.
390. Sulp.Sev., Chronicon 2.41.1 and 2.43.3; letter of Constantius to the bishops in Ariminium, Athan., De synodis 55.
391. Sulp.Sev., Chronicon 2.43.4.
392. Sulp.Sev., Chronicon 2.44.1.
393. Socr., HE 2.39; Athan., De synodis 12.1; Theodoret., HE 2.26.
394. Text in Epiph., Pan. 73.25.
395. Epiph., Pan, 73.26.
396. Quite a number of sources give information about the proceedings, Sulp.Sev., Chronicon 42; Hil.Pict., Contra Const. 12-24; Athan., De synodis. 12; Socr., HE 2.39-40; Sozom., HE 4.22, and still others.
397. Hil.Pict., Contra Constant. 12.
398. Socr., HE 2.41 (156).
399. Sozom., HE 4.23.
400. Text in Athan., De synodis 30.
401. Socr., HE 2.42; Sozom., HE 4.24-26.
402. Kopecek, Neo-Arianism II, Ch. 6.
403. Kopecek, Neo-Arianism II, 440.
404. Amm.Marc., 22.5.3.
405. Newman, Arians 354.
406. Hanson, Search 385.
407. Sozom., HE 4.30.
408. Hist.Ak. 8; Athan., Hist.Ar. 6-8. A telling example of the anti-orthodox slant which is so conspicuous in Hanson's book is that, although he states that the orthodox were not involved in this horrid deed, "they certainly did nothing to stop it", Hanson, Search 386. Can this author explain how they should have done this?
409. The discussion on the significance of Athanasius' theology is summarized by Ritschl, Athanasius, 7-19 Athanasius im Wechsel der Beurteilungen.
410. X. Le Bachelet s.v. 'Athanase', Dict.Théol.Cath. 1.2, 2169 (1923).
411. Tomus ad Antioch.

412. Athan. Epistula ad Rufinianum.
413. Tomus ad Antioch. 7; sources for this council Rufinus, HE 1.27-29; Socr., HE 3.6-9; Sozom., HE 4.12-13.
414. Newman, Arians 365-367. The problem was that the westerners had no equivalent term for 'hypostasis'; they translated it by 'substantia'. But 'substantia' was also the rendering of 'ousia'. The three 'hypostaseis' in the godhead could, in their opinion, mean that the godhead had three 'ousiai', in other words that there were three gods. So some vague suspicions lingered on.
415. Julian, Letters 6.
416. Julian., Letters 26.
417. Julian., Letters 51.
418. Socr., HE 3.14.
419. Hist.ak., ao. 363.
420. Narratio Athan. ad Ammon.
421. Hist.Ak. 4.7.
422. Athan., Epist. ad Jovian.
423. Sozom., HE 6.12; Socr., HE 4.12.
424. Sozom., HE 6.7.
425. Theodoret., HE 4.17.
426. Soocr., HE 4.21.
427. Socr., HE 4.22.
428. Theodoret., HE 4.19.
429. Bas.Magn., Ep. 225.
430. X. Le Bachelet s.v. 'Arianisme', Dict.Théol.Cath. 2.1, 1838 (1923).
431. Cod.Theod. 16.5.1-2.
432. Mt. 10:23.
433. Socr., HE 5.7.
434. 'Nullis haereticis', Cod.Theod. 16.5.6.
435. Sozom., HE 7.2.
436. Damasus, Prolegomena 14, PL 13 (1845).
437. Theodoret., HE 11.
438. Socr., HE 5.8-9; Sozom., HE 7.7-11; Theodoret., HE 5.6-8.

439. The question whether or not there was a 'Creed of Constantinople' is discussed by Hanson, Search 812-820. There was probably one which exhibits certain differences from the Nicene Creed. Most of the alterations are insignificant, with the exception of the words 'of the ousia of the Father' which figure in the Nicene Creed but not in that of Constantinople. If I understand Hanson well, not too much importance should be attached to this omission. The question has been amply discussed among theologians but it would take us too far to go into it.

440. Sozom., HE 7.17.

441. Kopecek, Neo-Arianism II, 540.

442. Kopecek, Neo-Arianism II, 542/543.

443. Cod.Theod. 16.1.3.

444. Cod.Theod. 16.5.8

445. Cod.Theod. 16.5.11.

446. Cod.Theod. 16.5.20.

447. See for this subject Knut Schäferdiek s.v. 'Germanenmission, arianische', TRE 12 (1984).

448. X. le Bachelet s.v. 'Arianisme', Dict.Théol.Cath. 2.1, 1859 (1923).

449. The traditional date is 496, baptism by bishop Remigius of Reims; however, the place could have been either Reims or Tours and the date 496, 498 or 499.

CHAPTER VII

THE STRUGGLE OVER THE NATURES OF CHRIST

PART I APOLLINARISM

1. Apollinaris père et fils

In the second half of the third century A.D. a man called Apollinaris (or Apollinarios) was born in Alexandria. He was a Christian who earned a reputation as a grammarian, well versed as he was in Greek literature. From the Egyptian capital he migrated to Berytus in Syria and from there to the Syrian town of Laodicea. In this town he acted as a presbyter around 335; his son, also named Apollinaris, a rhetor, was a lector in his church. Both used to frequent a certain sophist, named Epiphanius [1]. Theodotus, their bishop, fearing that they might be adversely influenced by this pagan, forbade them to go there, but "having a low opinion of their bishop, they continued to frequent the friendship of Epiphanius" [2].

This may throw some doubt on the orthodoxy of both father and son, but they were also great friends of Athanasius who, coming out of his second exile, stayed at their home in 346; they stood squarely behind the Nicene Creed. However, they had their share of the troubles, since the successor of Theodotus, George of Laodicea, excommunicated them because of their hospitality [3]. The younger Apollinaris [4] remained in correspondence with the bishop of Alexandria.

2. The fate of the literary production of Apollinaris jr.

The son was born around 315 [5]; he too became a cultivated man. We know little about the early part of his life, but around 360/361 he is identified as bishop of Laodicea [6]. He was a prolific writer, though precious little of his work remains [7], for later in his life he deviated from orthodoxy leading to the destruction of his books.

In his life of saint Ephraim the Syrian, Gregory of Nyssa relates an incident which perhaps is not wholly reliable but is too amusing to go unmentioned. Apollinaris, he tells us, entrusted the two books he had written to a woman who, as the rumour went, was willing to serve his lusts. Ephraim visited this woman and falsely pretending that he was interested, got the books from her. He then pasted all the pages together with fish-glue so that each of the volumes became one block, impossible to open. In this state he returned the books to the woman. A few days later he challenged Apollinaris to hold a disputation with some orthodox believers. Unwittingly putting his trust in his books, Apollinaris tried to open them in vain. This irritated him so immensely that he almost died as a consequence [8].

We are told that the Apollinarists circulated their master's writings under the name of perfectly orthodox authors like Athanasius and Pope Julius [9]. Palestinian monks living in the last decade of the fifth century wrote to Alcison, the bishop of Nicopolis, that Apollinaris could never be far wrong; they decided this on the strength of writings allegedly by Athanasius and Julius but which in reality were texts of Apollinaris that had been falsely attributed to orthodox authors by the Eutychians [10]. The fact is that Apollinaris himself naively but wrongly thought that his teaching was wholly in accordance with Athanasius' doctrine [11].

3. Apollinaris' deviation from orthodoxy

It is hard to tell what made Apollinaris, once such a great defender of 'Nicaea', deviate from the orthodox creed. Godet thinks that "his ardour in combating Arianism drew him into the opposed error" [12]. He had his problems with the two natures in Christ, the divine and the human nature. Was it conceivable that there existed two perfect and complete natures in one person? No, it was not! "There are not two natures in the one Son, of which the one (the divine) is to be worshipped and the other (the human) not; there is only one nature of the Logos of God who took on the flesh and that should be worshipped along with the human shape in the same adoration. There are not two Sons, one the Son of God, the true God who must be worshipped, and another who was generated like all of us, but, as I said, there is one Son of God who was born from Mary according to the flesh, and not another" [13].

Was it not so that a human nature would impinge on the divine one? For, unlike Arius, Apollinaris was intent on safeguarding Christ's perfect divinity at any cost. It is for this reason that Apollinaris sharply distinguished between the divine and the human element in Christ. Both exist in their own right; what belongs to the one does not belong to the other. This seems to jeopardize the concept of the unity of Christ's person, but he himself does not think so because the divine and the human proprieties are part of one and the same person [14].

The inevitable consequence, however, was that Christ's perfect humanity had to suffer. Apollinaris could hardly deny that Christ had a physical body and also not that this body was animated by a soul, a 'psuchê'. But what he did not have was a 'nous', a 'pneuma', which according to Platonic philosophy is the highest principle in the tripartite being that man is : pneuma/nous - psuchê - soma (spirit, soul, body).

4. Apollinaris' anthropology

The reason why Apollinaris was unable to see the two natures of Christ organically united in the person of Christ was that he recognized an anthropology of his own. In his view - but this was no exception in his days - the human person was composed of two imperfect and not comfortably cohabitating parts, the body and the soul [15]. In this composition - Apollinaris here applies Aristotelian principles - the soul is the mover and the body the moved which means that the soul is the guiding and superior element. What he is professing is a dichotomy of body and soul which comes very near to dualism, the soul being the superior and spiritual element, and the body - the 'sarx', the flesh - the material and wholly terrestrial one. Apollinaris was by no account the only Christian author to hold this opinion; it is not heretical in itself.

Apollinaris often speaks of the pneuma, the spirit, as though it is an aspect or mode of the soul. But we also find that the pneuma is spoken of as something different from the psuchê. The usual dichotomy is replaced then by a trichotomy, by the tripartite human being. The point, however, is that this pneuma, in Apollinaris' theology, does not really belong to Christ's humanity, but comes from above. And the spirit is that what makes a person really himself, into an identity which is wholly his own.

5. Two natures, two persons?

To the Christian consciousness of those centuries Christ was a unified being, one single person, that is. The question, however, in what manner the divine and the human were united in him had not yet been discussed and elucidated. But in the theological schools of Antioch which were so well-known to Apollinaris, this question had begun to play a role. The Antiochenes did not doubt that Christ was really God and really man. Starting from this tenet of the faith they drew the in their eyes unavoidable conclusion that just as there are two natures in Christ, there are two persons. Somehow, in a desperate attempt to reconcile faith and philosophy, they managed to believe, with the Church, that when all was said and done, these two persons were one Christ, but it is not surprising that Apollinaris reproached them to professing two Sons of God.

6. Apollinaris' answer : one nature, one person.

To combat them Apollinaris started not from the Bible and the common Christian faith but from philosophy. An individual person has a nature (his mode of being human) or is a nature, one single nature, that is. His

Christological conclusion was that Christ, being a person, one person, could have only one nature. In this one nature of Christ the divine and the human live side by side. This composition, however, is not so natural as the union of the psyche and the body is natural. In Apollinarian theology, the divine element may be considered the pneuma, the spirit, that, as an independent element from above, has been added to the human parts. It is the pneumatic, the divine element that really has the lead; it used the humanity as its visible instrument.

Is there dualism in this? At first sight there is not, for Apollinaris uses terms of unity for the symbiosis of the divine and the human in the one nature of Christ, words like 'enosis' and 'synthesis'. But there is also terminology with a dualistic tinge; he was not a stickler for theological precision. We hear him tell us that the divine pneuma is united with the body - 'sunthêtos' -, but at the same time it is 'asunthêtos', different from and more than the composition. Being adjoined to the human, the divine did not stop being itself. This leads, at least from an orthodox point of view, to curious consequences.

The person of Christ is not really an organic unity but a mixture - he used the Greek words 'mixis' and 'krasis' - of the two elements : he is neither wholly man nor wholly God but an intermediate between God and man (which does not mean that he was a half-god according to the concept dear to the Hellenes). He is not entirely man because he has no human pneuma (only a psyche and a body); he is also not God tout court, but an incarnated God, united to the flesh. I feel that once again we are in the presence of that horror materiae that was so wide-spread during this period; it appears that for Apollinaris too the idea that the divine is combined with the flesh somehow or other infringes on the pureness, the wholeness of divinity. I think it is for this reason that he allows the divine element an existence that does not remain confined to the physical presence. As the incarnated Word Christ is different from the Father because he inhabits a body, but at the same time he is absolutely equal to the Father.

Since the Gospels time and again mention emotions and human feelings in Jesus, Apollinaris was unable to deny that there was a physical side to him; the psyche was the source of the emotions. But the physical element does not have pride of place in Apollinaris' considerations; it certainly does not come on a par with the spiritual element. The body, the human part, is no more than a garment, an envelope [16]; it is only needed to make the eternal Word visible to mankind. It is something exterior and passive, without glory - which is tantamount to saying that it is inferior. It cannot be called a nature. Gregory of Nyssa expressed this metaphorically by writing that Christ, according to Apollinaris, had not taken the whole sheep on his shoulders but only the hide [17].

Not only in order to make the Word visible Apollinaris' Christ needs a body but perhaps still more because he has to suffer. In his view mankind is not redeemed, as in Arian doctrine, by following the ethical example of Jesus but, as in orthodox doctrine, by his passion and his death on the cross [18].

7. The dualism of Apollinaris

We can now answer the question whether or not Apollinaris' Christological doctrine is a case of dualism. Taking everything into account, I conclude that we are entitled to dub it relative dualism. In Christ the human, the physical element is dependent on the pneumatic, the spiritual element; therefore, the dualism is relative, not radical. But the human part is not congruent with the divine element, since it is inferior and must be moved and ruled by the pneumatic part; obviously the divine pneuma has to distance itself from the body in order to remain itself.

We see Apollinaris attempting to avoid colliding with two rocks. The first is that of Arianism according to which the Son is far more human than divine; the second is Antiochene theology according to which the divine Word could have no human proprieties; conversely, to the man Jesus no divine proprieties could be ascribed. The consequence is that, if Christ had two separate natures, he must also be two persons. Apollinaris might have chosen the orthodox solution contained (later) in the formula of Chalcedon : two natures, one person. But he was prevented from doing so because of his philosophical parti pris. Since in his vocabulary 'person' signified almost the same as 'nature', the fact that Christ could logically be only one person implied for him that he could possess but one nature. Apollinaris had to accept that in this one person-nature the divine and the human parts were very unhappily married.

8. Apollinarian doctrine disapproved of

Bringing forward insights of this kind was of course asking for trouble. Apollinaris was in for a series of condemnations. In 362 a council held at Alexandria expressed disapproval of Apollinaris' teachings, in particular of his opinion that the Redeemer had inhabited a body without a human soul [19]. But since this synod spoke of 'apsuchon', not making a difference between 'psuchê' (human soul) and 'pneuma' (spirit), Apollinaris could feel that the condemnation was not directed at him, since he did not deny that Christ had an animated soul [20]. He could also believe he was not envisaged because he was not mentioned by name.

9. Questions of terminology

In 374 Epiphanius, the great expert in matters of heresy, came to Antioch; his aim was to reconcile several factions with each other that were obviously orthodox but nevertheless quarrelled [21]. It seems that he did not meet Apollinaris in person; he did not believe he was heterodox but put the blame on his disciples who had misinterpreted him [22]. With these disciples he held a disputation but was unable to convince them. During this discussion he tried to clarify the terms his opponents were using. They said that Christ had no soul, no psyche. The Apollinarists seem to have equated 'psuchê' with 'nous', but Epiphanius introduced the term 'pneuma' which he said is something different from 'nous' (or 'psuchê'). If I understand him well, what he meant to say was that, in their terminology, they should not state that Christ had no 'psyche' but that he had no 'pneuma' [23].

By doing so Epiphanius either proved himself better informed than the Council of Alexandria twelve years earlier, or else he was referring to a later development in Apollinaris' teaching, that of the trichotomy. In his book 'Ancoratus' Epiphanius himself went on to profess the trichotomy in man who is composed of three distinct elements, body, soul, and spirit (pneuma or nous). The general opinion among the faithful was that Christ had been a perfect man; they found the idea that he had been truncated in some way or other abhorrent. The philosophically minded assumed that he, like everybody else, had been composed of the three elements mentioned above. For the Apollinarists this was no different : they too saw in Christ a perfect man [24]. Since in their opinion Christ did not possess a human pneuma, they substituted the divine Word for it in order to present him as a perfect man [25]. But, says Epiphanius, failing to assign a human spirit or intellect to Christ necessarily means making his person and his work of redemption 'deficient' or 'inadequate' [26].

10. The role of Vitalis

As I wrote above, during Epiphanius' visit to Antioch Apollinaris was probably not in town. Instead, he came into contact with one of his most important adherents, a priest called Vitalis [27]. The bishop of Antioch in these days, Paulinus, doubted this man's orthodoxy. Attempting to remain neutral in his role of pacifier, Epiphanius asked both Paulinus and Vitalis for a declaration of faith. The bishop was the first to do this, presenting an unexceptionally orthodox doctrinal statement [28]. What Vitalis held became apparent in a verbal form, when he was ever more closely interrogated by Epiphanius. No objections to what he said could be made until he was asked whether Christ had assumed a (human) mind (nous/pneuma); to this he answered point-blank : no. But how, Epiphanius pressed on, can you say then that Christ was a perfect (teleios) man? This is possible, retorted Vitalis, if we ascribe divinity to him instead of a mind and add body (sarx) and psyche to it. As a perfect man he consisted of divinity, body, and psyche, not of pneuma, body, and psyche [29]. After this statement it was impossible for Epiphanius to recognize Vitalis as orthodox.

Vitalis now went to Rome in order to present his case to the Holy See. It is not known whether he went there of his own accord in the hope of winning over Pope Damasus I or if he was sent by Paulinus. In 375 he was in Rome. What exactly happened there is problematic. In all probability he made a favourable impression on the Roman bishop [30], for he returned home with a papal letter admonishing Paulinus to receive Vitalis back into his flock. But after his departure Damasus seems to have got an uncomfortable feeling that he might have been taken in somewhat. In any case, he expedited a presbyter to Antioch with a letter telling Paulinus that he ought not reintegrate Vitalis and his friends until they had signed the Nicene Creed [31]. As a result Vitalis broke with his bishop and Epiphanius proved unable to reconcile him.

11. The Christian community beginning to split

In the years after 362 an Apollinarist sect came into being; it possessed some sort of ecclesiastical organization. Again, according to the ancient historian Sozomenos, the Apollinarists substituted songs composed by their prophet for the usual psalm singing [32]. In 373/374 we find Apollinaris himself in Antioch, having left or having been forced to leave Laodicea for one reason or other. He lectured there and once had the still young Jerome among his hearers. He had much success; one of the first Apollinarist communities was founded in the Syrian capital [33]. He made Vitalis the chief of his adherents in Antioch, and nominated one of his principal faithful, Timotheus, as bishop of Berytus; furthermore, he installed Apollinarist bishops in sees where there were already orthodox dignitaries.

The battle grew ever more acrimonious [34]. As a result, the Christian community of the Orient began to split. It was in these years, 375-377, that Apollinaris broke with the Church entirely and went his own way. His doctrine was condemned by three successive Roman councils, in 375, 376 and 380, and by that of Constantinople in 381.

In the Near East the position of Apollinarism must have been rather strong. According to Sozomenos, the whole region southward from Cilicia towards Phoenicia threatened to fall a prey to Apollinarism, whereas Eunomius' doctrine was capturing Asia Minor. That the Orient did not finally fall away Sozomenos ascribed to the monks of Syria and Cappadocia who stuck steadfastly to the Nicene Creed. The faithful of these regions trusted these monks more than any of the heterodox teachers, he concludes [35]. The Emperor Theodosius I judged it imperative to take measures against them. On 3d September, 383, he forbade the Eunomians and the Apollinarists to hold religious meetings in towns, villages, or wherever, and to ordain presbyters for their own sect. Wandering missionaries should be sent back to their home towns [36]. Above all, the Emperor would not tolerate them in the eastern capital : on 21st January, 384, he ordered their teachers and clerics to quit Constantinople [37].

Epiphanius, who knew many of them personally, distinguished two kinds of Apollinarists. Some of them, who visited him in Cyprus, he considered nitwits, stupid and ignorant people who did not really understand what their master taught and who occupied themselves with silly questions about the body of Christ [38]. They were brazen-faced fanatics [39]. But there was also another kind, more erudite and better cultivated. They too had their troubles with the fanatics who distorted the doctrine of Apollinaris. Epiphanius had discussions with them [40].

As a separate sect Apollinarism did not enjoy a long life. In the West it gained no foothold at all. They are mentioned for the last time in an imperial edict of 3oth May, 428 [41]. Many Apollinarists returned to the Roman Catholic Church; the remainder fused with other monophysite sects.

PART II THEODORE OF MOPSUESTIA'S THEOLOGY

As Wand wrote, "Apollinarianism was a reaction. We are now faced with a reaction against Apollinarianism" [42]. This reaction was not that of the main Church or of the orthodox Emperors, but that of Nestorius. This is a most interesting case, since the Nestorian Church is the only heterodox religious community to survive the vicissitudes of Antiquity. But although Nestorius is the name-giver of this sect, many scholars view Theodore of Mopsuestia as the real initiator of Nestorianism. First of all, however, with Apollinarianism as well as with Nestorianism we are moving within the orbit of monophysitism, that is, of those doctrines according to which Christ had only one nature (monê phusis), instead of two, as orthodoxy teaches.

1. Who was Theodore of Mopsuestia?

Theodore was an Antiochene, born in this city around 350 into a wealthy and influential family. While still a pagan, he, just as John Chrysostom, studied with the famous rhetor Libanius; later he converted to Christianity and was baptized [43]. Feeling an inclination towards an ascetic life, he decided to remain single; later he found he was not fit for this sort of life and wanted to marry. The austere John Chrysostom reproached him for this; in his eyes Theodore had 'lapsed' [44]. Theodore was penitent and became a monk. He had not yet become a priest then, for he was only ordained in 383. He lived in Tarsus for some time until he was called to the see of Mopsuestia in Cilicia in 392 [45]. He remained the bishop of this town for twenty-six years until his death in 418.

2, His literary output

Theodore was one of those prolific ecclesiastical authors who were not unusual in this period; he has brought quite a library to his name, consisting of exegetical, theological, and controversial works. Much of what he wrote did not survive the devastating effect of Turkish and Mongol raids on Syria. Nevertheless, several complete works have been preserved, some of them in Syriac translation (Theodore himself wrote in Greek); of the rest fragments remain. As Wand said, "he is so well-known from the writings of others that there is no real doubt about the positions he maintained" [46]. His nickname in Antiquity was 'the Interpreter', because of his exegetical method of interpreting Scripture, especially the New Testament; the humanity of Jesus was in the centre of his interest, for it was on this issue that he joined battle with the Apollinarists. He was no admirer of the allegorical method so beloved to Origen. He himself set out from the literal texts while paying strict attention to shades of grammar and wording that revealed the intentions of the biblical authors [47].

3. Godhead and humanity in Jesus according to Theodore of Mopsuestia

Theodore of Mopsuestia found his place amongst those theologians who defended the full humanity of Jesus. But in doing so they experienced difficulties with the relationship of the godhead (which they did not deny) and the humanity of Christ. Eusthatius of Antioch, for one, found it hard to imagine that Jesus could have suffered in his divinity; so he had to introduce a certain split in his personality, keeping the humanity somewhat apart. In the foregoing pages we saw how Apollinaris performed what we might call a surgical operation on Christ by amputating his human spirit (pneuma) and putting the divine Logos in its place.

    Reacting against both Arianism and Apollinarianism, Theodore steadfastly held that Jesus was perfectly God and perfectly man. But once again difficulties arose when the question how divinity and humanity were joined in him arose. Part of the problem was caused by his fundamental anthropology. He did not believe, as orthodox Christian teaching goes, that God creates a separate and individual soul for each human being; the body may come from the parents, but the soul comes from God. But Theodore instead thought that the whole human identity, body and soul, was transmitted by the parents to their child. Theodore was quite ready to accept that Jesus got his body from his mother, but what about his soul? He could impossibly say that Jesus also inherited his soul from Mary, for in that case he would have been as human as the rest of us and thus not divine. In Theodore's view, Jesus got his soul from God. This self-evidently ran counter to his own peculiar anthropology. In order to save Jesus' divinity he was forced to assume that what began in the womb of Mary was only physical. At the moment of conception of Jesus the Logos descended on him and joined himself with him.

Theodore spoke of Jesus Christ as "the one Lord who is of the divine nature of God the Father, who for our salvation put on a man in whom he dwelt and through whom he appeared and became known to mankind" [48]. Attention should be paid to the words 'put on a man in whom he dwelt'. What we encounter here is the theory of the indwelling Logos - a Logos who took up his abode in a man but did not become that man. He assumed a man but did not become really incarnated; Theodore did not do full justice to John's words "and the Word became (egeneto) flesh'. "If Apollinaris could not stick to the full humanity of Jesus, Theodore was unable to accept the fact of the Incarnation" [49]. Theodore, says Pelikan, thus had a theophany ('the man through whom he appeared') in mind rather than of an Incarnation [50].

4. Natures and persons

Are there two natures in Christ or one? Are there two persons in him or one? There cannot be the slightest doubt that Theodore assumed there were two natures in Christ, the divine and the human one. But since the Logos had 'assumed' the flesh, these two natures did not wholly fuse together; they remained separate to a certain extent. There is not one substance in Christ, not one essence, not one identity. There was no more than 'a close association or cohesion' which was not of an essential but of a moral or voluntary sort [51]. "The two natures are thus in danger of becoming two individuals" [52].

All this may make it rather hard to conclude whether Theodore held there were two persons in Christ or one. It was rather clumsy of him to refer, with regard to the two natures in Christ, to human marriage; his comparison was that in marriage also two natures are joined. True enough, in marriage man and woman become 'one flesh'; however, much as they become 'one flesh' (= sharing one common existence), they nonetheless remain two separate individuals and do not become one person in whom the two natures are joined.

5. Consequences of Theodore's Christology

A special problem was posed to Theodore by the passion of Jesus and his death on the cross. Did the divine element suffer together with the human one? It did not; he held this impossible. "The godhead was separated from the one who was suffering the trial of death, for it was impossible for him to taste the trial of death" [53]. As Pelikan writes : "Wherever there was a reference to the cross and the death of Christ or to the 'blood' as the instrument of salvation, this meant the man who had been assumed by the Logos, not the individual Logos himself, who was, as God, impassible" [54].

Another curious consequence of Theodore's Christology was his interpretation of the phrase : 'he shall come again in glory'. Who is this 'he'? It is only the Logos, stated Theodore, for the man has 'ascended to heaven' and would, therefore, not return; no human being ever came back to the earth after his or her death [55]. He found a confirmation for his opinion in the Letter to the Philippians where it is said that Jesus "was in the form of God; yet he laid no claim to equality with God , but he made himself nothing, assuming the form of a slave" [56]. He commented that the Apostle spoke "of Jesus as though of one person and combines into this one person things that by division of nature are different in force" [57].

6. The dualism of Theodore

The question with which we are now confronted is whether Theodore's Christology was dualistic. I think it was. It is no wonder that he had to defend himself against the reproach that, according to him, there were 'two Sons' in Jesus. This reproach is unjust; he did not hold nor say this, but he lay himself open to it. The two elements in his Jesus Christ do not really fit together; there is no organic, no substantial unity of the divine and the human in him. The human element is clearly inferior to the divine one : the celestial Logos 'assumes' the human shape. This inferiority also becomes apparent through the fact that, at the end of time, not the human shape wil return in glory but only the Logos.

The most important question is whether the two elements in Christ are opposed. I do not doubt that Theodore would vigorously defend himself against this idea, but I ask myself whether he would be able to get away with it easily. The fact that the divine element is far superior to the human part points to an opposition. The Logos did not use the body as his natural home on earth but rather as an instrument. This opposition remained veiled until Jesus' passion began. Theodore shrank back from the notion that the Logos could have suffered. It is as though the Logos stepped back not wanting to be involved in a suffering that was - beneath his dignity? incompatible with his divinity? I feel that we are here in the presence of something I have mentioned several times already, namely the 'horror materiae' that was a constitutional element of theological thought in these centuries. Somehow many theological thinkers were uncomfortable with the idea that the godhead could have something to do with the material, the physical, the body.

PART III NESTORIANISM

1. Who was Nestorius?

It was necessary to pay ample attention to Theodore's theology because it led straight to that of Nestorius. We do not know when exactly he was born nor from where he came. Whatever the case, his family resided in Germanicia (the present Mar'ash in Syria) [58], but he himself was probably born and educated in Antioch where he was taught by Theodore of Mopsuestia. He first became a deacon and later a presbyter. He had considerable success as a teacher and a preacher in the Syrian capital. In 428 he was the personal choice of Theodosius II for the post of bishop of Constantinople. Since there were two rivals for this see, the Emperor sought a way out through the appointment of an outsider, but, as Wickham writes, there remained a residue of bitterness in the capital [59].

2. Making enemies

For peace to reign in the great eastern metropolis a man of a conciliatory disposition was needed, but the new bishop was 'set on confrontation' [60]. He began his episcopate on April 10, 428 with an inflammatory sermon, delivered in the presence of the Emperor, in which he said : "Give me a world purgated of heresies, and I shall give you (the Emperor) heaven. Fight the heretics with me, and I shall wage war against the Persians with you" [61]. These last words demonstrated that he wanted to be a political bishop but, inexperienced as he was, he fell a prey to the intrigues of the court.

A war was certainly waged against the heterodox, the Arians, the Apollinarists, and others, in which the ruler assisted with imperial decrees [62]. Nestorius was a pastmaster in the gentle art of making enemies; he succeeded in an astonishingly short time in antagonizing almost everybody, the Emperor's equally combative sister Pulcheria, his fellow-bishops, the clergy and laity of the capital, the Gothic garrison, and just about everybody else. Add to this that he also provoked difficulties in the theological field to which I shall come back presently. These led to his condemnation by the Council of Ephesus in April 431, followed by his resignation in September of that year. He had been bishop for three years only. Nobody stood up for him. He returned to his monastery in Antioch, but the bishop of this town felt uncomfortable with his presence there; in 436 he was sent into exile, first to Egypt, then to Libya. He died in 450 or 451.

"In the orthodox Church Nestorius was even in his own time an ephemeral appearance ... He remained merely one of the most condemned heretics" [63]. How utterly lonely and abandoned he felt is shown by the moving words with which he concluded his 'Treatise of Heraclides'. "As for me, I have born the sufferings of my life and all that has befallen me in this world as the sufferings of a single day; and I have not changed all these years. And now I am already on the point to depart, and daily I pray to God to dismiss me - me whose eyes have seen his salvation. Farewell Desert, my friend, my upbringer, and my place of sojourning, and thou, Exile, my mother, who after my death shall keep my body, until the resurrection comes in the time of God's pleasure. Amen" [64].

3. Nestorius' literary output

Nestorius has many works to his name but most of them are lost. His writings were publicly condemned by an imperial decree of 435 [65]. No more than fragments remain, with the exception of the Syrian translation of one of the books, the aforementioned 'Treatise of Heraclides' [66]. His oeuvre embraced apologies, sermons, and letters.

4. The beginning of the theological battle

We saw that Nestorius caused quite a stir with his hard-handed approach against heterodox, really or allegedly so, groups; it did not make him very popular. As Amman writes, he believed himself above every suspicion, since he was, in his own opinion, perfectly orthodox [67]. But this is precisely the question. He was soon enough the centre of a theological battle. There are two versions of how it began, but perhaps they can be harmonized as follows [68].

Even before Nestorius arrived in the eastern capital, there existed certain divergent views of the theological status of Mary, the mother of Jesus. Was she the 'theotokos' = the God-bearer, or only the 'anthropotokos' = having born a human person? Those who held the latter opinion were accused of denying the divinity of Christ, mostly unjustly so, for to them the term 'anthropotokos' did not mean that Jesus was only human and not divine. In this context belongs a sermon by a certain presbyter Anastasius who was close to Nestorius. In this sermon he declared that "nobody should call Mary 'theotokos', for she was only a woman"; he obviously feared that giving Mary the title of 'God-bearer' would make her too divine what could lead to 'Mariolatry'. In a sermon offered in 429 or 430 Nestorius himself said that if anyone was simple enough to prefer the term 'theotokos', he had nothing against it; "only do not make a goddess of the Virgin" [69].

Anastasius' sermon led to great disturbance among clergy and lay-people. His bishop did nothing to allay the confusion but, instead, took up the theme himself by stating in a number of sermons that Mary should rather not be called 'theotokos' [70]. He preferred the term 'Christotokos' [71]. He did not deny that Jesus was divine, but he was pulling his divinity and his humanity apart by giving them a separate origin. The unity in the person of Christ was, he thought, not of an organic or hypostatic (essential) character, but consisted rather in the convergence of his will and work with that of his Father. He seems to have felt that a divinity that came to Jesus through Mary was, so to speak, of a lower quality than a divine status that was accorded to him directly by the Father.

5. A battle of theses

Of course, it was rumoured that the bishop did not believe in the godhead of Jesus at all. A battle of the sermons began. Proclus, a presbyter, told his audience, among which stood Nestorius, that Mary was really a 'God-bearer' who had not given birth to 'a mere man' [72]. Nestorius did not fail to retort. The fiercest attack came from an imperial official who later became bishop of Dorylaeum. He pasted up a placard in which he accused Nestorius of confessing the same errors of Paul of Samosata. In this placard he opposed two sets of theses, one by Paul and the other by Nestorius, in an attempt to show that they were more or less identical. The quintessence was that alledgedly to Nestorius Jesus was just a man who became 'adopted' by the godhead. In consequence, he was said to hold that there were two Christs and two Sons, namely a human person and the Logos, and to have put Jesus on the same line as the Jewish prophets who had also been inspired men [73].

    The accused defended himself with all the acerbity that was common to him. Counter-accusations and condemnations were at the order of the day. "This stupid garrulity of Nestorius disturbed the whole earth not a little", found Socrates. This church historian, having investigated the matter, thought the accusations were false. "In my opinion Nestorius imitated neither Paul of Samosata nor Photinus; he did not intend to say that the Lord was just an ordinary man. He is only afraid of a word (theotokos) as one is afraid of a bogey" [74]. Very well, but why was the word 'God-bearer' a bogey to him? Why did he think it would lead people astray? Was it not because, as I said already, it might suggest that Jesus, having received everything through Mary, would remain too much on the human side? He found that it smacked of Greek paganism if a god had a human mother. A creature like Mary could not create, bring forth what was not creational. Perhaps Nestorius had not yet distanced himself really far from orthodox doctrine, but that he was skating on thin ice is evident.

6. Cyril's epistolary offensive

Then Cyril, the bishop of Alexandria and the guardian of Alexandrian, Athanasian Christological doctrine, threw himself into the fray. He was well informed of the discussion, because he had been briefed by people in Constantinople; he was also in possession of all the Nestorian sermons. In the summer of 429 he addressed himself directly to his colleague in the eastern capital. His sermons had given him the impression that in the view of the orator Christ was only an 'organon', an instrument, that he was a 'God-bearing man'. What Cyril meant to convey was that to Nestorius the divinity was only added to or superimposed upon the humanity of Christ. What a scandal for the whole Church! Even Celestinus (I), the bishop of Rome (422-432), having informed himself in Alexandria, had been shocked by this all. Would Nestorius please declare as soon as possible that Mary really was 'theotokos' [75]?

Nestorius retorted, however, by stating that his alleged heterodoxy was something of Cyril's making; this bishop of Alexandria accused him falsely only to cover up his own doctrinal imperfections. "Since that time he (Cyril) became my (Nestorius') irreconcilable enemy and ready for anything. He started a quarrel in order ... to keep the charges brought against him in the background" [76]. Cyril was 'ready for anything', indeed. In the first months of 430 he read, as though armed with a magnifying glass, all the Nestorian writings that had come into his possession. The result was a bulky volume 'against the blasphemies of Nestorius' [77]. He also sought to interest the whole imperial family, by writing a long theological letter to the Emperor, Theodosius II [78], an interminable one to Eudoxia, the Empress, and Pulcheria, the sister of the ruler [79], and an equally long one to two younger sisters of Theodosius [80]. If he had hoped the members of the imperial family would really read all these, he must have been a very optimistic man. Cyril also contacted Pope Celestinus I. In the spring of 430 he sent him a letter indicting Nestorius of blasphemy; along with it he sent him a file containing his own letters and the Nestorian sermons, everything translated into Latin [81].

7. Celestinus investigates

Informations from Constantinople had made Rome somewhat distrustful of Nestorius; leading ecclesiastical circles could not quite understand what was wrong with that incriminated 'theotokos'. At the instigation of the Roman bishop, the archdeacon Leo, a future Pope, asked the advice of a learned monk in Marseille, called Cassianus; the relevant documents were sent to him. This monk, who also had an untiring pen, in due time produced a longish report [82]. His conclusion was that there was not much difference between the heresy of Pelagius (with whom Rome had already had its problems) and that of Nestorius [83]. As 'a disciple and imitator of Pelagius' Nestorius was said to believe that Christ was only a man who had obtained that the divine majesty associated himself with him by virtue of his living piously and religiously; he acquired this dignity not because of his sacred origin but only on account of his merits [84]. Whether this verdict did justice to Nestorius' thought may well be asked [85].

When Cassianus' report had, via the archdeacon Leo, come under the eyes of Celestinus, this Pope convened a synod in Rome. It duly condemned Nestorius as an heretic; the Roman bishop declared that it was perfectly legitimate to call Mary 'theotokos' [86]. After this synod Celestinus, on August 11th, 430, expedited four letters, to the clergy of Constantinople, to the Greek and oriental bishops, to Cyril of Alexandria [87], and to Nestorius [88]. The letter to Nestorius was the most important. He was invited (or ordered) to confess what the whole Church confessed; if not, he would be excommunicated. He was given ten days (after the receipt of this letter) to retract. The letter did not specify where exactly the bishop of Constantinople was wrong; the term 'theotokos' does not occur in this papal letter. But, curiously enough, it was not sent to the addressee directly; a papal envoy brought it to Cyril of Alexandria. It was as though Celestinus left the settlement of this affair to the Alexandrian bishop. It will be clear that this empowered Cyril to specify what Roman Catholic doctrine was on this point.

8. The affair entrusted to Cyril

Instead of hurrying at full speed to the oriental capital in order to deliver the knock-out blow to his opponent, Cyril in his turn convened a synod; he had no problem in ranging the Egyptian bishops behind him. The practical result was that Nestorius was requested to obey the orders of the Pope; to the final synodal statement twelve 'anathemas' were attached condemning opinions that were ascribed to Nestorius. The upshot of these condemnations was that nobody should think that there were two persons in Christ; there was only one single Son. The Gospels should not be read in this way that one set of expressions was taken to refer only to what is human in him and another to the divine element. One should not scruple to speak of Jesus as God, of the birth of God, of the passion of God. There was, therefore, not the slightest reason for denying Mary the title of 'theotokos' [89]. It was a forceful attempt to invalidate any idea of a dichotomy, a dualistic split, in the person of Christ.

A special envoy sped with the papal letter and with the synodal statement towards Constantinople; travelling via Jerusalem and Antioch, he delivered letters from Cyril to the bishops of these two towns [90]. Did John of Antioch see a schism lurking on the horizon? Anyhow, he gave the envoy a letter to his colleague of Constantinople adjuring him to keep his head cool, to reflect upon the question long and deeply, and to seek advice [91]. After all, the main point at issue was that 'theotokos'. And had not Nestorius himself declared that this term was, if not preferable, then at least acceptable ? But John knew nothing of the papal ultimatum [92].

9. The reaction of Nestorius

Nestorius' reaction was moderate. Having received the dossier on November 30, he pondered for a week on his answer and then, on December 6, delivered a sermon. He admitted that, from an orthodox point of view, no decisive objection could be made against the term 'theotokos', although he himself preferred the term 'Christotokos' as combining the concepts of 'theotokos' and 'anthropotokos'. He denied being tributary to the doctrine of Paul of Samosata. He declared that there was only one Son indeed, but added that this Son was a conjunction of the Logos and 'the temple' (= the body).

Nestorius probably felt that he might be accused of begging the question and that he had to be more explicit. Having consulted his clergy the next day, he produced a doctrinal statement. "Some, acting in this as sons of the Church, demand of us a more explicit affirmation; let us therefore express ourselves with greater precision ... Yes, the holy Virgin is the mother of God and the mother of the man - mother of God because the temple (the body), created in her by the Holy Spirit, was united to the divinity, and mother of the man, because God took from her the first beginnings of our own nature." So far so good. Celestinus might have felt satisfied ... if only he had had knowledge of Nestorius' declaration. But riddle of all riddles : Rome was not notified of all this [93].

10. The Council of Ephesus, 431

a. A Council convoked

Earlier in 430 Cyril had attempted to win the Emperor over for his cause. But Theodosius was not favourably disposed towards him; he accused the bishop of disturbing the peace in his capital and even of sowing discord in the bosom of the imperial family. A council would be convened in which everybody would be heard, not only Cyril and his party. The bishop of Alexandria was peremptorily told that he would have to accept the decisions of this council [94]. The idea of an ecumenical council seems to have been suggested to the Emperor by Nestorius who was well received at the court [95]. On November 19th, 430, that is before the papal ultimatum had arrived in Constantinople, the Emperor sent a letter to all bishops inviting to come to a synod to be opened in Ephesus on June 7th, 431 [96].

b. An unruly beginning

In that month of June, Ephesus saw the bishops marching in. Pope Celestinus, who had received the imperial invitation in the beginning of 431, sent a small embassy, with the instruction to execute what had already been decided in Rome [97]. It must be stressed that at that moment he knew nothing of the new doctrinal statement by Nestorius. The Roman bishop also tried to damp the fervour of Cyril somewhat; it was not the downfall of Nestorius that he wanted but his good [98]. The Emperor, who was much concerned about the outcome of the debates, sent a representative, count Candidianus; this official was not to take part in the discussions but would, instead, 'police' the proceedings [99]. The first to arrive was Nestorius with a retinue of bishops; since Memnon, the local ordinarius, was inimical to him, they were refused the use of the churches in town. Next came Cyril's party consisting of some fifty bishops and quite a number of other clerics and monks. It came to blows between Nestorians and Cyrillians [100]. In these circumstances a great deal of tact would have been needed to make the Ephesus synod a success, but tact was not the most outstanding quality of the main actors.

c. Cyril's coup d'état

Since not all bishops had arrived on the planned opening day of June 7th, the first session was postponed, especially at the wish of the imperial official. But Cyril had an advantage he would not let slip : the Antiochenes, with John, their bishop of whom a moderating influence was expected, had not yet turned up. Although nobody had committed Cyril to preside over the synod, he announced that it would start on June 21th, but sixty-eight bishops protested against this. Undaunted, Cyril convoked the Fathers for the next day, June 22nd, and one hundred and fifty-four of them appeared in the council hall [101]. Candidianus added his voice to the protest and then left angrily the meeting-room saying that he would appeal to the Emperor and tell him that he had been violently expelled [102].

Meanwhile Nestorius had been asked, and the third time even ordered, to appear before the council. This he refused. The assembled Fathers then resolved to proceed without him (and against him). Cyril made quite a show of it. He read the Nicene Creed to the assembly and after that the doctrinal statement he had sent to Nestorius in the beginning of 430 [103]. He then asked those present whether this statement agreed with the Nicene Creed. One hundred and twenty-bishops gave their assent to this. He had then read a doctrinal letter from Nestorius to Cyril [104]. Was this statement in conformity with the Nicene Creed? The Fathers found it was not. Nestorius was duly condemned and anathemized; he was also deposed as bishop of Constantinople [105].

May we believe Cyril himself, the condemnation of Nestorius was received by the faithful with great rejoicing, as though, in the words of Duchesne, "Mary had triumphed over Nestorius" [106]. Cyril and the other bishops were accompanied to their serail through an illuminated town by people carrying thousands of torches while clouds of incense rose up from the thuribles they swayed [107]. But Nestorius reports that much violence was done in the town to his adherents by the rowdies of Cyril and Memnon; the officers of the garrison expressed their displeasure with this but looked on passively [108].

According to Nestorius, the hand of his arch-enemy could be detected in everything. "He had gathered those who were sympathetic towards him, he is the public prosecutor, the Emperor and the judge ... It was Cyril who convoked this Council, it was Cyril was its president. Who was the judge? Cyril. Who was the accuser? Cyril. Who was bishop of Rome? Cyril. Cyril was everything. Cyril was bishop of Alexandria but he assumed the place of the saint and venerable bishop of Rome, Celestinus" [109]. There was not much love lost between the sees of Alexandria and Constantinople!

d. The breach complete

The breach was soon to be complete. On 26th June the Antiochene party arrived. They lost no time in convening with the Nestorian party, probably on the day of their arrival, highly irritated as they were to hear of Cyril's coup d'état. A gathering of Nestorians and Antiochenes condemned what the Council had done so far as contrary to ecclesiastical law, broke off all relations with the Cyrillians, and deposed Cyril and the bishop of Ephesus, Mennon [110]. This condemnation was signed by forty-three bishops. So there were now two synods, the majority one of Cyrillians and a minority one of Nestorians. The imperial and papal envoys parted ways, Candidianus supporting the Nestorian party, and the papal delegates siding with the Cyrillian group.

e. Imperial intervention

By couriers speeding to and fro between Ephesus and Constantinople, Theodosius II remained well-informed of the proceedings; he was highly dissatisfied with the turn things had taken. Soon a high imperial official, Palladius, arrived with a letter from the Emperor dated June 29th. All that had happened so far was null and void, wrote the ruler; the Fathers were forbidden to leave the town until a special envoy from his part had arrived [111]. Nestorius must have felt at that time that he was losing the support of the Emperor; to a suggestion from the imperial chancellery that he might retire to his monastery, he answered that he was willing to do so [112]. Maybe he was thoroughly fed up with the whole affair.

At the end of July or the beginning of August the special imperial envoy arrived, count John. He immediately declared all three depositions valid; he told the bishops that they should return home since the synod was

305

over [113]. Nestorius relates that the bishops loudly applauded when they heard that his deposition was confirmed, but that they vehemently protested when the same was declared of Cyril [114]. Count John went even further : he put the three main contestants under house arrest, apart from one another. With this measure he wanted to stop the proceedings, but the bishops remained in session for another short while. The Council ended without an agreement having been reached. As related already, Nestorius resigned in September 431 and returned to his monastery in Antioch. He was no longer even so much as mentioned at the court : "the Emperor loathed his name more than that of anyone else", wrote Theodoretus [115].

Theodosius asked the Fathers in Ephesus to send delegates to the capital, eight from each party [116]. They never reached their destination : the Emperor told them to stop at Chalcedon [117], because there was much unrest in Constantinople and he did not want to have more of it [118]. The Emperor crossed the Bosporus in person to join the delegates but did not succeed in bringing them to an agreement. He then ordered the synod in Ephesus to dissolve [119].

11. A schism prevented

The Council of Ephesus having brought no solution, the Church of the East remained divided from top to bottom. The question is what the real issue was, the personal enmity between Cyril and Nestorius, perhaps rather the hatred with which Cyril persecuted Nestorius, or the doctrinal question of the theotokos. All the elements for a schism were at hand. But the Emperor who probably had more than enough of the affair, decided to prevent this. In the middle of 432 imperial letters reached Cyril and John of Antioch asking to meet and come to an agreement. Bishop John, who had always supported Nestorius, was asked to abandon his friend; it would also greatly facilitate a solution if Cyril was ready to let fall or at least mitigate his anathemas [120].

This was asking much of both bishops. John must humble himself to the dust, and for Cyril invalidating the anathemas was tantamount to admitting that he had been wrong. The negotiations, conducted by imperial officials, were long and arduous. John abandoned Nestorius by acknowledging his successor as the legitimate bishop of Constantinople. Cyril did not withdraw his anathemas, but suggesting that they had no doctrinal significance, he declared they were directed against the person of Nestorius (he knew that high dignitaries at the court were very much irritated against the ci-devant bishop) [121].

There probably was a lot of window-dressing in this reconciliation, but the Emperor saw the road now free for a definitive solution. In 433 the contestants signed a formula of union with which the danger of a schism was averted [122]. The agreement (its content is doctrinal, the person of Nestorius being passed over in silence) was couched in the following terms. "We confess that our Lord Jesus Christ, the only Son of God, was really God and really composed of a rational soul and a body, that he had been engendered by the Father before all ages with regard to his divinity, and that with regard to his humanity he is born from the Virgin Mary at the end of times, for us and our salvation; that he is consubstantial with the Father according to his divinity, and consubstantial with us according to his humanity. For there has come into being a union of two natures ... We also confess that the Holy Virgin is the mother of God, the theotokos, because God the Logos has assumed the flesh, made himself man, and has united himself at the very moment of his conception with the temple (= the body) that he took from her." This agreement was communicated to all concerned, among them the Emperor and Pope Sixtus III (432-440). The only question is whether Nestorius himself would have been ready to sign this formula, but he was not invited to do so.

12. Taking stock of the situation

I feel we should pause here for a moment to review the situation, particularly in view of the fact that the schism that Theodosius II feared so much, was finally realized with the origination of the Nestorian Church. The dualistic element that was constantly present in this affair then became a hard fact. I find the Nestorian question the most difficult of all heterodox positions since it is so hard to state with the required precision how heterodox Nestorius was. We may ask, as Wand does, whether he was a 'Nestorian' himself [123].

I think all parties were to blame, least of all perhaps bishop John of Antioch, who was the most irenic of the contestants but who in the end was quite ready to jettison his friend. Pope Celestinus I deserves blame too, for it was not prudent of him to sail so confidently on the compass of bishop Cyril of Alexandria. It was this Cyril who succeeded in whipping up what was a minor doctrinal difference of opinion or perhaps even a misunderstanding into a major doctrinal question. And Nestorius himself? Well, we saw that he was not the most tactful man. His standing at the court would doubtless have been better had he not lashed out left and right against all who did not agree with him. The last thing Theodosius II wanted was trouble.

But the smoke was not without fire. Nestorius remained reticent with regard to the term 'theotokos', sensing there was paganism in it, because it might make a goddess of Mary. But when it came to the point, he did not object to the term. He did not even deny that there are two natures in Christ. Where his doctrine became somewhat dubious from an orthodox viewpoint is that in his opinion the fusion of the two natures was not of an organic or ontological nature. He held that the link between them was psychological or voluntary. The two natures, or substances, in Christ mean that there were also two persons (prosopa); the fusion which makes one entity of Christ is not that of the two natures but of the two persons who became the one person of Christ.

Nestorius came to this curiously artificial construction because he could not conceive of an organic fusion of the divine and the human in Christ. "One suspects it was really a desperate attempt to cover up the fact that Nestorius had already posited two complete persons in Christ ... It is difficult to see how in spite of this superhuman effort Nestorius can be acquitted of this charge" (namely that of holding there were not only two natures but also two persons in Christ) [124]. Orthodox or not, he surely laid himself open to misunderstandings and misinterpretations. The main doctrinal tenet of the later Nestorian Church (the founder of which is not Nestorius) is that there are two persons in Christ.

13. Nestorianism in the East

After the agreement of 433 in the West little or nothing was heard of Nestorianism. In the East the situation was somewhat different. There were clerics in the East who found that Cyril had conceded too much; for quite a number of others the deposition of Nestorius remained a sore point. Some of them even broke off relations with John of Antioch in whom they saw a traitor. We are already detecting the first contours of what was to become the Nestorian Church. This is not to say that Nestorianism really had a great future in the oriental half of the Empire. In the end only fifteen bishops refused to adhere to the agreement; they believed Cyril to be wrong [125]. Not wanting to remain isolated, they encountered kindred spirits in the Persian Empire.

Christianity must have penetrated already at a very early date into the regions east of the Euphrates and Tigris, but we have no idea how and when this happened. There exists an old tradition in the Persian Church that the apostle Thomas was its founder; for this reason it claims an apostolic origin. We know of Christian centres in the Parthian Empire in the second century, the most important of these being the Churches of Edessa and Nisibis. Their liturgical language was neither Greek nor Latin but Aramaic. In these East Syrian Churches there existed a strong tendency towards asceticism of which the doctrine of Tatian testifies.

We are never far from ethical dualism here. The original baptismal formula made it mandatory upon those receiving baptism to stay single or, if they were married, to live in continence. The hostility towards all forms of sexuality, even the marital one, is evident here. As this rule threatened the survival of the community, it was abandoned after 300. Instead, a bipartition was created between the 'Just' who had committed themselves to live a Christian life and were allowed to marry and have progeny, and the 'Perfect', charismatic persons whose lives were severely ascetic and who did not marry. This bipartition is reminiscent of that found in certain Gnostic sects, for instance Manichaeism.

Christianity spread even further eastward through the Parthian and Sasanian Empires; at the end of the fourth century it had reached the region of the Amu Darya and the town of Merw, profiting from the tolerant attitude of the rulers. For a long time there was no common ecclesiastical organization, but in 410 a general synod was held in Ctesiphon (Seleucia, the capital). There the Apostolic Church of the East was founded, consisting of six ecclesiastical provinces, each under a metropolitan. The metropolitan of Ctesiphon was the Katholikos. Although organizationally already at some distance from the Roman Catholic Church of the Roman Empire, it remained doctrinally in union with it, because it accpted the Nicene Creed and that of Constantinople in 381.

All organizational links with Rome were severed during a synod in 424, where it was stated that the patriarchs of the Empire, those of Rome, Constantinople, Alexandria, and Antioch, had no jurisdiction over the Apostolic Church of the East. The Katholikos was declared to be subject only to the tribunal of Christ. The dogmatic unity came to an end when this Church officicially adopted the 'Antiochene Christology', that is, the two-natures-doctrine with its dualistic flavour, the two natures remaining so distinct that it is almost impossible to speak of a real personal union. It may be said that since the synod that accepted this doctrine, that of Seleucia in 486, the Apostolic Church was a Nestorian Church. It was a Church that entertained no relations with the Roman Catholic Church and even stood opposed to it as a non-Roman Church.

It was with this Church that the deposed bishops and clergy of eastern Syria came into contact after 433. There existed an important centre of Nestorianism in Edessa, in eastern Syria, then still within the frontiers of the Roman Empire; it was in this town that they found a refuge. Edessa has had a fiercely anti-Nestorian bishop in the person of Rabbula (412-435), but when he had been succeeded by Ibas (435-457), the climate changed, although this Ibas was not an unconditional supporter of Nestorius. It was he who forged the link with the Apostolic Church of the East. He sent a letter to bishop Mari of Ardaschir within which he declared his sympathy for Nestorius and his aversion of Cyril; this letter was accompanied by translations of heterodox works of Theodore of Mopsuestia and others into Aramaic. Along this road Nestorian doctrine became known beyond the Euphrates. This development was helped by the fact that Rabbula had banished supporters of Nestorius from his town who then built up a new existence in Persia; one of them even became the metropolitan of Nisibis.

Edessa had a famous catechical school that under Ibas and after became a hotbed of Nestorianism. For this reason the Byzantine Emperor Zeno dissolved it in 489 and banished the Nestorians. They wandered over the border into Persia and greatly strengthened Nestorianism there.

So the schism, the dualistic split, so much feared by responsible authors as a consequence of the Nestorian struggle, had become a fact at last. The Nestorian Church had come to stay. Large sections of it were reunited with Rome in 1552; they form the so-called 'Chaldaean Church' with its own language and liturgy. They count presently some two hundred thousand Chaldaean Christians, to be found mainly in Iran, Iraq, and Syria, and, of course, as immigrants in the United States. They have their own patriarch. There are still some eighty thousand to one hundred thousand members of the old, non-reunited Nestorian Church, dispersed over Syria, Iraq, India, and, again, the United States.

PART IV MONOPHYSITISM

1. Continuing unrest in the oriental Church

The Church of the fifth century was not granted peace and harmony after the agreement of 433; the Christological discussion was not yet over. Soon enough much agitation was caused by some monks who left their monasteries in Armenia and began to wander throughout the eastern Empire. As itinerant preachers they drew large audiences where they went, in towns as well in religious houses. Although they did not proclaim this openly, they were adherents of Apollinarianism and of his doctrine of their being only one nature in Christ (the divine one). Apollinaris had taught that Christ, having only one

311

nature, was not 'consubstantial with us', i.e. did not possess a human nature [126]. This introduces us to the doctrine of monophysitism.

2. Cyril and monophysitism

The reader will perhaps remember two remarks made by the present author in the course of Chapter VI of this volume. The first is that Nestorius, a bishop of Constantinople, hit out against certain monks in his town whom he found unruly, the second that it was suggested in Nestorian circles that Cyril was so hotly after Nestorius because he wanted to camouflage deficiencies in his own theology. In the texts written by Cyril expressions occur not infrequently which might lend substance to this suspicion, namely that there was "one nature (mia phusis) of the divine Logos who became flesh" [127]. He sometimes squarely denied that there were two natures in Christ [128]. He was harking back then, probably unwittingly, to the doctrine of Apollinaris. He was, however, prudent enough to safeguard himself against the charge of Apollinarianism by declaring that out of the human and the suprahuman proprieties (of Christ) that go together some sort of one single intermediary (metaxu) was constituted [129]

3. Dioscorus, the guardian of Cyril's spiritual heritage

In the agreement of 433 between Cyril and John of Antioch, signed also by Cyril, it was stated expressly that in Christ there are two natures united in one person. But there was doubtless a hint of monophysitism in his doctrine. As long as nobody would press his own particular viewpoint too strongly the peace of 433 would hold. But Cyril, who had behaved loyally after 433, died in 444 and was succeeded by the much more fanatical Dioscorus. Meanwhile Celestinus I, who always walked in the footsteps of Cyril, was succeeded as bishop of Rome by Leo I (440-461), a man of a strong character who could not so easily be made the tool of whichever theologian. In 446 the influential sister of Theodosius II, the dea protectrix of the 433 agreement, saw herself relegated to a nunnery, while a certain Chrysaphius, an eunuch, became the most important person at the court. This Chrysaphius was the godchild of Eutyches, a monk [130]. With this name we make acquaintance with the man who reopened the hostilities in the oriental Church [131]. But before we turn to him and his role in the theological wars of his time, a word must be said of Dioscorus.

This bishop of Alexandria posed as the guardian of the secular and spiritual heritage of his predecessor. He was a harsh man who treated Cyril's family with a hard hand; the presbyter Athanasius, a nephew of Cyril, complained that Dioscorus had threatened him and his brother with death and made him flee to Constantinople, only to be put in prison there by Chrysaphius who was hand in glove with Dioscorus [132].

On the doctrinal plane, Dioscorus tried to out-Cyril Cyril by being still more anti-Nestorian than his predecessor had been. As the not very willing target of his attacks he chose Theodoretus, the bishop of Cyr and a widely read author. He had by hearsay that Theodoretus had used expressions that smacked of Nestorianism in a sermon. Instead of approaching his man directly, he denounced him to Domnus, the bishop of Antioch. Having been informed of Dioscorus' accusation, Theodoretus vehemently protested in a letter to his accuser [133]. Dioscorus, who wanted to see blood, was not convinced and even sent some bishops to the capital in an attempt to press his opponent as hard as possible [134]. He even went so far as to anathemize Theodoretus without having heard him; his victim complained of this high-handed move to Pope Leo [135]. With the transfer of the case to Constantinople we are coming into the orbit of the already mentioned Eutyches.

Dioscorus did not have to fear the reaction of the court. On February 18th, 448, an imperial decree appeared condemning not only Nestorianism, but also those authors who wrote against Cyril of Alexandria, according to Wickham, with mainly Theodoretus in mind [136]. Another imperial decree, summer 448, forbade this bishop to leave his diocese, which in practice meant that he was prevented from preaching in Antioch. Both he and Domnus might explain their attitude to Dioscorus as much as they wanted - Theodoretus even wrote an anti-monophysite treatise -, their enemy remained adamant. Once again the tension in the oriental Church rose to a dangerous level.

4. Eutyches steps forward

It was then, in the autumn of 448, that Eutyches stepped forward. He was a monk and a presbyter, and the superior, the 'archimandrite', of the big Hiob monastery in Constantinople. In 448 he had reached the age of seventy already, but this made him no less assertive and ambitious. May we believe Nestorius in his Liber Heraclidis, Eutyches, relying on imperial favour, wanted to play the role of 'bishop of bishops' (although he was not a bishop himself); having Flavian, the bishop of the capital, in his pocket, he was able to direct the affairs of the Church [137]. Making allowance for some exaggeration on the part of Nestorius, says Wickham, this picture may be largely correct [138]. Pope Leo did not have a high opinion of this Eutyches; 'very imprudent and inexperienced', he called him, and acting 'by want of learning rather than by subtlety of thought' [139].

Eutyches was not above suspicions of heresy. Already in the beginning of 448 bishop Domnus of Antioch had accused him in a letter to Theodosius II of being an Apollinarist, because he held that there is only one nature in Christ [140]. But at that moment Eutyches still enjoyed the favour of the Emperor; so nothing happened. The bubble burst, however, during a local synod in November 448 with bishop Flavian in the chair. Eutyches brought it down on his own head by his accusing, attacking and charging against everybody who professed there being two natures in Christ, thus confusing and troubling the Church [141]. During this synod bishop Eusebius of Dorylaeum reproached him for deviating from the Creed of Nicaea and from the canons of the Council of Ephesus [142]. Eusebius knew quite well what he was saying. He had had several conversations with Eutyches (they were still friends then) during which he had got convinced that the archimandrite was deviating from the path of orthodoxy [143]; in vain he had attempted to guide him back to it [144].

5. Eutyches condemned

Hoping to avoid disturbances in the Church, Flavian, a timid man, asked Eusebius to go and speak to Eutyches, but Eusebius, probably finding that he had already talked enough with his opponent, insisted that action should be taken. In consequence, delegates were sent to the archimandrite inviting him to appear before the synod [145]. At first the headstrong old monk refused to leave his monastery; he showed his lack of prudence by telling the delegates that "he scrutinized only the holy scriptures, so more solid than the expositions of the Fathers" [146]. A second delegation was sent but this came back with the news that Eutyches was too ill to attend the sessions [147]. A third delegation returned with two monks who told the synod how very ill their abbot was [148]. But having exhausted all his excuses, Eutyches finally appeared before the assembly on November 22nd. He did not come alone but was accompanied by a whole retinue of monks and even of soldiers and officials, put at his disposal by his godson Chrysaphius [149].

It did not help him at all. Asked to explain himself with regard to the union of the two natures in Christ, he defended himself clumsily, but it became sufficiently apparent that he professed neither the union of the two natures in Christ nor that Christ is consubstantial with us through his human nature [150]. Nobody raised a finger for him and even the meek Flavian saw himself forced to condemn him. He was declared blasphemous, deprived of his sacerdotal dignity, deposed as archimandrite, and expelled from the ecclesiastical community. Everybody following him in his (monophysite) errors would also be excommuncicated [151].

6. Eutyches' counter-attack

Since Eutyches had no intention whatsoever to stand back, a war was now on. Whilst the synodal Fathers were herding out of the hall after the closing session, Eutyches declared that he would appeal to the bishops of Rome, Alexandria, Jerusalem, and Thessalonike [152], as he did indeed. The ex-archimandrite, who was not popular in town, defended his position by having placards posted [153]. He may not have had the clergy and the faithful of the diocese on his hand, but he had the Emperor behind him, so that Theodosius wrote to Leo in his favour [154].

Feeling fortified by the support of the Emperor, Eutyches took the offensive. He complained that the acts of the synod that had condemned him had been adulterated with the complicity of Flavian; he asked the ruler to convoke another synod so that he could get due redress [155]. A synod of thirty-four bishops, with Flavian as chairman and with the assistance of three high-ranking imperial officials, came together in the capital in April, but having studied the synodal documents, the assembly did not find they had been falsified [156].

This was a success for Flavian, of course, but all the same his position was far from enviable. True enough, he enjoyed the support not only of his own (secular) clergy but also that of Pope Leo. Flavian informed him accurately on the situation to which the Pope answered that the affair had his close attention and that he would state his position as soon as possible. Since Leo spoke of the 'bad error, occurring in Constantinople', its bishop might be certain that the Pope's reaction would be favourable for him [157].

On the other hand, Flavian felt the hot breath of Eutyches in his neck, of "that terrible inquisitor who confused the whole East with his intemperate zeal and whose feeble brain was haunted by the spectre of Nestorianism" [158]. Of course, after all Eutyches was only a monk who could do no great harm to his bishop, but after the monk was the Emperor, his protector, who was far from favourably disposed towards Flavian. Taking his chance with Theodosius who was under the influence of his chamberlain Chrysaphius, and supported by Dioscorus, the bishop of Alexandria, Eutyches asked for another ecumenical council. The ruler granted his request and, on March 30th, 449, told the metropolitans to assemble with a number of their suffragans in Ephesus on the first of August [159].

7. The 'Robbers' Council'

This council became known as the infamous 'Latrocinium', the 'Robbers' Council', perhaps the most undignified episode in the turbulent history of the ancient Church. In fact, the Council opened a week later than planned, on August 8th, but six weeks earlier Leo had unequivocally stated his position in a letter to Flavian, the famous 'Tomus ad Flavianum' [160]. In it the bishop of Constantinople was mildly censored for his weak leadership; for the teachings of Eutyches he had no good word. Although an official papal document, the Tomus must not be seen as an ex-cathedra statement; nevertheless, it is a highly important doctrinal declaration of the faith of the Church. It should be remarked, however, that Leo, learned as he was, knew no Greek; since he was relying on Latin translations of Greek documents, some of the subtleties of the discussion may have escaped him.

Leo stated that Christ possessed two natures in one person. He belonged totally to the supernatural world and just as much as he did to humanity. Being divine, he enriched the human nature; being human did not infringe upon his divinity. The two natures did not fuse into one but remained distinct. As a person Christ was sui generis 'through a new order', since no other human person possessed two natures. Each nature in him had its own peculiar properties, but they, although forming two distinct sets, were relative to one single person. This is what in theologicis is called the 'communicatio idiomatum', the harmonious cohabitation of two natures in one person. Leo accused Eutyches of not understanding this, for in his Christ there was such a wide gulf between his divinity and the bodily shape that one might ask how it was possible that God's Son had suffered and died. By using the term 'solvere Jesum', i.e. to 'separate his human nature from him', Leo implicitly accused Eutyches of dualism [161].

Armed with this Tomus, the papal legates departed to Ephesus. There they found some one hundred and thirty bishops assembled; the Emperor had dispatched some officials to represent him. From which quarter the wind would blow became evident when, on the orders of Theodosius, Dioscorus took the chair. Immediately after the official opening the papal legates (who could not speak Greek and were severely handicapped as a consequence) asked that the 'Tomus' should be read. Knowing or sensing that this contained a magisterial condemnation of the Eutychian doctrine, Dioscorus refused them the platform; in the course of the sessions they were never allowed to take the floor. A very dangerous split between East and West, dualistic in nature, here becomes apparent : Dioscorus, supported in this by a substantial majority of the assembly, did not recognize the authority of the bishop of Rome.

Then Eutyches was brought in and his appeal against his condemnation by Flavian was read. At this point, the imperial envoy, count Elpidius, intervened; he desired that Flavian and all those who had supported the condemnation of Eutyches or who were supposed to be sympathetic to it, would be excluded from voting. The majority acquiesced in this so that a minority of forty-two bishops lost their voting rights. Through this indefensible manoeuvre the council was henceforward packed.

The next stage was that Eutyches was reinstated into his dignities, whereas Flavian and bishop Eusebius of Dorylaeum were deposed. When Flavian heard Dioscorus proposing this, he cried ; "I repudiate you!", whereupon one of the papal legates took his side by crying : "He (Dioscorus) must be contradicted". Poor Flavian was not only deposed but also banished; he died from exhaustion before he had reached his place of exile. More depositions followed, those of Ibas of Edessa, Domnus of Antioch, and Theodoretus of Cyr. Eutyches got off scotfree with a vague declaration of adherence to the Creed of Nicaea. He acknowledged that there were two natures in Christ, but with this proviso that there were two natures before the union (before the Incarnation) but only one after it [162]. If the reader does not understand this, I cannot help him. He denied that Jesus was as human as we are, because his body was not consubstantial with us (but the Holy Virgin was) [163].

Jugie judges that "the old archimandrite wanted to remain faithful to orthodoxy, and sometimes spoke in this way but because of his ignorance and his lack of intelligence sometimes expressed himself as an heretic" [164]. If his formula 'two natures before the union' meant anything at all, it could only signify that Christ's human soul was pre-existent. This smacked of Origenism, and Leo characterized it as 'an absurd and perverse opinion' [165]. The question is whether Eutyches had ever read Origen or was consciously referring to him. For if he said that the two natures were pre-existent, he implied that the human nature, the humanity (with body and soul), was pre-existent too - which, from whichever angle we look at it, is complete nonsense. Anyhow, the baleful result of the Robbers' Council [166] was that the East was now so firmly pitted against the West that a schism could hardly be avoided.

8. Leo tries to redress the situation

Pope Leo was highly displeased with the way things had been handled; he would have felt personally slighted, but he must also have feared greatly for the unity of the Church. The breach that finally became a fact in 1054 might have occurred already a thousand years earlier. The papal envoys returned to Rome as though they were refugees, just as bishop Eusebius who had been thrown into prison but had managed to escape. Flavian, on his way to his place of exile and his death, sent a 'libellus appellationis', an appeal, to Rome.

Leo wrote to Theodosius asking him to convene another more truly ecumenical council; it characterized the distance between East and West that he insisted that it should be held in Italy [167]. On the same day he asked Pulcheria's support for this plan [168]. Similar letters went out to the secular and regular clergy and the faithful of Constantinople [169]. Since Theodosius did not react, Leo wrote again on Christmas Day 449, pressing his request [170]. The papal offensive gathered momentum when Theodosius' co-emperor for the West, Valentinianus III (424-455) visited Rome in February 450, accompanied by his mother, the famous Galla Placidia, a daughter of Theodosius I, and his wife, Licinia Eudoxia; all three were orthodox believers. At Leo's request they each wrote a letter to Theodosius II, telling him that he should convene a council of all the bishops in the world, to be held in Italy. Valentinianus expressly recognized the Roman bishop as the supreme authority in the Church and as the judge of faith and bishops [171]. Since Theodosius did not react to this spate of letters either, Leo kept up the bombardment with new letters, written in March, to Pulcheria, to the monks and secular clergy of Constantinople, and to the faithful of this town [172].

In April 450, the Emperor at last sent an answer but not to Leo; he wrote to his co-emperor and to the two western Empresses. He had, he said, never deviated from the religion of his ancestors. Nothing had been wrong with the Council of Ephesus; it had acted in complete independence. The great offender, Flavian, had been banished; since his removal peace and concord reigned once again in the Church. But not a word about a new council [173]!

9. A schism averted

And then, all of a sudden, something happened that the anguished faithful of these days must have considered providential. Theodosius had a fatal accident on July 25th, 450; he left no offspring. Leaving the monastery to which she had been confined, Pulcheria took the reigns of government into her hands. She married a general, Marcianus, who became Emperor (450-457). One of his first acts was to send the all-powerful chamberlain Chrysaphius to his death. The Emperors and Empresses of both East and West were all orthodox now, which meant that the fate of Eutyches and his party was sealed.

Shortly after his accession to the throne Marcianus acknowledged the Roman bishop's supreme authority over the Church [174] in a letter to Leo. This signified that, at least officially, East-West relations had been restored. Marcianus also acquiesced to the papal wish for a council 'to take away the ignomious error". Everything now came round full circle. The Emperor ordered that the body of Flavian be brought back to Constantinople where it was laid to rest in the basilica of the Apostles amongst his predecessors. His successor on the see of the capital, Anatolius, was forced to recognize the authority of Rome [175]. The only thing Marcianus did not concede was a council in Italy; it would be held in the East in a town to be chosen by the Emperor [176].

10. The ecumenical Council of Chalcedon

a. The management of the Council

On May 17th, 451, Marcianus sent out letters convoking a council at Nicaea (the choice of this town was, of course, not accidental); it opened on September 1st, 451 [177]. Leo had to accept this; he did not go himself but, instead, sent legates [178]. Quite a number of bishops had already arrived in Nicaea, when the Emperor changed his mind and asked them to assemble at Chalcedon (now Kadiköy), just opposite the capital on the Bosporus; he wanted to be as near to the Council as possible without having to go there himself [179]. The opening date had to be postponed to October 8th. When the Council of Chalcedon at last was opened in the church of Saint Euphemia, there were some six hundred bishops present, the greatest ecclesiastical gathering the world had ever seen. Leo desired that his legates would conduct the syndodal affairs [180], but once again he was overruled. The Emperor appointed an office of eighteen laymen who had to fix the order of the day. The legates kept the place of honour but saw the imperial commissars constantly intervening in the proceedings.

b. Measures against persons

Eutyches' cause was lost beforehand, but there was also Dioscorus, the powerful bishop of Alexandria, whose position had not been a subject of discussion thus far. When this ferocious man arrived at Nicaea with a retinue of Egyptian bishops, that is, before the Council began, he declared that Leo was excommunicated [181]. He overplayed his hand with this unwarranted move; in the third session, when the imperial commissars were absent, the case of Dioscorus was put on the agenda at the request of Eusebius of Dorylaeum; he was duly condemned, deposed, and reduced to the lay-state [182]. He did not return to his see but was sent to Gangres, a Paphlagonian town, where he died three years later. Eutyches had already been expelled from his monastery and confined to some place in the vicinity of

Constantinople; he did not attend the Council. Later he was banished further from the capital, we do not know where to, nor when he died. On July 28th, 452, Marcianus condemned Eutyches' writings to the fire.

c. The doctrinal result

The main result of the Council of Chalcedon in the doctrinal field is the condemnation of every form of monophysitism. It rejected the notion that there would have been two natures in Christ before the Incarnation but only one after it. "We teach unanimously that there is only one and the same Son, our Lord Jesus Christ, complete with regard to his divinity, complete also with regard to his humanity, truly God and at the same time truly man, composed of a rational soul and a body, consubstantial with the Father through his divinity, consubstantial with us through his humanity, similar to us in every respect except sin ... We recognize (in him) two natures, with no confusion or transformation or division or separation between them, for the difference between the two natures is in no way abolished by their union. Quite the contrary! The proprieties of each nature are safeguarded and subsist in one single person and one single hypostasis" [183].

11. The end of Eutychianism

This great doctrinal statement put an end to 'Eutychianism'. I place this word between inverted commas, because the question is justified whether a doctrine with this name ever really existed. Eutyches was much too inconsequential and too much of a muddle-head to found a theological school or to present some sort of coherent doctrine. Nevertheless, he succeeded in causing an enormous turmoil in the Church - a turmoil that finally led to the most explicitly anti-dualistic statement the Church had ever produced.

NOTES TO CHAPTER VII

1. Not be confused with that other Epiphanius, the bishop of Salamis in Cyprus.

2. Socr., HE 2.46.

3. Sozom., HE 6.25. According to Socr., HE 2.46, they were exommunicated on account of their frequentation of Epiphanius. According to Lietzmann, Apollinaris 2, the hospitality offered to Athanasius was the real reason for their excommunication which he ascribes to Theodotus, since this bishop was an Arian who wanted to gag those eloquent spokesmen of the orthodox party. The two Apollinaris's did penance and were accepted again.

4. Dräseke in his 'Apollinarios' (see Bibliography), Part I, wrote extensively about his life.

5. Leontius Byz., Adv. fraudes Apoll. (col. 1976).

6. Athan., Tomus ad Antioch. 9.

7. Dräseke, Apoll., Part II; Lietzmann, Apoll., Ch. IV Schriften des Apollinaris.

8. Greg.Nyss., De vita Ephr., col. 840/841.

9. Leontius Byz., Adv. fraudes Apoll., col. 1948. For this fraud see Voisin, L'Apollinarisme, IIe partie, Ch. I, § 2 La fraude des Apollinaristes.

10. Evagrius, HE 3.31 (363).

11. Athan., Letter to the bishops of Diocaesarea, Dräseke, Apoll. 392.

12. P. Godet s.v. 'Apollinaire et les Apollinaristes'. Dict.Théol.Cath. 1.2, 1506 (1923).

13. Apoll., Ep. ad Imp. Jovianum, Dräseke, Apoll. 341/342.

14. Apoll. Treatise on the unity of Christ's body with regard to his divinity, Dräseke, Apoll. 343.

15. Apoll. said literally that man existed imperfectly of two parts, Treatise on the unity of Christ, Dräseke, Apoll. 344, 18. Voisin, L'Apollinarisme 273 : Apollinaris "est, avec la généralité de ses contemporains, partisan de la dichotomie et, quoique les nécessités de la polémique l'aient fait changé d'avis, sa conception est toujours resté dichotomite : l'âme et le corps sont deux éléments imparfaits qui constituent la nature humaine".

16. Apoll., Contra Diodorum. Dräseke. Apoll. 365, 23.

17. Greg.Nyss., Adv.Apoll. 16.

18. Throughout this whole section I have been gratefully relying on Voisin, L'Apoll., IIIème partie, Ch. I, § 4, Le mode d'union.

19. Athan., Tomus ad Antioch. 7.

20. Lietzmann, Apoll. 7.

21. Lietzmann, Apoll. 16/17.

22. Epiph., Pan. 77.2.
23. Epiph., Pan. 77.3.
24. Epiph., Pan. 77.23.1.
25. Epiph., Pan. 77.20.
26. Epiph., Ancor. 77.3.
27. Epiph., Pan. 77.20.
28. This statement in Epiph., Pan. 77.21.
29. Epiph., Pan. 77.23.
30. We find Vitalis' profession of faith in Cyr.Al., De recta fide 10 (51).
31. Damasus, Ep. ad Paulinum Antiochenum Episcopum. Mansi 3, 425/426; this letter is usually referred to as 'per filium'.
32. Sozom., HE 6.25.
33. Sozom., HE 6.25.
34. Voisin, Apoll. 85.
35. Sozom., HE 6.26.
36. Cod.Theod. 16.5.12.
37. Cod.Theod. 16.5.13.
38. Epiph., Pan. 77.15.
39. Epiph., Pan. 77.19.
40. Epiph., Pan. 77.24.
41. Cod.Theod. 16.5.65.
42. Wand, Heresies 89.
43. Sozom., HE 8.2 (326).
44. Jo.Chrysost., Ad Theodorum Lapsum, I and II.
45. Sozom., HE 8.2 (326).
46. Wand, Heresies 92.
47. É. Amann s.v. 'Théodore de Mopsueste. Herméneutique', Dict.Théol.Cath. 15.1 (1946), 248-255.
48. Theod.Mops., Catechetical Homilies 3;5, quoted Pelikan, Christ.Trad. I, 250.
49. Lohse, Epochen 92.
50. Pelikan, Christ. Trad. I, 251.
51. Wand, Heresies 94.

52. Wand, Heresies 93.
53. Theod.Mops., Catechical Homilies 89, quoted by Pelikan, Christ.Trad. I, 254.
54. Pelikan, Christ.Trad. I, 254.
55. Theod.Mops., Catechetical Homilies 7.6.7, quoted by Pelikan, Christ.Trad. I, 255.
56. Phil. 2.6-7.
57. Theod.Mops., Comm.to Phil.2.6-7, quoted by Pelikan, Christ.Trad. I, 256. Somewhat belatedly, in the middle of the sixth century, Theodore found a staunch defender in the person of Facundus, bishop of Hermiane. In his 'Pro defensione trium capitulorum' (see Bibliography) he stated that Theodore, as bishop Leo I of Rome had done, should not be seen as the teacher of Nestorius since he had explicitly rejected the theory of Paul of Samosata (3.3.3-4); he had never taught that Jesus was a mere man (3.7). Many Fathers, he said, had taught things that resembled very much the teachings of Theodore of whom he cited several in his Liber XI. If these holy Fathers were erring sometimes a little from orthodoxy, it was not their intention to do so; therefore, they should not be thought of as heretics (11.6). The implication is, of course, that if we do not condemn them, we should not condemn Theodore either.
58. Socr., HE 7.29.
59. Lionel R. Wickham s.v. 'Nestorius/Nestorianischer Streit', TRE 24, Lief. 1/2 (1994), 276/277.
60. Lionel R. Wickham s.v. 'Nestorius/Nestorianischer Streit', TRE 24, Lief. 1/2 (1994), 278.
61. Socr., HE 7.29.
62. Cod.Theod. 16.5.65, 30.V.428.
63. Loofs, Nestorius 16.
64. Loofs, Nestorius 16/17, translation Loofs.
65. Cod.Theod. 16.5.66, 30.VII.435.
66. For this book, in the edition of Nau, see the Bibliography. An overview is to be found in É. Amann s.v. 'Nestorius. Oeuvres' in Dict.Théol.Cath. 11.1 (1931), 75-84; more recent is Lionel R. Wickham s.v. 'Nestorius/Nestorianischer Streit', TRE 24., Lief. 1/2 (1994), 281-284.
67. É. Amann s.v. 'Nestorius', Dict.Théol.Cath. 11.1. (1931), 92.
68. I am following Friedrich Loofs here s.v. 'Nestorius', Realenc.prot.Theol.u.Kirche 13 (1903), 739.

69. Quoted Loofs, Nestorius 31/32.
70. Socr., HE 7.32.
71. Nest., Heracl., ed. Nau 91/92. It is quite possible that Nest. did not consdier the term 'theotokos' downright heretical, but he found 'Christotokos' safer. Loofs, Nestorius 30. To Pope Celestine I he wrote that he was very averse of the term, but all the same "it may be tolerated", Loofs, Nestorius 31.
72. Proclus, Oratio 1.2.
73. Mansi 4, col. 1009.
74. Socr., HE 7.32.
75. Cyrillus Al., Ep 2.
76. Nest., Heracl., ed. Nau 93, English translation Loofs, Nest. 36.
77. Cyrillus Al., Adversus Nestorii blasphemias, PG 76 (1863).
78. Cyrillus Al., De recta fide ad Theodosium Imperatorem, PG 76 (1863).
79. Cyrillus Al., Ad reginas de recta fide oratio altera, PG 76 (1863).
80. Cyrillus Al, Ad reginas de recta fide, PG 76 (1863).
81. Cyrillus Al., Ep. 11.
82. Joannes Cassianus, De incarnatione Christi libri septem, PL 50 (1846).
83. Jo.Cass., De incarn. 6.14.
84. Jo.Cass., De incarn. 5.1.
85. É. Amann s.v. 'Nestorius', Dict.Théol.Cath. 11.1 (1963), 100/101, argues that Cassianus' own theology was not much different from that of Nestorius.
86. Arnobius, Conflictus 2.13.
87. Mansi 4, 1026-1050.
88. Mansi 4, 1026-1035.
89. Cyrillus Al., Ep. 17.
90. Cyrillus Al., Ep. 13 and 16.
91. Mansi 4, 1061-1077.
92. É. Amann s.v. 'Nestorius', Dict.Théol.Cath. 11.1 (1931), 104/105.
93. I am following here the relation, with the relevant texts, by É. Amann s.v. 'Nestorius', Dict.Théol.Cath. 11.1 (1931), 105/106; see also Synodicon 5.
94. Mansi 4, 1109-1112.

95. Evagrius, HE 1.7 (256); he spoke of it in a letter to John of Antioch in which we also find a copy of his doctrinal sermon, Synodicon 3, Epistola Nestorii ad Joannem Antiochenum.
96. Mansi 4, 1111-1115.
97. Coelestinus, Ep. 17, PL 50 (1846).
98. Coelestinus, Ep. 16, PL 50 (1846).
99. His commission in Mansi 4, 1117-1120.
100. Synodicon 8.
101. Mansi 5, 765-768, with the name of the protesters; same in Synodicon 7.
102. Synodicon 9.
103. Cyrillus Al., Ep. 4.
104. Cyrillus Al., Ep. 5.
105. Mansi 5, 1123-1226, presents a long report of this dramatic session, with the interventions of the individual bishops. Nestorius gives his own version with his refutation of the accusations made against him in his Liber Heracl., ed. Nau 116-290.
106. Quoted by É. Amann s.v. 'Nestorius', Dict. Théol.Cath. 11.1 (1931), 114.
107. Cyrillus Al., Ep. 24.
108. Nest., Heracl., ed. Nau no. 367-368, pp. 236/237.
109. Nest., Heracl., ed. Nau, pp. 177, no. 195. Nestorius conveniently forgot that the idea for an ecumenical council was his own.
110. Mansi 4, 1259-1270.
111. Mansi 4, 1377-1380.
112. Mansi 5, 792/793.
113. Mansi 4, 1396-1398.
114. Nest., Heracl. p. 248, no. 387.
115. Theodoret., Ep. ad Alexandrum Hieriopolitanum, Mansi 5.800.
116. The two sets of instructions in Mansi 4, 1399-1402 and 1457-1464.
117. The site is where Kadiköy now stands.
118. Ep. episcoporum orientalium, Mansi 4, 794.
119. Ep. Theodosii ad Synodum Ephesinam, Mansi 5, 1465-1466.
120. Ep. Theodosii et Valeriani ad Joannem Antiochae, Mansi 5, 277-282.

121. Ep. Joannis ad Cyrillum, Mansi 5, 289-292; Cyr., Ep. 39 (ad Joannem), PG 77.
122. The Greek text of this formula is found in the letter of Cyril to John, Ep. 39, PG 77 (1864); in Latin in Liberatus, Breviarium 8 (De pace Cyrilli et Joannis), PG 68 (1847).
123. Wand, Heresies 97.
124. Wand, Heresies 97-99; the quotation is from p. 99.
125. Liberatus, Breviarium 8.
126. Liberatus, Breviarium 10.
127. Cyr.Al., Ep. 17 (73), PG 77 (1863), Adv.Nest. 2 (31), PG 76 (1863), and elsewhere.
128. Cyr.Al., Quod unus sit Christus (736), PG 77 (1863).
129. Cyrl.Al., Directa fide 40. This points into the direction of two natures in one person indeed.
130. Liberatus, Breviarium 11.
131. See for this passage Lionel R. Wickham s.v. 'Eutyches/Eutychianism', TRE 10 (1982).
132. Libellus Athanasii Presbyteri contra Dioscorus, Mansi 6.1021-1030.
133. Theodoret., Ep. 83 ad Dioscurum. PG 83 (1864).
134. Theodoret., Ep. 86 ad Flavianum, PG 83 (1864).
135. Theodoret., Ep. 113 ad Leonem. PG 83 (1864).
136. Lionel R. Wickham s.v. 'Eutyches/Eutychianischer Streit', TRE 10, 560.
137. Nestorius, Liber Heracl. 460, ed. Nau p. 294.
138. Lionel R. Wickham s.v. 'Eutyches/Eutychianischer Streit', TRE 10.560.
139. Leo Magnus, Ep. 28. PL 54 (1846).
140. Facundus Herm., Pro defensione 8.5.
141. Nest., Liber Heracl. 460, ed. Nau p. 295.
142. The interpellation of Eus. in Mansi 6.657-660.
143. Report of these conversations in Nest., Liber Heracl. 462-466, ed. Nau pp. 296-298.
144. Mansi 6.655.
145. Mansi 6.655.
146. Mansi 6.700.

147. Mansi 6.706.
148. Mansi 6.712.
149. Mansi 6.732.
150. The discussion in Mansi 6.748.
151. Mansi 6.748.
152. Mansi 6.817.
153. Leo Magnus, Ep. 23.1. PL 54 (1846).
154. Nest., Liber Heracl. 466, ed. Nau p. 298; Leo Magnus, Ep. 24.1. PL 54 (1846).
155. Mansi 6.763-766.
156. Report of this synod Mansi 6.753-764.
157. Leo Magnus, Ep. 27 ad Flavianum. PL 54 (1846).
158. M. Jugie s.v. 'Eutychès et Eutychianisme', Dict.Théol. Cath. 5.1, 1584 (1924).
159. Mansi, 6.587-590.
160. Leo Magnus, Ep. 28 ad Flavianum. PL 54 (1846).
161. Lionel R. Wickham s.v. 'Eutyches/Eutychianischer Streit', TTE 10, 562 (1982), characterizes Leo's position as 'the most strongly dualistic interpretation of the formula of union of 433'. It is true that Leo, in order to combat Eutyches' monophysitism, stressed diophysitism (the two natures) as much as possible by distinguishing the two natures as being of a different order. But I feel that Wickham employs the term 'dualistic' somewhat loosely. If taken literally, it would mean that the two natures remain separated by an unbridgeable gulf, with the consequence that one could not conceive of one person. But this is, of course, just the opposite of what Leo wanted to convey.
162. Mansi 6.744.
163. Mansi 6.741.
164. M. Jugie s.v. 'Eutychès et Eutychianisme', Dict.Théol.Cath. 5.1, 1593 (1924).
165. Leo Magnus, Ep. 28 ad Flavianum 6. PL 44 (1846).
166. The Acts of this Council in Mansi 5.827 sqq.
167. Leo Magnus, Ep. 43, 13.X.449, ad Theodosium. PL 44 (1846).
168. Leo Magnus, Ep. 45 ad Pulcheriam. 13.X.449. PL 44 (1846).
169. Leo Magnus, Ep. 50 and 51. PL 44 (186).
170. Leo Magnus, Ep. 44 ad Theodosium, 25.XII.449. PL 44 (1846).

171. Ep. 55 Valentianus ad Theodosium, Ep. 56 Galla Placidia ad Theodosium, Ep. 57 Licinia Eudoxia ad Theodosium. Galla Placidia also wrote to Pulcheria, Ep. 58. PL 44 (1846).

172. Leo Magnus, Ep. 60 ad Pulcheriam, 17.III.450, Ep. 59 ad clerum et plebem Constantinopolis, Ep. 61 ad presbyteros et archimandritos. Pl 44. (1846).

173. Ep. 62 Theodosius ad Valentinianum, Ep. 63 ad Gallam Placidiam, Ep. 64 ad Liciniam Eudoxiam. PL 44 (1846).

174. Ep. 73 Valentinianus et Marcianus ad Leonem. PL 44 (1846).

175. Ep. 77 Pulcheria ad Leonem. PL 44 (1846).

176. Ep. 76 Marcianus ad Leonem. PL 44 (1846).

177. Mansi 6.551-554.

178. Leo Magnus, Ep. 87 ad Marcianum, 24.VI.451. PL 44 (1846).

179. Mansi 6.557-558.

180. He repeated this wish in several letters to Marcianus and Pulcheria, Ep. 89, 90, 94, 95. PL 44 (1846).

181. Mansi 6.1007.

182. Mansi 7.47.

183. Acts of this Council in Mansi 6.539-1102 and 7.1-627.

CHAPTER VIII

THE BATTLE OVER THE STATUS OF MAN

1. Point and counter-point

The great and doctrinal statement, unanimously accepted in the fifth session of the Council of Chalcedon, was a historic decision. It brought the theological discussions of the foregoing centuries to a close; it also, although this was not expressly or consciously intended, called a halt to the ever present dualistic tendencies in the theology of the Church. But if this was a point, there was also a counter-point. In this same period a doctrine arose that tackled the problem of dualism from quite another angle. This doctrine was Pelagianism. "It could be said that, from the fifth to the seventeenth century, the doctrinal work of Christian intelligence consisted of discussion and definition of the principles determining the supernatural bonds that can exist between God and man, that is to say, the total of the relational functions that are subsumed under the two notions, whether conjugated or contrarious, of grace and freedom" [1].

I am quoting Plinval here who elsewhere depicts the situation of the Christian masses. Innumerable converts were constantly streaming into the Church, pious people surely, but not well-instructed in Christian doctrine, there being not enough clergy to cater for them. They had many intimate links with paganism, since family, neighbours, and colleagues were still pagans. These Christians fervently believed in Jesus and put all their trust in his cross. What Christianity meant to them was that their sins were pardoned and that their salvation was assured. There was something magical in this certainty, for they did not fully realize that their baptism required a strictly moral life - with the result that there was often a somewhat painful distance between their professed faith and their conduct. But there were also those who led an examplary moral life; one of these was Pelagius [2].

2. Who was Pelagius?

We remain in the dark about much of Pelagius' life. It is fairly certain that he came from Britain, as several sources testify [3]. He was born in this island some time after 350. Since his name is Greek or hellenized, he may have had an educated background. He seems to have been stoutly built, with a tendency to obesity. Jerome, who did not intend to be flattering, described him as having "the shape and the strength of an athlete; he is becomingly corpulent [4], ... with the shoulders of a Milo (= the most famous athlete of Antiquity, ca. 540 B.C. - F.) [5], ... and moving at the pace of a tortoise" [6]. Was Jerome perhaps somewhat afraid of "this big and fat dog from Albion, that can do more harm with his boots than with his teeth" [7]? Did he suspect an uncouth barbarity under the civilized exterior [8]?

Pelagius was certainly not without erudition, although his culture was predominantly Latin [9]; he did not have much knowledge of Greek. He was well-read in the Bible and demonstrated his acquaintance with pagan and Christian authors; he had also some knowledge of philosophy [10]. Pelagius is sometimes referred to as a 'monk', but there can be no doubt that he, a 'cradle Catholic', was and remained a lay-man, never lived in a monastery nor belonged to a regular religious community [11]. The German scholar Greshake supposes that he and his friends were not monks in the ordinary sense but 'servi Dei', living with another in some sort of community without having made vows, but striving nonetheless for evangelical perfection [12]. We may assume that the unmarried Pelagius lived in the frontier zone between clerics and lay-people without belonging to either of them. This may explain his objections against the clericalism in the Church of his time [13] and why he stressed the function of the laity. "Lay-people should possess the word of

Christ, not only in a sufficient but even in a superabundant measure; they also should teach one another reciprocally" [14].

For a long time we hear nothing of his whereabouts. Did he travel? We do not know. But at some date before 400 he established himself in Rome. There he acquired quite a reputation because of his severely ascetic way of life; the moral laxity of his fellow-Christians in the centre of Christianity shocked and pained him. He went to any lenghts in his moral rigour : oaths were wrong, and the rich could not enter the Kingdom of heaven [15]. In Rome Pelagius made a friend, a certain Caelestius, a young man who was a lawyer with an aristocratic background. This man became, to employ a modern term, Pelagius' pr-officer; he was the Aaron who could speak to the Moses who couldn't, 'the master and leader of that army', said Jerome [16].

When the Visigoth armies of Alaric were approaching Rome in 409, both friends left for North Africa. They first went to Hippo where they failed to meet Augustine, and then moved on to Carthage. Later, leaving Caelestius behind, Pelagius travelled to Jerusalem where he enjoyed a considerable freedom of expression and was in vogue as a spiritual leader. At the synod of Diospolis in 415 he succeeded in clearing himself of a charge of heresy. But in 418 Pope Zosimus (417-418) excommunicated both him and Caelestius for their heretical opinions to which judgment the Emperor Honorius added a sentence of banishment. Pelagius left Jerusalem and nothing more was heard of him.

3. Pelagius' literary output

A lot of writings are associated with Pelagius' name among which Greshake distinguishes three categories ; writings that with reasonable certainty can be ascribed to Pelagius himself; writings of which we cannot be certain that he was their author but that have a close connection with him; and writings of which he presumably was not the author but that belong to an early stage of Pelagianism [17].

4. How Pelagianism began

In Rome in 405 Pelagius heard a sermon - and this was 'the first certain event in his life' [18] - preached by a bishop (was it perhaps Paulinus of Nola?) who took as his text a prayer of Augustine : "Da quod iubes and iube quod vis" [19], "give what you (God) command, and command what you will". This made the hearer suspect; he did not agree with it at all. Could this mean that man is no more than a puppet on a string, manipulated by God and without any contribution by himself? Did a human person have no autonomy or free will whatsoever? He protested and almost quarrelled with the bishop in question [20].

Perhaps it was in connection with this incident and in the same period that Pelagius wrote a letter to Paulinus in which he admitted that we can do absolutely nothing without the help of God's grace. But Augustine, who had read this letter (which is not extant), said that there was hardly anything else in it than the faculties and possibilities of (human) nature; only lip-service was paid to the concept of divine grace in passing. He was unable to discover what Pelagius meant by grace : forgiveness of sin or the teaching of Christ on the way we have to behave or perhaps the great love that God kindles in us [21].

It is highly probable that it was at Rome that Pelagius wrote his commentary on the epistles of saint Paul. He certainly was an original mind, but he was a lay-man without a thorough theological training. In this commentary he sailed, partly at least, on the compass of a somewhat older commentary on the Pauline epistles, the so-called 'Ambrosiaster' [22]. This commentator did not deny original sin - Adam's sin brought death to all mankind -, but he laid a strong accent on the free will of the human person who alone is responsible for his moral behaviour. But man is in need of salvation all the same. It will be clear that Ambrosiaster diminished the role of grace somewhat. Pelagius may have found a source of inspiration in him.

5. Pelagian doctrine

In spite of some measure of dependence on his Latin predecessor, Pelagius "enriched", to quote Plinval, "the Latin tradition, while continuing it, with a personal and to some extent new work" [23], this work being the commentary on Paul [24]. Its author follows Paul closely where the apostle polemized against Judaism. Perhaps he judged the threat of Judaism, or rather that of judaizing, as not yet over [25]. But on other points he deviates from Pauline theology. He does not deny that the first couple did sin, but that was their own affair and responsibility. Their fault, in the form of an original and hereditary sin, should not be visited upon their entire progeny [26]. It is true that Paul had written that "Scripture had assigned all without exception to the custody of sin" [27], but Pelagius found this statement not in accordance with the notion he himself had of God's grace on the one hand and of human freedom on the other. God is always ready to forgive us our own sins, but how could he impute the sins of others to us [28]? This would mean denying the justice of God; there would be no godhead, if there is no justice [29].

Pelagius did not contend that mankind lives innocently and goes its way through live unblemished. There is sin, of course, but we do not sin because we are physically, anthropologically, determined to do so. We sin because we personally and freely choose to sin, imitating the example of Adam and from sheer habit [30]. This could not be true if man was the prey of original sin. "There is, to be sure, a certain kind of necessity imposed by habit, but this is a necessity which man has prepared for himself" [31]. People are not perfect; they forget that one possesses this faculty of freedom and that it is possible for one not to sin. So one sins because one thinks one has to [32]. Pelagius distances himself as far as possible from the Manichaean doctrine that there is in every human being an evil substance that is dominating him or her [33]. Quite the contrary! Man is perfectly free to use his body and his members for good or for evil [34]. For Pelagius free will and (human) nature are identical; in Manichaeism nature means being inexorably drawn towards evil [35]. God, said Pelagius, gave man the faculty not to sin. "If sin is natural (i.e. if it is a basic part of the conditio humana - F.), it is not voluntary; if it is voluntary, it is not inborn. These two definitions are mutually contradictory as are necessity and (free) will" [36].

6. Pelagius confronting Manichaeans and Arians

Perhaps this is the right place to state that Pelagius always attempted to steer a middle course between the heresies of his days, all those heresies that threw doubt on either the true humanity or the true divinity of Christ; he acknowledged both. Consequently, as Greshake says, in his commentary on the Pauline epistles he polemizes almost as often against the Manichaeans as against the Arians, against all those erring spirits who "somehow or other show a tendency to determinism or particularism ... In contrast to all dualistic trends Pelagius programmatically stresses the unity of the Old and New Testaments, of nature and underline{universal} (Greshake's underlining) grace" [37].

With this 'universal grace' is meant that to Pelagius the freedom of human nature is a grace given to all mankind [38]. Freedom is "a faculty common to all people ... existing on account of (human) nature" [39]. Even pagans possess this freedom. What pagans do not have is the grace that comes to Christians through their baptism.

7. Human nature and grace

Augustine, one of the great opponents of Pelagius and one whose own ideas on grace were to profoundly influence the development of Christian theology, accused Pelagius of equating nature and grace [40] and so virtually denying the necessity of grace, that is, of God's help [41]. But this is not wholly correct. "We confess a manifold grace of Christ", said Pelagius [42]. So, when Augustine stated that his opponent "agitated against grace" [43], he misread and misjudged him [44]. Pelagius left no doubt that grace is necessary for leading a Christian life. He did not hold that grace is the same as human nature, although it cannot exist without that nature. "God helps us through his doctrine and revelation ...; he shows us the future so that we do not remain confined to the actual situation; he explains the snares of the devil to us; and he illuminates us through the manifold gift of his grace" [45]. Grace lifts our lives to a higher plane; it enables us to live a life superior to that of those who live by their senses [46].

But when all is said and done, Pelagius' main aim seems to have been to safeguard man's freedom. This freedom does not mean that it is an indifferent thing if a man chooses for good or for evil. One should opt for the good wholeheartedly. But there would be no freedom if not also the possibility existed to opt for evil. "For one who is unwavering in the good there is no virtue at all, if he could not equally go for evil ... But the endlessly good Creator wished that ... we would do only one thing, namely what is good" [47]. This raises the question whether we are really entitled to use the term 'autonomy' in connection with Pelagius' doctrine.

With regard to the difference between God and man in respect of grace, Pelagius made a philosophical distinction. There is ability, there is will, there is acting. The ability to offer grace is with God, and with him alone; it is not in the power of man. But the will to do the good and the actual doing it are entirely human [48]. When it would be held that the alleged fact of original sin necessitated an abundance of divine grace, this meant, in the opinion of the Pelagians, that the idea of free will is completely abandoned and that a doctrine of fate is introduced under the flag of grace [49]. This would signify that God implants a desire to do good in one who does not ask for it and who rejects it [50]. If grace would be understood as being of a coercive nature, there would be no need of redemption.

8. The necessity of baptism

Pelagius created a problem for himself when it came to the necessity of baptism. He stated in as many words that he believed everything according to the doctrine of the Holy Catholic Church [51]. The Nicene Creed confesses 'one baptism for the forgiveness of sins'. If babies are baptized, their sins are forgiven. With 'sins' nothing but original sin can be meant. Pelagius did not turn himself against infant baptism. "Infants are to be baptized in order that they may be with God in the Kingdom of Christ" [52]. So far so good. But in

Pelagius' opinion baptism is not for the forgiveness of original sin, since there is no original sin. "Infants are baptized not for the purpose of receiving remission of sin, but that they may be sanctified in Christ" [53]. Baptism enables us to lead an exemplary life more easily than otherwise would be the case; Pelagius actually used the word 'more easily' ('facilius') [54].

It should be understood that in Pelagius' view "the death of Christ and his resurrection are only examples that lack an actual redeeming value". They do not redeem but, instead, reveal something significant to man. "According to his nature man has always been 'conciliatus' with God"; there has been no rupture as a consequence of original sin. Pelagius does not deny that people are sinning; their bad deeds make them enemies of God. Therefore, a reconciliation is necessary, a restoration of the harmony between God and man that is part of the original conditio humana. This reconciliation is effected by baptism : "baptism restores the human freedom that is an element of creation". That baptism has this salutary effect is the fruit and merit of Jesus' death on the cross [55]. Reading this I wonder if Pelagius is not bringing in the necessity of baptism through the backdoor.

9. Pelagius under crossfire

The stone got rolling only when Pelagius came to Palestine leaving his friend Caelestius behind in Carthage. He won friends and adherents and continued his epistulary activity from Jerusalem; Jerome even said that his letters "were flying over the streams of Ethiopia" [56]. It was in Palestine that he wrote his two main theological works, 'On nature' and 'On free will' of which only fragments remain. And it was also there that he was confronted by two powerful opponents, Jerome and Orosius.

Modern scholars are convinced that Pelagius' opponents, Augustine in particular, did not do full justice to him, as though he had severely underrated the role of grace. Now there are clearly two main elements in his theology, free will and grace. But his polemic against Manichaeism caused him to stress free will so heavily that the role of grace became somewhat obscured. In this way he opened the way for misunderstandings and made himself the object of attacks from the orthodox side [57].

a. Jerome contra Pelagius

Jerome, as an heresy-watcher only to be compared to Epiphanius, was soon alerted. In 413 he spoke of the revival of the hydra with its new offshoot [58]. A year later he spoke of 'that impious and criminal doctrine that was once current in Egypt and parts of the East', meaning with this the doctrine of Origen - a doctrine that now was resurging again, as an hereditary evil, with which evil he meant the Pelagian doctrine, for he saw little difference between the teachings of Origen and Pelagius [59]. So far he had not mentioned Pelagius by name, nor did he do so when he wrote of a stupid calumniator who had had the insolence of criticizing his commentary on Paul's Epistle to the Ephesians; but since he described his opponent as coming from Scotland (sic), there can be no doubt whom he was aiming at [60].

Only a little later, did he make a direct hit at Pelagius (still not mentioned by name) in a long letter to a certain Ctesiphon who was an adherent of his enemy. This new doctrine is a concoction of the poisons of all the heretics, he wrote [61]. Singling out the doctrine of his usual suspect, he said that "your doctrine is a small branch of Origen" [62]. He accused Pelagius above all of holding that man is impeccable, as the consequence of his free will. "They (the Pelagians) say that because of free will the help of God (= his grace) is not at all necessary" [63] - something that Pelagius did not teach.

A stronger approach proved necessary. Pelagius was gaining support in Jerusalem, not only of some women in religion but perhaps even of bishop John. Alarmed by this, Jerome hurled three thunderbolts at Pelagianism or what he understood by it, his 'Dialogues against the Pelagians' [64], in which he returned to the charge while amplifying it. That Pelagius was acquainted with the thinking of Origen, either directly or indirectly (we don't know whether he knew Greek), is not a matter of doubt. But scholars differ as to the amount of Origenist influence. Plinval, for one, does not make much of it; he thinks that the principal influence was that of Ambrosiaster [65]. On the other hand, Evans [66] and Bohlin [67] think that he was 'heavily indebted' to Origen, or rather to the way Rufinus had interpreted him. If this is correct, then "Jerome is not entirely without basis in claiming that Pelagius is a spokesman for both Rufinus and Origen" [68].

b. Orosius charges too

Meanwhile Paulus Orosius had arrived in Jerusalem from North Africa armed with an anti-Pelagian treatise by Augustine, 'De peccatorum meritis'. Jerome now knew that he had two powerful allies. Orosius was a Spaniard, having been born in Tarragona between 380 and 389. Feeling threatened by the invading Vandals and Alans, he fled his native country in 415 and went to Augustine in Hippo. This Father of the Church found the young man 'very holy' and a great student, and highly eloquent too; he was a presbyter then [69]. Augustine sent him on to Jerome who was glad to have him [70].

John, the bishop of Jerusalem, wanting to make an end of the growing confusion in his diocese, in July 415 convoked a council in the Holy City. Jerome did not go; he was no friend of John. But Orosius did. Travelling from Bethlehem to Jerusalem, he encountered Pelagius with whom he had a short conversation. To the synod Orosius related what had happened at Carthage where Caelestius had been condemned already (to which we shall come back). John, who was in the chair, then allowed Pelagius to take the floor. Orosius, our source for this synod, vividly describes how he slowly entered the hall, impeded by his great bulk. He was reminded of the fact that such a great theologian as Augustine was writing against him. Pelagius was imprudent enough to retort : "What is Augustine to me?", a remark the Fathers found impertinent.

Next Orosius attacked. Pelagius had stated to him that "my teaching is that a man can, if he will, live without sin and easily keep God's commandments". Pelagius admitted that he had indeed said this. Asked what he meant by 'sinlessness', he said he did not mean that "human nature had a natural endowment of sinlessness"; if one did not sin, this was an effect of the will and of grace. The synod did not feel this was an heterodox position;

consequently, Pelagius was not condemned [71]. There was a linguistic problem throughout the proceedings, since John did not speak Latin and Orosius no Greek.

c. Allies of Jerome and Orosius

Later in that same year two bishops arrived in Palestine who had been driven from their sees by political circumstances, Heres of Arles and Lazarus of Aix. We see them framing an indictment of Pelagius, the 'libellus'; there is reason to suspect that they were acting on behalf of Jerome and Orosius. They presented this indictment to the metropolitan of Caesarea, Eulogius, the highest ecclesiastical functionary in Palestine, who convoked a synod in Diospolis (Lydda). It came together in December 415. Neither Jerome nor Orosius was present, but John was and also Pelagius himself. The accused defended himself to the best of his ability and once again got away scotfree. The fifteen bishops who took part declared that he belonged to the Catholic ecclesiastical community [72]. It is, however, probable that Pelagius modified his views somewhat in order not to be anathematized. Whatever the case, Jerome was furious : what a miserable synod! [73].

10. What had happened in Carthage

We must now make a flash-back to Carthage where Caelestius had stayed when his friend and mentor sped on to Palestine. In this city he had an altercation with Paulinus of Milan, a deacon who had been secretary to Ambrose; this pillar of orthodoxy was soon convinced that Caelestius' doctrine was heretical. He framed a statement that contained a number of heterodox positions of his opponent. 1. Even if Adam had not sinned, he would have died; 2. Adam's sin harmed himself, but not his progeny; 3. new-born infants are in the same (innocent) state as Adam before his fall; 4. children can obtain eternal life without baptism; 5. it is not correct that all humanity will die as a consequence of Adam's fall nor is it true that all humanity will rise (i.e. go to heaven) as the fruit of Christ's resurrection [74]. Two things will be evident.

Firstly, this is neither biblical nor Roman Catholic doctrine; secondly, Caelestius put a much sharper edge on Pelagius' original teaching. For this reason some scholars feel that what we call Pelagianism hails back to Caelestius rather than to Pelagius himself.

Paulinus duly denounced Caelestius to the bishop of Carthage, Aurelius, who convoked a synod; this met at the end of 411 or at the beginning of 412. Caelestius did not deny that the propositions contained his doctrine but refused to renounce them, after which he was exommunicated [75]. He left Carthage and went to Ephesus where he was ordained as a priest. In the first half of 416 Orosius returned to Carthage where he related all that had happened in Palestine. The clerics of Carthage were stupified to hear that Pelagius had not been condemned by two Palestinian synods. What! They had exommunicated Caelestius for exactly the same errors from which Pelagius had been acquitted! Once again, the East-West, the Greek-Latin division becomes apparent here. If the oriental bishops were so weak with regard to Pelagianism, it was no wonder that it was gaining ground.

11. An appeal to Rome

Both sides appealed to Rome where Innocentius I (401-417) was bishop. Those of Carthage almost fell over their feet to be the first to present their case. A whole dossier was sent to the Holy See. An episcopal letter that accompanied it and that was signed by the North African bishops stated that a man who held that human nature in itself was sufficient to avoid sin and that infant children did not need baptism, should be anathemized [76]. A second urgent letter followed after the Synod of Milevum in Numidia where Augustine was one of the sixty-one participants; it asked the attention of the Holy See for the great danger the Church was running [77]. One of them, bishop Julius, was sent to Rome, charged with documents [78].

After some deliberation the Pope sent three letters to North Africa in which he endorsed the verdict of the Carthaginian and Milevian synods; he declared both Pelagius and Caelestius excommunicated [79]. In a sermon in Carthage Augustine said : "causa finita est" [80]; this saying is the origin of the famous : "Roma locuta, causa finita". But although Rome had indeed spoken, the affair was not yet over. The Pelagians too were intent on gaining the support of Rome [81]. Pelagius did not go to Rome in person, but sent, instead, a letter to Innocentius, accompanied by a confession of faith, a 'libellus fidei'. The addressee died before this letter arrived. The one who went to the Eternal City was Caelestius; when it became known that he had been excommunicated, he was expelled first from Ephesus and then from Constantinople, and now he went to Rome to plead his cause. In the meantime Innocentius had been succeeded by Zosimus (417-418), probably an oriental. It was Zosimus who received Pelagius' letter and also a confession of faith by Caelestius in which he retreated somewhat from his advanced positions, for instance on the (non-)necessity of baptism.

12. Zosimus occupies himself with the question

Zosimus convoked a Roman synod where Caelestius, acting as his own counsel for the defence, was present. He knew how to play his audiences. He said he was ready to abjure his heresies and submitted himself to the judgment of the Pope. Zosimus was not wholly convinced by the good intentions and the humility displayed by Caelestius. He gave himself two months time in order to come to a conclusion. In the meantime the penitent could show his good will by abstaining from disputations which were not edifying but, instead, causing ruin [82]. That he was not unfavourably disposed towards Caelestius he showed by writing to the African bishops that they had been too hasty with their condemnation; they should come to Rome to plead their cause.

Having pondered on the question, Zosimus called together the assembly again and read to them the profession of faith sent by Pelagius; he wrote in that same letter to Africa mentioned above, that some of those present had been unable to hold back their tears in hearing calumniated men of such perfect faith (i.e. Pelagius and Caelestius). There was nothing wrong with their faith. Pelagius had always been unwavering in the service of God and in performing good works. Zosimus said the African bishops should be glad that men of such a blameless character had been acquitted of the accusations brought against them [83].

13. Conflict between Zosimus and the North Africans

But the Africans did not rejoice. They obviously did not realize that they had left the field in Rome entirely to their enemies; not one accuser of the two men had taken the trouble to go to Rome. No wonder, then, that Pelagius' victory was complete. As Plinval wrote, "while he had not been forced to make any unpleasant disavowal, the See of Peter the authority of which he recognized proclaimed the mendacious inanity of the accusations brought against him and acknowledged the correctness of his doctrine as well as his personal merits" [84]. Bishop Aurelius of Carthage addressed himself directly to Zosimus, expressing his discontent with the papal attitude in no uncertain terms. He found that the Roman bishop had allowed himself be taken in by Caelestius who had not explicitly withdrawn his heretical opinions; this might induce the faithful to believe that Rome condoned them [85].

The reaction of Zosimus on March 21st, 418 may seem authoritarian at first sight. He assumed a high tone in reaffirming the authority of the Roman see but then let it transpire that in his view the case of Caelestius had not yet been definitely closed [86]. The next stage was a council held in Carthage in May 418 in which more than two hundred bishops took part, some coming from as far away as Spain. It issued nine canons all conforming orthodox doctrine with regard to the fault of Adam, original sin, infant baptism, and the necessity of justifying grace [87]. Zosimus felt cornered, the more so because there was also opposition to his attitude in Rome. And the Emperor Honorius, informed by Aurelius, issued a decree, dated April 20, 418, ordering the Roman prefect to persecute the heretics and to expel Pelagius and Caelestius (but Pelagius was then not in Rome) [88].

Under all this pressure Zosimus changed his course. He summoned Caelestius before him, but he did not come; instead, he fled Rome and Italy. The Pope then abandoned the Pelagian cause completely. He published the Tractoria, an encyclical letter sent to all the bishops of the Church. This letter is not extant but its main contents are known from other sources. Caelestius was now declared to be wrong; Pelagius was also involved in his errors. Zosimus confirmed all the objections of Innocentius I against them. This meant that he too excommunicated them both [89]. Pelagius' last hope evaporated when a council held at Antioch somewhat later ordered him to leave Palestine for ever [90]. Everyone abandoned him now; his cause was lost.

14. The fate of Caelestius

From this time onwards, Pelagianism steadily lost ground, although hot debates in which Augustine vigorously took part went on for some time. Nothing more was heard from Pelagius, but Caelestius reappeared in Rome in 429, when Celestinus II was Pope. A decree of banishment drove him from Italy [91]. He went to Constantinople where he was received with sympathy by Nestorius who was still bishop of that town then; he even wrote to Rome on Caelestius' behalf. But, as mentioned earlier, they went down hand in hand at the Council of Ephesus in 431 where both were condemned.

15. Augustine's doctrine of grace

Let us now see what this Church Father's doctrine of grace looked like. We must do this for two reasons, first because it stands in linear opposition of Pelagius' teaching, secondly because its later influence was so immense.

Augustine's position may be sketched in short as follows. Adam's fault, the original sin, had a devastating effect. Sharing in it, all humanity became a 'massa damnata', doomed, in principle, to eternal perdition. Who would be temerarious enough to say that God would be unjust, if he would doom all mankind to the last one, nobody excepted? Human beings cannot, like the Baron Münchhausen, draw themselves up by their own hair from the marsh in which they find themselves; nobody is capable of saving him- or herself by his or her own efforts. But God is not only sublimely just, he is also sovereignly good. Because he is merciful, he is ready to save, no, not everyone, but certain people of his own choice. He is entirely free in doing so; nobody can lay claim to it. There is nothing in man that may merit it. We should, therefore, not protest if only part of humanity is saved, the people of his predestination. To those who are elected he gives his grace in abundance.

Augustine does not deny the free will, the liberum arbitrium; neither sin nor grace will destroy it. Free will distinguishes a human person from animals that cannot choose between good and evil and are, in consequence, not morally responsible for their deeds. But man is. However, that the will is free does not mean that a man or a woman will choose spontaneously for the good. Free will is not freedom (libertas). Real freedom would mean always choosing for the good, but exactly this capacity got lost. Human beings are fundamentally condemned to opt for sin, for evil. And in sinning one does not run counter to oneself; one necessarily follows the impulse of human nature. There is no grace in human nature.

Nevertheless, Augustine does not deny that man, everyone, is created in the image of God, as Genesis says. This explains how it is possible that sinful people may commit good deeds, as even the pagans do. But true as this is, it does not save a person. For salvation man is entirely dependent on divine grace; there is nothing else that can help. Does this mean that in the bishop's view all unbaptized persons are irrevocably doomed? No, he does not go to this extreme length. According to him, the divine order of salvation existed since the promise to the first couple in Paradise; on the strength of this order it is possible that some pagans will be saved. But here too Augustine does not deviate from his concept of predestination : God gives his illumnination only to those he chooses. As Greshake whose exposition I am following and paraphrasing states : Augustine distinguishes two sets of men, those who are illumined and blessed by Christ, and those who are not [92]. I add that the difference between these two groups is enormous, for the first category is saved and the second is doomed.

I am still following Greshake where he writes that the conflict between Pelagius and Augustine was the outcome of a fundamentally different experience. We have entered the fifth century A.D., the last century of the Roman Empire, the last of the period we use to call Antiquity. All certainties seemed to have gone afloat. In 410 Roma Aeterna was sacked by the Goths.

Wasn't this a sure sign that the end of the world was near? Man had been firmly embedded in the structure of the Empire which in its turn was an image, a mikrokosmos, of the makrokosmos; just as the cosmos was ruled by unalterable laws, was the Empire governed by an unwavering hand. All this was coming to an end now. Men and women were no longer citizens in a well-ordered socio-political entity. They were increasingly becoming individuals thrown back upon themselves and their own resources.

If anybody in Late Antiquity realized this, it was Augustine. His 'Confessions' are considered the first ego-document ever. He knew what was coming, for he died when the Vandals stood before his town of Hippo. The citizens could no longer refer to an Empire; the Christians could no longer appeal to a God who revealed himself and acted through the cosmological order. Man was alone now and helpless. But God had not withdrawn his hand from mankind. He reached out to at least a number of people whom he wanted to save from eternal perdition. That he did not reach out to everyone, who would dare to object against it? Was it not incomparably merciful of him to give the help of his grace to at least part of the human race?

Pelagius, on the contrary, was still tributary to the old conceptions; his view of human life and of the Christian's relation to God was still optimistic. Fundamentally, there was nothing wrong. Man was not alienated from God on account of a defect in his nature. If Augustine betted on grace, he betted on freedom. I conclude with a direct quotation from Greshake's book. "In 'Pelagian man' for the last time flares up what was powerful and unbroken in ancient religiosity; Augustine's man understands himself as pure receptivity and as being radically thrown upon God" [93].

16. Were Pelagius and Augustine dualists?

The question remains whether or not Pelagius' and Augustine's doctrines were dualistic. The Pelagian doctrine was definitely undualistic. In his opinion man is not fundamentally, existentially estranged from and rejected by God. God is with mankind and mankind is with God. Of course, hitches will originate in the relationship of individuals with their Creator, because man is not sinless. But then there is God's grace to help them along.

In principle Augustine's doctrine of grace is without any doubt dualistic. Original sin has put God and man as far apart as possible. God is sovereignly just and condemns mankind, essentially sinful as it is, to eternal damnation. In practice this remains true for the majority, the 'massa damnata', but God will bridge the gap for a minority by extending his grace to them. However, the elected will also remain utterly helpless; nothing they can do will be of any value.

It must be stressed that Augustinian doctrine did not become the official orthodox teaching. We saw already that Augustine went beyond the canons of the Council of Carthage in 418; the Council of Orange in 529 affirmed that there can be in man an 'initium fidei', that is, a natural, an independent striving after the truth. Man is not entirely helpless and lost.

17. Semi-Pelagianism

a. Vitalis' protest against Augustianism

Just as there were Semi-Arians, there existed Semi-Pelagians. But whereas Semi-Arianism is a term of ancient standing, dating from the fourth century, 'Semi-Pelagianism' is rather recent, in any case from long after the Middle Ages [94]. Amann defines this Semi-Pelagianism as 'a fierce anti-Augustianism'. The main Augustinian tenet to which the Semi-Pelagians objected was that, in Augustine's opinion, man had become absolutely powerless as a result of original sin; he needed God's grace for everything, even for the most feeble beginnings of a rational belief in God or for the most simple expression of human goodness.

The first to protest against this was a certain Vitalis, a Carthaginian, who addressed a letter to the bishop of Hippo. He was no Pelagian; he freely admitted that God's grace is absolutely necessary. But an initiative from the side of the human person was also needed : God offered the faith and a man or woman might or might not accept this gift. The first step towards supernatural life is, therefore, an act that is totally dependent on the will of an individual person [95]. This letter dates from the period 420-427.

b. Monks protesting

An incident that took place in 426 or 427 illustrates how much havoc could be caused by Augustine's stern doctrine. In 418 the Church Father had written a letter to the presbyter Sixtus (the later Pope) in Rome in which he expounded his doctrine on grace [96]. A monk called Florus later sent this letter to the monks of the monastery where he belonged, at Hadrumetum in Fenicia (which no longer exists). Many monks there were greatly upset by Augustine's tenets; the whole community was in turmoil [97].

The centre of resistance to the Augustinian doctrine of grace did not become this Fenician monastery but, instead, from a group of religious communities in southern France, in Marseille, Lérins, and surroundings. The monks of these houses were not Pelagians and had originally been admirers of the bishop of Hippo, but his severity now made them uncertain and confused. The great man was Cassianus, founder and abbot of the monastery of Saint Victor at Marseille, who had several books on monastic life to his name. He agreed with Augustine with regard to the doctrine of original sin and the necessity of grace. But he also found that, if a person showed only some weak form of an initiative towards faith, God would help him or her with his grace. Whoever strives after perfection needs grace, and much grace too, but nevertheless free will remains operative; grace will never suppress it [98].

As the anti-Augustinian champion Cassianus was relayed later in the century by Faustus, a Briton, who became bishop of Riez in the Provence in 458. As a preacher and a publicist he was very active. He is known as a combater of Arianism which cost him his see, for the Visigoth King Euric expelled him 477. Faustus held that there is in man a natural drive towards the good; this is what he called 'free will' in his book 'De gratia Dei'. God's grace must come to the assistance of this faculty of good will, but God forces nobody to be good.

c. Allies of Augustine

Augustine could count on two fervents defenders of his doctrine, Prosper of Aquitaine and Hilarius, bishop of Arles. There is with respect to our overall theme no need to describe the discussions between pro- and anti-Augustinians. In any case, the waves ran high. Prosper and Hilarius having appealed to Pope Innocentius I to intervene in favour of the Augustinian party, the Roman bishop met them only half-way. He admonished the bishops of southern France to keep their parish priests under better control, for he had heard that simple curates discussed these matters from their pulpits, thus causing a lot of confusion [99].

d. Condemnations of the Semi-Pelagian position

The spread of such Semi-Pelagian ideas, so close to vintage Pelagianism, caused unrest in Rome and in Constantinople. Pope Gelasius I (492-496), a North African who was profoundly inimical to Pelagianism, was unable to detect any difference between this and its variant [100]. In his famous 'Decretum Gelasianum de libris recipiendis et non recipiendis' [101] (a kind of Index avant la lettre) he ranged the works of Prosper and Augustine among the commendable books but those of Cassianus and Faustus among the heretical ones.

The fate of Semi-Pelagianism was finally sealed at the Council of Orange in 529. The most influential participant was Caesarius, bishop of Arles since 503; he was in the chair. The canons of this Council condemned the Semi-Pelagian doctrine of Cassianus and Faustus. Original sin, it was stated, affected both body and soul, so that free will is impaired to a certain extent. As a consequence man experiences difficulties in striving after the good. It was acknowleged that there can be in a man or woman a natural beginning of faith - the 'initium fidei' -, but this has to be sustained from its inception by the grace of God. If someone sincerely wants to be morally good, this desire is already the work of the Holy Ghost. Grace is permanently necessary, not only in the beginning of life but during its whole duration.

Cassianus had wrongly made a distinction between those who are totally dependent on divine grace and those who can acquire it by their own free will. Faustus was wrong to think that free will was still strong enough to choose the good and give assent to the precepts of the Gospel without being illuminated by the Holy Spirit.

The upshot of this century-long debate is that the Roman-Catholic Church found both free will and grace necessary; it is impossible to say which went first. Man is neither totally autonomous nor entirely helpless. One could say that God and man, when it comes to salvation and leading the morally good life, collaborate very closely. The Church did not accept Pelagian and Semi-Pelagian doctrine, but neither did she go all the way with Augustine.

NOTES TO CHAPTER VIII

1. Plinval, Pélage 19.
2. Plinval, Luttes pélagiennes 79/80.
3. Aug., Ep. 186.1 : 'Brito'. See also Rees, Pelagius XIII.
4. Hier., Ep. 50.4.
5. Hier., Dialogus 1.28.
6. Hier., Dialogus 3.16.
7. Hier., Comm. in Jer. III Prologus (col. 923/924).
8. Friedrich Loofs s.v. 'Pelagius und der pelagianische Streit', Realenc. 15, 750, calls Jerome's description 'häßliche(s) Geschimpf'.
9. Hier., Ep. 50.2 : 'homo latinissimus'.
10. Ferguson, Pelagius 41/42. See for this subject Plinval, Pélage, Ch. III Les lectures de Pélage. Rees, Pelagius XIII.
11. Rees, Pelagius XIII.
12. Greshake, Gnade 35, note 51.
13. Ferguson, Pelagius 144.
14. Pel., Expositiones 468, quoted Greshake, Gnade 34/35.
15. Hilarius ad Augustinum, Aug., Ep. 156.
16. Hier., Ep. 133.5.; Hier. does not mention the name of Caelestius here but does speak of 'unus discipulus eius'.

351

17. Greshake, Gnade 311; this author presents a list of authentic Pelagian writings on pp. 311/312.
18. Ferguson, Pelagius 47.
19. Aug., Conf. 10.40.
20. Aug., De dono 20.53.
21. Aug., De gratia 35.38.
22. Erasmus ascribed it to Ambrosius, or rather to a 'Pseudo-Ambrosius'. But although it is also sometimes ascribed to Hilary of Poitiers, the safest thing to say is that the author has remained anonymous. See Alfred Stuebler s.v. 'Ambrosiaster', TRE 2 (1978).
23. Plinval, Pélage 135.
24. Pelagius, Expositiones (see Bibliography).
25. Plinval, Pélage 148.
26. Pelagius, Exp. Rom., ed. Souter 5.15.
27. Gal. 3.22.
28. Pelagius, Exp.Rom., ed. Souter 5.15.
29. Aug., Opus imp. 1.38.
30. Aug., Opus imp. 2.74.
31. Evans, Pelagius 104.
32. Pelagius, Ep. ad Demetrium 16.
33. Bohlin, Theologie 104, says "... dass Pelagius' Theologie sich von einer antimanichäischen Fragestellung aus strikt und einheitlich durchgeführt erweist, worin sowohl ihre Stärke als auch gleichzeitig ihre Begrenzung liegt".
34. Pelagius, Exp. Rom., ed. Souter 6.19.
35. Bohlin, Theologie 18.
36. Aug., Opus imp. 4.93.
37. Greshake, Gnade 53.
38. Greshake, Gnade 77.
39. Aug., De gratia 1.31 and 33.
40. Aug., De gratia 35.38.
41. Aug., De gestis 10.22.
42. Aug., Opus imp. 1.94.
43. Aug., Ep. 181.4.

44. Not that modern theological scholarship did more justice to him; more often than not he is seen as the one for whom nature is self-sufficient and grace superfluous. He was reproached of being irreligious, according to Harnack even fundamentally atheistic, or a positivist. See Greshake, Gnade 31/32. Evans, Pelagius 66, says he "is one of the most maligned figures in the history of Christianity".

45. Aug., De gratia 7.8.
46. Aug., Op.imp. 1.94.
47. Pel., Ep. ad Dem. 3.
48. Aug., De gratia 3.3-4.
49. Ep. Prosperi ad Ruf. 3.89.
50. Aug., Contra duas ep. 2.5.10.
51. Aug., De gestis 19.43.
52. Aug., De pecc. 1.21.30.
53. Aug., De pecc. 1.30.58.
54. Aug., De gratia 29.30.
55. Bohlin, Theologie 31. An important source for these ideas is Pel., Ep. ad Dem.
56. Hier., Dial.c.Pel. 2.12.
57. Bohlin, Theologie 45.
58. Hier., Comm.Ez. 6.18 (197).
59. Hier., Ep. 130 16 (193).
60. Hier., Comm.Jer., Prologus 835/836.
61. Hier., Ep. 133 ad Ctes. 1 (1026).
62. Hier., Ep. 133 ad Ctes. 3 (1031).
63. Hier., Ep. 133 ad Ctes. 6 (1033).
64. Hier., Dial.adv.Pel.
65. Plinval, Pélage Ch. III, § VII L'influence d'Ambrosiaster.
66. Evans, Pelagius 19.
67. Bohlin, Theologie pp. 77 sqq. Die Origenes-Renaissance.
68. Evans, Pelagius 20.
69. Aug., Ep. 169, 4.13.
70. Hier., Ep. 134.1.
71. Orosius, Liber apol. 3-8, quoted Ferguson, Pelagius 83/84.

353

72. The source is Aug., De gestis.
73. Hier., Ep. 143.2.
74. These propositions and some more are to be found in Mercator, Commonitorium 1.1.
75. Mansi 4.289-292.
76. This letter in PL 33 (1861), Ep. 175.
77. This letter in PL 33 (1861), Ep. 176.
78. Ep. 177, letter of five bishops, among them Aurelius and Augustine, PL 33 (1861).
79. These three letters in PL 33 (1861), Ep. 181, 182, 183.
80. Aug., Sermo 181.10. PL 38 (1845).
81. Possidius, Vita Aug. 18.
82. Ep. Zosimi ad Aurelium Episcopum, PL 45 (1861), col. 1719-1721.
83. Ep. Zosimi ad Africanos Episcopos, PL 45 (1861), col. 1721-1723.
84. Plinval, Pél. 317.
85. Aug., Contra duas ep. 2.3.5.
86. Ep. Zosimi ad Africanos Episcopos, PL 45 (1846), col. 1725-1726.
87. Mansi 3, 810-823.
88. Imperator Honorius Palladio Praefecto praetorio, PL 56 (1846), col. 490-492.
89. Prosper Aq., Liber contra coll. 21; Mercator, Commonit. 2.
90. Mercator, Commonit. 3.5.
91. Prosper Aq., Coll. 21.2.
92. Greshake, Gnade 202.
93. Greshake, Gnade 250; for this passage see his book Kap. IV, § 3.3 Pelagius und Augustinus.
94. Friedrich Loofs s.v. 'Semipelagianismus'. Realenc.prot.Theol.u.Kirche 18, 192 (1906); É. Amann s.v. 'Semi-Pélagiens', Dict.Théol.Cath. 14.2. 1795 (1941).
95. Aug., Ep. 217 ad Vitalem.
96. Aug., Ep. 194 ad Sixtum Presbyterum.
97. Aug., Ep. 216, Valentinus ad Aug.
98. Jo. Cassianus, Collatio 13.8.
99. Coelestinus, Ep. 21 ad Episcopos Galliorum. PL 50 (1846).

100. Gelasius, Ep. 5 and 6 ad Honorium Episcopum. PL 59 (1847).
101. In PL 59 (1847).

EPILOGUE

1. A red-hot issue

In this volume we have travelled through a landscape alien to the modern reader who, even if he or she was not completely indifferent to religion, would be totally unacquainted with theological subtleties. We heard venerable bishops addressing synods in a rapidly spoken Greek full of incomprehensible theological jargon. We witnessed them getting excited, screaming at their opponents, hurling insults about, pulling another's beards, and resorting to other dirty tricks. We saw learned scholars scribbling away during their nightly studies with the oil-lamps on their writing-desk, filling vellum after vellum with texts studded with terms that have become meaningless to the student of today : homoousios, homoiousios, homoeusios, homoios, anhomoios. Diligently they produced tome after tome of the bulky volumes which, in the Patrologiae graeca et latina, now form impressive and daunting rows on the shelves of theological libraries.

We also passed through the narrow streets and odorous alleys of oriental towns where we witnessed groups of ordinary people - artisans, shopkeepers, bath attendants - standing together and discussing theological issues. What they lacked in professional knowledge they certainly made up by zeal, for we heard them yelling at each other at the top of their voices and getting red in the face. We were frequently treated to the spectacle of opponents resorting to blows. Theology was certainly a red-hot issue in the fourth and fifth centuries A.D.

2. Why all the fuss?

The points of discussion may seem nugatory to the modern reader. Why all that fuss? Why depose and banish respectable clerics for the sake of a iota, the difference between homoousios and homoiousios? Was it not the great historian Edward Gibbon who found it absolutely ridiculous to get excited over the smallest letter of the Greek alphabet? But this is missing what really was at stake.

Today people work themselves up over football results; they often come to such blows over these that the police must intervene. Sometimes there are tough battles in the streets, windows being smashed and cars overturned. Issues like these, however, have a highly ephemeral character : today they are all important, tomorrow they are forgotten. But what the professional and amateur theologians of the centuries we have studied discussed was of great and lasting importance; they were issues that were to determine the course and nature of European intellectual history. It is not inconceivable that the reader has been somewhat confused by the seemingly endless succession of theological opinions, synods, councils, and statements. I fancy, therefore, that it would be useful to summarize what we have found; the charts at the end of this volume may act as a signpost to help the reader to find his or her way. But let me first of all make a few general remarks about things that struck me when I was preparing and writing this volume.

3. Some general remarks

The first is our prelates' love of travel and the ease with which they journeyed along the highroads of the Empire. It took them longer that it would take us today to arrive at their destinations, but it was certainly not more dangerous that it is now. How often didn't the bishops meet! They went from synod to synod. It gives us an idea of the coherence of the infrastructure of the Roman Empire. A second remark is that the theological discussion was mainly conducted in the East, just as most of the theological material was written in Greek. But not wholly, for there were also Latins involved, on the orthodox side, for instance, Augustine and Hillary of Poitiers, and on the other side Priscillian and Pelagius. North Africa, the home of the Donatist movement, was a Latin domain. But with all this taken into account, the centre of gravity lay in the oriental world; it was there that the main battles were fought.

Attention must be paid to two differing backgrounds. It is important to realize that the Church of the fourth century had two and a half centuries of persecution and discrimination behind it. Christians had led an abnormal existence; nobody could be really sure that he or she would not be the next victim. A situation like this one must have caused a kind of general neurosis the traces of which did not disappear quickly and smoothly. Questions of martyrdom - 'to be or not to be a martyr' - stood at the cradle of Montanism and Donatism and even of Arianism, and constituted a powerful personal motive for a man like Origen.

One may compare this to the mental plight of countries like France or the Netherlands that were once occupied by the Nazis. Until the present day every now and then something from that past surfaces again causing pain and trouble. The misery of the occupation period is still with us, as it is, to quote an example, with the children of Dutch national-socialists, who are often despised because the sins of their fathers are visited upon them. I have the impression that the tensions, the fears, and the nervosity of the times of persecution still conditioned the mentality of the people of the fourth century, although they will probably not have always been aware of this. The poison remained in their veins for a long time yet and made them react more fiercely than they would have done in normal days. We should not forget that the last persecution ended only in 305, with an aftermath in the East under Licinius until 312. And the Council of Nicaea took place in 325!

4. 'Horror materiae'

In the background of all these theological discussions was what I dubbed 'horror materiae', a repugnance to all that is material, physical, bodily. This aversion is conspicuous in many of the scholars whose doctrines we studied, but it was not solely restricted to the field of Christian theology. It was also strongly present in Gnostic ideology in which abhorrence of matter, of the body, of sexuality was one of the main constituents. But it is to be found in pagan philosophy and mentality also. During these last centuries of Antiquity there existed a somewhat forced striving after spirituality which tended to put spirit and matter further apart than was normal and healthy.

This was perhaps a reaction against Roman decadence. Possibly it was also caused by the horrors of the civil wars in which the lust for power and sheer greed had played so great a role and which human lives had counted for nothing. Sincere people wanted to distance themselves from all this. And it might also be that the people of the Late Roman Empire secretly read the signs of the times; they may have had a fin-de-siècle sentiment feeling that the Roman imperial system was steadily on the wane, so that they attempted to find a refuge in an immaterial, spiritual world.

5. Political interventions

Something should also be said of the interventions by the Christian Emperors. There was nothing new in this, for pagan rulers had always occupied themselves with religion; the Christian princes only continued an age-old tradition. Many of them may not have been deeply religious men and certainly they were no experts in theology. This does not necessarily mean that they were insincere. But as the statesmen they were, their main interest was political. Just as the pagan Empire had always acknowledged only one religion, the Christian Empire should, in the view of its rulers, also be ecclesiastically and religiously one; they considered a unified religion as the fundament of a unified state. It is for this reason that they actively intervened in theological disputes, even to the point of convoking synods and banishing unwelcome bishops. Seen from this viewpoint, it did not really matter whether an Emperor was orthodox or Arian, although the practical results would be different.

6. The lines of dualism

The intended summary will have to proceed along the lines of the main theme of this whole series, that of dualism. There was certainly dualism in this struggle between orthodoxy and heterodoxy, even a twofold dualism, one of really or allegedly irreconcilable theological doctrines, the other between contestants on both sides.

A modern scholar, of whatever discipline, who knows how acrimonious scholarly debates can be, how sour and unjust reviews sometimes are, how opinions and theses can acquire quite a different aspect when referred to by opponents, to put it as charitably as possible, will not be greatly surprised to hear how the theologians of the ancient Church handled one another. In this respect both sides are to be blamed. Slander and vituperation were ordinary weapons, used freely and indiscriminately. Distortion of the tenets of opponents occurred frequently. It was not always wilfully done, but was often caused by the fervour of an author in defending what he saw as truth; this made him see things through magnifying or distorting glasses. It must be stated, however, that there were also examples of discussions that were in accordance with good scholarly standards and, we might add, with the precepts of Christian love. I am thinking here, for instance, of the debate between the orthodox bishop Optatus and his Donatist colleague Parmenian.

I do not intend to say that there was dualism solely because the controversy became so bitter nor was there dualism because personal ambitions, sympathies and antipathies played so great a role (bishops are human after all). But it is the backdrop against which the developments must be seen. Whereas theologians fought with words, their retinues occassionally used their sticks. The ordinary faithful did not always find the good example of Christian love in their pastors. They certainly knew, interested in such problems as they were, that essential things were at stake. Fired by the theological debate, specific groups of faithful began to feel that they, and they alone, were the guardians of the truth. They were the orthodox, the others the heretics.

When such people found each other out, sects began to originate, sometimes even counter-Churches. It was not always only theological tenets that were constitutive in the formation of these sects and Churches. In some cases, as for instance in the origination of Donatism, they were even completely absent; I think it would be hard for a Circumcellion to tell us what exactly his doctrine was. There were enough non-theological elements to replace doctrinal thought; in the many cases in which theology was indeed involved, it served to widen the gap that separated people from the main Church. It remains a moot point whether in North African sectarianism factors of ethnicity were the background of the deviations. But it is an historic fact that the Maghreb (Morocco, Algeria, Tunisia) had always been highly averse to Roman rule; it has a long history of never ending rebellions [1]. Just as there was revolt after revolt against Roman imperialism, there was also fierce opposition to ecclesiastical domination by Rome. Large sections of the North African population simply did not want to be incorporated in an all-encompassing structure, be it political or ecclesiastical.

There was a marked inclination among sectarian groups to distance themselves from Roman orthodoxy and Roman ecclesiastical rule, so much so that we are entitled to speak of dualism. I refer again to the Donatist Church which set itself up as an anti-Roman counter-Church. The same tendency is also to be found in Montanism, Arianism, Priscillianism, Nestorianism, and other deviant sects. The Nestorian Church, which still exists, has always been both un-Roman and anti-Roman.

The relationship between orthodoxy and heterodoxy was also dualistic because it closely resembled warfare. Of course, there were no bloody battles, but theological riots sometimes resulted in fatal victims. Failing to acknowledge a reciprocal right of existence, both sides attempted to bring each other down. The principal weapon used was to anathemize an opponent and depose him when he was a bishop. Several sees changed hands more than once. The Emperors often completed the work by banishing unwelcome bishops and clerics; Arian Emperors sent orthodox bishops into exile and orthodox rulers did the same to heterodox ones. Imperial intervention, albeit by a usurper, was the cause of the death of Priscillian and his friends, the first heretics ever to be executed. The Emperors acted against sectarian groups with decrees of prohibition.

7. The positions of East and West

It must have struck the reader that heterodoxy hardly had a foothold in the West; not one of the great heresies originated there, with the exception perhaps of Semi-Pelagianism. As I already wrote, the centre of gravity lay in the East. How can this be explained? Of course, the oriental world was more civilized and culturally and intellectually more advanced than the West; its civilizations were incomparably older than the occidental ones. The oriental theologians could draw upon the rich heritage of Greek and Hellenistic philosophy and they indeed frequently did. Oriental thought was, as a consequence, far more sophisticated than that which existed in the western world, while the Greek language was a much better vehicle for subtleties than its Latin counterpart. There was a linguistic barrier. This was not only so because many western Fathers, bishops of Rome among them, knew little or no Greek, and therefore did not feel at home in oriental synods (which they sparsely visited). Another problem was that Greek theological terms were hard to render in Latin; for instance, was 'consubstantialis' the exact translation of 'homoousios'? There was ample opportunity for misunderstandings, which were wilfully exploited sometimes.

This was already sufficient ground for alienation, but there is more. In Chapter VII of Volume XI I described the relationship between the occidental and oriental halves of the Roman Empire - that between Latins and Greeks - as problematic and even relatively dualistic. There was not much love lost between them; East and West deeply distrusted each other. In the Hellenistic world there was a deep-seated resentment for having been subjugated by the Romans and having been incorporated willy-nilly in their Empire. The orientals with their ancient civilizations and their once mighty Empires had now to acknowledge those uncouth barbarians from the West as their masters. And they did not like it at all!

It is hardly conceivable that something of this anti-Latin, anti-Roman sentiment would not flow over into the ecclesiastical relationship. Today the Greek world and that of the Middle East is almost to a man either orthodox or Islamitic. Roman Catholics are sparse there. The cradle of Christianity once stood in the regions that are now overwhelmingly Islamitic ; it has originated there, it grew there, it spread from there. In the first centuries the bulk of the faithful lived in the East; for every western bishop, for every western believer there were ten orientals. Where the West had only one great ecclesiastical centre, there were three or four in the East : Constantinople, Alexandria, Antioch, to say nothing of Jerusalem. The patriarch of Constantinople was second in rank to the bishop of Rome.

Add to this that the eastern capital, with the main imperial residence, was an all-Christian city, whereas in Rome paganism still lingered on. To many orientals the western capital must have seemed only an outpost; they were not inclined to accept orders and invitations from there, feeling perfectly able to mind their own business. Was it purely accidental that there was a sudden change in the situation of Pelagius, when Zosimus, who was in all probability a Greek, became bishop of Rome?

8. The Roman Catholic Church finally triumphant

In the long run, after two eventful centuries, the Roman Catholic Church, not without imperial help, remained triumphant. At the end of the fifth century heterodoxy was either a thing of the past or on the wane, the great exception being the rule of Arian Germanic tribes in the West and in North Africa. This does not mean, however, that heresy had been extirpated root and branch. This is hardly conceivable since heterodox doctrines had had so many adherents in their heydays and the great heresiarchs so many sympathizers. We saw how incredibly tough Donatism was in North Africa, while in the East Nestorianism could never be subdued. There always remained a residue of protest, a hidden agenda in theologicis, which goes a long way towards explaining why the oriental world later so easily became the prey of Islam.

9. The non-dualism of the Roman Catholic Church

So much for the practical, the organizational, the ecclesiastical side of the question. But there is also a conceptual side, that of the great difference of theological opinions. Earlier I mentioned Greshake's apt remark that Pelagius rejected all kinds of dualism; this is exactly what the Roman Catholic Church did too. The Church and Pelagius were at one in this, although the actual contestants did not realize it. We see the Church of these centuries, with its magisterium and its leading orthodox theologians, constantly seeking its way between the dualistic rocks of the time. It firmly rejected all forms of Gnosis, the most overt form of dualism in Late Antiquity. It repudiated overstrong tendencies to asceticism, with its implicit aversion to all that is material and physical. Refusing to stress the merits of martyrdom too much, the Roman Catholic Church was far more merciful to lapsed Christians than Montanists and Donatists.

In all the non- or not wholly orthodox opinions that have been reviewed, with the notable exception of Pelagianism, there was some mesaure of dualism. I am thinking here of the more or less veiled attempts to keep God the Father as far as possible from the work of creation, as though he were too sublime to occupy himself with it. Some Fathers, Origen being the most outspoken among them, propagated, to escape from the dilemma, a 'double creation', one in two stages, first a spiritual and then a physical one, as though the two components had to be carefully kept apart. Finally, the Nicene Creed emphatically declared that we believe 'in one God, the almighty Father, Creator of heaven and earth, of all things visible and invisible', which is, from our point of view, an unequivocal and categorical anti-dualistic statement.

10. The battle over the doctrinal status of Jesus Christ

But the main battle was fought over the doctrinal status of Jesus Christ. Was he a mere man? Was he human but also somewhat more than human? Was he divine only? Did he possess a body only in appearance? Was he divine and human at the same time, but was there no organic unity between the two elements? Or was he a real God-man in whom humanity and divinity were harmoniously united? Had Christ one nature in one person? Two natures in one person? Two natures in two persons? All these questions were hotly debated.

a. No Trinity, no Logos

There is dualism in the assumption of the Ebionites and the Docetists that Jesus had a body only in appearance, for they saw the physical as something highly inferior to the spiritual, to be kept down as deeply as possible. There is dualism too in the position of the Adoptionists the first instance of which is the 'Pastor' of Hermas. The main tenet of the Adoptionists is that Jesus was human; however, later in his life, at the occasion of his baptism or else at his death, he was 'adopted' by God, that is, made more than human but not divine. Whichever name an Adoptionist sect may have had - Monarchian, Patripassionist, Modalist, Sabellian, Paulinian -, they were all 'a-logoi', that is, they rejected the Logos-doctrine, which said that the divine Son, the Logos, the Word, became man. In their theology there was either no Son at all (so that there was also no Trinity) or the Son was a 'mode' of the Father, not numerically different from him. The Logos is no more than a name then. Their problem was that they were unable to conceive of a God who could communicate himself to mankind; in consequence, there could be no Logos, no Word becoming flesh.

All these heterodox teachers were, as I wrote before, balancing on the brink of the dualistic abyss. Denying the possibility of a divine person who became man and thus constituted the link between the godhead and humanity, they were very near - although they shrank back from the ultimate consequence - to positing an unbridgeable distance between God and man.

b. No God-man

Arius, to whom God was ineffable, put him at an immeasurable distance from creation. God cannot communicate his being to what is created. He cannot have a Son who shared divinity with him, for then there would be two Gods. In consequence, the one whom we call Son and Logos is not God. He is a man but not a mere man; he is an exceptional and privileged man. Orthodox thinkers had attempted to bridge the gap between God and the world that is so dualistically wide in the Gnosis; their means to do this was the Logos-doctrine. Arius widened this gap again; he found the idea horrifying that God could have suffered in the person of Jesus Christ. We are in the frontier-zone of dualism here, a frontier that later Arians did not hesitate to cross. The problem of the One and the Many that had so long bevilled philosophy, had found a solution in the concept of the Trinity, of the essential unity of the three in the One. By denying the Trinity, Arius tore this connection apart again and sent godhead and mankind on different ways.

In the middle of the fourth century Aetius and Eunomius radicalized the original Arian position. In their opinion there was absolutely no similarity, let alone identity, between the Father and the Son. They heavily stressed the 'aseity' of God, which means that God exists only for himself and can and will not communicate himself to anyone, not even to a Son. The distance between the Father and the suffering Son was made immeasurably wide, with the result that mankind, the human brothers of the Lord, found itself severed from God by a dualistic gap. Older and newer Arians never made it clear how this gap could be bridged.

c. 'Christological dualism'

Later in the fourth century, and especially in the East, a debate on the ontological status of Christ began, centering on the admittedly difficult question of the relationship of divinity and humanity in him. By far the easiest solution seemed to be to consider Jesus as either entirely divine or entirely human. But this is a solution only in appearance. For if Jesus was entirely divine, were the Jews of his days then deluded, when they believed to see a real man walking about and speaking to them? Must we assume that he, when on earth, was a kind of spectral apparition without any human substance? And if he was human and not more than that, then what made him more exceptional than other great teachers of wisdom, than other shining moral examples? And in particular, what then was the value and the significance of his death on the cross? What about salvation?

In the course of the decades this theological problem became ever more acute. In fact, none of the great heresiarchs saw Jesus as being just as human everybody else. He was always something more, steadily growing to a more elevated status, so that he could be adopted by the Father. Even for Arius he was not an ordinary man, since he was sinless and enjoyed a special relationship with the Father. And Eustathius of Antioch held that Jesus was a 'God-bearing man'. But nowhere in these doctrines an organic unity of the two natures in Christ was posited. This problem of the two natures became the hub of the theological debate between 350 and 450.

Apollinaris started it. He found it inconceivable that there would be two natures in one person. In one person there could only be one nature; he opted for the divine nature, the divine pneuma, that used humanity as its instrument. That was around 360. A generation later, around 390, Theodorus of Mopsuestia readily acknowledged that Jesus was both fully divine and fully human, but was somewhat at a loss when it came to explaining how these two natures were united. He distanced himself from a literal 'incarnation' - the Word becoming flesh - and held that the Logos was 'indwelling' in the human person of Jesus. So there was no Incarnation but rather a 'theophany'. Again a generation later came Nestorius. Declaring that he preferred to call Mary 'anthropotokos' = man-bearing rather than 'theotokos' = God-bearing, he implicitly affirmed that to him Jesus was more human than divine.

There is in all these theological doctrines something that is sometimes called 'Christological dualism'. During the first centuries of the Church dualism was never far off. It was overwhelmingly present in all Gnostic doctrines with their double dualism of the chosen and the damned and of the 'above' and 'below' with the watertight separation of both spheres. Christian theologians were no Gnostics; they combated the Gnosis. But they too were not wholly proof against the dualistic temptation. Many of them had an urge to make God so sublime, so high, so ineffable, that he threatened to disappear beyond the horizon of human ken. The threat that the relation of God and man would become dualistic, in this sense that he would be unapproachable, unanswerable, was averted by the fact that all these theologians acknowledged that there was a servant of God, a certain Jesus of Nazareth, who, by his word and his example, taught people how to come into contact with the Father.

Opinions differed widely, however, on how Jesus himself related to the Father. But whichever solution chosen, he never became wholly one with the Father, just as much God as the Father was. And since to all these heterodox theologians Jesus was somewhat more, or even much more, than purely human, they had their problems with defining how much humanity and how much more-than-humanity there was in him and how the two natures - if there were two natures - related to each other. Not one of them succeeded in wholly solving this problem. The Council of Nicaea had stated that Jesus was 'consubstantial' with the Father, but obviously this term, the Greek 'homoousios', was not unequivocal enough. It was constantly reduced to similarity or even less. But to these theologians it never meant ontological identity.

In no case the human and the divine went harmoniously together. They never became an organic unity. If two natures were assumed, it seemed as though the divine nature was superimposed on the human one. Or the rather absurd solution was chosen that there were in Jesus not only two natures but even two persons. In all these cases we are close to dualism, if there was not downright dualism. It was obviously hard to imagine that divine and human elements could fuse together in one single entity and share one single identity.

d. The orthodox solution

This disharmony, this remaining apart and separated, not rarely even opposed of the two elements in Jesus, might have had evil consequences for Christian self-consciousness. In orthodox Christian doctrine, Jesus Christ, the Son of God, restored the disturbed relation of God and man, the breach between heaven and earth, between divinity and humanity, between 'above' and 'below', between Creator and created. Jesus did this in a personal, existential and historical manner, namely by being the God-man, the one in whom the divine element and the human element became integrated in one and the same person. For all mankind he became the link, the organic connection, with the Father. It is through him that people come to God : 'Who sees me is seeing the Father" [2]. This is what orthodox doctrine teaches. Every doctrine that disconnects the two natures, that puts them ever wider apart, even to the point of making disappear the one or the other, endangers the relationship of the Father and mankind, not rarely making it tenuous to the breaking-point.

11. The dualistic temptation

Dualism was the great temptation of Late Antiquity. It always is a liability, in all ages, but particularly so when the established politico-religious order is at risk. When its fabric is cracking and people are beginning to feel destabilized and at a loss, dualism rears its head. Those who have an inborn inclination towards radicalism then look for solutions that will forcefully express their disarray. The further we come in the history of the Late Roman Empire, the more we see it falling apart, the more uncertain the future becomes.

No wonder that in these centuries Gnostic sects, with their inexorable dualism, had so great a success, especially Manichaeism. No wonder that downright dualistic sects like Ebionites and the Docetists won so many adherents. No wonder that we detect in many Christian authors the 'horror materiae' that was an expression of their discontent with the situation of their days; it prevented them from accepting that God was ready to enter into communication with a world that was as it was.

12. Overcoming dualism

a. The optimism of Pelagius

There were two great attempts to overcome this creeping or overt dualism. The first is Pelagian doctrine. It moved within a Christian orbit, but there can be no doubt that its was unorthodox, what with its denial of original sin. It is exactly this denial that interests us here, for it was formally a denial of the rejection of mankind by God. According to this doctrine the initial harmony is not destroyed, although it becomes disturbed when people use their free will in order to sin. But then there is individual grace to restore the relationship. Pelagianism and Semi-Pelagianism, optimistic and undualistic as they are, would have a future before them.

b. Roman Catholic anti-dualistic statements

The second great attempt, the solution that was to dominate all the Middle Ages, was that of Roman Catholic orthodox doctrine. It is contained in two great anti-dualistic statements. The first we find in the Creed of Nicaea. It declares that God is the Creator of all things visible and invisible. With this it distances itself from the 'horror materiae'. It still more does so when it first repeats seven times in different terms that the Son is just as much God as the Father, and then that he took the flesh from Mary, became man, suffered, and was crucified. The second great doctrinal statement, specifying that of Nicaea, was the result of the Council of Chalcedon in 451. It declared that Jesus is truly God and truly man, and that his two natures cohabitate harmoniously, without impairing, hurting, or diminishing each other, in one organic unity, in one single person.

  These two climactic doctrinal statements made it clear that there is an unblocked channel between heaven and earth. Their significance is that they, at least on the doctrinal, liturgical, and pastoral levels, outlawed every form of dualism within the Roman Catholic Church. Whereas the erstwhile dominant entity, the Roman Empire, was rapidly ceasing into nothingness, the Church stood ready to take its place and become the ground on which medieval civilization would be built.

NOTES TO THE EPILOGUE

1. See Vol. XI, Ch. IV, Part I.6.

2. Jo. 14:9.

CHRONOLOGY

1st/2nd cent. Ebionism
1st/2nd cent. Docetism
1st/2nd cent. Encratism

± 150 Justin the Martyr
± 160 Hermas
± 170 Athenagoras
± 170 Praxeas
± 170 Montanus
± 180 Theophilus
184/185-253 Origen

180/200 Noetus
± 190 Theodotus I
± 217 Sabellius
200-220 Theodotus II
± 250 Paul of Samosata
268 Council of Antioch : Paul deposed

303-305 Persecution of Diocletian
after 307 Donatus bishop of Casae Nigrae
311 Schism in the North African Church

318 Arius steps forward with his theology
after 318 Asterius Arian propagandist
325 Council of Nicaea : Arianism condemned;
     Arius banished

321 Imperial decree tolerating Donatism
after 330 Circumcellion terrorism

328 Athanasius bishop of Alexandria
± 330 Eustathius, bishop of Antioch, deposed
335-337 Athanasius in exile
336 death of Arius
337 Athanasius returns to his see
336 bishop Marcellus of Ancyra deposed;
     Basil bishop of Ancyra
338 death of Eustathius
339-346 Athanasius in exile
339-345 Gregory bishop of Alexandria
343 Council of Serdica
345 death of Gregory
346 Athanasius returns to his see

346 Donatism proscribed
356-361 Athanasius in exile

356-361 Georgius bishop of Alexandria
358 Council of Ancyra
359 Councils of Rimini and Seleucia
± 360 Aetius and Eunomius
361 death of Georgius; Athanasius returns to his see

± 360 Apollinaris

361 Julian the Apostate favours Donatism
after 363 Donatism repressed again

362-363 Athanasius in exile
363 Athanasius returns to his see
365-366 Athanasius in exile
366 Athanasius returns to his see
373 death of Athanasius
374 death of bishop Basil of Ancyra
381 Council of Constantinople : Nicene Creed reaffirmed

385 Priscillian and companions executed

392 Theodorus bishop of Mopsuestia

after 384 pro-Donatist rule of Gildo in North Africa
388 Optatus Donatist bishop of Timgad
388-391 heyday of Donatism
391 Schism among the Donatists
398 end of Gildo and Optatus
411 Council of Carthage : Donatism condemned

410 Pelagius and Caelestius
411/412 Caelestius condemned
416 Pelagius and Caelestius excommunicated by Rome
418 Anti-Pelagian decree of the Emperor Honorius
431 Council of Ephesus : Pelagius and Caelestius condemned

428-431 Nestorius bishop of Constantinople
431 Council of Ephesus : Nestorius deposed
433 doctrinal agreement
448 imperial decree against Nestorianism
after 448 heterodoxy of Eutyches
449 Council of Constantinople

during the 5th cent. anti-Augustinian reaction in southern France; Semi-Pelagianism; Cassianus, Faustus
529 Council of Orange : Semi-Pelagianism condemned

during the 5th cent. Germanic Arianism

BISHOPS OF ROME	EMPERORS
Victor I ± 189-198/199	
Zephyrinus 198/199-± 217	
Callistus I ± 217-222/223	
	Diocletian 284-305
Miltiades 311-314	Constantine I the Great 305-337
Sylvester I 314-335	
Julius I 337-352	Constans 337-350
	Constantine II 337-361
Liberius 352-366	Constantius II 337-361
(Felix II 355-365)	Julian the Apostate 361-363
Damasus I 366-384	Valentinianus I 364-375
	Valens 364-378
Siricius 384-399	Valentinianus II 375-392
	Theodosius I 379-395
Innocentius I 401-417	Honorius 395-423
	Arcadius 395-408
Zosimus 417-418	Theodosius II 408-450
Bonifatius I 418-422	
Celestinus I 422-432	

SCHEMES
OF
THEOLOGICAL SYSTEMS

THE APOLOGISTS

Difficult transition from
the absolute state of
existence of God to
the contingency of creation
(Ch. III)

± 150 Justin the Martyr (§ 3)
Father not concerned with creation;
Logos (Son) is Demiurge

± 170 Athenagoras (§ 3)
Father averse to matter;
Son generated and secondary
to the Father

184/185-253 Origen (§§ 6,7)
Souls preexistent;
all souls (angels too) have
fallen, preexistent spirit
of Christ being the only exception;
Son = Logos;
present condition of cosmos the
result of the Fall;
difference of simple and
perfect believers;
perfect have higher knowledge
(surpassing the Bible)

ADOPTIONISM
Ch. IV

1st/2nd cent. Ebionism
§ 1, see also Vol. XII, Ch. III, § 3

Jesus born as a human being;
at baptism adopted by God;
remains human, does not become divine

1st/2nd cent. Docetism
§ 2

Jesus not human, but divine only;
human only in appearance

± 160 Hermas, 'Pastor';

Son not preexistent;
Holy Ghost = Son;
Holy Ghost preexistent;
servant = redeemer, made heir
of God, but not divine

MONARCHIANISM
Ch. IV, § 5

Monê archê =
God is unitary;
no Trinity;
no Son-Redeemer

± 170 Praxeas forerunner (§ 5a)

180-200 Noetus (§ 5b)
no Trinity;
no Son-Redeemer;
Patripassianism =
the Father underwent the Passion,
not the Son

MODALISM
Ch. IV, § 6

Father and Son not persons,
but modes of being in God (§ 6a)

220 Sabellius main spokesman
for the Modalists, Sabellianism (§ 6c)

THE ALOGOI

Rejection of the Logos-doctrine

± 190 Theodotus I (§ 7)
200-220 Theodotus II (§ 7)
Jesus born as man,
but became Christ at his baptism
and God only after his resurrection
= dynamic Monarchianism

250 Paul of Samosata (§ 9)
Christ only a man, not the Logos;
unitarian concept of God;
Christ mouthpiece of God,
but also the Redeemer
= Paulinianism

ASCETIC TENDENCIES
Ch. V

ENCRATISM
§ 1

Total sexual abstinence propagated;
vegetarianism, no alcohol;
world intrinsically bad

2nd cent. Cassianus (§ 2)
Jesus no physical body;
woman-unfriendly

2nd cent. Tatianus
Father and Son substantially one;
Spirit not present in the cosmos;
matter abhorred;
God's spirit given to a few people only;
two races of men

MONTANISM
§ 5

± 170 Montanus (§ 5b)
and the Montanist sect (§ 5c)
Glorification of martyrdom,
rigoristic, ascetic, and exalted
character of movement (§ 5f);
visionaries and charismatics (§ 6c)

Trinity acknowledged,
but role of Holy Ghost heavily stressed;
eschatology very important (§ 7c);
the New Jerusalem coming (§ 5d);

DONATISM

4th cent. Donatus (§ 12)

Ecclesiological sanctity (§ 14)
Church = Church of the martyrs;
condemnation of lapsed Christians,
should be rebaptized if repenting;
extremist view of Christian life (§ 21);
Christianity and paganism irreconcilably opposed;
Roman Catholic Church rejected,
considered schismatic and impure

PRISCILLIANISM
§ 35

± 385 Priscillianus

No Trinity;
rejection of matter, only spirit is good;
glorification of martyrdom;
opposed to Roman Catholic Church and her hierarchy

ARIANISM
Ch. VI

308 Arius (Part I, § 1, 2)
The Son is generated, but before all time;
the Son does not participate in God's being;
the Son is called Logos only metaphorically;
the Son is human and not divine,
but has a special relationship with the Father;
Jesus 'one of many brothers',
accent placed on his human characteristics;
redemption effectuated by following Jesus' ethical example
(Part I, § 4)

325 Council of Nicaea (Part II, § 4)
Arianism condemned;
the Son 'consubstantial with the Father'

325 and after Eustathius of Antioch (Part III, § 5)
Jesus not the God-man but a 'God-bearing man';
no organic unity of the divine and the human in him

NEO-ARIANISM
Part VI

355 and after Aetius, Eunomius (§ 1)
God cannot communicate himself;
Son is created;
no consubstantiality,
Son is 'heteroousios';
Son is inferior to the Father,
but superior to all other creatures

SEMI-ARIANISM
Part VI, § 2

336 and after Basil of Ancyra
Son is like the Father (homoios);
no identity of substance

381 Council of Constantinople (§ 8c)
Nicene Creed reaffirmed

THE NATURES AND PERSONS OF CHRIST
Ch. VII

APOLLINARISM
Part I

± 360 Apollinaris
Not conceivable that there are
two natures in the one person of Christ;
Christ = one person
with one nature (the divine);
divine pneuma uses his humanity
as an instrument

NESTORIANISM
Part II

± 395 Theodorus of Mopsuestia (§§ 1-4)
Jesus fully human and fully divine;
<u>but</u>
Logos is 'indwelling', not really incarnated;
a theophany rather than an incarnation;
not one single identity in Jesus

± 430 Nestorius (Part III)
Prefers calling Mary 'anthropotokos'
rather than 'theotokos';
Jesus more human than divine?

431 Council of Ephesus (§ 10)
Nestorius condemned

451 Council of Chalcedon (Part IV, § 10)
Mary declared 'theotokos'

BIBLIOGRAPHY

I ORIGINAL SOURCES

A COLLECTIONS

CODEX THEODOSIANUS. Ed. Thomas Wiedemann. London (1981).

COLLECTANEA ANTIARIANA PARISINA. CSEL 65 (1916).

COLLECTIO SCRIPTORUM ECCLESIASTICORUM LATINORUM (CSEL).

CORPUS SCRIPTORUM CHRISTIANORUM. Series latina.

ENCHIRIDION SYMBOLORUM. Eds. H. Denzinger/A. Schönberger. Barcelona-Freiburg i. Breisgau-Rome-New York, 1967^{25} (referred to as Denzinger/Schönberger).

GESTA COLLATIONIS CARTHAGINIENSIS. PL 11. Paris, 1845.

PATROLOGIA GRAECA (referred to as PG).

PATROLOGIA LATINA (referred to as PL).

SACRORUM CONCILIORUM COLLECTIO. Ed. J.D. Mansi. Florence, 1759 (quoted as Mansi).

TEXTE ZUR GESCHICHTE DES MONTANISMUS. Herausgegeben von Nathanael Bonwetsch. Kleine Texte für Vorlesungen und Übungen. Bonn, 1914.

URKUNDEN ZUR ENTSTEHUNGSGESCHICHTE DES DONATISMUS. Herausgegeben von Hans von Soden Neue durchgesehene Auflage von Hans von Campenhausen. Kleine Texte für Vorlesungen und Übungen. Bonn, 1950.

B INDIVIDUAL AUTHORS

ALEXANDER
Depositio Arii. PG 18. Paris, 1857.

AMBROSIUS
1. Epistulae. PL 16. Paris, 1845.
2. De fide. PL 16. Paris, 1845.

AMMIANUS MARCELLINUS
Historiae. The Histories. Ed. J.C. Rolfe. 3 vols. Loeb Classical Library. Cambridge (Ms)/London.

ANONYMUS
Contra Fulgentium Donatistam. PL 43. Paris, 1861.

APOLLINARIS fils
1. Letter to the bishops of Diocaesarea. In : Dräseke.
2. Epistula ad Imperatorem Jovianum. In : Dräseke.
3. Treatise on the unity of Christ's body with regard to his divinity. In : Dräseke.

ARNOBIUS
Conflictus de Deo trino et uno. PL 53. Paris, 1847.

ATHANASIUS
1. Apologia contra Arianos. PG 25. Paris, 1857.
2. Apologia de fuga sua. PG 25. Paris, 1857.
3. Apologia ad Imperatorem Constantium. PG 25. Paris, 1857.
4. Chronicon Athanasii. PG 26. Paris, 1857.
5. De decretis Nicaenae synodi. PG 26. Paris, 1857.
6. Epistola ad Afros Episcopos. PG 26. Paris, 1857.
7. Epistola encyclica ad Episcopos. PG 25. Paris, 1857.
8. Epistola ad Episcopos Egyptiacos. PG 25. Paris, 1857.
9. Epistola ad Jovianum. PK 26. Paris, 1857.
10. Epistola ad Rufinianum. PG 26. Paris, 1857.
11. Epistola ad Serapionem de morte Arii. PG 25. Paris, 1857.
12. Historia Arianorum. PG 25. Paris, 1857.
13. Narratio Athanasii ad Ammonium Episcopum et alios. PG 26. Paris, 1857.
14. Orationes contra Arianos. PG 26. Paris, 1857.
15. De synodis. PG 26. Paris, 1857.
16. De Vita Antonii. PG 26. Paris, 1857.
17. Tomus and Antiochenos. PG 26. Paris, 1857.

ATHANASIUS PRESBYTER
Libellus Athanasii Presbyteri adversus Dioscurum. In : Mansi 6.

ATHENAGORAS
Legatio. PG 6. Paris, 1857.

AUGUSTINUS
1. De baptismo contra Donatistas. PL 43. Paris, 1861.
2. Breviculus collationis cum Donatistis. PL 43. Paris, 1861.
3. Confessiones. Eds. E. Tréhorel and G. Bouissou (Latin text with French translation). Bibliothèque augustinienne. Oeuvres de Saint Augustin Vols. 13 and 14. Louvain, 1962.
4. Contra Cresconium grammaticum et Donatistam. PL 43. Paris, 1861.
5. Ad Donatistas post collationem. PL 43. Paris, 1861.
6. De dono perseverantiae. PL 45. Paris, 1861.
7. Epistola ad Catholicos contra Donatistas. PL 43. Paris, 1861.
8. Epistolae. PL 33. Paris. 1861. CSEL 57. Prague/Vienna/Leipzig, 1911.
9. Contra Epistolam Parmeniani. PL 43. Paris, 1861.
10. Contra duas Epistolas Pelagianorum. CSEL 60. Vienna/Leizpig, 1913.
11. Contra Gaudentium. PL 43. Paris, 1861.
12. De gestis Pelagii. PL 44. Paris, 1841.
13. De gratia Christi. PL 44. Paris, 1841.
14. De haeresibus. PL 42. Paris, 1861.
15. Ioannis Evangelium tractatus. PL 35. Paris, 1861.
16. Contra literas Petiliani. PL 42. Paris, 1861.
17. Opus imperfectum Juliani. PL 45. Paris, 1861.
18. De peccatorum meritis et remissione. PL 44. Paris, 1841.
19. Psalmus contra partem Donati. PL 43. Paris, 1861.
20. Sermo 2, 46, 88, 181, 311. PL 38. Paris, 1841.
21. De utilitate credendi. PL 42. Paris, 1861.

BASILIUS MAGNUS
1. Epistolae. PG 32. Paris, 1857.
2. Liber Apologeticus. Appendix operum S. Basilii Magni. PG 30. Paris, 1857.

CASSIANUS, Johannes
1. Collatio. PL 49. Paris, 1869.
2. De incarnatione Christi libri septem. PL 50. Paris, 1846.

CLAUDIANUS
De bello Gildonico. War against Gildo. Ed. M. Platnauer. Loeb Classical Library 135. Cambridge (Ms)/London, 1922.

CLEMENS ALEXANDRINUS
Stromateis. Les Stromates. Texte et traduction de Marcel Casier et autres. Série : Sources chrétiennes 38, 278, 279. Paris, 1954-1981.

COELESTINUS I
Epistolae. PL 50. Paris, 1846.

CONSTANTINUS
Universis episcopis per Africam. CSEL 26, Appendix VIII. Slso Maier, Dossier I.

CYPRIANUS
1. De ecclesiae catholicae unitate. PL 4. Paris, 1844.
2. Epistola 7, 75. PL 3. Paris, 1845.

CYRILLUS ALEXANDRINUS
1. Epistolae. PG 77. Paris, 1864.
2. Adversus Nestorii blasphemias. PG 76. Paris, 1863.
3. De recta fide ad reginas. PG 76. Paris, 1863.
4. Ad reginas de recta fide oratio altera. PG 76. Paris, 1863.
5. Quod unus sit Christus. PG 75. Paris, 1863.

DAMASUS
1. Epistola ad Paulinum Antiochenum Episcopum. In : Mansi III.
2. Prolegomena. PL 13. Paris, 1845.

DIDYMUS ALEXANDRINUS
De Trinitate. PG 39. Paris, 1863.

EPIPHANIUS
Panarion haeresium, alias Haeresium fabularum compendium. Die griechischen christlichen Schriftsteller der ersten drei Jahrhunderte. Epiphanius I. Herausgegeben von Karl Holl. Leipzig, 1915. Also PG 41. Paris, 1863.

EUSEBIUS OF CAESAREA
1. Epistolae. PG 20. Paris, 1857.
2. Historia ecclesiastica. Die griechischen christlichen Schriftsteller der ersten drei Jahrhunderte. Eusebius II.1. Herausgegeben von Eduard Schwartz. Leipzig, 1915 (referred to as Eus., HE).
3. Contra Marcellum. PG 24. Paris, 1857.
4. Liber de martyribus Palaestinae. PG 20. Paris, 1857.
5. De Vita Constantini. PG 20. Paris, 1867.

EVAGRIUS
Historiae ecclesiasticae. PG 86bis. Paris, 1864.

FACUNDUS
Pro defensione trium capitulorum libri XII. PG 18. Paris, 1857. Facundi Episcopi Ecclesiae Hermianensis opera omnia. Corp.script.christ. Series latina XCA. Turnhout (B), 1974.

FILASTRIUS
De haeresibus. CSEL 38. Prague/Vienna/Leipzig, 1888.

GELASIUS CYZICENUS
Historia concilii nicaeni. PG 85. Paris, 1864.

GELASIUS, episcopus Romae
1. Decretum Gelasianum de libris recipiendis et non recipiendis. PL 59. Paris, 1847.
2. Epistolae. PL 50. Paris, 1846.

GESTA COLLOQUII CARTHAGINIENSIS. PL 11. Paris, 1845.

GESTA APUD ZENOPHILUM. CSEL 26. Prague/Vienna/Leipzig, 1893.

GREGORIUS MAGNUS
Epistola 11, 32. PL 11. Paris, 1849.

GREGORIUS NYSSENUS
1. Adversus Apollinarem. See Dräseke.
2. Contra Eunomium. PG 45. Paris, 1863.
3. De vita S. Patris Ephraim Syri. PG 46. Paris, 1863.
4. De deitate Filii et Spiritus Sancti. PG 46. Paris, 1863.

HERMAS
Pastor. The Shepherd. With an English translation by Kirsopp Lake. Loeb Classical Library 25. Cambridge (Ms)/London (1970, 1913[1]).

HIERONYMUS
1. Apologia adversus libros Rufini. PL 23. Paris, 1845.
2. Chronicon. PL 27. Paris, 1846.
3. Commentarium in Epistulam ad Galatos. PL 26. Paris, 1845.
4. Commentarium in Ezechielem. PL 24. Paris, 1845.
5. Commentarium in Jeremiam. PL 24. Paris, 1845.
6. Dialogus adversus Pelagianos. PL 23. Paris, 1845.
7. Epistola ad Joannem Episcopum (translated into Latin by Jerome). PL 43. Paris, 1864.
8. Epistolae 50, 57, 58, 82, 130, 133, 134, 143, 412, 414. PL 22. Paris, 1845.
9. Liber contra Joannem. PL 23. Paris, 1845.
10. De viris illustribus. PL 23. Paris, 1845.

HILARIUS POTEVINENSIS
1. Contra Constantium. PL 10. Paris. 1845.
2. Fragmenta ex opero historico. PL 10. Paris, 1845.
3. De synodis. PL 10. Paris. 1845.
4. Textes narratives. CSEL 65.
5. Contra Vigilantium. PL 10. Paris, 1845.

HIPPOLYTUS
1. Commentarium in Danielem. Hippolyte, Commentaire sur Daniel. Ed. Maurice Lefèvre. Sources chrétiennes 14. Paris, 1947.
2. Contra haeresin Noeti cujusdam. PG 10 (Paris, 1857).
3. Refutatio omnium haeresium. Die griechischen christlichen Schriftsteller der ersten drei Jahrhunderte. Bd. 26, Hippolytus. 3. Bd. Ed. Paul Wendland. Leipzig, 1916.

HISTORIA AKEPHALE
Histoire acéphale et index syriaque des lettres festales d'Athanase d'Alexandrie. Ed. Annik Martin. Sources chrétiennes 317. Paris, 1985.

HONORIUS
Imperator Honorius Palladio Praefecto praetorio. PL 56. Paris, 1846.

IGNATIUS ANTIOCHENUS
1. Ad Trallianos. The Apostolic Fathers I. With an English translation by Kirsopp Lake. Loeb Classical Library 24. Cambridge (Ms)/London (1975, 1912[1]).
2. Ad Smyrnaeos. The Apostolic Fathers I. With an English translation by Kirsopp Lake. Loeb Classical Library 24. Cambridge (Ms)/London (1975, 1912[1]).

INNOCENTIUS I
Epistolae. PL 33. Paris, 1861.

IRENAEUS LUGDUNENSIS
Adversus haereses. Contre les hérésies. Eds. Adelin Rousseau and Louis Doutreleau. Vol. 2 Textes latin et grec avec traduction. Paris, 1982.

ISIDORUS
De ecclesiasticis officiis. PL 83. Paris, 1850.

JOANNES ANTIOCHENUS
Epistola Joannis ad Cyrillum Alexandrinum. In : Mansi 5.

JOHANNES CHRYSOSTOMUS
1. Laudatio Eustathii. PG 49-50. Paris, 1862.
2. Ad Theodorum lapsum. PG 47. Paris, 1863.

JULIANUS APOSTATA
Juiani imperatoris epistulae et leges. Ed. J. Bidez et F. Cumont. Collection Budé 50. Paris, 1922.

JUSTINUS MARTYR
1. Apologia 1. PL 6. Paris, 1857.
2. Apologia 2. PL 6. Paris, 1857.
3. Dialogus. PL 6. Paris, 1857.

LEO I MAGNUS
　Epistolae. PL 54. Paris, 1846.

LEONTIUS BYZANTINUS
　1. Adversus fraudes Apollinistarum. PG 82bis. Paris, 1865.
　2. De sectis. PG 86. Paris, 1933.

LIBERATUS
　Breviarium (De pace Cyrilli et Joannis). PG 68. Paris, 1847.

LIBERIUS
　1. Epistula Liberii ad Constantium. CSEL 65 (1916).
　2. Epistula Liberii ad orientales episcopos. CSEL 65 (1916).
　3. Epistula Liberii ad Ossium. CSEL 65 (1916).

LUCIFER CARALIENSIS
　1. De Athanasio. CSEL 14.
　2. De non parcendo in Deum delinquentibus. CSEL 14.

MERCATOR, Marius
　Commonitorium super nomine Coelestii. PL 48. Paris, 1846.

NESTORIUS
　Liber Heraclidis. Le Livre d'Héraclide de Damas. Traduction français par F. Nau. Paris, 1910.

NICEPHORUS CALLISTUS
　Historia ecclesiastica. PG 146. Paris, 1865.

OPTATUS
　1. Historia Donatistarum. PL 11. Paris, 1845.
　2. Contra Parmenianum. PL 11. Paris, 1845.
　2. De schismate Donatistarum. PL 11. Paris, 1845.

ORIGENES
　1. Commentaria in Evangelium Joannis. PG 14. Paris, 1862.
　2. Homilium in Matthaeum. PG 13. Paris, 1862.
　3. Peri archoon. De principiis. PG 11. Paris, 1857.

OROSIUS
　1. Commonitorium de errore Priscillianistarum et Origenistarum. Ed. G. Schepes. CSEL 18. CSEL 18. Prague/Vienna/Leipzig, 1889.
　2. Historiae. Histoires. Texte établi et traduit par Marie-Pierre Arnaud-Lindet. Paris, 1991.

PAMPHILIUS
　Apologia Pamphilii Martyris pro Origene. PG 17. Paris, 1857.

PASSIO SANCTAE CRISPINAE. Maier, Dossier I.

PASSIO SANCTORUM DATIVI, SATURNINI PRESBYTERI ET ALIORUM. Acta Saturnini. PL 8. Paris, 1844. Also in Maier, Dossier I (annotated).

PASSIO DONATI. PL 8. Paris, 1844.

PASSIO SANCTI FELICIS EPISCOPI. Maier, Dossier I.

PASSIO MARCULI. PL 8. Paris, 1844.

PASSIO SANCTARUM MAXIMAE, SECUNDAE ET DONATILLAE. Maier, Dossier I.

PASSIO MAXIMINIANI ET ISAAC. PL 8. Paris, 1844.

PASSIO PERPETUAE ET FELICITATIS
The Passion of S. Perpetua. Newly edited from the mss. with an introduction and notes by J. Armitage Robinson. Nendeln (Liechtenstein), 1967 (photostatic reprint of the edition Cambridge, 1891).

PELAGIUS
1. Epistola ad Demitriadem de vera humilitate. Ed. M.K.C. Krabbe. A Critical Text and Translation with Introduction and Commentary. Washington, 1965.
2. Pelagius' Expositions on Thirteen Epistles of St. Paul. Ed. Alexander Souter. Texts and Studies, Vol. IX. Cambridge, 1922.

PHILOSTORGIUS
Historia ecclesiastica. PG 65. Paris, 1864.

PHOTIUS
Myriobiblon alias Bibliotheca. PG 103. Paris, 1860.

POSSIDIUS
Vita Augustini. PL 22. Paris, 1845.

PRISCILLIANUS
1. The Pauline Canons. Ed. G. Schepes. CSEL 18. Prague/Vienna/Leipzig, 1889.
2. The Würzburg Tractates. Ed. G.Schepes. CSEL18. Prague/Vienna/Leipzig, 1889.

PROCLUS
Oratio. PG 65. Paris, 1864.

PROSPERUS AQUITANUS
1. Epistola Prosperi Aquitani ad Rufinum de gratia et libero arbitrio. PL 45. Paris, 1846.
2. Liber contra collatorem. PL 51. Paris, 1846.

PSEUDO-LEONTIUS
Contra Nestorium et Eutychium. PG 86. Paris, 1933.

PSEUDO-TERRULLIANUS
Adversus omnes haereses. CSEL 47. Vienna/Leipzig, 1906.

RUFINUS
1. De adulteratione librorum Origenis. Corpus Scriptorum Christianorum. Series latina XX. Tyranii Rufini Opera. Turnhout, 1961).
2. Apologia in S. Hieronymi libros duo. PL 21. Paris, 1849.
3. Praefatio ad Macarium. PG 17. Paris, 1857.
4. Prologus in libros Peri archoon. PG 11. Paris, 1857.

SERMO DE PASSIONE S. DONATI ABIOCALENSIS. Maier, Dossier I.

SOCRATES
Historia ecclesiastica. PG 67. Paris, 1864.

SOZOMENOS
Historia ecclesiastica. Sozomenus, Kirchengeschichte. Ed. Joseph Bidez. Die christlichen griechischen Schriftsteller der ersten drei Jahrhunderte. Bd. 50. Leipzig, 1960.

SULPICIUS SEVERUS
1. Chronica. CSEL 1. Vienna, 1866.
2. Dialogus. CSEL 1. Vienna, 1866.

SYNODICON. PG 84. Paris, 1864.

TATIANUS
Oratio ad Graecos. PG 6, Paris, 1857.

TERTULLIANUS
1. De anima. PL 2. Paris, 1844.
2. De corona. PL 2. Paris, 1844.
3. De cultu feminarum. PL 1. Paris, 1844.
4. De exhortatione ad castitatem. PL 2. Paris, 1844.
5. De fuga in omni persecutione. PL 2. Paris, 1844.
6. De idolatria. PL 1. Paris, 1844.
7. De ieiuniis. PL 2. Paris, 1844.
8. Adversus Marcionem. PL 2. Paris, 1844.
9. De monogamia. PL 2. Paris, 1844.
10. De praescriptionibus. PL 1. Paris, 1844.
11. Adversus Praxean. PL 2. Paris, 1844.
12. Ad uxorem. PL 2. Paris, 1844.
13. De virginibus velandis. PL 2. Paris, 1844.

THEODORETUS
1. Epistolae. PG 83. Paris, 1864.
2. Epistola ad Alexandrum Hieropolitanum. In : Mansi 5.
3. Haereticarum fabularum compendium. PG 23. Paris, 1864.
4. Historia ecclesiastica. PG 82. Paris, 1864.

THEODOSIUS II
1. Epistola Theodosii ad Synodum Ephesinum. In : Mansi 5.
2. Epistola Theodosii et Valentiniani ad Joannem Antiochiae. In : Mansi 5.

THEOPHILUS
Ad Autolycum. PG 6. Paris, 1857.

ZOSIMUS
Epistolae. PL 45. Paris, 1861.

II SECONDARY WORKS

A WORKS OF REFERENCE

Dictionnaire de théologie catholique. Paris.

New Catholic Encyclopedia, Vol. 8. New York (1967).

Paulys Real-Encyclopädie der Classischen Altertumswissenschaft. Neue Bearbeitung herausgegeben von Georg Wissowa. Stuttgart. (PW).

Realencyclopädie für protestantische Theologie und Kirche.

Theologische Realenzyklopädie (quoted as TRE). Berlin.

B COLLECTIONS

Arianism : Historical and theological Reassessments. Papers from the Ninth International Conference on Patristic Studies. Oxford, September 5-10, 1983. Patristic Monograph Series, no. 11. Ed. Robert C. Gregg. Philadelphia, 1985.

Atti del Colloquio Internazionale per l'Encratismo, Milano 20-23 Aprile 1982. Ed. Ugo Bianchi. Roma, 1985.

Maier, Jean-Louis, Le dossier du Donatisme. Tome I Des origines à la mort de Constance II (303-361). Texte und Untersuchungen zur Geschichte der altchristlichen Literatur. Band 134. Berlin, 1987.

The making of orthodoxy. Essays in honour of Henry Chadwick. Ed. Rowan Willians. Cambridge (1989).

Origenes. Herausg. Ulrich Berner. Erträge der Forschung 147. Darmstadt, 1981.

Origenes. Vir ecclesiasticus. Herausg. Willem Geerlings/Hildegard König. Symposion zu Ehren des Herrn Prof.Dr. H.-J. Vogt. Bonn (1195). Reihe : Hereditas. Studien zur Alten Kirchengeschichte 9.

Urkunden zur Geschichte des arianischen Streites. Athanasius' Werke. III. 1. Berlin/Leipzig, 1934. Herausg. Hans-Georg Opitz.

C MONOGRAPHS

ALèS, Adhémar d', Priscillien et l'Espagne chrétienne à la fin du IVe siècle. Paris, 1936.

ARMSTRONG, Karen, A History of God. From Abraham to the Present : the 4000-year quest for God. London, 1993.

BABUT, E.-.Ch., Priscillien et le Priscillianisme. Bibliothèque de l'École des Hautes Études. Sciences historiques et philosophiques, fasc. 169. Paris, 1909.

BALTHASAR, Hans Urs von, Origenes. Geist und Feuer. Ein Aufbau aus seinen Schriften. Salzburg (1951², 1938¹).

BARDY, Gustave, Paul de Samosate. Étude historique. Spicilegium sacrum lovaniense. Études et documents, fasc. 4. Louvain/Paris, 1923.

BARNARD, Leslie William, The Meletian Schism.

BARNES, Timothy D., Athanasius and Constantius. Theology and Politics in the Constantinian Empire. Cambridge (Ms)/London, 1993.

BELLINI, Enzo, Alessandro e Ario. Un esempio di conflitto tra fede e ideologia. Documenti della prima controversa ariana a cura di --. Series : Teologia 18, fonti 3. Milano, 1974.

BENJAMINS, Hendrik Simon, Eingeordnete Freiheit. Freiheit und Vorsehung bei Origenes. Doctoral thesis Un. of Groningen, 1993.

BIANCHI, Ugo, Le thème du colloque en tant que problème historico-religieux. Atti del Colloquio Milano 1982.

BOHLIN, Torgny, Die Theologie des Pelagius und ihre Genesis. Uppsala Universitets Arskrift1957. Uppsala/Wiesbaden, 1957.

BRISSON, Jean-Paul, Autonomisme et Christianisme dans l'Afrique romaine de Septime Sevère à l'invasion vandale. Paris, 1958.

BROWN, Peter, St. Augustine's Attitude to Religious Coercion. Religion and Society in the Age of Saint Augustine. London (1972).

BÜTTNER, Theodor and WERNER, Ernst, Circumcelliones und Adamites. Zwei Formen mittelalterlicher Häresie. Berlin, 1959.

CADIOU, René, La jeunesse d'Origène. Histoire de l'École d'Alexandrie du début au IIIe siècle. Paris, 1935. Études de théologie historique.

CHADWICK, Henry
1. The Fall of Eustathius. Journal of Theological Studies 49. (1948).
2. Priscillian of Avila. The occult and the charismatic in the early Church. Oxford, 1972.

CLARK, Elizabeth A., The Origenist Controversy. The cultural construction of an early Christian debate. Princeton NJ, 1992.

CROUZEL, Henri, Origène. Paris/Namur (1984).

DANIÉLOU, Jean, Origène. Paris (1948). Série : La génie du Christianisme.

DOCUMENTO FINALE DEL COLLOQUIO MILANO 1982 (Atti del Colloquio). Proposte concernenti l'uso dei termini encratismo ed enkrateia. La tradizione dell'Enkrateia. Motivazioni ontologiche e protologiche.

DRÄSEKE, Johannes, Apollinarios von Laodicea. Sein Leben und seine Schriften. Nebst einem Anhang : Apollinarii Laodiceni quae supersunt dogmatica. Leipzig, 1892.

ELZE, Martin, Tatian und seine Theologie. Forschungen zur Kirchen- und Dogmengeschichte. Bd. 9. Göttingen, 1960.

EVANS, Robert F., Pelagius. Inquiries and reappraisals. New York (1968).

FAYE, Eugène de, Origène. Sa vie, son oeuvre, sa pensée. Volume premier : Sa biographie et ses écrits. Paris, 1923. Volume deuxième : L'ambiance philosophique. Paris, 1927. Volume troisième : La doctrine. Paris, 1928. Bibliothèque de l'École des Hautes Études. Sciences religieuses. Vols. 37, 43 and 44.

FERGUSON, John, Pelagius. Cambridge, 1956.

FISHER, George Paul, History of Christian Doctrine. Edinburgh (1949^7, 1896^1).

FRANCHI DE 'CAVALIERI, Pio, La 'Passio' dei martiri Abitensi. Note agiografiche. Fasciculo 8. Studi e Testi 65. Città del Vaticano (1935).

FREND, William H.C., The Donatist Church. A movement of protest in North Africa. Oxford, 1952.

GIRARDET, Klaus M., Kaiser Konstantius II. als 'Episcopus Episcoporum' und das Herrscherbild kirchlichen Widerstandes (Ossius von Cordoba und Lucifer von Calaris). Historia, Band XXVI.1 (1977).

GRASMÜCK, Ernst Ludwig, Coercitio. Staat und Kirche im Donatistenstreit. Bonner Forschungen. Bd. 22. Bonn, 1964.

GREGG, Robert C., and GROH, Dennis E., Early Arianism - A View of Salvation. London, 1981.

GRESHAKE, Gilbert, Gnade als konkrete Freiheit. Eine Untersuchung zur Gnadenlehre des Pelagius. Mainz (1972).

HAGEMANN, Hermann, Die römische Kirche und ihr Einfluß auf Disziplin und Dogma in den ersten drei Jahrhunderten. Nach den Quellen aufs neue untersucht. Freiburg im Breisgau, 1864.

HALL, Stuart G., The Thalia in Athanasius' Accounts. In Gregg (Ed.), Arianism.

HANSON, R.P.C.
1. The Arian Doctrine of the Incarnation. in : Arianism.
2. The Search for the Christian Doctrine of God. The Arian Controversy 318-381. Edinburgh (1988).

HARNACK, Adolf von, Lehrbuch der Dogmengeschichte. 3 Vols. 1894-1897[3] verbesserte und vermehrte Auflage (1886-1890[1]).

HEIMANN, Peter, Erwähltes Schicksal. Präexistenz der Seele und christlicher Glaube im Denkmodell des Origenes. Tübingen (1988).

HEINE, Ronald E., The Montanist Oracles and Testimonia. North American Patristic Society. Patristic Monograph Series 14. Macon GA, 1989.

HILGENFELD, Adolf, Die Ketzergeschichte des Urchristentums urkundlich dargestellt. Hildesheim, 1963 (photomechanischer Nachdruck von Leipzig, 1884).

KANNENGIESSER, Charles, The Blasphemies of Arius : Athanasius of Alexandria De Synodis 15. In : Gregg (Ed.) Arianism.

KOBUSCH, Theo, Origenes, der Initiator der christlichen Philosophie. In : Geerlings/König, Origenes.

KOCH, Hal, Pronoia und Paideusis. Studien über Origenes und sein Verhältnis zum Platonismus. Berlin/Leipzig, 1932.

KOPECEK, Thomas A., A History of Neo-Arianism. Patristic Monograph Series no. 8. Published by the Philadelphia Patristic Foundation, Ltd. 1979.

KOSCHORKE, Klaus, Hippolyts Ketzerbekämpfung und Polemik gegen die Gnostiker. Wiesbaden, 1975.

LABRIOLLE, Pierre de,
1. La crise montaniste. Thèse pour le doctorat ès-Lettres. Paris, 1913.
2. Les sources de l'histoire montaniste. Textes grecs, latins, syriaques, publiés avec une introduction critique, une traduction française, des notes et des indices. Paris, 1913.

LAMIRANDE, Émilien, Church, State and Toleration. The Saint Augustine Lecture 1974. Villanova University Press, 1975.

LIETZMANN, Hans, Apollinaris von Laodicea und seine Schule. I Texte und Untersuchungen. Hildesheim/New York, 1970 (reprographischer Nachdruck der Ausgabe Tübingen, 1904²).

LOHSE, Bernhard, Epochen der Dogmengeschichte. Stuttgart (1963).

LOOFS, Friedrich,
1. Nestorius and his place in the history of Christian doctrine. Burt Franklin : Research & Source Works Series. Philosophy & Religious History Monographs 158. New York (1975, reprint of the edition Cambridge 1914).
2. Paulus von Samosate. Eine Untersuchung zur altkirchlichen Literatur- und Dogmengeschichte. Leipzig, 1924.

LORENZ, Rudolf, Arius judaizans? Untersuchungen zur dogmengeschichtlichen Einordnung des Arius. Forschungen zur Kirchen- und Dogmengeschichte. Bd. 31. Göttingen, 1979.

LYMAN, J. Rebecca, Christology and cosmology. Models of divine activity in Origen, Eusebius, and Athanasius. Oxford, 1993.

NAUDIN, Pierre, Origène. Sa vie et son oeuvre. Paris, 1977. Série : Christianisme antique I.

NEWMAN, John Henry, The Arians of the Fourth Century. New Impression 1901. (1833¹).

PELIKAN, Jaroslav, The Christian Tradition. The History of the Development of Christian Doctrine. 1 The Emergence of the Catholic Tradition (100-600). Chicago and London (1975⁴, 1971¹).

PETERSEN, William L., Tatian's Diatesseron. Its creation, dissemination, significance, and history in scholarship. Supplements to Vigiliae christianae. Vol. XXV. Leiden/New York/Köln, 1994.

PLINVAL, Georges de,
1. Les luttes pélagiennes. Ch. IV of 'Histoire de l'Église depuis les origines jusqu'à nos jours. Eds. Augustin Flicke & Victor Martin. Vol. 4 De la mort de Théodore à l'élection de Grégoire le Grand. 1939.
2. Pélage. Ses écrits, sa vie et sa réforme. Étude d'histoire littéraire et religieuse. Lausanne, 1943.

QUISPEL, Gilles, The Study of Encratism. Atti del Colloquio Milano 1982.

REES, B.R., Pelagius, a reluctant heretic. Woodbridge, GB (1991).

RITSCHL, Dietrich, Athanasius. Versuch einer Interpretation. Theologische Studien. Heft 76. Zürich (1964).

SCHEPELERN, Wilhelm, Der Montanismus un die phrygischen Kulte. Eine religionsgeschichtliche Untersuchung. Freiburg, 1929.

SELLERS, Robert V., Eustathius of Antioch and his place in the early history of Christian doctrine. Cambridge, 1928.

SFARMENI GASPARRO, Giulia, Le motivazioni protologiche dell'Enkrateia nel Cristianesimo dei primi secoli e nello Gnosticismo : Osservazioni sulla loro specifità storico-religiosa. Atti del Colloquio Milano 1982.

SPANNEUT, Michel, Recherches sur les écrits d'Eustathe d'Antioche avec une édition nouvelle des fragments dogmatiques et exégétiques. Mémoires et travaux des facultés catholiques de Lille. Lille, 1948.

STROEHLIN, Ernest, Essai sur le Montanisme. Un chapitre de l'histoire de l'Église au second siècle. Strasbourg, 1870.

THÜMMEL, Wilhelm, Zur Beurteilung des Donatismus. Halle, 1893.

TIETZE, Walter, Lucifer von Calaris und die Kirchenpolitik des Constantius II. Zum Konflikt zwischen dem Kaiser und der nikänisch-orthodoxen Opposition. Athanasius von Alexandria, Hilarius von Poitiers, Ossius von Cordóba, Liberius von Rom und Eusebius von Vercellae. Stuttgart, 1976.

TURNER, H.E.W., The Pattern of Christian Truth. A Study in the Relation between Orthodoxy and Heresy in the Early Church. Bampton Lectures 1954. London (1954).

VILLAIN, Maurice, La querelle autour d'Origène. Saint Épiphane et l'Inquisition à Jérusalem. Paris, 1937. Série : Recherches de science religieuse. Tome XXVII.

VOISIN, Guillaume, L'Apollinarisme. Étude historique, littéraire et dogmatique sur le début des controverses christologiques au IVᵉ siècle. Diss. Louvain. Louvain/Paris, 1901.

WAND, J.W.C., The Four Great Heresies. London, 1967[4] (1955[1]).

WIDDICOMBE, Peter, The Fatherhood of God from Origen to Athanasius. Oxford, 1994. Series : Oxford Theological Monographs.

WILES, Maurice,
   1. Archetypal Heresy. Arianism through the Centuries. Oxford, 1996.
   2. Eunomius : hair-splitting dialectician or defender of the accessibility of salvation. In : The making of orthodoxy.

WILLIAMS, Rowan D.,
   1. Arius : Heresy and Tradition. Oxford, 1987.
   2. The Quest of the Historical Thalia. In : Gregg (Ed.), Arianism.

GENERAL INDEX

Aaron, 332
Abitenae (Mdjez el-Bab), town in North Africa, martyrs of, 97, 98, 113, 133
Abraham, 23, 266
Acacius, bishop of Caesarea, 246, 247
Achillas, bishop of Alexandria, 166
Acquitaine, 146
Acts of the Apostles, apocryphal, 73
Adam, 73, 79, 80, 333, 334, 340, 343
Adoptionism, Adoptionists, 27, Ch. IV passim, 363
Advocata (Avioccala) = Sidi Amara in Tunisia, 113
Aelafius, governor of North Africa, 111
Aetians, 238, 22
Aetius, Neo-Arian bishop, 237-240, 243, 247, 275, 365
Africa Proconsularis, 134
Aix, town in France, 340
Ajax, Dutch football team, 203
Alans, 339
Alaric, Visigoth king, 257, 332
Alcison, bishop of Nicopolis
Alemans, 230
Alès, Adhémar d', 146, 163
Alexander, bishop of Alexandria, 166, 168, 184, 185, 186, 187, 189, 192, 193, 199, 200, 214, 259, 260, 262, 263, 264
Alexander, bishop of Constantinople, 189, 213, 218, 259, 265
Alexander, presbyter in Alexandria, 167
Alexander Severus, Roman Emperor, 83
Alexandria(n)(s), 24, 25, 33, 40, 43, 75, 165, 166, 167, 168, 169, 185, 186, 191, 193, 196, 198, 199, 200, 201, 208, 213, 217, 218, 219, 220, 221, 222, 226, 227, 232, 235, 237, 249, 252, 253, 259, 262, 264, 275, 280, 298, 300, 304, 309, 362

Algeria, 98, 114, 115, 117, 136, 152, 360
Alogoi, 58-59, 60
Amann, É, 7, 57, 68, 275, 296, 323, 325, 326, 347, 353
Ambrose, bishop of Milan, 144, 163, 195, 254, 256, 266, 351
Ambrosiaster, Christian commentator, 333, 338
Ammia, Christian prophetess, 81
Ammianus Marcellinus, 159, 233, 268, 274, 277
Amu Darya, river, 309
Anastasius I, Pope, 43
Anastasius, presbyter in Constantinople, 296, 297
Anatolia, 192
Anatolius, bishop of Constantinople, 319
Anchialos, town in Asia Minor, 83
Ancyra, the modern Ankara, 192, 208, 209, 241, 242
Andrew, apostle, 8
Anomians, 238
Anselm of Canterbury, 182
Anthropomorphism, anthropomorphists, 23, 38, 42
Anthony, patron saint of the hermits, 200, 219
Antioch in Caria, 255
Antioch in Syria, Antiochene, 22, 60, 63, 66, 70, 165, 186, 190, 192, 193, 196, 204, 205, 212, 218, 219, 220, 222, 223, 224, 225, 226, 227, 229, 237, 248, 252, 255, 260, 269, 286, 287, 288, 290, 295, 300, 305, 309, 312, 344, 362
Antiochene school of theology, 283, 285, 309
Antonia Melania, Christian lady, ca. 400, 41

Annulinus, proconsul in North Africa, 110
Anullinus, proconsul of North Africa, 97-98, 113
Apelles, Gnostic prophet, 20
Apollinaris (Apollinarios), père, 280
Apollinaris, fils, 280-289, 291, 292, 311, 322, 366
Apollinarism, Apollinarists, 280-289, 289, 290, 291, 295, 310, 311
Apollonius, ancient author, 150
Apologists, Ch. III passim
Apostles, 1, 2, 9, 11, 14, 15, 20, 54, 141
Apostolic Church of the East (Nestorian Church), 309-310
Aptungi (Aptugni), town in North Africa, 152
Aquileia (Venice), 226, 230, 236
Arab(ia)(n), 25, 60, 148, 192, 212
Aramaean Christianity, 73
Aramaic, 308, 310
Arcadius, Roman Emperor, 95, 238
Archbishop of Canterbury, 7
Archelaus, governor of Palestine, 39
Ardaban, Phrygian town, 81
Arian(s), 5, 147, Ch. 6 passim, 284, 295, 322, 335, 358, 362, 365
Arianism, 4, 37, Ch. 6 passim, 281, 285, 291, 348, 357, 360
Ariminium (Rimini), 243, 245, 277
Aristotle, Aristotelian, 22, 23, 36, 238, 282
Arius, 164, 165-179, 181-187, 188, 189, 190, 192, 193, 195, 198, 199, 201, 207, 208, 213, 214, 215, 216, 222, 224, 230, 238, 240, 244, 245, 259, 260, 261, 262, 263, 265, 268, 282, 364-365, 366
Arles, 111-112, 230, 340
Armenia, 310
Armstrong, Karen, 173, 174, 263
Arnobius, 325
Arnold, Gottfried, 3, 4
Arsenius, a Meletian bishop, 215, 216, 271
Ascalon, town in Palestine, 39
Asceticism, Ch. V passim
Asia Minor, 9, 54, 80, 83, 84, 169, 185, 186, 218, 242, 253, 289
Asiatic, 58, 59, 84, 90

Asterius, Arian sophist, 189-191, 208, 222, 253, 260, 266
Astorga, town in Galicia, 146
Atarbius, Christian apologist, 37
Athanasius, Father of the Church, 70, 173, 179, 193, 196, 199-201, 203, 208, 209, 210, 211, 212, 213, 214-218, 218-229, 220-221, 221-222, 224, 225-227, 227-228, 230, 231, 232, 232-235, 236, 240, 241, 247, 248, 249-253, 259, 261, 262, 263, 264, 266, 267, 268, 269, 270, 271, 272, 273, 274, 275, 276, 277, 278, 280, 281, 322
Athanasius, a presbyter, 312
Athenagoras, Christian apologist, 21, 23, 24, 44
Athens, 76
Augustine, Father of the Church, 15-17, 19, 24, 35, 95, 102, 103, 109, 114, 115, 118, 121, 132, 133, 134-135, 136, 137, 152, 153, 154, 155, 156, 157, 158, 159, 160, 161, 332, 333, 335, 337, 339, 341, 344-347, 347, 348, 349, 350, 351, 352, 353, 357
Aurelianus, Roman Emperor, 63
Aurelius, bishop of Carthage, 134, 341, 343, 353
Aurès mountains in Algeria, 122
Avila, 143
Axido, commander of the Circumcellions, 121

Babut, E.-Ch., 162
Bacaulis, quarter in Alexandria, 165, 166, 167, 259
Bachelet, X. le, 165, 250, 253, 258, 260, 261, 265, 268, 272, 274, 275, 277, 278, 279
Bagai (Ksar-Bagaï or Baraï), town in Algeria, 122, 123, 133
Balaam, 9
Balanae, town in Syria, 185
Balkans, 218
Balthasar, Hans Urs von, 35, 47
Barbelo-Gnostics, 20
Bardy, G., 44, 66, 69, 70, 79, 92, 148, 151, 163, 260
Bareille, G., 52, 67, 153, 156, 265
Barnard, Leslie Willam, 215, 218, 219,

225, 226, 228, 270
Barnes, Jules, 240
Barnes, Timothy D., 240, 271, 272, 273, 274, 275, 276
Basil of Caesarea, Father of the Church, 239, 253
Basil, bishop of Ancyra, 241-244, 247
Basilides, 11, 20, 251
Basilidians, 13
Battle of Adrianople, 254
Bellini, Enzo, 184, 261, 264
Benjamins, Hendrik Simon, 45
Berber, 104, 135
Bergman, Jan, 72, 147
Bernadette Soubirous, the seeress of Lourdes, 86
Beroea, town in Thrace, 192, 204, 234, 236
Beryllus, bishop of Bostra, 60
Berytus, town in Syria, 280, 288
Besan-Duc, monastery in Palestine, 39
Bethlehem, 37, 39, 41, 339
Betz, Hans-Dieter, 4, 7
Bianchi, Ugo, 46, 147
Bible, 2, 5, 24, 25, 32, 35, 62, 63, 85, 142, 166, 174, 179, 180, 182, 199, 229, 239, 243, 250, 283, 290, 330
Bithynia(n), 185, 187
Bohlin, Torgny, 339, 351, 352
Bonaventura, medieval theologian, 173
Bonifatius, Roman general, 135
Bonwetsch, R., 48, 149, 154
Book of Genesis, 263, 345
Book of Revelation, 9
Bordeaux, 143
Bordeaux, Synod of, 144
Bosporus, 305
Bostra, Arabian town, 60
Bossuet, Jacques-Bénigne, 6
Boudarli, village in Turkey, 150
Brisson, Jean-Paul, 105, 106, 109, 119, 154, 155
Britain, 144, 330
Brown, Peter, 19
Büttner, Theodor, 157, 158
Bulgaria, 218
Burgundians, 257
Buruma, Ian, 276
Byzantium, Byzantine, 58, 95, 137, 138

399

Cadiou, René, 44, 45
Caecilianus, archdeacon in Carthage, later bishop of this town, 98, 99, 102, 103, 109, 110, 111, 112, 113, 115, 116, 193
Caelestius, friend of Pelagius, 332, 337, 339, 340-342, 342, 344, 350
Caesarea, town in Palestine, 26, 27, 185, 186, 216, 246, 340
Caesarea, town in Cappadocia, 219, 239
Caesarius, bishop of Arles, 349
Calaris (Cagliari), town in Sardinia, 229, 249
Calixtus (Callistus) I, bishop of Rome, 13, 57, 58
Candidianus, Roman comes, 302, 303, 304
Cappadocia(n), 83, 192, 219, 220, 237, 238, 253, 289
Carmel of Lisieux, 85
Carmel of Nevers, 86
Carmelite, 85
Carpocratians, 20
Carthage, Carthaginian, 54, 55, 88, 92, 96, 97, 101, 102, 103, 104, 105, 108, 110, 111, 115, 123, 125, 128, 132, 133, 134, 135, 136, 193, 210, 332, 337, 339, 340, 341, 343
Casae Nigrae, town in Algeria, 101
Cassianus, Julius, Encratite heresiarch, 73, 74-75, 75
Cassianus, Johannes, Christian author, 299, 325, 348, 349, 350, 353
Castellum Tingitanum (Orléansville), town in Algeria, 115
Cataphronicus, Roman prefect of Egypt, 234
Cathar(s), 6
Cebarussa (Cabarussa), town in Algeria, 132
Celestinus I, bishop of Rome, 298, 299-300, 301, 302, 304, 307, 311, 325, 326
Celestinus II, 344, 353
Cerdon, Gnostic prophet, 20
Cerinthus, a Gnostic prophet, 20, 58
Chadwick, Henry, 44, 143, 161, 162, 163, 269
Chalcedon, town in Asia Minor, 305, 320
Chaldaean Church, Chaldaean

Christians, 310
Charlemagne, 258
Chrestos, bishop of Syracuse, 155
Christian(s), 3, 10, 12, 13, 15, 17, 18, 21, 23, 24, 25, 33, 34, 35, 36, 37, 38, 71, 75, 76, 77, 78, 83, 84, 90, 92, 93, 94, 95, 96, 98, 99, 100, 101, 108, 111, 113, 116, 118, 119, 126, 130, 138, 140, 141, 152, 164, 165, 166, 172, 173, 174, 175, 176, 178, 181, 183, 184, 188, 189, 190, 191, 193, 198, 214, 218, 220, 224, 225, 230, 247, 249, 250, 253, 254, 255, 256, 257, 280, 283, 288, 291, 308, 330, 331, 332, 335, 357, 358, 359, 363, 366, 367, 368
Christianity, 2, 3, 4, 8, 10, 13, 17, 20, 24, 31, 33, 44, 47, 50, 69, 71, 74, 76, 80, 81, 82, 86, 92, 97, 129, 136, 173, 175, 178, 181, 189, 240, 248, 249, 252, 257, 258, 308, 309, 330, 332, 346, 352, 362, 366
Christology, Christological, 52, 53, 54, 62, 69, 90, 176, 207, 310, 365-367
Chrysaphius, a courtier, 311-312, 314, 315, 319
Church of England, 2, 7
Cilicia, 243, 247, 289, 290
Circumcellions, Donatist terrorists, 96, 117-122, 127, 128, 130, 131, 139, 360
Cirta (Constantine) town in Algeria, 99, 100, 114, 152
Clark, Elizabeth, 31, 46, 47, 48, 49
Claudianus, ancient author, 160
Clement of Alexandria, 15, 75, 81, 148, 149
Cleomenes, Monarchian, 56, 57
Clovis, Frankish king, 258
Constans, Roman Emperor, 122, 123, 124, 125, 127, 210, 211, 212, 214, 221, 225, 226, 227, 228
Constantia, sister of Constantine the Great, a wife of the co-Emperor Licinius 186, 199
Constantine I the Great, 95, 110, 111, 112, 113, 114, 115, 117, 127, 129, 155, 156, 168, 186, 189, 191, 192-193, 193, 194, 196, 198, 199, 201, 203, 205, 208, 209, 210, 213, 214, 215, 216, 217, 218, 234, 241, 266, 267, 268, 269, 271, 272
Constantine II, 214, 218, 221
Constantinople, 189, 199, 209, 213, 216, 217, 218, 224, 238, 245, 246, 247, 248, 254, 255, 261, 270, 289, 294, 295, 299, 300, 302, 304, 305, 309, 312, 315, 318, 319, 321, 342, 344, 349, 362
Constantius II, Roman Emperor, 127, 209, 210, 211, 212, 214, 217, 218, 219, 220, 221, 222, 224, 225, 226, 227, 228, 229, 230, 231, 232, 233-235, 236, 239, 241, 243, 244, 246, 247, 248, 250, 252, 273, 275, 277
Cordoba, 143, 191
Corinth, Church of, 87
Council of Alexandria 352, 228
Council of Alexandria 362, 250-251, 286, 287
Council of Antioch, 264, 61, 69
Council of Antioch, 26, 63, 191-192
Council of Arles, 230-231
Council of Carthage 418, 343, 347
Council of Chalcedon, 50, 285, 320-321, 330, 369
Council of Constantinople 360, 247
Council of Constantinople 381, 188, 255-256, 256, 257, 288
Council of Ephesus, 431, 295, 301-305, 305, 313, 344
Council of Ephesus, 449, the 'Robbers' Council', 316-318, 319
Council of Jerusalem, 208
Council of Milan, 224
Council of Milan, 231-232, 233
Council of Nicaea, 325, 66, 115, 164, 167, 192-197, 198, 200, 201, 202, 203, 204, 208, 243, 244, 257, 259, 260, 357, 367
Council of Orange 529, 347, 349
Council of Rimini, 244-245
Councils of Rome, 288
Council of Seleucia, 245-246
Council of Serdica, 210-211, 212
Council of Toledo, 400, 28
Council of Trent, 193
Council of Tyre, 216-217, 218
Council of Vaticanum I, 193
Creed of Nicaea, 197, 202, 203, 204, 211, 214, 223, 224, 230, 231, 237, 238, 241, 242, 244, 246, 248, 249, 251, 253, 254, 255, 256, 259, 279, 280, 281, 288, 289, 303, 309, 313, 317, 336, 363, 369

Cresconius, Donatist author, 125
Crispina of Thagora, 98
Crouzel, Henri, 30, 45, 47
Ctesiphon (Seleucia), capital of the Sasanian Empire), 309
Ctesiphon, adherent of Pelagius, 338
Cybele, 80, 81
Cyprian, bishop of Carthage, Father of the Church, 91, 108-109, 119, 120, 130, 150, 154, 155
Cyprus, 15, 43, 289
Cyrillus of Alexandria, Christian author, 200, 268, 298-299, 299, 300, 301, 302-304, 305, 307, 308, 311, 312, 325, 326, 327
Cyril, bishop of Jerusalem, 247

Damasus I, Pope, 144, 254, 255, 256, 278, 287, 323
Daniélou, Jean, 24, 44
Decius, Roman Emperor, 26, 120, 229
Demetrius, bishop of Alexandria, 25, 26
Demiurge, 74, 174
Demophilus, bishop of Beroea, 236
Demophilus, bishop of Constantinople, 254
Dictinus, bishop-coadjutor of Astorga, 146
Didymus Alexandrinus, Christian author, 68
Diocletian, Roman Emperor, 96, 97, 120, 165, 189, 214
Dionysius, bishop of Alexandria, 11
Dionysius, bishop of Nicaea, 231, 232
Dionysius, bishop of Rome, 11
Dionysius the Areopagite (Pseudo-Dionysius), 173
Dioscurus, bishop of Alexandria, 311, 312, 315, 316, 320
Diospolis (Lydda), synod of, 332, 340
Ditheism, ditheists, 55, 67
Docetism, Docetists, 14, 22, 44, 51-52, 54, 75, 168, 363, 368
Domnus, bishop of Antioch, 312, 313, 317
Donatism, Donatist(s), 16, 19, 95, 96-139, 192, 193, 215, 257, 356, 359, 360, 362, 363
Donatus, founder of the Donatist Church, bishop of Carthage, 101, 102, 103, 105, 111, 115, 122, 123, 153
Donatus, bishop of Advocata, 113
Donatus, Donatist bishop of Bagai, 122
Dorylaeum, town, 297
Dositheus, Gnostic, 13
Dräseke, Johannes, 322
Dualism, dualistic, 2, 5, 8, 9, 10, 17, 20, 23, 24, 31, 33, 34, 45, 50, 51, 53, 65, 66, 72, 74, 75, 77, 78, 80, 92, 94, 105, 106, 116, 120, 123, 136, 139, 140-141, 143, 147, 171, 176, 177, 207, 211, 222, 226, 230, 234, 240, 283, 284, 285, 293-294, 300, 306, 308, 309, 310, 316, 317, 328, 330, 335, 346-347, 359-361, 363, 364, 365, 366, 367, 368-369
Duchesne, L., 303
Dulcitius, Roman magistrate, 137
Dumanli, village in Turkey, 150
Dutch, 148, 203, 357
Dynamic Monarchianism, 59

Earth Mother see Cybele
Ebionite(s), 50-51, 58, 363, 368
Edessa town in Syria, 226, 308, 309
Egypt(ian), 24, 25, 43, 72, 75, 165, 169, 175, 184, 185, 187, 189, 191, 198, 199, 200, 203, 216, 217, 218, 220, 226, 234, 235, 246, 252, 253, 259, 280, 295, 300, 320, 338
Eleutheropolis. town in Palestine, 39
Elizabeth II of Britain, 7
Elkasaites, 13
Elze, Martin, 76, 77, 80, 148, 149
Encratism, Encratite(s), 72-80
English, 240
Enlightenment, 4
Ephesus, 55, 302, 304, 315-318, 341, 342
Ephraim the Syrian, 281
Epigonus, Monarchian, 56
Epiphanius, Christian author, 15, 26, 28, 36, 36-43, 45, 47, 48, 49, 58, 67, 68, 88, 149, 150, 151, 166, 167, 168, 169, 185, 213, 239, 260, 261, 265, 270, 275, 276, 286-288, 289, 321, 322, 323, 338
Epiphanius, sophist, 280
Erasmus, 351
Ethiopia, 337

Essenes, 1, 12
Eucharist, 6, 84, 85, 97
Euchrotia, Christian woman, 162
Eudoxia, wife of Theodosius II, 299
Eudoxius, bishop of Constantinople, 253, 260
Eulogius, bishop of Caesarea, 340
Eunomians, 238, 242, 243, 255, 256, 289
Eunomius, Neo-Arian, 237-240, 243, 248, 253, 256, 275, 276, 365
Euphrates, 8, 75, 308, 310
Euphrates, bishop of Cologne, 212
Euphration, bishop of Balanae, 185
Euric, Visigoth king, 257, 348
Europe(an), 129, 192, 356
Eusebian(s), 214-215, 216-217, 221, 222, 224, 236
Eusebius of Caesarea, 12, 18, 25, 44, 45, 46, 54, 59, 61, 67, 68, 69, 70, 81, 82, 88, 149, 150, 152, 156, 185, 186, 187, 192, 193, 194, 195, 196, 197, 201-203, 204, 205, 207, 208, 209, 213, 214, 223, 260, 261, 262, 265, 266, 267, 268, 269, 270, 271
Eusebius, bishop of Dorylaeum, 313, 314, 317, 318, 320, 327
Eusebius, bishop of Nicomedia, later of Constantinople, 185, 185-186, 187, 190, 193, 195, 197, 198, 201, 208, 213, 215, 217, 218, 219, 222, 224, 260, 266
Eusebius, bishop of Vercellae, 231, 232
Eusebius, Palestinian monk, 42
Eusebius, Roman official, 233
Eustathius, bishop first of Beroea and later of Antioch, 192, 193, 202, 203, 204-207, 267, 268, 269, 291, 366
Eutychian(s), Eutychianism, 281, 317, 321
Eutyches, abbot, 312, 313-317, 319, 320, 321, 328
Evagrius, Christian author, 322, 326
Evans, Robert F., 339, 351, 352
Eve, 73

Facundus, bishop of Hermiane, Christian author, 268, 324, 327
Fall (biblical), 73, 74
Fasir, commander of the Circumcellions, 121

Fathers of the Church, 2, 5, 10, 15, 16, 17, 20, 21, 51, 52, 64, 314, 324
Fausta, Christian lady in Rome, 111
Faustus, Christian author, 348, 349, 350
Faye, Eugène de, 29 , 36, 44, 45, 46, 47
Felicitas, 88, 91, 113
Felix, bishop of Aptungi (Aptugni), 152
Felix, bishop of Thibiuca, 97, 103
Felix, Donatist bishop of Zabi, 126
Felix, bishop of Rome, 236
Fenicia, 348
Ferguson, John, 350, 351, 352
Filastrius, Christian author, 157
Firmilianus, bishop of Caesarea, 150
Firmus, Mauretanian prince, 127, 130
Fisher, George Paul, 43
Flavianus, Nicomachus, vicarius Africae, 127-128, 159
Flavianus, bishop of Constantinople, 313, 314, 315, 316, 317, 318, 319
Flavius Taurus, prefect of Italy and Africa, 244
Florus, Fenician monk, 348
Flumen Piscensis, town in Algeria, 126
Fontainebleau, 234
Fortunatus, bishop of Aquileia, 236
France, 348, 349, 357
Franchi de 'Cavalieri, Pio, 152, 153
Franks, 164, 258
French, 85
Frend, W.H.C., 100, 103, 104, 105, 106, 113, 115, 116, 126, 131, 133, 135, 137, 139, 147, 149, 153, 154, 156, 157, 158, 159, 160, 161
Fritz, G., 49
Fundanus, bishop of Abitenae, 97, 98

Galatians, 9
Galicia(n), 146, 147
Galla Placidia, daughter of Theodosius I and mother of Valentianus III, 318, 319, 329
Gangres, town in Paphlagonia, 320
Gasparro, Sfameni, 45
Gaudentius, Donatist bishop of Timgad, 137, 161
Gaul, Gallic, 95, 111, 123, 146, 198, 228, 230, 244
Gelasius Cyzicenus, Christian author, 70

Gelasius I, bishop of Rome, 349, 353
Genseric, Vandal king, 257
Georgius, bishop of Alexandria, 235, 237, 243, 246, 249-250, 253
Georgius, bishop of Laodicea, 280
German(s), 72
German tribes, 257-258, 362
Germanic, 147, 164, 257
Germanicia (Mar'ash) town in Syria, 294
Gibbon, Edward, 200, 356
Gildo, governor of North Africa, 130-134, 134, 159
Girardet, Klaus M., 229, 230, 273, 274
Glossolaly, 87
Gnosis, 13, 20, 21, 22, 28, 32, 79, 94, 141, 142, 174, 183, 358, 363, 365, 366
Gnostic(s), 5, 6, 8, 11, 12, 13, 14, 15, 20, 21, 28, 29, 30, 32, 33, 34, 46, 50, 53, 58, 74, 75, 78, 79, 80, 92, 140, 141, 143, 173-174, 209, 251, 308, 366, 368
Godet, P., 281, 322
Gondobald (Gundobald), Burgundian king, 257
Gospel(s), 8, 9, 14, 74, 90, 141, 179, 238, 284, 300
Gospel of John, 21, 55, 59, 171, 174, 180, 206
Goth(ic), 247, 257, 258, 295
Grasmück, Ernst Ludwig, 122, 124, 130, 155, 156, 158, 159, 160, 161
Gratianus, Roman Emperor, 143, 254
Gratus, bishop of Carthage, 116, 122, 125
Great Britain, 7
Greece, 25, 77, 290
Greek(s), 1, 21, 22, 28, 34, 35, 37, 39, 44, 45, 51, 59, 71, 73, 76, 77, 92, 148, 150, 174, 175, 194, 196, 222, 251, 252, 266, 276, 280, 284, 298, 299, 308, 316, 317, 326, 330, 338, 340, 341, 355, 356, 361, 362, 367
Gregg, Robert C., 177, 181, 182, 263, 264
Gregory I the Great, Pope, 96, 137-138, 152, 161
Gregory of Nazianze, Father of the Church, 253
Gregory of Nyssa, Father of the Church, 147, 188, 238, 253, 265, 275, 276, 281, 284, 322
Gregory, bishop of Alexandria, 220-221, 222, 226, 235
Greshake, Gisbert, 331, 332, 335, 345, 346, 350, 352, 353, 363
Groh, Dennis E., 177, 181, 182, 263, 264

Hadrumetum, town in Fenicia, 348
Hagemann, Hermann, 65, 70
Hall, Stuart George, 68, 262
Hanson, R.P.C., 169, 173, 190, 192, 193, 203, 206, 211, 221, 222, 230, 232, 239, 242, 259, 260, 261, 262, 265, 266, 267, 268, 269, 270, 271, 272, 274, 275, 276, 277, 279
Harnack, Adolf von, 34, 35, 36, 47, 52, 54, 62, 67, 68, 69, 70, 169, 261, 262, 352
Hebrew, 178, 263
Hegesippus, Christian author, 12-13
Heimann, Peter, 30, 31, 45, 46
Heine, Ronald E., 150, 151
Helena, mother of Constantine the Great, 205, 269
Hellenistic, 77, 361
Heraclianus, comes Africae, 135
Heraclitus, 21
Heraclius, Roman general, 234
Heres, bishop of Arles, 340
Hermas, Christian author, 52-54, 67, 363
Hermogenes, Roman general, 224
Herod, 229, 230
Hierapolis, 81
Hilarius, bishop of Arles, 349, 350
Hillary of Poitiers, 223, 228-229, 246, 249, 270, 272, 274, 277, 351, 357
Hilgenfeld, Adolf, 18, 19
Hiob monastery in Constantinople, 313
Hippo Regius (Bône), 95, 121, 132, 134, 135, 160, 332, 339, 346
Hippolytus, Christian author, 13, 57, 58, 64, 67, 68, 91, 151
Holophernes, 229
Honoratus, bishop of Sicilibba, 113, 136
Honorius, Roman Emperor, 95, 131, 135, 136, 332, 343, 353
Hyginus, bishop of Cordoba, 143, 145

Ianuarius, Donatist bishop of Flumen Piscensis, 126

Ibas, bishop of Edessa, 309, 317
Iconium (Konya), 84
Ignatius of Antioch, 51, 67
Illyria, 198, 205
Imperialism, 360
Innocentius I, Pope, 95, 341, 349
Inquisition, 86
Iran, 310
Iraq, 310
Irenaeus of Lyons, 11, 12, 13, 18, 75, 79, 147, 148, 149, 152
Isaac, a Donatist, 123
Isidore, Egyptian presbyter, ca. 400, 40
Isidorus, Christian author, 157
Islam(it)(ic), 71, 117, 139, 362
Israel, 12
Ithacius, bishop of Ossobona, 143, 144, 146
Italy, Italian, 63, 105, 111, 135, 156, 184, 192, 221, 228, 318, 319, 344

James, apostle, 180
James, first bishop of Jerusalem, 12, 13
James II, King of England, 7
Jeanne d'Arc, 85
Jerome, Father of the Church, 19, 26, 37, 38, 39, 41, 43, 45, 48, 49, 75, 81, 95, 148, 149, 152, 163, 236, 238, 265, 268, 269, 275, 288, 330, 332, 337, 338-339, 339, 340, 350, 352, 353
Jerusalem, 12, 37, 38, 41, 48, 84, 300, 332, 337, 338, 339, 362
Jesus Christ, 5, 6, 8, 10, 11, 12, 14, 15, 22, 31, 33, 34, 36, 50, 51, 52, 54, 55, 56, 59, 60, 62, 63, 64, 69, 71, 75, 78, 80, 89, 90, 119, 120, 140, 141, 142, 167, 168, 174, 176, 177, 178, 179, 180, 181, 182, 183, 184, 190, 191, 196, 206, 207, 208, 209, 239, 282, 283, 285, 291, 292, 293, 296, 297, 298, 300, 317, 324, 330, 332, 335, 337, 345, 363-368, 369
Jew(s), Jewish, 10, 12, 13, 15, 18, 56, 92, 149
Jewry, 1
Jezabel, 9
Joachim da Fiore, Joachimite, 90
Joel, biblical prophet, 88
Johannes Chrysostomus, 269, 290, 323
John, apostle, 141, 180, 292

John the Baptist, 8
John, bishop of Antioch, 300, 302-303, 305-306, 307, 308, 311, 326
John, bishop of Jerusalem ca. 400, 37-43, 48, 338, 339, 340
John, Roman comes, 304-305
John Arcaph, Meletian leader, 216, 217
Jordan, 8, 50, 59
Josephus, Flavius, 1, 6
Jovianus, Roman Emperor, 127, 252
Judah, the tribe, 12
Judaism, 174, 175, 334
Judaizing, 174, 334
Judas, 229
Jude, apostle, 9
Jugie, M., 317, 328
Julia Mammaea, Roman Empress, 25
Julian the Apostate, Roman Emperor, 125, 126, 127, 247, 249, 252, 253, 278
Julianus, bishop of Apamea, 83
Julius I, bishop of Rome, 209, 210, 211, 219, 221, 222, 223, 225, 226, 228, 281
Julius, a bishop, 341
Justin the Martyr, 10-12, 18, 21, 22-23, 44, 75
Justina, widow of Valentinianus I, 256

Kadiköy, town in Turkey
Kannengiesser, Charles, 262
Katholikos of the Nestorian Church, 309
Kingdom of God (Christ), 73, 119
Kobush, Theo, 33, 46
Koch, Hal, 32, 46
Kopecek, Thomas A., 237, 240, 248, 256, 259, 275, 276, 277, 279

Labriolle, Pierre de, 81, 84, 92, 147, 149, 150, 151, 152
Lamirande, Émilien, 19
Laodicea, town in Syria, 280, 281, 288
Lateran Hill in Rome, 111
Lateran Palace in Rome, 233
Latin(s), 39, 42, 92, 94, 104, 135, 136, 148, 193, 222, 223, 251, 258, 276, 308, 315, 326, 330, 334, 340, 341, 356, 357, 361
Law, Mosaic, 90
Lazarus, bishop of Aix, 340
Lemellfense (Khirbet Zembia, Toqueville),

town in Algeria, 126
Leo I, bishop of Rome, 299, 311, 312, 313, 315, 316, 318, 319, 320, 324, 327, 328, 329
Leo III the Isaurian, Byzantine Emperor, 95
Leonas, Roman official, 246
Leonidas, father of Origen, 24-25
Leontius, bishop of Antioch, 237, 260
Leontius Byzantinus, Christian author, 61-62, 69, 322
Lérins, town in southern France, 348
Letter to the Colossians, 9
Letter to the Galatians, 9
Letter of Ignatius of Antioch, 51
Letters of John, 51
Letter of Jude, 9
Letter of Peter, Second, 10
Letter to the Ephesians, 338
Letter to the Philippians, 9, 293
Letter to Timothy, First, 9, 10
Libanius, rhetor, 290
Liberatus, Christian author, 326
Liberius, bishop of Rome, 228, 230, 231,, 240 233-234, 236-237, 243, 272, 275
Libya(n), 57, 165, 184, 185, 189, 197, 295
Licinia Eudoxia, wife of Valentinianus III, 318, 319
Licinius, Roman co-emperor, 165, 186, 189, 191, 357
Lietzmann, Hans, 322
Limata, town in Algeria, 102
Lisieux, 85
Logos, 52, 54, 55, 58, 61, 62, 64, 65, 77-78, 90, 171-172, 174, 176, 190, 195, 196, 206, 207, 209-210, 263, 282, 292, 293, 294, 311, 364, 366
Lohse, Bernhard, 24, 44, 323
Longobards, 257
Loofs, Friedrich, 69-70, 275, 324, 325, 353
Lorenz, Rudolf, 207, 62, 263, 265, 269
Lot, 266
Lucian, Christian martyr, 165
Lucian, scholar, 186, 190, 260
Lucifer, bishop of Calaris, 229, 231, 232, 249, 273, 274
Lucilla, Christian widow in Carthage, 99, 102, 103, 114
Lucius, bishop of Adrianople, 212
Lucius, bishop of Alexandria, 253, 254
Lyman, J. Rebecca, 46
Lyons, 210, 228

Macarius, philosopher, c. 400, 41
Macarius, high Roman official, 122, 124, 129
Macarius, presbyter, 270
Macedonia, 205
Macedonius, bishop of Constantinople, 224-225
Macomades, town in Algeria, 138
Macrina, sister of Basil of Caesarea and Gregory of Nyssa, 253
Macrobius, Donatist bishop of Hippo, 121
Marculus, Donatist bishop, 124
Maghreb, 116, 117, 128, 138, 257, 360
Magnentius, Roman Emperor, usurper, 227, 228, 230
Maier, Jean-Louis, 152, 153, 154, 155, 156, 158
Majorinus, lector in the Church of Carthage, later bishop of this town, 102, 103, 104
Malchion, Christian sophist, 63. 70
Mamre, oak of, 23
Mandaeans, 8
Manichaeans, Manichaeism, 16, 20, 72, 73, 134, 139, 140, 143, 144, 251, 308, 334, 334, 337, 368
Mansi, J.D., 266 , 267, 323, 325, 326, 327, 328, 329, 353
Marcella, Christian woman in Rome, 95
Marcellinus, Roman official, 135-136
Marcellus, bishop of Ancyra, 203, 208-210, 210, 211, 212, 212-213, 221, 222, 223, 255, 261
Marcianus, Roman Emperor, 319, 320, 321, 329
Marcion, Gnostic prophet, 5, 11, 12, 13, 20, 79, 209
Mari, bishop of Ardasch, 309
Marmarice, town in Libya, 185
Marseille, 299, 348
Martin, bishop of Tours, 144-146
Martin, Thérèse, known as Saint Teresa of Lisieux, the Little Flower, Little Tessie,

85
Martinianus, Christian martyr, 95
Mary, mother of Jesus, 62, 89, 142, 206, 209, 282, 291, 296, 297, 298, 299, 300, 303, 306, 307, 317, 366, 369
Mascazel, Mauretanian prince, 131
Mass, Roman Catholic, 197
Mauretania(n), 106, 115, 126, 127, 130, 133
Mauricius, Byzantine Emperor, 138
Maximilla, Montanist prophetess, 81, 82, 83, 89, 149
Maximinanists, Donatist sect, 133-134, 160
Maximinianus, a Donatist deacon, 123, 132
Maximinus, Roman co-emperor, 166
Maximinus, bishop of Treves, 217, 225
Maximus, Roman Emperor, 144-146, 162, 163
Mediterranean, 136
Meletius, bishop of Lycopolis, Meletians, 165, 166, 214, 215, 216, 260, 271
Membressa, town in Algeria
Memnon, bishop of Ephesus, 302, 303, 304
Menander, Gnostic, 11, 12, 13, 20
Mensurius, bishop of Carthage, 97, 98, 99, 101, 109
Mercator, Marius, 353
Merw, town in Parthia, 309
Michels, Rinus, Dutch football trainer, 203
Middle Ages, 3, 6, 61
Milan, 144, 225, 231, 233, 254
Milan, congress of -, 1982, 73
Milevis (Mila) town in Algeria, 100, 125, 341
Milo, famous Greek athlete, 331
Miltiades, bishop around 180, 81, 82
Miltiades, Pope, 101, 110, 111
Modalism, Modalists, 56-58, 58, 59, 64, 68, 70, 142, 168, 363
Modalist Monarchianism, 56, 58, 59, 363
Moderator of the Free Church Federal Council, 7
Monarchianism, Monarchians, 27, 54-56, 56, 59, 60, 61, 64, 65, 67, 88, 142
Mongol, 290

Monica (Monnica), mother of Saint Augustine, 135
Monophysitism, Monophysite(s), 289, 310-321, 328
Mons Caelius, Rome, 42, 43
Montanism, Montanist(s), 6, 14, 80-96, 96, 147, 149, 357, 360, 363
Montanus, founder of the Montanist Church, 81-82, 88, 89, 90, 149, 202
Mopsuestia, town in Cilicia, 290
Mopsukrene, 247
Morocco, 115, 360
Moses, 62, 332
Moslim, 117, 138
Mount of Olives, 37, 39, 41
Munatiana, town in Algeria, 132
Mursa (Osijek in East Slavonia), 231
Musonianus, Roman official, 205, 210
Mystic(al), mysticism, 4, 85-88, 173

Napoleon I, 234
Natalis, schismatic bishop, 59
Naudin, Pierre, 45
National-socialists, 357
Nazis, 357
Nectarius, Roman official, 256
Neo-Arians, Neo-Arianism, 237-249, 275
Neo-Platonic, Neo-Platonists, 34, 275
Nero, 229
Nestorian Church, 289, 360
Nestorian(s), Nestorianism, 290, 294-310, 311, 312, 315, 360, 362
Nestorius, bishop of Constantinople, 289, 290, 294-307, 308, 310, 311, 313, 324, 325, 326, 327, 328, 344, 366
Netherlands, 357
Nevers, 86
New Testament, 5, 6, 9, 10, 31, 32, 62, 247, 290, 335
Newman, John Henry, 3, 215, 223, 237, 249, 260, 264, 270, 271, 272, 275, 277
Nicaea, 192-193, 193, 201, 204, 208, 231, 243, 278, 320
Nicene Fathers, 22
Nicephoras Callistus, 267
Nicolaites, 9, 20
Nicomedia, 185, 187, 191, 205, 215, 216, 243, 260, 267
Nicopolis, town in Palestine, 281

Nike, town in Thrace, 245, 247
Nile, 252
Nisibis, town in Mesopotamia, 308, 310
Noetus, Monarchian, 55-56, 67, 68
Noetism, 55-56, 56
Nominalism, nominalistic, 64-66
North Africa(n), 57, 58, 91, 95, 96-139, 156, 192, 193, 215, 332, 339, 341, 349, 356, 360, 362
Nova Petra (Henchir Encedda) fortress-town in Algeria, 124
Numidia(n), 99, 101, 102, 103, 104, 105,, 134 114, 117, 122, 123, 126, 131, 132, 133, 135, 137, 138, 341
Nundiniarius, deacon in Cirta, 114

Octavensis, town in North Africa, 121
Old Testament, 5, 31, 140, 335
Olympian gods, religion, 22, 23, 77, 174
Ophites, 20
Opitz, Hans-Georg, 259, 260, 261, 262, 265, 266, 267, 268
Optatus, Church historian, 103, 122, 125, 128-130, 153, 154, 155, 156, 157, 158, 159, 359
Optatus, Donatist bishop of Thamagudi, 131-132, 134, 137
Origen, 15, 21, 23, 24-43 passim, 45, 46, 47, 60, 69, 77, 147, 168-171, 174, 176, 200, 208, 261, 262, 263, 269, 291, 318, 338, 339, 357, 363
Origenism, Origenist(s), 33, 37-43, 47, 49, 74, 169, 211, 318, 338
Orosius, Christian author, 159, 160, 161, 337, 339-340, 340, 341, 352
Orphism, 72
Ossius, bishop of Cordoba, 191, 192, 210, 211, 225, 229, 234, 266, 274
Ossobona, town in Spain, 149
Ostrogoths, 257

Paganism, 28, 202, 258, 298, 307
Palestine, Palestinian, 25, 26, 39, 41, 42, 43, 142, 185, 187, 212, 218, 227, 281, 337, 340, 341, 344
Palladius, imperial official, 304
Palmyra, Kingdom of, 60
Pammachius, friend of Jerome, 40
Pammachius, Roman senator, ca. 400, 42

Pamphylian, 204
Pamphilius of Caesarea, Christian apologist, 27, 41, 42
Panteles, Byzantine comes Africae, 138
Pantheism, 55
Papias, bishop of Hierapolis, 81
Paradise, 93
Parmenian, Donatist bishop of Carthage, 123, 125, 128-130, 131, 158, 359
Parthia, Parthian Empire, 127, 308, 309
Pastoral epistles, 73
Patripassianism, Patripassianists, 55, 64, 363
Paul, apostle, 9, 80, 82, 87, 130, 141, 150, 240, 293, 333, 334, 338
Paul, bishop of Constantinople, 214, 218, 224, 225
Paul, bishop of Samosata, 60-64, 64, 66, 69, 70, 86, 208, 223, 297, 301, 324
Paul, bishop of Tyre, 215
Paula, Christian lady, ca. 400, 41
Paulianianism, Paulinian(s), 60-64, 66, 67, 86, 363
Paulinidas, brother of Jerome, 39
Paulinus, bishop of Antioch, 287-288
Paulinus, bishop of Nola, 333
Paulinus, bishop of Treves, 231
Paulinus, bishop of Tyrus, 186, 187, 195, 208
Paulinus, a cleric in Milan, 340-341
Paulus, high Roman official, 122, 123, 124
Pelagianism, Ch. VIII passim, 363, 369
Pelagians, 16
Pelagius, Christian author, 299, 331-344, 345, 346, 346-347, 350, 351, 352, 357, 362, 363, 368-369
Pelikan, Jaroslav, 21, 44, 68, 292, 293, 323, 324
Pepuza, town in Phrygia, 83, 95, 150
Perpetua, Christian martyr, 88, 91, 113
Persia(n)(s), Persian Empire, 61, 225, 295, 308, 310
Peter, apostle, 3, 141
Peter, bishop of Alexandria around 310, 165, 166, 214
Peter, bishop of Alexandria 374, 253, 254
Petersen, William L., 148
Petilian, a Donatist author, 109, 125, 136

Pietistic, 4
Phaeno mines, 165
Pharisees, 1, 12
Philadelphia (in Asia Minor), 81
Philippi, town in Macedonia, 205
Philippopolis, town in Thrace, 211, 226
Philo, Jewish philosopher, Philonic, 34
Philosophy, philosophical, 2, 31, 33, 34, 36
Philostorgius, ancient scholar, 197, 200, 201, 239, 260, 261, 267, 268, 269, 275, 276
Phoenicia, 289
Photinus, a heretic, 297
Photius, Byzantine scholar, 27, 31, 45, 275
Phrygia(n), 80-81, 82, 93, 95, 149, 243
Pinetum, hill in Rome, 41
Pistus, bishop of Alexandria, 217, 219, 220
Pius VII, Pope, 234
Platonic, Platonism, Platonists, 2, 28, 33, 35, 72, 263, 282
Plinval, Georges de, 330, 334, 338, 343, 350, 351, 352, 353
Poitiers, 249
Polis, 175
Pontus, 83, 90
Possidius, 353
Postmodernist, 4
Praxeas, Monarchian, 54-55, 55, 64, 68
Presocratics, 77
Primianus, Donatist bishop of Carthage, 132, 133, 136
Prisca or Priscilla, Montanist prophetess, 81, 82, 89, 90, 149
Priscillianism, Priscillianist(s), 17, 28, 139-147, 161, 163, 360
Priscillianus, bishop of Avila, 139-147, 161, 162, 163, 357, 360
Processus, Christian martyr, 95
Proclus, presbyter in Constantinople, 297, 325
Procula, Christian girl, 162
Prosper of Aquitaine, Christian author, 349, 353
Protestant, 3, 7
Provence, 230
Pseudo-Dionysius see Dionysius the Areopagite
Pseudo-Leontius, 70
Pseudo-Tertullian, 89, 147, 149, 151
Ptolemais, town in Egypt, 185
Pulcheria, sister of Theodosius II, 295, 299, 311, 318, 319, 329
Punic, 104, 133, 135
Puritanism, puritanical, 80, 81, 140
Purpurius, bishop of Limata in North Africa, 100, 101, 102, 103
Pythagoras, 62, 179
Pythagoreans, 28

Quadratus, Christian prophet, 81
Quispel, Gilles, 147

Rabbula, bishop of Edessa, 309, 310
Ramadan, 71
Ramsay, W.-M., 150
Rees, B.R., 350
Reeves, Marjorie, 151
Reformers, Reformation (Churches of the), 2, 3, 4, 258
Reims, 279
Remigius, bishop of Reims, 279
Riez, town in the Provence, 348
Rimini see Ariminium
Ritschl, Dietrich, 277
Ritter, Adolf Martin, 164, 239, 259, 275
Roman, 76, 81, 92, 104, 111, 115, 120, 122, 126, 130, 132, 135, 144, 250, 255, 272, 276, 358, 360, 361
Roman Catholic(s), 7, 35, 85, 89, 111, 116, 120, 121, 125, 126, 127, 128, 129, 132, 133, 134, 135, 136, 137, 138, 139, 144, 146, 213, 239, 258, 266, 300, 331, 341, 362, 369
Roman Catholic Church, 1, 2, 3, 5, 6, 7, 8, 10, 11, 12, 13, 15, 16, 17, 21, 28, 32, 35, 40, 42, 43, 47, 51, 52, 55, 56, 59, 63, 64, 66, 71, 72, 73, 75, 81, 83, 84, 85, 86, 87, 88, 90, 92, 93, 95, 96, 97, 101, 104, 105, 106, 108, 109, 110, 112, 117, 125, 126, 128, 129, 134, 136, 138, 139, 142, 144, 164, 167, 169, 172, 186, 188, 189, 191, 194, 197, 199, 200, 201, 210, 211, 214, 215, 222, 229, 230, 232, 236, 241, 247, 249, 251, 258, 260, 283, 288, 289, 295, 298, 300, 309, 310, 316, 318, 330,

336, 340, 341, 343, 350, 357, 359, 360, 362-363, 366, 369
Roman Empire, 16, 17, 60, 93, 104, 105, 112, 116, 117, 129, 130, 134, 135, 138, 139, 142, 164, 167, 192, 210, 217, 218, 221, 228, 241, 243, 248, 254, 256, 257, 308, 309, 310, 345, 346, 356, 358, 361, 368, 369
Romanus, comes in North Africa, 127
Rome (city), 13, 25, 40, 42, 54, 55, 56, 57, 58, 59, 60, 75, 92, 95, 106, 110, 112, 116, 130, 136, 143, 156, 162, 209, 217, 219, 221, 225, 228, 230, 233, 236, 243, 299, 302, 309, 318, 332, 333, 342, 343, 344, 345, 348, 349, 362
Roosevelt, Theodore, 166
Rufinus, Christian author, 26, 37, 38, 39, 40, 41, 42, 43, 45, 48, 49, 193, 199, 267, 268, 278, 339
Russicade, town in North Africa, 160

Sabellian(s), Sabellianism, 56, 58, 62, 167, 203, 204, 206, 207, 208, 211, 242, 251, 255, 363
Sabellius, Monarchian, Modalist, 56, 57-58, 62, 167, 202, 223
Sadducees, 1, 12
Salamis, town in Cyprus, 15, 37, 43, 321
Salvius, Donatist bishop of Membressa, 133
Samaritans, 12
Samosatian doctrine, 61-63, 251
Sanhedrin, 229
Saragossa, Synod of, 143
Sardinia, 229
Sasanian Empire, 309
Satan, 9
Saturnilus, Gnostic prophet, 11, 13, 20, 79
Saturninus, priest in Abitenea, 97, 98
Schäferdiek, Knut, 279
Schepelern, Wilhelm, 149, 150
Schepes, G., 161
Schindler, Alfred, 4, 7, 15, 19, 104, 106, 110, 120, 152, 153, 154, 155, 157
Schwarz, E., 266
Scilly Islands, 145
Scotland, 338
Scripture see Bible

409

Sebastianus, Roman commander, 235
Secundus, bishop of Tigisis, Primate of Numidia, 98, 99, 100, 101, 102, 103
Secundus, nephew of bishop Secundus, 101
Secundus, bishop of Ptolemais, 185, 197, 198, 219
Seeck, Otto, 159
Seleucia, gtown in Cilicia, 243
Sellers, Robert V., 204, 206, 268, 269
Seleucia, synod of, 309
Semi-Arian(s), 241-242, 347
Semi-Pelagianism, 347-350, 361, 369
Senate, Roman, 131
Septimius Severus, Roman Emperor, 25, 120
Serapis, Temple of, 153
Serdica, 226 (Sofia), 210, 225
Severus Alexander, Roman Emperor, 25
Sex(ual)(ity), 72-73, 73, 74, 75, 80, 308
Sfameni Gasparro, Giulia, 147
Sicilibba, town in North Africa, 113, 156
Side, town in Pamphylia, 204
Silvanus, bishop of Cirta, 99-100, 102, 114, 116, 153
Silvester, Roman comes in North Africa, 122
Silvester I, bishop of Rome, 192, 193
Simon the Magician, 11, 13, 14, 15, 20
Siricius, Pope, 43, 145, 162, 163
Sirmium, town on the Middle Danube, 234, 237, 243
Sixtus III, bishop of Rome, 306, 348
Slavonia, 231
Smyrna, 51, 55
Socianism, 258
Socrates, the philosopher, 21, 62, 179
Socrates, Christian historian, 69, 149, 167, 168, 193, 202, 206, 208, 224, 260, 261, 262, 265, 266, 268, 269, 270, 271, 272, 273, 274, 275, 277, 278, 297, 322, 324, 325
Sozomenos, Church historian, 48, 184, 193, 195, 196, 200, 205, 209, 242, 260, 261, 262, 265, 266, 267, 268, 270, 271, 272, 274, 276, 277, 278, 279, 288, 289, 322, 323
Spain, Spanish, Spaniard, 86, 95, 123, 140, 143, 144, 145, 146, 147, 339, 343

Spiritualist, 4
Stephanus, bishop of Antioch, 212
Stilicho, chief minister of the Empire, 131
Stoa, Stoic, 182, 183
Stroehlin, Ernest, 89, 150, 151, 152
Stuebler, Alfred, 351
Sulpicius Severus, Christian author, 145, 162, 163, 245, 266, 274, 277
Sylvester I, Pope, 112, 116
Synod see Council
Synod of Cirta, 100, 103
Syracuse, 155
Syria, 84, 90, 185, 189, 192, 204, 212, 218, 222, 227, 280, 288, 289, 290, 294, 296, 308, 309, 310
Syriac, 266, 290
Syrianus, Roman general, 232

Tarragona, town in Spain, 339
Tatian, Encratite heresiarch, 36, 73, 75-80, 148, 149, 308
Taurinus, Roman comes in North Africa, 121-122
Tebessa, town in Algeria, 115
Teilhard de Chardin, Pierre, 142
Teresa of Avila, 85-86
Tertullian, 13-15, 19, 21, 23, 54-55, 57, 64, 65, 67, 68, 69, 70, 88, 89, 90, 91-94, 95, 96, 119, 120, 130, 150, 151, 152, 157, 196
Tetz, Martin, 215, 271
Thagaste (Soukh Ahras), town in Algeria, 135
Thamugudi (Timgad), town in Algeria, 115, 131, 135, 137
Thebaid (Egypt), 215
Thebutis, Jerusalemite heretic, 12-13
Themison, the first treasurer of the Montanists, 82, 83
Theodore of Mopsuestia, 289-294, 294, 310, 323, 324, 366
Theodoretus, Father of Church, 51, 67, 70, 157, 188, 193, 196, 205, 234, 239, 260, 261, 265, 267, 268, 269, 270, 275, 278, 305, 312, 317, 326, 327
Theodoric, Ostrogoth king, 257
Theodosius, comes in North Africa, 127
Theodosius I, Roman Emperor, 95, 130, 238, 253, 254, 256, 289, 318

Theodosius II, Roman Emperor, 95, 294, 295, 299, 301, 302, 303, 304, 305, 306, 307, 311, 313, 315, 316, 318, 319
Theodotians, 69
Theodotus, heretic, cobbler, 58-59
Theodotus, banker, heretic, 59
Theodotus, bishop of Laodicea, 280, 322
Theognis, an Arian bishop, 198
Theonas, bishop of Marmarice, 185, 197
Theophilus, Christian apologist, 21, 22, 23, 24, 44
Theophilus, bishop of Alexandria, ca. 400, 40, 41, 43, 48
Theophronos, bishop of Tyana, 223
Thermae Gargilianae, bath house in Carthage, 136
Thessalonike, 189, 254
Thibiuca, town in North Africa (Henchir Zougitina), 97, 152
Tigris, 308
Thomas, apostle, 308
Thomas of Aquinas, 36
Thrace, 205, 211, 226, 234, 236
Thümmel, Wilhelm, 104, 154
Tietze, Walter, 273, 274
Timotheus, Apollinarist bishop of Berytus, 288
Toledo, Synod of, 146
Tours, 144, 279
Traianopolis, town in Thrace, 205
Treves (Trier), 144, 146, 210, 217, 218, 225, 226, 231
Trinitarian(s), 67, 70
Trypho, Jewish scholar, 23
Tunisia(n), 113, 133, 134, 138, 152, 360
Turin, Synod of, 146
Turkey, Turkish, 150, 290
Turner, H.E.W., 1, 3, 5, 6, 7, 179
Tyconius, Donatist author, 118, 127
Tymion, town in Phrygia, 83, 150
Tyrus, 186, 187, 215, 216

Ulfilas (Wulfila), 247, 258
Unitarian(s), unitarianism, 60, 62
United States, 310
Universalia, 65

Valens, Roman Emperor, 252-253, 254
Valens, bishop of Mursa, 231

Valentinianus I, Roman Emperor, 253, 256
Valentianus II, Roman Emperor, 127, 144, 256, 257
Valentianus III, Roman Emperor, 318, 319
Valentianism, Valentinian(s), 6, 12, 13, 14
Valentinus, Gnostic prophet, 11, 12, 20, 209, 251
Vandals, 137, 257, 339, 346
Vercellae, 231
Victor, a fuller in Cirta, 100
Victor of Garba, Donatist bishop, 116, perhaps the same person as Victor the fuller
Victor, Donatist bishop of Munatiana, 132
Visigoth(s), 332, 345, 348
Vitalis, a priest in Antioch, 287-288, 323
Vitalis, a Semi-Pelagian, 347-348
Vegesala (Ksar el-Gelb), town in Algeria, 124
Victor I, Pope, 54, 59
Villain, Maurice, 37, 40, 48, 49
Viminacium, town in Bulgaria, 218, 219
Vincentius, a bishop, 16
Vincentius, bishop of Capua, 212
Vincentius, a priest, ca. 400, 40
Virgins of Thuburbo, Christian martyrs, 98
Visigoths, 147, 254, 257
Voelter, Daniel, 154
Voisin, Guillaume, 322, 323

Waldensians, 6
Wand, J.W.C., 21, 43, 184, 263, 264, 267, 289, 290, 307, 323, 324
Werner, Ernst, 157, 158
Westminster Cathedral, 7
Wickham, Lionel R., 294, 312, 313, 324, 326, 328
Widdicombe, Peter, 35
Wiles, F. Maurice, 259, 263, 276
William of Ockham, 65
Williams, D.H., 259
Williams, Rowan D., 35, 47, 164, 258, 259, 260, 261, 262
Würzburg Tractates, 161

Yugoslavia, 231

Zabi, town in Algeria, 126
Zebedee, father of John and James, 180
Zeo, Byzantine Emperor, 310
Zenobia, Queen of Palmyra, 61, 63, 69
Zenophilus, governor of Numidia, 114
Zephyrinus, Pope, 57, 58, 59
Zoroaster, 179
Zosimus I, bishop of Rome, 332, 342, 342-344, 353, 362
Zotikos, bishop of Cumana in Phrygia, 83